The
Multibus
Design
Guidebook

JAMES B. JOHNSON
STEVE KASSEL

The Multibus Design Guidebook

Structures, Architectures, and Applications

McGraw-Hill Book Company

New York   St. Louis   San Francisco   Auckland
Bogotá   Hamburg   Johannesburg   London   Madrid
Mexico   Montreal   New Delhi   Panama   Paris
São Paulo   Singapore   Sydney   Tokyo   Toronto

Library of Congress Cataloging in Publication Data

Johnson, James B.
  The multibus design guidebook.

  Includes bibliographical references and index.
  1. Microcomputers—Buses. 2. Computer architecture.
I. Kassel, Steve. II. Title.
TK7895.B87J63   1984   621.3819'535   83-16258
ISBN 0-07-032599-5

1 2 3 4 5 6 7 8 9 0   DOC/DOC   8 9 8 7 6 5 4

ISBN 0-07-032599-5

The editors for this book were Roy Mogilanski and Janet B.
Davis, the designer was Riverside Graphics, and the
production supervisor was Thomas G. Kowalczyk. It was set in
Caledonia by University Graphics, Inc.

Printed and bound by R. R. Donnelley & Sons Company.

Multibus is a registered trademark of Intel Corporation.

Photographs, tables, and figures are used courtesy of Intel
Corporation, Santa Clara, California.

This book is dedicated to our parents, who furnished us guidance and gave us the educational opportunities to pursue our careers, and to our wives, Nancy and Nancy, who provided support and understanding during the development of this book.

Contents

Preface

The Multibus/IEEE-796 is a commercial-quality industry-standard bus structure for use in microprocessor-based systems. Additionally, three separate buses have been developed to complement and extend the capabilities of the Multibus structure. Together these four structures form the Multibus family of structures. The Multibus family consists of the Multibus system bus, which is the center of all Multibus-based systems; the iSBX bus, a low-cost local (on-board) input-output expansion bus; the Multichannel bus, a very high speed cable bus designed to move blocks of data between peripherals and intelligent subsystems and Multibus-based systems; and the iLBX bus, a high-speed memory execution bus that allows a microprocessor on a single-board computer to expand its local memory using multiple boards.

This book provides the reader with a basic understanding of the structures, architectures, and detailed hardware designs of the various modules that can be used in association with the Multibus system bus, the iSBX local input-output bus, the Multichannel high-speed cable bus, and the iLBX local execution bus. It describes these various bus structures using simple concepts, and then builds on them until the reader understands the different architectures that can be constructed. The book, which is intended for board- and system-level hardware design and evaluation engineers and their managers, is essential for anyone involved with Multibus-based products. It provides detailed bus interface information and also serves as a quick reference for those designing Multibus-based systems. The text is supported by a wealth of examples and illustrations.

The book is divided into three parts: (1) structures, in which the electrical and mechanical specifications of the Multibus family members are described; (2) architectures, in which the different architectures are described that can be built on and around the Multibus family members; and (3) applications, in which hardware design examples are given for interfacing modules to the various Multibus family members.

The structures section reviews each of the different Multibus family structures. First the structures are described conceptually; then the functions and the electrical and mechanical specifications of the bus are described in detail.

The Multibus family of structures supports a wide spectrum of system architectures, from simple, low-cost uniprocessing systems to sophisticated, distributed multiple-processor systems yielding high throughput. The architectures section considers the benefits and trade-offs of each of these different architectures in detail. Examples of several types of systems, including uniprocessing, multicomputing, and multiprocessing systems, are used to explain the major architectural approaches, interconnection schemes, and related hardware and software trade-offs. Other topics covered include an overview of system design issues and some discussion of highly reliable computers.

The applications section gives the reader examples of various interface circuits for the Multibus family structures. Each example provides enough detail to make it possible to actually implement the module or interface. This section also provides evaluation criteria for purchasing Multibus-compatible products.

James B. Johnson
Steve Kassel

Acknowledgments

We wish to acknowledge the help of many colleagues at Intel's OEM Microcomputer Operations group (Hillsboro, Oregon) over the years during which most of these ideas, specifications, and applications were formulated and refined. The special efforts of Clark Allsworth, who provided constructive criticism of the early manuscript, have been most helpful. The final manuscript also has benefited greatly from the careful reading and comments of Craig Kinnie and Mary Slamp. The assistance of the engineering staff of Intel Corporation—especially Phil Drain, Pete MacWilliams, John Deignan, Scott Tetrick, and Ron Dilbeck—is also acknowledged.

PART 1

The Multibus Family of Bus Structures

1

Introduction

This chapter provides a basic framework for evaluating microprocessor system buses and offers a little history of some of the most popular of such buses: the Multibus/IEEE-796 system bus and its extensions: the iSBX bus, the iLBX bus, and the Multichannel bus.[1] Basic system architectures of the Multibus/IEEE-796 family will also be defined.

1.1 OBJECTIVES AND GOALS OF MICROPROCESSOR-BASED SYSTEM BUSES

The system bus is the foundation of any computer system; it will influence the flexibility, cost, performance, and reliability of the system for its entire operating life. Advances in very large scale integration (VLSI) technology result in increased system complexity. The system bus, as a result, is recognized as the primary architectural resource, and it can frequently be the limiting factor in performance, reliability, and modularity. The most basic portion of a system bus is the bus structure, which defines all the signals and how the various system components interact with each other. These signals run along the backplane, where they can be supplied to the interface modules. A typical bus structure defines the word length, data types, and address length, as well as data transfer protocols such as memory reads, input-output (I/O) writes, and direct memory accesses (DMA). It will also specify some type of intermodule signaling such as interrupts, as well as a protocol to exchange control of the bus to various bus modules.

[1]Multibus, iSBX, iLBX, and Multichannel are trademarks of Intel Corporation, Santa Clara, California.

1.1.1 Do You Need a System Bus?

Not all users need a bus-oriented system. Such a system is generally more flexible, easier to upgrade, and easier to implement, but it is more expensive, module for module, than a specialized system. This expense is due to the greater component count required to meet the bus interface specification. Typically, a bus specification requires that each signal line be buffered. That can result in excess drive capacity, since most system designs use only a small fraction of the allowable receivers permitted on a signal. The buffers also require additional area on the board and increase power consumption. The additional parts increase the component cost, assembly time, and test time, which results in increased manufacturing cost.

In applications with lesser volume it will generally be found that the added cost of using standard bus design methodologies will be favorably offset by lower development costs during the shorter development time. In many instances, complete systems can be configured with off-the-shelf board-level products. In applications in which some custom design is required, standard bus design methodology is still applicable. The system design can be divided into two parts: the custom boards and the standard boards. The customized portion of the system can be completed with less expenditure of time and money because the system bus interface is already designed. The entire system development cost is lower because part of the system uses standard products. Bus-oriented systems also have a greater degree of configuration flexibility because different modules can be mixed and matched to produce a particular product or version. Products can easily be configured to meet the exact need of the end user.

Another important aspect of using standard bus-oriented systems is the ability to buffer a system design from the rapid technological changes in VLSI components. If a design needs more speed, it can be upgraded by plugging in a new bus-compatible module that uses a faster microprocessor or faster memory. Even using new technology such as converting a current design which used an 8-bit microprocessor to a 16-bit microprocesor would be permitted if the module met the bus interface requirements.

In summary, in applications that have very high volume, such as terminals or low-cost test equipment, it will be found that the use of a standard bus system adds undesirable cost to the end product. Systems that are dominated by manufacturing costs and do not need a great deal of configuration flexibility should use specialized configurations to avoid the costs of unnecessary parts and interconnections. On the other hand, systems that are dominated by development costs or need configuration flexibility should use a system bus scheme.

1.2 PICKING YOUR MULTIBUS FAMILY STRUCTURES

The Multibus system bus is a commercial quality bus for use in microprocessor-based systems. Some Multibus boards are shown in Fig. 1-1. The Multibus struc-

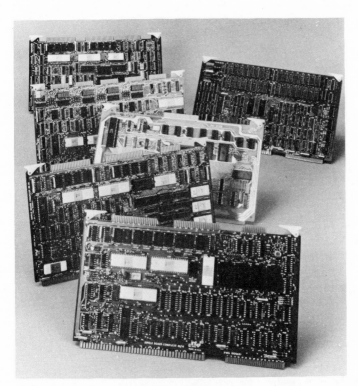

FIGURE 1-1 Multibus compatible boards.

ture provides all the necessary signals for easy system expansion with additional memory, I/O, or microprocessor modules. The Multibus system architecture has been developed to expand beyond the capabilities of the basic system bus structure with three new bus structures. They are (1) the iSBX bus, a low-cost local (on-board) I/O expansion bus, (2) the Multichannel bus, a high-speed path for block data transfers between a Multibus-based system and peripherals or other remote computer systems and (3) the iLBX bus, a high-speed memory-only execution bus that makes it possible to expand the local memory of a microprocessor on a single-board computer (SBC) by using multiple boards.

These three extensions—the iSBX bus, the Multichannel bus, and the iLBX bus—were developed to optimize a particular aspect of the basic Multibus system. The Multibus system bus, along with its three extensions, comprises the Multibus family (Fig. 1-2). The three extensions complement the Multibus system bus, which permits a system designer to make the best cost-performance trade-offs during the system design. The Multibus family provides a complete set of system building blocks for use in a wide variety of system architectures.

Picking the right system bus for a specific application is a very important and difficult task. When different system bus structures are evaluated, the following objectives need to be considered:

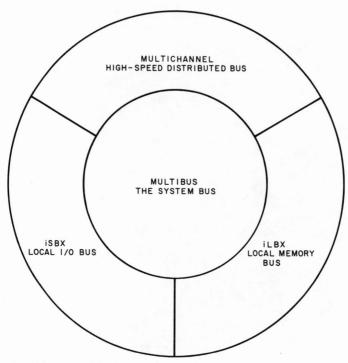

FIGURE 1-2 The Multibus family.

- Support of a wide range of system architectures

- A conceptually simple structure

- A structure that can quickly incorporate new VLSI

- A reliable, cost-effective structure

- A well-defined, documented, and controlled standard

Each of the above objectives will be discussed to provide a basis for understanding its effect on system design. Then the Multibus family will be examined in light of all the objectives.

1.2.1 Support of a Wide Range of System Architectures

The bus structures provide the groundwork for the system hardware architecture; they must support many different architectures ranging from simple, single-master monolithic designs to complex multiple-processing, locally distributed designs. These different system architectures are briefly defined, and their effects on the bus structures are explored. (In Chaps. 6 to 8 the different architectures are explored in more detail.)

SINGLE-PROCESSOR ARCHITECTURE

A system with single-microprocessor architecture can have only one user-reprogrammable microprocessor. Although the system can have other bus masters with microprocessors, such as peripheral controllers, on them, these microprocessors are dedicated to particular tasks and cannot be reprogrammed—they simply replace logic and do it more cost-effectively. Two types of single-microprocessor architectures will be discussed. The first is a very traditional approach used by most of the basic minicomputer and microprocessor systems; the second is an evolution of the first that is driven by the effects of VLSI technology.

The most straightforward microprocessor system bus architecture is a split-bus or common-bus architecture, in which both the microprocessor and the system have equal access to the memory and other system resources. Examination of Fig. 1-3 reveals four basic blocks: the SBC unit, the global memory unit, the global I/O unit, and the DMA unit. The microprocessor unit is responsible for

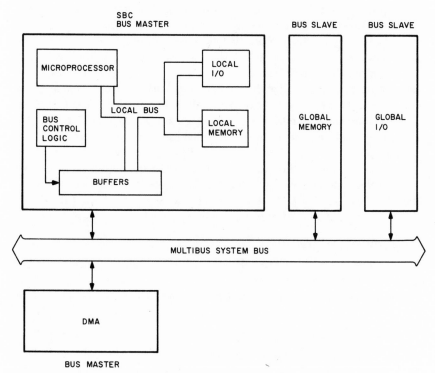

FIGURE 1-3 Common-bus architecture.

all execution of code, all communication in the system, and most of the low-speed I/O tasks, and it can control the system bus (a bus master). The memory unit holds or stores all system data and program execution code and can respond only to bus commands; it is a bus slave. The I/O unit is responsible for interfacing to all the low-speed I/O in the system and is a bus slave; it interfaces to such devices as printers, control lines on machines, and front panels of boxes. The fourth block is the DMA unit; it handles all high-speed I/O devices such as disks, graphics stations, and video cameras without the aid of the microprocessor. This block's main task is to transmit high-speed data between the system peripherals and the system memory unit. The DMA unit is a bus master and can control the system bus. The microprocessor unit initializes the DMA unit for each block of data transfer, and then the DMA unit sustains independent activity. The microprocessor unit tells the DMA unit the direction of the data flow and where to put or get the data in system memory. Once the block transfer is complete, the DMA unit notifies the microprocessor unit via an interrupt.

The common-bus approach is very popular in minicomputer designs and early microprocessor systems. It was used in the first systems based on the Multibus system bus and in many personal computers such as the Apple II[2] and the TRS-80.[3] The microprocessor uses the system bus to execute out of the memory and to perform all I/O operations. In this configuration, the system bus is used as an execution bus. The advantages of this approach are simplicity and architectural consistency, which means that all system resources are accessible from the system bus and are made global; there are no resources in the system that only one of the bus masters can access. As an example, the microprocessor and disk controller can access all of the memory; that is, the memory is made global. System capacity is easily expanded by installing new modules. The limitations of the common-bus system are (1) the high utilization of the system bus required by most new microprocessors, which leaves no system bus bandwidth for other system activities such as DMA, and (2) the slow throughput, which is due to both arbitration time to gain control of the system bus and the extra delays of the multiple layers of buffers used to get to and from the system bus. The addition of another DMA device could slow the system down if the system bus cannot support all the bus master's memory bandwidth needs.

SINGLE-BOARD COMPUTERS

The 1970s produced VLSI technology, which increased the performance and capabilities of silicon devices and at the same time reduced the number of devices and cost to implement complex functions. It became possible to inte-

---

[2]Apple II is a trademark of Apple Corporation, Cupertino, California.

[3]TRS-80 is a trademark of Radio Shack Division of Tandy Corporation, Fort Worth, Texas.

grate on a single circuit board all of the basic elements of the common-bus computer architecture. This resulted in the first SBC. (Figure 1-4 is a block diagram of an SBC, and Fig. 1-5 shows the implementation.) A typical SBC in the 1970s consisted of the generation of the system clock, read and write memory (RAM), real-only memory (ROM), I/O ports and drivers, serial communications interface, and bus control logic and drivers. The SBC is really a self-contained computer system which offers an inexpensive, yet expandable, way to computerize a product with minimal engineering effort.

The key advance that VLSI technology provided was reduction of device count that in turn reduced the amount of printed-circuit board (PCB) area required to support system functions. An example is the serial communications area: the 8251 programmable communications interface chip reduced the serial communication interface logic from 30 in^2 (193.56 cm^2) to less than 4 in^2 (25.8 cm^2). Similiar VLSI advances in devices that implement other system functions permitted the first SBC to be built. The trend in Multibus-compatible SBCs is toward enhancement of existing features as well as the addition of new ones. These trends can be seen in Heurikon Corporation's MLZ-91A SBC, which

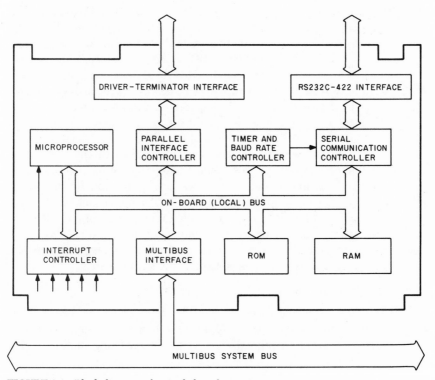

FIGURE 1-4   Block diagram of a single-board computer.

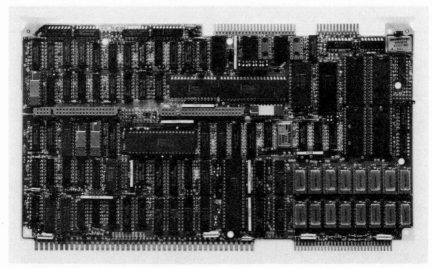

FIGURE 1-5   Single-board computer.

includes a 4-MHz Z80A[4] microprocessor, 64K bytes of RAM, DMA controller, a double-density floppy disk drive controller, hard disk and tape interfaces, and hardware mathematics support. Another example of the enhancement of features on an SBC is Intel Corporation's iSBC 86/30, which includes an 8-MHz 8086 microprocessor, 128K bytes of dual-ported RAM, four 28-pin sites, 24 parallel I/O lines, an RS-232 serial port, two iSBX connectors for inexpensive I/O expansion and high-speed mathematics support via an 8087 coprocessor.

The architecture of an SBC is designed to permit access of local resources (memory and I/O on the SBC) by the local microprocessor without accessing the system bus. Local resources are accessible only by the local microprocessor; no other system bus device can access them. The microprocessor operates fastest when using local resources because it does not have to arbitrate for the system bus and the design can be optimized for a particular implementation. This is particularly useful in multiple-processing applications, since all the SBCs can perform true parallel processing when executing out their local resources. The potential disadvantage is that system consistency is lost. Another master in the system, such as a disk controller, cannot access the local resources.

MULTICOMPUTING AND MULTIPROCESSING

The VLSI explosion has continued to reduce the cost of a microprocessor to such a low level that applying multiple microprocessors to meet system performance requirements has become an attractive and viable option. Using multiple micro-

---

[4]Z80A is a trademark of Zilog Corporation, Cupertino, California.

processors in a system design not only enhances system performance and throughput but also improves system reliability and system real-time response. Instead of doing one task at a time, a microprocessor-based system can increase throughput because the work is divided among a number of microprocessors. Another way of improving performance is by reducing the number of individual tasks any given microprocessor must handle. The time a new request for service will wait is thereby reduced, and so is the real-time response of the system.

A simple definition of multicomputing is the use of multiple microprocessors that are capable of independent instruction execution and are able to communicate with each other over some local interconnection mechanism. The system is statically partitioned in that each microprocessor does a predetermined task. The processing units can be heterogeneous or homogeneous. A multicomputing system may have some shared resources, but that is not a requirement. The key is that the processing units' tasks are independent and require little interunit communication. A basic multicomputing configuration is shown in Fig. 1-6.

Using SBCs in a multicomputing system moves the bus activity from the system bus to the SBCs' local bus; this reduces the bandwidth needed on the system bus. The local execution of a program on an SBC becomes very important in multicomputing applications, since the different SBCs can execute their programs without using the Multibus system bus as long as all their code is located in local memory. Thus, providing true parallel processing with all microprocessors operating independently is possible with SBCs. The reduced system bus demand permits additional microprocessors (SBCs) to be added to the system and thereby increases overall system throughput.

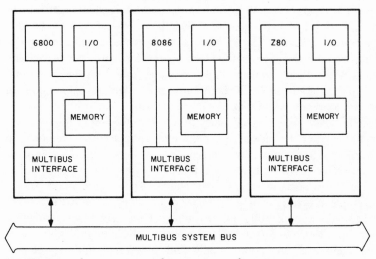

FIGURE 1-6 A heterogeneous multicomputing configuration.

Similar to multicomputing is multiprocessing, which is defined as the use of multiple homogeneous microprocessors that are capable of independent instruction execution, are able to communicate with each other over some interconnection mechanism, and have shared memory and I/O. All the microprocessors in the system have exactly the same available resources. The coupling between the processing units is much tighter. The System is dynamically partitioned in that each microprocessor is assigned a task on a next-available-microprocessor basis. This must be done in such a way that the process is invisible to the user code being executed. A basic multiprocessor configuration is shown in Fig. 1-7.

In a common-bus architecture, adding more microprocessors to the system, as in multiprocessing systems, eventually causes the system bus to become saturated. When microprocessors are added to an already saturated system bus, each microprocessor must wait longer to gain access to the system bus, so the performance of each of the modules decreases. The net effect is lower total system throughput. A well-planned multiple microprocessor system bus structure will allow new microprocessors to be added to the system in a modular fashion. When new system functions, such as more peripherals, are added to the system, more processing power can be applied to handle them without affecting existing processor performance. This is a result of having extra system bus bandwidth as in the case of a multiprocessor system (needed to support another microprocessor executing on the system bus), or, in a multicomputing system, having enough bandwidth to support the communication and data transfer needs of the additional microprocessor. In addition, the bus structure must provide a communication path for microprocessors to signal each other.

Multiprocessing and multicomputing are supported on the Multibus system bus. Two to sixteen microprocessors (bus masters) are supported on the same system bus. Each of these microprocessors can be homogeneous or heterogeneous: one an 8-bit, another a 16-bit, one running at 1 MHz, and another at 16 MHz. Another aspect of heterogeneity is that the resources available to each microprocessor are different. The Multibus system bus also provides an arbitration and bus control exchange method that guarantees that a bus master can access the system without another master obtaining it, and it provides several reliable communication methods between bus masters through common resources such as memory and I/O.

Advances in semiconductor technology have driven the cost of microprocessors down to the point at which peripherals are the most expensive resources in the system. To design for maximum efficiency and economy, the designer must keep the expensive peripherals highly utilized. It is possible to do so only if multiple microprocessors are using the peripherals. The point can best be seen with an example. A system with an 8-in hard disk, a floppy disk, 512K bytes of RAM, and a single-user operating system running on one central processing unit (CPU) costs from $5000 to $10,000. The peripherals (the hard and floppy disks) and the packaging (the box, power supply, and cables) represent over 80 percent of the system cost. Adding a second microprocessor and a multiuser oper-

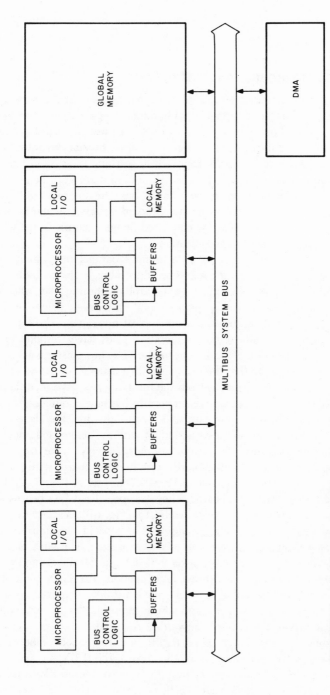

FIGURE 1-7 A multiprocessor configuration.

13

ating system to the system could roughly result in doubling throughput with only a 5-percent cost increase.

1.2.2 A Conceptually Simple Structure

A system bus structure must be easy to learn and use, and at the same time it must be flexible in order to support a wide range of applications. Documentation is a very important aspect of "easy to use"; it must be well structured to help the user understand the bus system. It must be broken down to give the user a step-by-step building-block approach to learning the system bus structure. Application examples of how to use the bus also are very helpful. They can give the user practical experience with the bus structure without having to actually build a prototype. An experienced board designer should be able to understand a new structure in a few hours and design a simple board within a few days after reading the bus specifications.

The Multibus system bus is an asynchronous parallel bus which can be divided into five signal categories: a 24-line address bus, a 16-line bidirectional data bus, eight multilevel interrupt lines, control and timing lines, and power distribution lines. The system bus operates on a master-slave principle. Figure 1-8 shows a typical bus master and some typical bus slaves. The bus master controls the system bus and starts all operations. Bus slaves respond to commands put on the system bus by the bus master. The bus master is interlocked to the bus slave module in that the bus master first issues a command and then must wait for an acknowledgment from the receiving bus slave module before continuing. This interlocking mechanism permits bus slave modules of different speeds to be on the same system bus, since each individual bus slave controls the amount of time it waits before responding with the acknowledgment.

The iSBX concept allows the designer to inexpensively customize standard cost-effective Multibus-compatible boards (or any other board) with particular I/O features. This is done with small (2.85 × 3.7 in; 7.24 × 9.4 cm) I/O modules called iSBX Multimodule boards. They are specialized I/O boards which plug piggyback style onto a variety of baseboards (Fig. 1-9) and thereby provide very low cost local I/O functional expansion. The concept is optimized around VLSI technology and small increments of I/O expansion. The iSBX boards are connected to the baseboard's local bus via the iSBX bus interface, and they convert the iSBX bus signals to a defined I/O function. The iSBX Multimodule boards enable the user to configure exactly the capabilities required for the system, which keeps both system size and cost at minimum levels. Since the I/O expansion is local, no system bus bandwidth is required.

By providing a standard high-speed, tightly coupled connection between the microprocessor and its memory on another board, the iLBX bus permits the expansion of an SBC's local memory in a modular manner (without using the Multibus system bus) beyond what can fit on an SBC. The iLBX bus is opti-

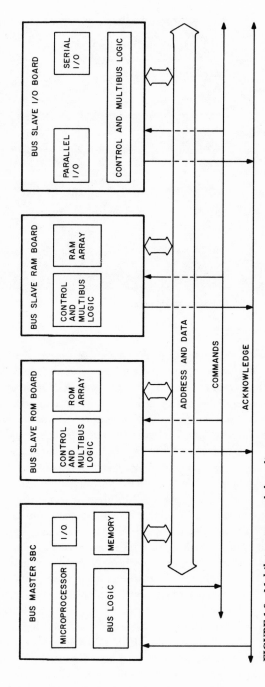

FIGURE 1-8 Multibus master and slave diagram.

15

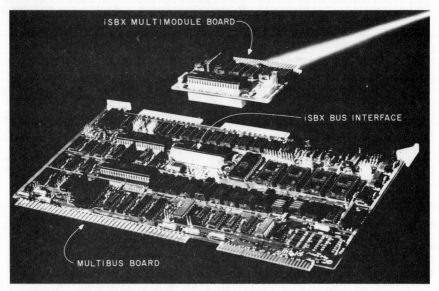

FIGURE 1-9 The iSBX Multimodule board concept.

mized for high-speed memory access. It supports two types of data transfer: a noninterlocked mode for maximum performance and an interlocked mode to support slower memory modules. The bus structure is built upon the master-slave principle, whereby the bus master (the SBC) places address and commands on the bus and the slave board (the memory module) decodes and acts on the command. This private bus between the microprocessor and the memory frees the Multibus system bus for DMA or other bus master traffic. Figure 1-10 is a block diagram of an SBC and a memory board connected via the iLBX bus.

The Multichannel bus provides a standard high-speed (8M bytes per second) block-oriented gateway into and out of a Multibus-based system. By utilizing a standard interface, the bus allows multiple heterogeneous devices such as different high-speed I/O and memory modules to be connected together. Figure 1-11 is a simplified block diagram of a Multichannel system. The bus structure is an asynchronous parallel bus built upon the master-slave principle with interlocked 8- and 16-bit data transfers. The Multichannel bus has the ability to link together up to 16 devices that are distributed over a distance of up to 50 ft (15 m) via a twisted pair flat ribbon cable. It has addressing capability of up to 16M bytes of memory and 16M bytes of I/O space on each bus device. Figure 1-12 shows Intel's iSBC 589, a high-speed intelligent DMA controller, which connects the Multibus system bus to the Multichannel bus. The 60-pin connector on the top of the board is the Multichannel bus connector.

Another important feature of both the Multibus structure and the Multichannel bus is the ability to put multiple master modules on the same bus for multiprocessing configurations. A method is defined to transfer control of the bus between master modules, and it guarantees that only one bus master controls the bus at a given time. Both buses also support priority interrupts. This capability permits bus modules to request interruption of normal activity and have a special event serviced by the master microprocessor.

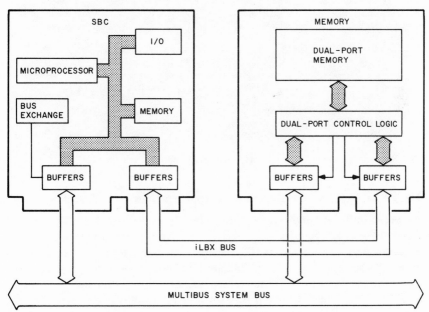

FIGURE 1-10 The iLBX memory expansion bus concept.

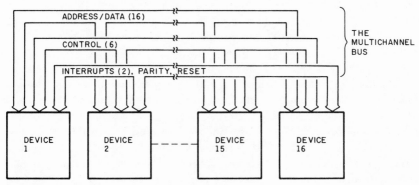

FIGURE 1-11 The Multichannel bus block diagram.

FIGURE 1-12   Multibus board with a multichannel interface.

1.2.3   A Structure That Can Incorporate New VLSI Quickly

Advances in VLSI technology have resulted in performance and complexity doubling every 2 to 3 years (Fig. 1-13). As an example, Intel Corporation's 8008 microprocessor, introduced in 1972, had a 30-μs average instruction execution time and was able to address a maximum of 16K bytes of memory. In 1982, Intel introduced the iAPX 80286 microprocessor, which has an average instruction time of less than 1 μs and is capable of addressing a maximum of 16M bytes of memory. This technology explosion presents the system designer with the opportunity to design systems that have lower cost, higher performance, increased density, and greater reliability. But it also means quick obsolescence for systems that are not designed to permit the incorporation of future generations of VLSI components. The system designer has the challenge of creating competitive systems that can easily assimilate successive generations of VLSI technology.

Historically, new VLSI components required new system designs, especially for new microprocessors. Designers would implement new system boxes each time a new microprocessor was introduced, which meant completely new memory, I/O, and microprocessor board designs. The new designs were dedicated to supporting only a few functions with very basic and limited I/O. There was very little flexibility in the design to handle future VLSI technology or new peripherals without a major redesign. It became clear that a universal system box was needed; it would permit the use of previously designed memory and peripheral modules. From this exercise came the Multibus system bus, the first standard microprocessor system bus, and its family members: the iSBX bus, the Multichannel bus, and the iLBX bus.

In this age of rapid technological change, the use of standard system structures helps designers to quickly incorporate new VLSI technology into both new and old designs. They do so by tying the new VLSI devices to solid universal interfaces which are the gateway to all system resources such as memory and peripherals. The system must be developed in a functionally partitioned manner. Each of the functional units may be designed with the best technology available for that particular task and to interface to the system bus standard. When future generations of VLSI devices permit it, a superior replacement functional unit can be designed provided it meets the interface standard. Since the interface remains unchanged, the new unit can replace the old one and minimize the impact it has on the other functional units in the system.

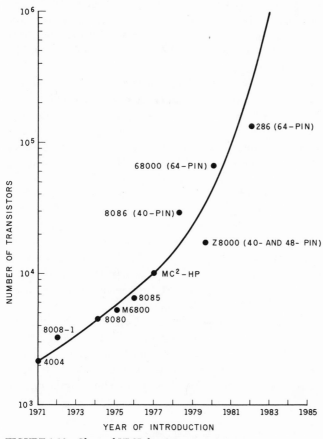

FIGURE 1-13   Chart of VLSI density versus time.

Success in adapting future VLSI devices to microprocessor-based systems is measured by the effectiveness of the system's organization in alleviating the highly irregular structures of past and present microprocessors. The key lies in so defining the system bus structure that it is decoupled from any particular VLSI device. It must be architecture-independent; that is, it must be flexible enough to support many different families of VLSI devices. It should not have special signals that only one device supports. However, the interface must be similar to typical VLSI component interfaces to minimize the extra transistor-transistor logic (TTL) required to convert the component interface to the universal interface. The board designer can design the VLSI device to the universal bus interface provided the new device has the ability to communicate quickly and easily with the rest of the system.

As an example, let us examine a three-board system: a CPU board based on a 5-MHz Z80,[5] a memory board, and a disk controller board. Assume that in the next design, a new CPU board is needed to get higher performance. The system designer needs to have the freedom to build an 8-MHz 80286-based CPU board. A properly defined bus structure would permit this new microprocessor board, which operates 10 times faster, to replace the old microprocessor board without affecting the rest of the system. The memory and disk controller boards would not have to be modified or replaced.

Another goal of a bus structure must be longevity. One way to achieve longevity is to support many different types of microprocessors and other VLSI devices over a 10- to 15-year lifespan. This requires that the bus structure support generic microprocessor attributes such as memory address space, I/O address space, some form of mutual exclusion, interrupts, different widths of address and data lines, and multiple-bus master-control capability. The bus must also be independent of microprocessor, memory, and I/O device speed.

The Multibus system bus provides a very basic set of generic functions which support a wide range of microprocessor families. Two data path widths permit the use of both 8- and 16-bit microprocessors. That includes a very wide range of 8-bit microprocessors such as 8080, Z80, 6800, and 8088. In the 16-bit world, there are Multibus-based SBCs with 8-MHz 80286s, 8-MHz 68000s, and 8-MHz Z8000s. Addressing is flexible; it permits the choice of 64K bytes, 1M byte, or 16M bytes of memory address space. Separate I/O address space, which can be either a 256K- or a 65K-byte location, is also supported.

In applications in which the microprocessor requires more bandwidth from the system bus than it can deliver, the iLBX bus provides an alternative. Microprocessor memory bandwidth needs have increased at a greater rate than memory subsystems have. The system bus which connects the two modules together can easily become the bottleneck. One solution is to use two buses in the system:

<hr>

[5]Z80 is a trademark of Zilog Corporation, Cupertino, California.

one bus for execution (which must be very tightly coupled to the microprocessor–memory subsystem pair) and a second bus for system communication and data movement. The iLBX bus provides this tightly coupled connection. The iLBX bus expands the local memory of the SBC, saving system bus bandwidth and supporting multicomputing architectures that require multiple SBCs with more memory than can fit on a single board.

1.2.4 A Reliable, Cost-Effective Structure

The most important aspects of a bus structure's basic .cost are the form factor and interface costs. The cost of a module is generally proportional to module area. For a given area of PCB there is a minimum established cost; it is the cost of a two-layer PCB plus the system bus interface and some minimal circuitry. The complexity of implementing the system bus interface is proportional to the board area occupied. Smaller form factors cannot support extensive system bus features because of the additional circuitry required. The bus interface logic should occupy only 10 to 20 percent of the PCB area. Thus, in applications with minimal computer requirements a bus standard with a small board area should be chosen. Ideally, the form factor would support just enough components to accomplish the task at hand and future upgrades. The boards should be small enough for easy and inexpensive replacement in the field. That also makes repairs simple and fast.

If the form factor is too small, designers may run into problems in implementing reasonable functions in the system on a single board. Often the designer must resort to numerous board-to-board interconnections. Small board size may result in a greater than 20 percent board area to implement the bus interface. That leaves less space to implement the required function. A larger board has more area for interface logic, which in turn makes room for more complex functions to be supported. For applications which require a lot of computer power it is necessary to choose a bus standard with a larger form factor. The upper limit of the board size is typically limited by power-to-ground and signal-noise considerations. A standard Multibus board can safely handle 30 to 40 W of 5-V power. The limiting factor is the voltage drop across the P1 connection, which becomes too large. It subtracts from the voltage margin of the components on the board, which reduces the reliability of the board. Other factors that limit board size are (1) the envelope of the enclosure in which the board is used and (2) the warpage of the board, which can become severe.

The Multibus system bus provides solutions to a wide range of microprocessor-based systems. The form factor is small enough to be cost-effective in low-density designs and large enough to support a wide range of functions on a single board. At the low end, the VLSI support has reduced the bus interface logic to 10 percent of the board area. The Multibus system bus is also modular, which permits low-end designs to implement only part of the total bus capability and yet still operate with other Multibus boards. This leaves most of the board area available to accomplish the function of the design on a low-density two-layer circuit board. At the high end, a single Multibus board can accommodate a basic computer system consisting of a 16-bit microprocessor, nine interrupts, 24 parallel I/O lines, an RS-232 serial channel, 128K bytes of ROM capacity, and 512K bytes of RAM.

There are three options for I/O expansion: a Multibus module, an iSBX Multimodule board, and a Multichannel module, each with a different cost, performance, and capability range (Fig. 1-14). The iSBX Multimodule board provides the lowest-cost expansion for small increments of local I/O capacity. The iSBX Multimodule board is small (10.5 in^2; 26.7 cm^2), which keeps costs low. The interface was so designed that very little or no interface logic is required on the iSBX Multimodule board, so almost all the PCB area (typically >90 percent) can be used to implement the desired I/O function. An example of an iSBX Multimodule board is a serial communication module which has one or two complete serial channels. A Multibus module provides more flexibility and capacity, as well as global accessibility, but at a higher cost because of the

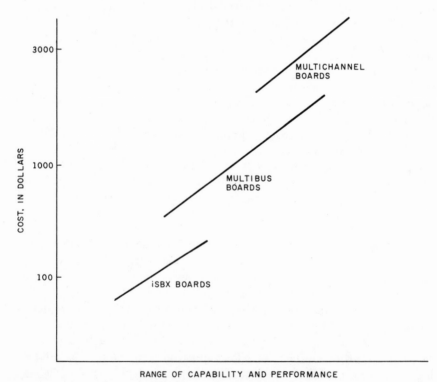

FIGURE 1-14 **Multibus family I/O expansion flexibility.**

greater PCB area (81 in^2; 522.6 cm^2) and the greater bus interface cost of implementing more complex functions. An example of a Multibus I/O board is a communication module with eight complete serial channels and a microprocessor with memory. The maximum data rates into and out of the board are limited by the Multibus lines (about 1M bytes per second). If more bandwidth is required, the Multichannel bus can be used; it provides up to 8M bytes per second transfer rates.

1.2.5 A Well-Defined, Documented, and Controlled Standard

The bus structure must be very well defined so multiple-board designers can design boards that will operate together on the system bus. Each signal must be documented and explained so clearly that there is no room for user misinterpretation. This includes signal definition, timing and loading requirements, and application examples. The signals in the system must cross a multiplicity of physical interfaces between the microprocessor and memory or I/O, including the system bus. Careful consideration must be given to these interfaces—solder connections, wire-wrap connections, and plug-in card connections—if they are to meet long-term-reliability goals. In addition, there must be limits on the physical dimensions of the system bus modules to permit construction of economical packaging systems to house the modules. All of this must be properly documented in a publicly available specification.

The specification must be properly controlled by an accepted authority in the industry. This controlling body has the responsibility to maintain and make updates and extensions to the bus specification. The changes and extensions must be so implemented that they support all old designs that met the earlier specification. The adoption of standards results in connectability, portability, and interchangeability of the different products designed to meet that standard. This protects the investment in many of the board designs when the boards are used in newer and more powerful systems. A custom I/O board can be used in two or three generations of systems, which saves time and development expense. This is a very important aspect of the evolution of a system bus to a solid and reliable foundation for system designs for years to come.

Developed standardized industrial buses used to build a microprocessor-based system provide a proven, reliable foundation. They are implemented by experienced designers who take into account very important electrical attributes, such as bus length, ground-plane effects, line reflections, ringing, noise coupling, signal skew, and connector reliability, that could easily be overlooked in a new bus design. Also, standardized industrial buses have been thoroughly tested and have demonstrated long-term reliability in field applications.

The Multibus/IEEE-796 bus set the standard for what a well-defined bus structure should be. It was first defined by Intel in the Multibus specification and later refined by the Institute of Electrical and Electronics Engineers (IEEE)

Standards Committee in the form of the IEEE-796 bus standard. The iSBX bus is following a similar path. The initial definition, by Intel, was later updated by the IEEE Standards Committee in the form of the IEEE-P959 standard. Both specifications were written to define all operations completely; no user interpretation is required. In 1984, just 9 years after the introduction of the Multibus system bus, more than 120 different vendors were making more than 2000 compatible products. After only 3 years following the introduction of the iSBX bus, six vendors were making 35 different iSBX-compatible products. This is an indication of the popularity and quality of the specifications. The IEEE standardization efforts on both the IEEE-796 and IEEE-P959 will help assure the user community that the compatibility and high commercial quality of these buses will be maintained. The result is bus-compatible products from different manufacturers that will operate together reliably. The Multichannel and iLBX buses also have controlling specifications available to the general public. They were written with the same basic goals of the Multibus and iSBX specifications and will most likely follow the same standardization path.

The Multibus system bus and its other family members are very popular, and buyer's guides for them are available. The *Multibus Buyers Guide* is published semiannually by Ironoak Company (La Jolla, California). The *Buyers Guide* lists all the Multibus-family-compatible board-level products currently available. This publication provides the system designer, original equipment manufacturer (OEM) integrators, and manufacturers with a survey of the entire market.

The Multibus family of structures has been the basis of many designs in many different applications and environments from controlling bank teller machines to controlling steel mills. During the first 5 years of Multibus availability, more than 100,000 systems were shipped. This training ground has resulted in a proven and reliable bus structure.

1.3 BRIEF HISTORY OF THE IEEE-796/MULTIBUS AND ITS EXTENSIONS

The Multibus system bus was originally developed at Intel Corporation in 1975 by the company's microprocessor systems group. The first product in which the new standard system bus was used was the group's Microcomputer Development System, the Intellec 800,[6] which provided design engineers with the software and hardware tools needed to implement microprocessor-based designs. The system architecture was a simple split-bus approach (Fig. 1-15). In addition to using the development system to implement their projects, some customers built custom boards and incorporated all of the boards into their own boxes. Intel Corporation then distributed the Multibus system bus specification to give

---

[6]Intellec is a trademark of Intel Corporation, Santa Clara, California.

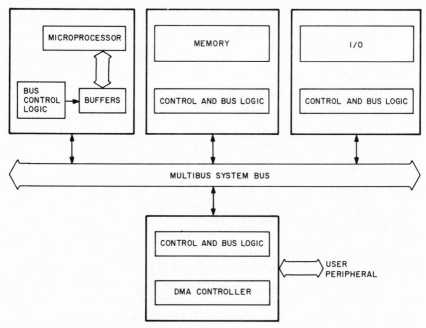

FIGURE 1-15 Split-bus architecture.

other vendors the basis for building Multibus-compatible products. The original Multibus structure supported only 8-bit transfers and 16 address lines.

Intel perceived the need for board-level solutions. In 1976 it provided the first commercially available SBC, the iSBC 80/10, that integrated on a single PCB a microprocessor, memory, and I/O. This new iSBC product line was based on the Multibus system bus, and it was the first Multibus-compatible board with a complete microprocessor system on a single board. The product line was very successful, and hundreds of competitive and complementary products followed from Intel Corporation and other vendors. All these products were compatible with the commercial-quality Multibus because of the effective documentation of the Multibus specification, which was made available by Intel Corporation and later by the IEEE Standards Committee with the IEEE-796 bus specification.

In 1977 the first silicon support for the bus was developed. Intel's 8218 and 8219 bipolar Multibus system bus controller for MCS-80 and MCS-85 families reduced the PCB area required to support the bus exchange logic and command generation from 5 in^2 (32.26 cm^2) to 1 in^2 (6.45 cm^2), which reduced the dollar cost of the Multibus interface. These chips contain all the control logic required by a bus master to interface with other masters on the Multibus system bus and share memory and I/O. They permit any designer to implement the bus exchange logic and command generation with a proven, reliable method and thereby reduce the possibility of design errors. The bus structure was extended in 1978 to dynamically support both 8- and 16-bit devices. The Multibus system bus became the first microprocessor bus to permit both 8- and 16-bit devices to communicate with each other over the system bus. These evolutionary extensions made it possible for the Multibus system bus to support a new generation of 16-bit microprocessors and increased the useful lifespan of the bus as an industry standard.

In 1978 the Task 796 Working Group of the IEEE Computer Society's Microprocessor Standards Committee was set up to standardize the Multibus system bus. The 796 bus specification has its roots in Intel's Multibus system bus. Intel's specification was reviewed and refined by representatives from many different companies throughout the industry. During the standardization task some minor bus modifications were incorporated and improvements in documentation were made. One of the modifications was to extend the address bus to support 16M bytes by providing 24 address lines. The IEEE Standards Committee serves as a single point of control, which ensures that the specification of the bus will not change. A solid specification which does not change assures that products built by different vendors will be compatible. And, finally, the IEEE Standards Committee puts the specification into the public domain. The standardization work was completed in December 1982.

The iSBX bus was originally developed at Intel in 1979 by the OEM Microcomputer Systems Operation (OMO) group in Hillsboro, Oregon, to extend the SBC architecture with low-cost local I/O expansion. The concept was accepted immediately, and multiple vendors started producing iSBX Multimodule-compatible boards. In 1982 the IEEE Computer Society's Microprocessor Standards Committee was formed to standardize the iSBX bus. The Multichannel and iLBX buses were developed by Intel Corporation in 1982 by the OMO group.

2

The Multibus
System Bus

This chapter provides the basis for a conceptual understanding of the Multibus system bus. Included in it are the logical description of the functions of the bus and a detailed look at the electrical and mechanical specifications. The information in it was based on the Intel Multibus Specification (9800683-03) dated April 1981 and the Microcomputer System Bus Standard (796 bus) dated October 1980. It is recommended that anyone designing on the Multibus system bus obtain the latest versions of those specifications from Intel Corporation.

2.1 NOTATION

In this section, as well as throughout the book, a consistent notation for signals has been followed, and the memory read command (MRDC) will be used to explain it. The terms "true-false" and "one-zero" can be ambiguous and will be avoided. We will use the terms "electrical high (H)" and "low (L)." A slash or an asterisk following the signal name, as in MRDC*, indicates that the signal is active-low. For example,

$$\text{MRDC}* = \text{MRDC}/ = \text{MRDC}- = \overline{\text{MRDC}} = \text{asserted at 0 V}$$

Table 2-1 further explains the notation used in this book.

During the Multibus system bus standardization work by the IEEE Standards Committee, which produced the IEEE-796 bus specification, two basic notation standards were used. They differed from those of the original bus specification by Intel in two ways: (1) the change from the slash (/) to denote an active-low signal to an asterisk (*) and (2) the use of decimal instead of hexadecimal notation. For example, in the original Multibus specification DAT0/ to DATF/ represented the 16 data lines; in the new IEEE-796 specification DAT0* to

TABLE 2-1 Notation Summary

Signal name	Definition			
	Label	Electrical	Logical	State
IORC	H High	$\geq +2.0$ V	1 True	Active, asserted
	L Low	$\leq +0.8$ V	0 False	Inactive
IORC*	L Low	$\leq +0.8$ V	1 True	Active, asserted
	H High	$\geq +2.0$ V	0 False	Inactive

DAT15* is used to represent them. In the original IEEE-796 specification hexadecimal notation was used, and it is to be converted to decimal notation over a 5-year period. By 1987 decimal notation must be used in all IEEE-796-compatible documentation. This chapter uses the notation of the IEEE-796 specification, which is hexadecimal, and an asterisk (*) to indicate an active-low signal. The other specifications in this book use decimal and asterisk notation. Readers will encounter the variant forms of notation on some figures and tables, and should be aware of their meaning and validity.

Also, these numeric conventions will be followed: to indicate decimal notation, (1) the letter D will follow the number (e.g., 120D) or (2) a number without any following letter will be assumed to be decimal. Binary numbers will be followed by the letter B (e.g., 10001110B), and hexadecimal numbers will be followed by the letter H (e.g., 10BDH).

2.2 LOGICAL DESCRIPTION OF THE MULTIBUS SYSTEM BUS

The Multibus system bus is a commercial-quality bus used in microprocessor-based systems. The bus supports both 8- and 16-bit data paths in the same system, and it can be configured to support up to 16M bytes of memory address space and 64K bytes of I/O address space. Multiple masters are supported with up to 16 bus masters. The basic command protocol of the bus is asynchronous (the bus masters and bus slaves can operate with independent clocks) and interlocked, and all bus cycles require a positive acknowledgment from the bus slave before the bus master can continue. The maximum bus transfer rate is 5 megawords per second.

A Multibus-compatible board measures 6.75 × 12.00 in (17.5 × 30.48 cm). The Multibus interface consists of two edge card connectors, P1 and P2. The P1 connector has 86 pins and handles the regulated +5-, +12-, and −12-V power, the 8- and 16-bit data bus, 20 bits of addressing (1M byte), the bus control lines, and the bus arbitration lines. The P2 connector has 60 pins and is used for the upper four address lines (16M bytes) and the iLBX bus. The iLBX bus is a high-speed memory execution bus used to expand the local memory capacity of an SBC without using the Multibus system bus. The iLBX bus is discussed in more detail in Chap. 5.

2.2.1 Bus Devices

There are three basic types of elements that interface with the Multibus system bus: bus masters, bus slaves, and bus hybrid modules.

BUS MASTERS

A bus master is any module that can control the bus and initiate data transfers. The Multibus system bus supports up to 16 bus masters on the same system bus. Control of the bus is passed from one bus master to another through its bus exchange logic. Any one of these 16 bus masters can make a data transfer by (1) requesting control of the bus through its bus exchange logic, (2) aquiring the bus once it is granted access, and (3) driving the command and address lines to perform data transfers. Figure 2-1 is a block diagram of a basic bus master, which consists of a microprocessor, bus exchange logic, and data-address buffers. A more complex master, a typical SBC bus master, is shown in Fig. 2-2. The SBC also includes its own memory and I/O logic. Typical bus masters are CPU modules, SBC modules, disk controller modules, and DMA controllers. All bus masters either process or move data in the system.

BUS SLAVES

A bus slave is any module that can respond to bus commands generated by a bus master. It can control only three parts of the bus: (1) the interrupt lines when generating interrupts, (2) the data lines when performing a read command, and (3) the acknowledge line. Bus slaves simply decode the address and command information on the system bus and perform the requested operation and acknowledge the master once the operation is completed. Memory and I/O expansion modules are examples of typical bus slaves; they are low-cost vehicles that extend the system capabilities by providing data storage or I/O capability to the system. Some bus slaves are shown in Fig. 2-3.

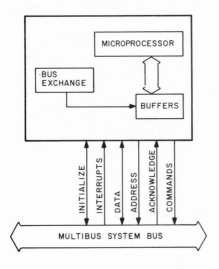

FIGURE 2-1 Basic Multibus master.

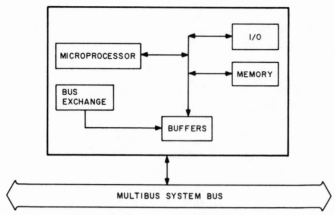

FIGURE 2-2 Block diagram of a typical SBC bus master.

HYBRID MODULES

A hybrid module has all the attributes of a bus master and most of the attributes of a bus slave on one module. Like a bus master, it can control the bus, and it has resources that can be used by other bus masters. The latter make it look like a bus slave to the other bus masters. Figure 2-4 shows two hybrid modules. The first one is an SBC with dual-port memory, which is memory which can be accessed by the microprocessor on that module, as if it were a private resource, and by another bus master via the Multibus system bus. The dual-port memory is both a local resource, which can be accessed by the local microprocessor without using the system bus, and a global resource, which is accessible to all bus masters. The second hybrid is a simple combination of a memory module and a bus master on one board. Each of the functions, however, is logically independent.

Hybrid modules are an outgrowth of the VLSI explosion; today an entire system can be built on one Multibus board. Some examples of hybrid modules are intelligent communication boards such as Interphase Corporation's LNC5180 Local Area Network Controller and SBCs such as Intel's iSBC[1] 86/30 board and National Semiconductor's BLC[2] 80/30 board. These boards are considered hybrid modules because they have (1) the ability to control the bus through their bus exchange logic and (2) the RAM that can be accessed from the system bus through their dual-port control logic.

[1]iSBC is a trademark of Intel Corporation, Santa Clara, California.

[2]BLC is a trademark of National Semiconductor Corporation, Santa Clara, California.

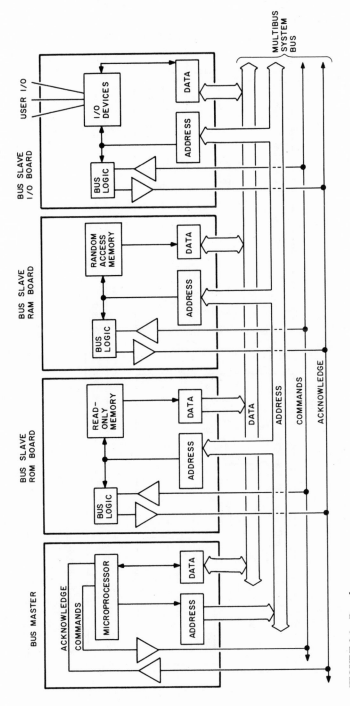

FIGURE 2-3 Bus slaves.

31

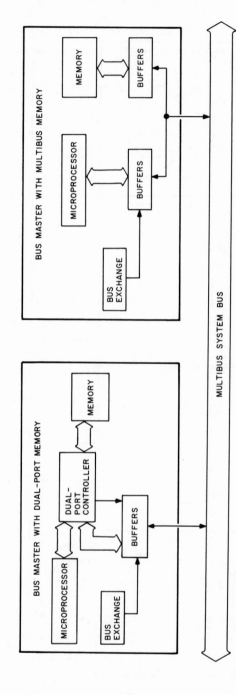

FIGURE 2-4 Hybrid Multibus modules.

2.3 BUS SIGNAL DEFINITIONS AND OPERATION OVERVIEW

In this section the signals that make up the bus are described, and basic Multibus operations are discussed. The Multibus system is composed of 90 signal lines that can be broken into several classes: address (25 bus lines), inhibit (2), data (16), control (9), interrupts (9), bus exchange (5), and power (24). The different classes are explained in the following sections.

2.3.1 Address, Inhibit, and Data Lines

The address, inhibit, and data lines can be broken down into four groups:

Class	Signal	Function
Address	ADR0*–ADR17*	Address lines (0–9, A–F, 10–17) in hexadecimal notation
Byte control	BHEN*	Byte high enable
Inhibit	INH1*–INH2*	Inhibit 1 and 2
Data	DAT0*–DATF*	Data lines 0 to F in hexadecimal notation

ADDRESS

The 24 address lines ADR0* to ADR17* carry the binary address of the memory location or I/O device that the bus master is referencing. ADR0* is the least significant bit of the address. The bus master indicates to the bus slaves which type of address (memory or I/O) is on the address lines by using the appropriate command line. The IORC* and IOWC* commands are used for I/O port accesses, and the MRDC* and MWTC* commands are used for memory accesses. The Multibus system bus supports many address ranges—three for memory modules and two for I/O modules. The three memory address ranges are those that address 16M bytes, those that address 1M byte, and those that address 64K bytes. The I/O address ranges are those that address 256 devices' addresses and those that address 64 kilodevices' addresses (see Fig. 2-5). These various ranges are discussed in Sec. 2.6. Different ranges are needed to support various microprocessors. The 8080 microprocessor can address only 64K bytes of memory and 256 I/O devices, whereas Intel's iAPX 80286 microprocessor can address 16M bytes of memory and 64K bytes of I/O devices.

All signals on the Multibus system bus are negative true; that is, the active state is low, and they are terminated with a pull-up resistor. These termination resistors cause all signals which are not driven to be in the inactive (high) state. If a bus slave looks at the address bus and no bus master is driving it, the bus slave reads an address of 000000H. This permits a memory board (a bus slave) to decode all 24 address bits and still respond to a microprocessor that can generate only 16 address bits. In this case all the nondriven address lines will be in the inactive state. (ADRX* = high, so the upper eight address lines ADR10*

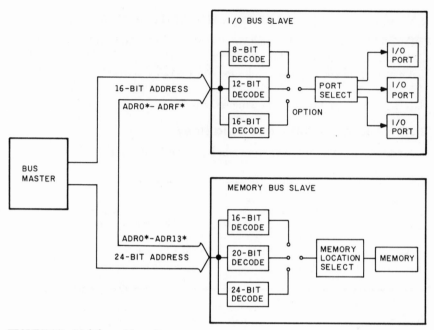

FIGURE 2-5 Multibus address line usage.

to ADR17* will be decoded as TTL low.) Thus if an 8080 microprocessor were to generate a memory read command of location 1000H (hexadecimal), the address on the system bus as seen by the memory board would be 001000H. The microprocessor module would drive ADR0* to ADRF*, and the termination resistor would drive ADR10* to ADR17*.

BYTE HIGH ENABLE

Byte high enable (BHEN*) is used to select the upper byte (DAT8* to DATF*) of a 16-bit word. BHEN* is used only in 16-bit systems. It is an extension of the address bus that supports 8-bit-byte operations on 16-bit words.

The Multibus structure supports both byte and word addressing (see Fig. 2-6). A byte location is the smallest addressable unit of storage. There are two types of byte address locations: an even-byte address (ADR0* = high) and an odd-byte address (ADR0* = low). Two consecutive byte locations form a word. The Multibus structure can transfer a word only if the first byte location of the word is an even address (ADR0* = high). If the first byte location of the word is an odd address (ADR0* = low), the bus master must perform two byte accesses and assemble the word.

A bus master accesses a byte on the system bus by placing the binary address (even or odd) on the address lines and driving BHEN* = high (inactive). Access to a word location is gained by placing the binary address on the address lines with ADR0* = high (an even address) and BHEN* = low (active). Again, word access on odd-address boundaries must be divided into two byte bus accesses, and the bus master must reassemble the word. This is summarized below:

	BHEN* = low	BHEN* = high
ADR0* = low	Reserved	Odd-byte access
ADR0* = high	Word access	Even-byte access

INHIBIT

Inhibit INH1* and INH2* is used by a bus slave to hold off another bus slave's bus activity. This permits a bus slave (the inhibiting slave) to turn off another bus slave (the inhibited slave). The inhibit lines can be used during a memory read or memory write operation. The inhibit signal is generated by the inhibiting bus slave based on the bus address lines. If the address is in its address range, an inhibit signal is activated. Then the inhibited bus slave will disable all its drivers from the system bus (data and acknowledge) and may perform the operation internally (locally to the module). The inhibiting bus slave must not return its acknowledge until 1.5 μs after the command is generated. This long

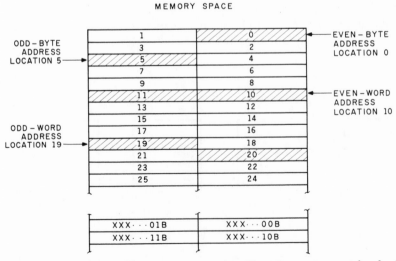

FIGURE 2-6 Multibus address memory mapping. (Note: Bus master must break odd-word address access into two byte accesses and reform the word.)

bus cycle is required to give all inhibited bus slaves enough time to return to a normal state, since an internal operation may have occurred.

Bus slaves that support inhibit operations can be classified as having top, middle, or bottom inhibit priority. The top inhibit priority module can inhibit all other memory bus slaves; a middle inhibit priority module can inhibit or can be inhibited by another bus slave; and a bottom inhibit priority module can be inhibited by but cannot inhibit another bus slave. The signal INH1* is used by a middle inhibit priority slave memory device that wants to prevent another slave memory device (bottom inhibit priority) at the same address from responding to the requested bus operation under certain specified conditions. For example, this permits ROM to overlap RAM when both are assigned the same address. Effectively, this allows ROM boards, which are typically small or memory-mapped I/O devices, to override the RAM in the system which could occupy the whole memory space. INH2* is used by top-priority modules to prevent middle-priority modules, such as ROM memory modules, from responding to the memory command request. Top inhibit priority modules should also assert INH1* to inhibit bottom inhibit priority modules.

Figure 2-7 demonstrates a bootstrap application which also has diagnostic software in ROM. There are three modules that can occupy the same memory location: (1) the bootstrap ROM, which has top inhibit priority, (2) the diagnostic ROM, which has middle inhibit priority, and (3) the RAM, which has bottom inhibit priority. When the system is first turned on, the boot ROM is enabled. The bus master accesses memory from its reset starting point, where the RAM is normally located. Since the boot ROM is enabled, it generates the INH1* signal which turns off the RAM module, the bottom inhibit priority. It also enables the INH2* signal which turns off the diagnostic ROM module, the middle inhibit priority. Once the bootstrap operation is complete, the bootstrap module is disabled, which disables its INH1* and INH2*.

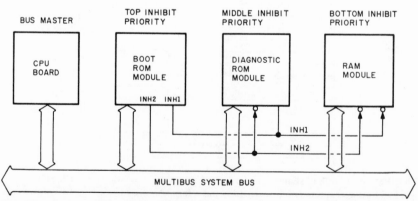

FIGURE 2-7   Bootstrap inhibit application.

Next the system software will confirm that the system hardware is operational by executing the diagnostic software installed in the diagnostic ROM module, which is enabled via an I/O command. Each access to the ROM module would cause the INH1* signal to be activated, which would turn off the RAM module. Once the diagnostic program is complete, the system software can disable the ROM module. This disables the INH1* signal, and the bus master can now access the RAM.

The inhibit lines can be used during both read and write operations. During read operations the inhibited module will not cause its stored data any adverse effects. This means that data written into a RAM module and then accessed after a previously inhibited access will remain valid. During write operations, the contents of the memory location may or may not be changed. If data is changed, it will be only the one byte or word that is addressed. No other data in the inhibited module may be altered. Thus, the inhibit lines cannot be used to protect memory.

DATA LINES

The 16 data lines DAT0* to DATF* are used to transmit or receive information to or from a memory location or I/O device. DAT0* is the least significant bit for both byte and word transfers. The Multibus permits both 8- and 16-bit bus masters by supporting three types of data transfer (Fig. 2-8): (1) even-byte transfers on DAT0* to DAT7*, (2) odd-byte transfers on DAT0* to DAT7*, and (3) word data transfers on DAT0* to DATF*. All byte transfers use data lines DAT0* to DAT7*. DAT8* to DATF* are not defined during byte transfers. All odd-byte transfers, which when local to a 16-bit microprocessor are transferred on the high-order data byte, are swapped from the local high-order data byte to the lower-order data byte while on the Multibus system bus. They are swapped back to the high-order byte once they are back on the local bus of the 16-bit microprocessor. This is done by using a byte-swapping technique that permits both 8- and 16-bit bus masters to operate on the same bus because all byte transfers occur over the lower byte of the data lines.

Two signals control the data flow: byte high enable (BHEN*) and ADR0*. (The data flow is summarized in Fig. 2-9.) Even-byte transfers require both ADR0* and BHEN* = high (inactive). Odd-byte transfers require ADR0* = low and BHEN* = high. The data is swapped from the high byte of the word and sent over the low-byte portion of the data bus. A 16-bit microprocessor would swap the data back to the odd byte of the word. An 8-bit microprocessor would simply read the data on its data lines. During word transfers, the address put on the address lines must be an even address; ADR0* = high and BHEN* = low (active). There are two consecutive byte addresses for each word. The even-byte address (ADR0* = high) corresponds to the word data bits DAT0* to DAT7*. Conversely, the odd-byte address, which is the address on the address lines plus 1, corresponds to the word data bits DAT8* to DATF*. Only word transfers use data lines DAT8* to DATF*.

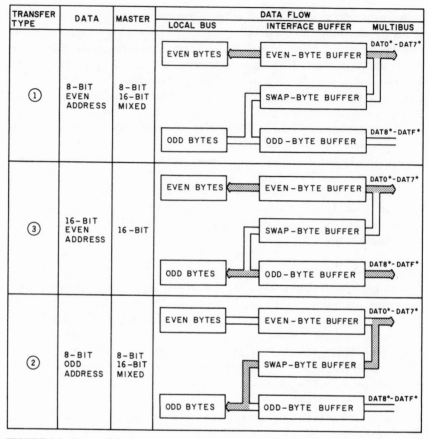

FIGURE 2-8 Types of data transfers.

2.3.2 Control Lines

The control lines define the data transfer protocol on the system bus. They can be broken down into four basic groups.

Class	Signal	Function
Mutual exclusion	LOCK*	Lock
Utilities	CCLK*	Constant clock
	INIT*	Initialize
Commands	MRDC*	Memory read command
	MWTC*	Memory write command
	IORC*	I/O read command
	IOWC*	I/O write command
Acknowledge	XACK*	Transfer acknowledge

MUTUAL EXCLUSION

Mutual exclusion (LOCK*) is used by a bus master to guarantee that no other bus device or microprocessor can access a resource until that bus master has finished using it. In systems with multiple microprocessors, there must be an established method for the microprocessors to communicate with one another. One very popular method is through the use of shared memory (RAM). It

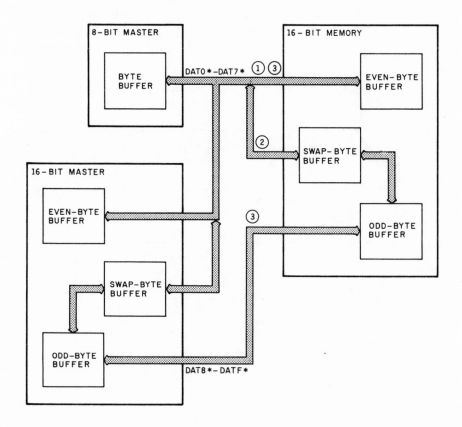

TRANSFER TYPE	DATA TRANSFER	BHEN *	ADRO *
①	8-BIT EVEN ADDRESS	HIGH	HIGH
②	8-BIT ODD ADDRESS	HIGH	LOW
③	16-BIT EVEN ADDRESS	LOW	HIGH

FIGURE 2-9 Data flow on Multibus data lines.

requires no special mechanisms between the microprocessors—they communicate by passing messages stored in the RAM. The message is guarded by a flag (a byte in the RAM) which indicates if there is a valid message. When this

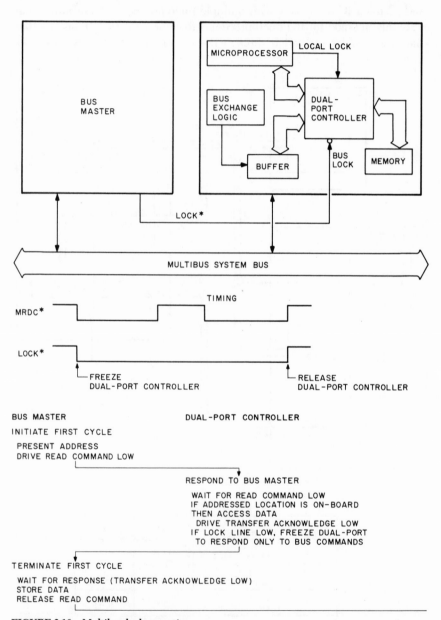

FIGURE 2-10 Multibus lock operation.

method is used, there are many cases in which one of the microprocessors must have exclusive access to the flag. While one of the microprocessors is updating the flag, another microprocessor must not be permitted to have access to it. A microprocessor must have the ability to read the flag, test it for validity, and write back into the flag in order to let other microprocessors know that it now owns the flag and corresponding message (without another microprocessor intervening). This operation, called read, modify, and write, provides the microprocessor with exclusive access to or mutual exclusion of a memory location for both the read and the write operations.

The Multibus system bus provides for mutual exclusion between bus masters simply by holding the bus until the operation is completed. The bus master can gain control of the system bus, perform a read operation, test the data, and then perform the write operation. The LOCK* line allows this mutual exclusion to be extended off the bus. This signal is required only in multiple-port RAM board designs when the bus master needs to prevent the microprocessor on another module from getting access to its own multiple dual memory (memory with multiple paths into it). Figure 2-10 is an example of how LOCK* is used

TERMINATE RESPONSE

WAIT FOR READ COMMAND HIGH
RELEASE DATA AND TRANSFER
   ACKNOWLEDGE
CONTINUE TO FREEZE DUAL-PORT
   TO RESPOND ONLY TO BUS COMMANDS

RELEASE ADDRESS

INITIATE SECOND CYCLE

PRESENT ADDRESS
DRIVE READ COMMAND LOW

RESPOND TO BUS MASTER

WAIT FOR READ COMMAND LOW
IF ADDRESSED LOCATION IS ON-BOARD
THEN PRESENT DATA
   DRIVE TRANSFER ACKNOWLEDGE LOW

TERMINATE BUS CYCLE

WAIT FOR RESPONSE
STORE DATA
RELEASE READ COMMAND AND
   LOCK LINE

TERMINATE RESPONSE

WAIT FOR READ COMMAND HIGH
RELEASE TRANSFER ACKNOWLEGE
   AND DATA LINES
RELEASE DUAL-PORT CONTROLLER TO
   RESPOND TO ON-BOARD REQUESTS

RELEASE ADDRESS LINES
INITIATE NEXT CYCLE

FIGURE 2-10 (*Continued*)

in a dual-port design. The bus hybrid locks its dual-port memory to the Multibus system bus when it is addressed and the LOCK* signal is active. The dual-port logic on the bus module will not permit access to the memory by the local microprocessor until LOCK* is driven inactive.

CONSTANT CLOCK

Constant clock (CCLK*) is a general-purpose clock used by bus modules. The frequency is approximately 10 MHz. The most common use of CCLK* is on bus slave modules for acknowledge generation logic.

INITIALIZE

Initialize (INIT*) is used to put the system in a known state before bus cycles are started. INIT* is typically used at power-up time in order to guarantee that the system starts in the same way each time and also when a major error occurs and the only recovery is a complete system restart. All bus masters should both receive and drive the INIT* signal. This causes the entire system to start at the same time, because the INIT* signal will not become inactive until the slowest board reset is completed.

COMMAND LINES

The command lines (MWTC*, MRDC*, IOWC*, IORC*) are controlled by the bus master and are used to request an operation of a bus slave device. There are four commands: memory read and write and I/O read and write. Each has a unique signal on the bus. The four commands are used to support two types of operations: memory and I/O. Microprocessors such as the 8085 have instructions dedicated to I/O operations; that is, there are specific output and input instructions. These instructions initiate special machine cycles which cause information to flow between the microprocessor and an I/O port location.

An active command indicates to the bus slave that the address lines are valid and that the bus slave should perform the specified operation. Only one of the four commands can be active at a time. A read command is used by the bus master to request that data be sent from the bus slave. Conversely, a write command is used by the bus master to send data to the bus slave.

TRANSFER ACKNOWLEDGE

Transfer acknowledge (XACK*) is used by the bus slave to inform the current bus master that the requested operation is complete. For a memory write cycle, an active XACK* indicates (to the bus master) that the data on the data lines is now stored in the memory location specified on the address lines. For an I/O read cycle, it means that the data on the data lines from the addressed I/O device is valid. This signal permits the bus master to proceed to the completion of the bus cycle.

The bus master command and bus slave transfer acknowledge relationship provides the interlocking mechanism which permits modules of different speeds to be on the system bus. The bus master initiates the bus data transfer and then waits for the bus slave to inform it when the operation is completed via the transfer acknowledge (XACK∗) signal. Thus, if there are two bus slaves, one that can transfer data at a 1M byte per second rate and another that can transfer data at a 2M bytes per second rate, both can operate at maximum rate. This also permits a module to be replaced with a faster or slower module without modification of the bus masters.

If a bus slave fails to generate an XACK∗, the bus master will not be able to complete the bus cycle. Since the bus master continues to wait, the system will stop. This situation will occur only if the bus master tries to access a resource that was not present on the system bus. One way to prevent the stoppage is to provide a time-out function which will terminate the bus cycle, after some fixed period of time, by generating XACK∗. This capability is used in systems with different amounts of RAM when the system software needs to find out how much memory is available. The software starts at the beginning of RAM and does a test on that location. If the RAM can be written into and that same data read back, the location is in the system. The software continues through memory until it finds a bad location which it interprets as being top of memory. The time-out function is a separate piece of logic which typically is on all bus masters.

2.3.3   A Data Read Operation

A memory read cycle is shown in Fig. 2-11; it is assumed that the bus master has control of the system bus. (Bus exchange techniques are discussed later in this section.) The data read operation sequence is as follows:

1. The bus master takes the first action by placing the address on the address lines.

2. Then, after a wait for the address setup time (time for the bus slave modules to decode the address), the transfer is initiated by activating the read command (MRDC∗) signal. All the bus slaves look at the address and command information on the bus. The slave with the requested memory location accesses the data.

3. That bus slave then puts the data on the data lines.

4. In doing so, the bus slave activates the transfer acknowledge (XACK∗) line.

5. The bus master strobes in the data and terminates the data transfer cycle by putting the MRDC∗ signal in the inactive state.

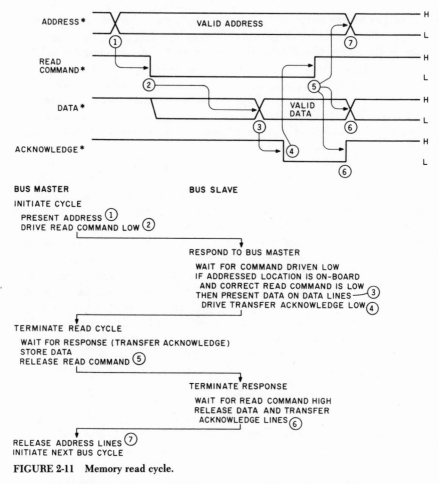

FIGURE 2-11 Memory read cycle.

6. This causes the XACK* signal and read data from the bus slave.

7. The address from the bus master then becomes inactive.

An I/O read operation is the same as the memory read operation except the I/O read (IORC*) command is used and an I/O port location instead of a memory location is accessed.

2.3.4 A Data Write Operation

A typical memory write cycle is shown in Fig. 2-12. Again it is assumed that the bus master has control of the system bus. The data write operation sequence is as follows:

1. The bus master places the address on the address lines.

2. The bus master also places the data to be written on the data lines.

3. After waiting to meet the address and data setup time (time for the bus slave modules to decode the address and get the data through its data buffers), the transfer is initiated by activating the memory write command (MWTC*) signal. All the bus slaves look at the address and command information on the system bus; the bus slave with the requested memory location stores the data on the data bus into that memory location.

4. When the operation is completed, the bus slave activates the transfer acknowledge (XACK*) line.

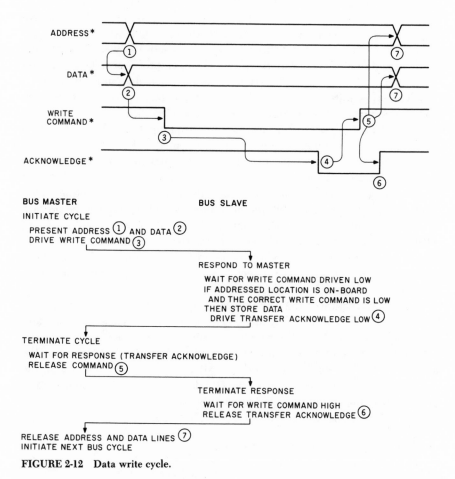

FIGURE 2-12   Data write cycle.

5. The bus master terminates the data transfer cycle by driving MWTC*
inactive.

6. This, in turn, causes the memory board to drive XACK* inactive.

7. The address and data then become invalid.

An I/O write operation is the same as the memory write operation except that
the I/O write (IOWC*) command is used and the I/O port location instead of
a memory location is accessed.

2.3.5 Interrupt Lines

An interrupt is typically used in a real-time execution-type system in which an
external event must be acted upon with minimal delay. Any system with interrupt capability must have a set of interrupt servicing routines in its executive
software. Each of these interrupt service routines is a task activated by a particular interrupt level or number; this type of control is well suited to the
machine and process control marketplace. The microprocessor is the destination
of all interrupts. Each of the interrupt sources is assigned an interrupt number
which determines its priority level. When multiple interrupts occur at the same
time, the interrupt with the highest priority is serviced first.

Most microprocessors have a hardware interrupt input pin which, when activated, causes the program currently being executed to be automatically suspended. Then the state of the machine is saved and the program execution
control is transferred to an interrupt service routine that corresponds to the
device that caused the interrupt. The particular interupt service routine is chosen by the hardware, which tells the microprocessor where to go in the progam
by sending it an interrupt vector address. The interrupt vector address is not
necessarily the exact memory address of the starting location of the service routine; some microprocessors modify the address before using it. The resultant
address is then used as a lookup vector in a table of jump commands which
points to the various service routines.

The basic structure of the Multibus interrupt system is shown in Fig. 2-13.
The microprocessor in this diagram is controlling some external machine and
processes. The machine will generate interrupts when service is needed. The
microprocessor then stops executing its current progam and starts executing the
interrupt service routine for that device. After it has completed servicing the
machine, the microprocessor signals the I/O device to turn off its interrupt and
then returns to the program it was previously executing.

The interrupt lines can be broken down into two groups:

Interrupt request	INT0*–INT7*	Interrupt 0–7
Interrupt hold	INTA*	Interrupt acknowledge

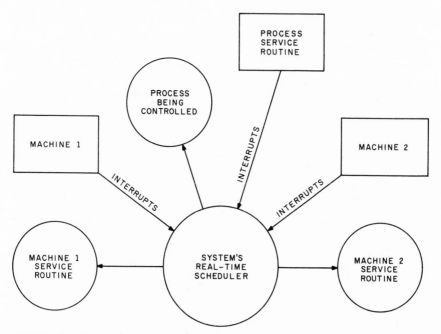

FIGURE 2-13 Interrupt system structure.

INTERRUPT REQUEST

The interrupt request lines (INT0* to INT7*) are used by any bus module to activate an interrupt service request from the system master. The requesting device activates the interrupt signal and keeps it active until serviced. INT0* has the highest priority.

INTERRUPT ACKNOWLEDGE

Interrupt acknowledge (INTA*) is generated during interrupt cycles on the bus. It is used to freeze the interrupt status of all the interrupt controllers in the system and then get the interrupt vector address from another module in the system. The Multibus supports two types of interrupt implementation schemes: non-bus-vectored and bus-vectored.

NON-BUS-VECTORED INTERRUPTS

Non-bus-vectored (NBV) interrupts are handled totally on the bus master and do not require the Multibus interface for the interrupt vector address. The interrupt vector address is generated by the interrupt controller on the bus master and transferred to the microprocessor over the local bus. The device that generates the interrupts can reside on the bus master or on a bus slave module. In the latter case it uses the Multibus interrupt request lines (INT0* to INT7*) to generate its interrupt requests to the bus master. In both cases the bus master performs its own interrupt operation by generating the interrupt vector address locally and executing the interrupt service routine. This routine will service the interrupting device and command it to remove the interrupt request. Figure 2-14 shows two examples of NBV interrupt implementation, one with the interrupting device on the bus master module and one with the device on a bus slave module.

BUS-VECTORED INTERRUPTS

For bus-vectored (BV) interrupts the bus master requires the aid of the interrupting module. After receiving an interrupt, the bus master requests the interrupting bus module to send the appropriate interrupt vector address. The

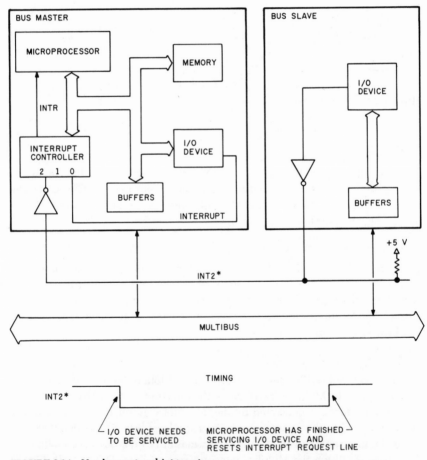

FIGURE 2-14 Non-bus-vectored interrupts.

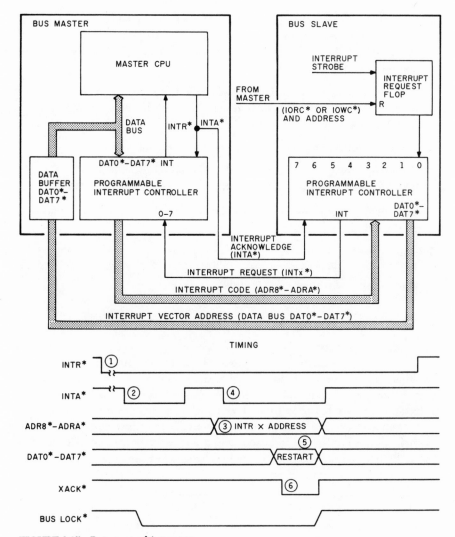

FIGURE 2-15 Bus-vecotred interrupts.

interrupt vector address is sent to the bus master over the Multibus data lines (DAT0* to DAT7*) by the interrupting bus slave. The bus master uses the INTA* signal to request the interrupt vector address.

Figure 2-15 shows a BV interrupt implementation. When the interrupt is requested,

1. The slave interrupt controller notifies the master interrupt controller on the bus master, which causes the microprocessor on the bus master to process the interrupt.

2. The microprocessor then generates an INTA* command on the system bus, which freezes the state of the priority of the interrupt logic on all bus modules. Each of the slave interrupt controllers is assigned a unique interrupt controller address.

3. Next the bus master puts the address of the bus slave's interrupt controller on the Multibus address lines (ADR8* to ADRA*) that had the highest-priority interrupt request.

4. The bus master also generates a second INTA* command.

5. The second INTA* command asks the selected interrupt controller to put its interrupt vector address on the Multibus data lines (DAT0* to DAT8*).

6. The bus slave activates the XACK* signal when the interrupt vector address on the data lines is valid.

7. This causes the bus master to terminate the interrupt cycle by removing the INTA* signal. The microprocessor will then transfer program control to the appropriate interrupt service routine.

2.3.6 Bus Arbitration and Exchange

As microprocessor costs continue to decrease, it has become economically feasible to use multiple microprocessors to meet system performance requirements. Multiple microprocessors must be able to share global resources. The Multibus system bus supports multiple bus masters (microprocessors) with a hardware arbitration and exchange scheme. Two basic types of bus arbitration methods, serial and parallel, are supported. One method of bus exchange also is supported. All bus arbitration and exchanges are made in synchrony with the bus clock (BCLK*). The bus arbitration and exchange lines can be broken down into three groups:

Class	Signal	Function
Control	BUSY*	Busy
	BCLK*	Bus clock
Bus request	BREQ*	Bus request
	CBRQ*	Common bus request
Bus priority	BPRN*	Bus priority in
	BPRO*	Bus priority out

BUS BUSY

Bus busy (BUSY*) indicates the state of the bus; it is supplied to all bus modules. The inactive state means the bus is not being used. All bus masters monitor and can drive the BUSY* signal. The controlling bus master uses BUSY* to indicate to the other bus masters that the bus is in use by driving BUSY* in the active state. A requesting bus master must wait until it has priority and the bus is not being used (BUSY* inactive) before it can gain control of the system bus.

BUS CLOCK

Bus clock (BCLK*) is the bus exchange logic master clock; all bus exchanges are in synchrony with it. BCLK* is bused to all bus modules and can be slowed, stopped, or single-stepped. Single-stepping is very useful during the debug phase of a project. The bus clock frequency is very important in determining the speed of a bus control transfer (bus exchange). The number of masters supported by the serial-priority arbitration method (discussed later in this section) is a function of the BCLK* frequency. BCLK* normally operates at about 10 MHz.

BUS PRIORITY IN

Bus priority in (BRPN*) is used to indicate to a particular bus master that, of all current bus requests, it has the highest-priority request for the system bus. BPRN* also indicates that the master can take control as soon as the system bus is not busy. BPRN* is not bused, and its connection is based on the arbitration method used.

BUS PRIORITY OUT

Bus priority out (BPRO*) is used in a serial or daisy chain bus arbitration scheme (Fig. 2-16) to pass the bus priority along. It is not bused. The BPRN* of the highest-priorty master is always active (low, or tied to ground); its BPRO* is connected to the BPRN* input of the master with the next-lower priority. This, in turn, can be repeated. If the highest-priority master does not need the system bus, it will activate its BPRO* and pass the system bus priority to the next-lower-priority master. This causes the BPRN* of the next bus master to become active, which indicates that it now has the highest priority. If it does not need the system bus, it passes the priority on. A master making a system bus request simply causes its BPRO* to become inactive. That, in turn, causes the next-lower-priority master to lose its bus priority because its BPRN* has become inactive. It then causes its BPRO* to become inactive because it has lost its priority.

The biggest advantage of a bus arbitration scheme using a daisy chain system is its simplicity. Very few control lines are required, and the number of lines is independent of the number of devices. More devices can be added simply by connecting them to the system bus, provided the AC timings are met.

The biggest disadvantage of the daisy chain scheme is its susceptibility to failure. A failure that occurred in the arbitration circuitry of a device could prevent succeeding devices from ever getting control of the system bus or allow

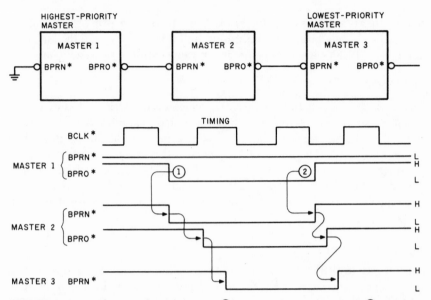

FIGURE 2-16 Serial-priority bus arbitration: ① Master 1 done with the bus. ② Master 1 requests the bus.

more than one device to gain control of the system bus. However, the logic involved is very simple, and a redundant circuit would increase its reliability. Another disadvantage is that the priority structure is fixed. The devices farthest from the highest-priority master could be locked out by higher-priority masters if they had a high demand for the system bus.

The maximum number of bus masters in a system is determined by gate delays through the daisy chain logic, which must be less than one BCLK* period. Figure 2-16 also shows the timing associated with a serial arbitration scheme. A bus arbitration operation can be made each BCLK* cycle (falling edge to falling edge). This requires that all priorities be passed in one bus clock period. The maximum number of bus masters is determined by dividing the amount of time it takes a bus master to pass through the bus priority by the bus clock period. For example, if the bus clock period is 100 ns and a serial pass through delay is 30 ns, the number of masters that can be supported by a serial arbitration method is three (with 10 ns of margin). A more detailed look at serial-priority bus arbitration is taken in Sec. 2.4.

BUS REQUEST

A bus request (BREQ*) is used by a bus master which does not have control of the system bus and wants it. The signal is used only in a parallel arbitration method (Fig. 2-17). Each bus master has a separate pair of bus request (BREQ*) and bus granted (BPRN*) lines which are used for communicating with the central parallel bus priority resolution circuitry (CPR). A BREQ* and BPRN* pair of signals need not be assigned a fixed priority. When a bus master requires use of the system bus, it sends a request to the CPR circuitry. The circuitry selects the next bus master to receive the bus grant and notifies the bus master

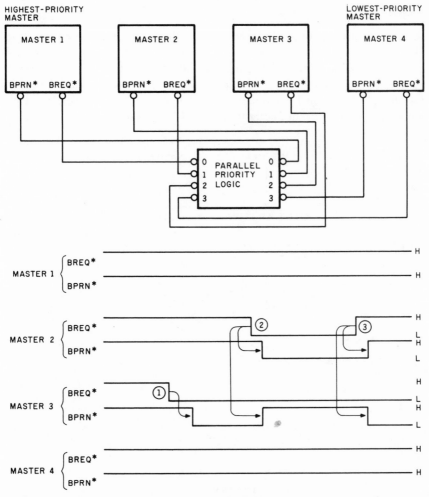

FIGURE 2-17 Parallel-priority bus arbitration: ① Master 3 requests the bus. ② Master 2 requests bus and takes priority away from master 3. ③ Master 2 done with bus and master 3 regains bus priority.

by activating the appropriate BPRN* signal. Up to 16 bus masters can be supported by using this method.

The overhead time required for bus allocation can be shorter than for a daisy chain scheme, since all the bus requests are presented to the CPR circuitry simultaneously. The bus priority can also be dynamically assigned by using a different method such as fixed, adaptive priority, or round robin. The major disadvantage of the parallel-priority method is the additional circuitry of the CPR module.

COMMON-BUS REQUEST

A common-bus request (CBRQ*) indicates to the bus master in control that no other masters are requesting the bus. This allows the bus master to retain control of the bus without contention during each bus cycle and permits it to execute faster because the bus exchange overhead for each cycle is eliminated. A request for control of the bus by another bus master would activate CBRQ*, which would inform the current master to relinquish control of the bus.

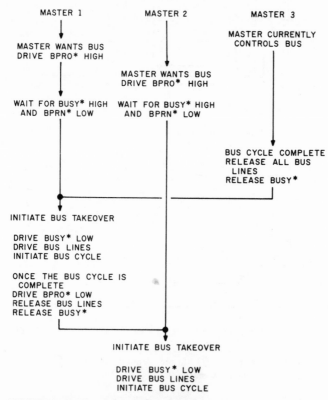

FIGURE 2-18   Bus exchange flow diagram.

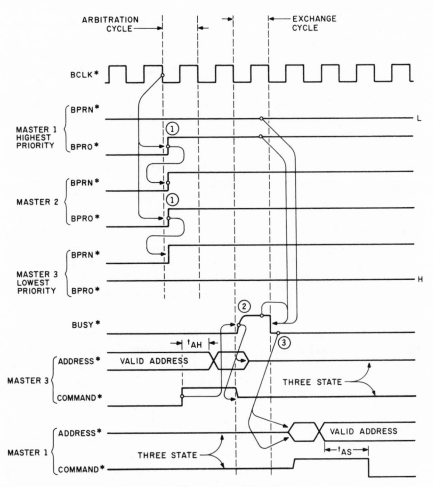

FIGURE 2-19 Bus arbitration and exchange timing diagram.

2.3.7 Bus Exchange

Figures 2-18 and 2-19 illustrate the sequence of events which take place when bus master 1 (the higher-priority bus master) and bus master 2 request the system bus simultaneously and bus master 3 (the lowest-priority bus master) is currently in control of the system bus. Figure 2-18 is a flow diagram; Fig. 2-19 shows the system bus exchange timing of the event. In this example a serial-priority method is used to resolve the bus request arbitration, but the flow diagram and system bus exchange timing would be basically the same if a parallel-priority method were used. All the system bus exchange signals are synchronized to BCLK*. This means that all the output system bus exchange signals

(BPRO∗, BREQ∗, BUSY∗, and CBRQ∗) change state on the falling (high-to-low transition) edge of BCLK∗ and all input system bus exchange signals (BPRN∗, BUSY∗, and CBRQ∗) are in valid states before the next falling edge of BCLK∗. In order to gain control of the system bus, three conditions must be met. First, the bus master must want control of the system bus. Second, the bus master must have the highest priority, which is indicated by an active BPRN∗. Third, the system bus must be free, which is indicated by an inactive BUSY∗ signal.

1. The sequence begins (Fig. 2-18) when bus masters 1 and 2 request the system bus at the same time, which causes the BPRO∗ of both to go inactive on the next falling edge of BCLK∗. On the next falling edge of BCLK∗ both bus masters sample their BPRN∗ and BUSY∗ signals. Bus master 1 detects that it has the highest bus priority, but the system bus is busy and will wait. Bus master 2 detects that it does not have bus priority and will wait. Bus master 1 waits until bus master 3 finishes with the system bus by sampling BUSY∗ on every falling edge of BCLK∗. When bus master 3 finishes the current bus cycle, it checks whether it must give up the system bus by looking at its BPRN∗ signal.

2. Since BPRN∗ is in the inactive state, this causes bus master 3 to initiate releasing the system bus by driving BUSY∗ to the inactive state and disabling all of its system bus drivers. This permits the actual exchange to occur. On the next falling edge of BCLK∗, bus master 1 samples its BPRN∗ and BUSY∗ signals.

3. Since bus master 1 still wants control of the system bus, which is indicated by the state of its BPRO∗ (inactive) signal, it takes control of the system bus by driving BUSY∗ into the active (low) state and enables its system bus drivers. This action must be taken before the next falling edge of BCLK∗. Bus master 2 will continue to sample its BPRN∗ and BUSY∗ signals while waiting for its turn on the system bus.

It is possible for bus master 3 to retain control of the system bus by activating an internal (on-board) signal, called override or bus lock, which goes to the bus master's bus exchange logic. The internal override signal is used to prevent any other bus master from gaining control of the system bus even though it has higher priority. The signal keeps BUSY∗ active and thereby keeps bus master 3 in control of the bus. This procedure guarantees that bus master 3 can have consecutive bus cycles for such software functions as semaphores (test and set).

2.4 DETAILED ELECTRICAL DESCRIPTION

In this section all the timing, loading, and drive specifications of the Multibus system bus are described.

2.4.1 Logical State and Electrical Level Relations

The signal names indicate if the signals are active-high or active-low. If the signal name is followed by an asterisk, the signal is active-low and has the following logical state and electrical level relations, in which L = low and H = high:

Logical state	Electrical level	At receiver	At driver
0	H = TTL high state	$5.25 \text{ V} \geq H \geq 2.0 \text{ V}$	$5.25 \text{ V} \geq H \geq 2.4 \text{ V}$
1	L = TTL low state	$0.8 \text{ V} \geq L \geq -0.5 \text{ V}$	$0.5 \text{ V} \geq L \geq 0 \text{ V}$

If the signal name is not followed by an asterisk, the signal is active-high and has the following logical state and electrical level relations:

Logical state	Electrical level	At receiver	At driver
0	L = TTL low state	$0.8 \text{ V} \geq L \geq -0.5 \text{ V}$	$0.5 \text{ V} \geq L \geq 0 \text{ V}$
1	H = TTL high state	$5.25 \text{ V} \geq H \geq 2.0 \text{ V}$	$5.25 \text{ V} \geq H \geq 2.4 \text{ V}$

These specifications are based on TTL when the power source is 5 V ± 5 percent, referenced to logic ground (GND).

2.4.2 Signal Line Characteristics

The rise and fall times of a signal on the bus must not exceed the following limits:

	Open collector	Totem pole	Three-state
Rise time, ns	—	10	10
Fall time, ns	10	10	10

The timing parameter t_{PD} is the maximum signal propagation delay on the bus. It is measured from the edge of any one board plugged into the backplane to any other board plugged into any other slot, and can be expressed as

$$t_{PD(max)} = 3 \text{ ns}$$

t_{PD} is very important when timing on the bus is to be determined. The setup, hold, and any other times are measured at the edge of the board where it is plugged into the bus. This means that all board-internal and bus delays must be taken into account.

The settling time for all command, acknowledge, clock, and inhibit lines after a transition is zero. On these lines the ringing cannot go beyond the noise immunity levels. The control signals are used to determine the state of the bus, and ringing beyond the noise immunity levels could cause system failures. Address and data lines can ring beyond the noise immunity levels; the only requirement is that they be stable for their setup times. The setup, hold, and command ringing are summarized in Fig. 2-20.

2.4.3 Bus Power Specification

Three voltages ($+5$, $+12$, and -12 V) and ground are provided on the Multibus system bus; eight pins each are assigned to $+5$ V and ground, and two pins are assigned to each of the remaining two voltages. All other voltages should be derived from the three standard voltages. Table 2-2 provides all the bus power specifications.

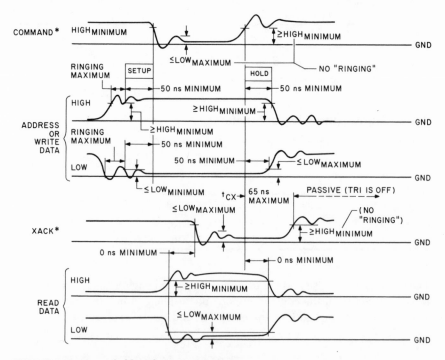

FIGURE 2-20 Setup, hold, and ringing summary.

TABLE 2·2 Multibus Power Specification

	Ground	+5	+12	−12
Mnemonic	GND	+5 V	+12 V	−12 V
Bus pins	P1 − 1,2, 11,12, 75,76, 85,86	P1 − 3,4, 5,6, 81,82, 83,84	P1 − 7,8	P1 − 79,80
Nominal output, V	Ref.	+5.0	+12.0	−12.0
Tolerance from nominal,[a]	Ref.	4.9 to 5.2	11.8 to 12.5	−12.5 to −11.8
Ripple (Pk-Pk),[b] mV	Ref.	50	50	50
Transient response time,[c] μs		500	500	500
Transient deviation,[d] %		±10	±10	±10

[a]Tolerance is worst case, including initial voltage setting, line and load effects of power source, ripple, temperature drift, and any additional steady-state influences.

[b]As measured over any bandwidth not to exceed 0 to 5 MHz.

[c]As measured from the start of a load change to the time an output recovers with ±0.1% of final voltage (50% load change).

[d]Measured as the peak deviation from the initial voltage.

2.4.4 Temperature and Humidity Limits

All bus parameters and specifications must be met within the following temperature and humidity limits:

Temperature 0 to 55°C (32 to 131°F); free moving air across modules and bus (200 LFM recommended)

Humidity 90% maximum relative (no condensation)

2.4.5 Bus Timing

In this section all the timing specifications of the Multibus system bus are described; they are summarized in Table 2-3. The timing diagrams show, for clarity, only the minimum or maximum value required for each parameter; Table 2-3 should be referred to for complete minimum or maximum information. The timing diagrams show how all the parameters are defined in relation to the signals involved. All timing is measured at 1.5 V with loading capacitance C_o and the terminations specified in Table 2-4.

READ OPERATIONS (I/O AND MEMORY)

A read operation transfers data from a memory location or an I/O device to the bus master that is controlling the system bus. Figure 2-21 shows the signals involved in and the timing specifications for a read operation. The bus master must drive the address lines with a valid address a minimum of 50 ns (t_{AS})

TABLE 2·3 Multibus Timing Specification

Parameter	Description	Minimum	Maximum	Units
t_{BCY}	Bus clock period	100	∞ (DC)	ns
t_{BW}	Bus clock width	$0.35t_{BCY}$	$0.65t_{BCY}$	ns
t_{SKEW}	BCLK* skew		t_{PD}	ns
$t_{PD(typ)}$	Standard bus propagation delay		3	ns
t_{AS}	Address setup time (at slave board)	50		ns
t_{DS}	Write data setup time	50		ns
t_{AH}	Address hold time	50		ns
t_{DHW}	Write data hold time	50		ns
t_{DXL}	Read data setup time to XACK	0		ns
t_{DHR}	Read data hold time	0	65	ns
t_{XAH}	Acknowledge hold time	0	65	ns
t_{CCY}	C-clock period	100	110	ns
t_{CW}	C-clock width	$0.35t_{CCY}$	$0.65t_{CCY}$	ns
t_{INIT}	INIT* width	5		ms
t_{INITS}	INIT* to MPRO* setup time	100		ns
t_{XACK}	Acknowledge time	0	8	μs
t_{CMD}	Command pulse width	100	t_{TOUT}	ns
t_{ID}	Inhibit delay	0	100 (Recommend $<$100 ns)	ns
t_{XACKA}	Acknowledge time of an inhibited slave	t_{IAD} + 50 ns	1500	ns
t_{XACKB}	Acknowledge time of an inhibiting slave	1.5	8	μs
t_{IAD}	Acknowledge disable from inhibit (an internal parameter on an inhibited slave; used to determine t_{XACKA} min.)	0	100 (Arbitrary)	ns
t_{INTA}	INTA* width	250		ns
t_{CSEP}	Command separation	100		ns
t_{BREQL}	↓BCLK* to BREQ* low delay	0	35	ns
t_{BREQH}	↓BCLK* to BREQ* high delay	0	35	ns
t_{BPRNS}	BPRN* to ↓BCLK* setup time	22		ns
t_{BUSY}	BUSY* delay from ↓ BCLK*	0	70	ns
t_{BUSYS}	BUSY* to ↓BCLK* setup time	25		ns
t_{BPRO}	↓BCLK* to BPRO* (CLK to priority out)	0	40	ns
t_{AIZ}	Address to inhibit high	0	100	ns

TABLE 2-3 Multibus Timing Specification (*Continued*)

Parameter	Description	Minimum	Maximum	Units
t_{AD}	Address disable		100	ns
t_{BPRNH}	BPRN*↑ to ↓BCLK*	5		ns
t_{BPRNO}	BPRN* to BPRO* (priority in to out)	0	30	ns
t_{CBRO}	↓BCLK* to CBRQ* (CLK to common bus request)	0	60	ns
t_{CBRQS}	CBRQ* to ↓BCLK* setup time	35		ns
t_{CMPH}	XACK↓ to command↑ delay	20		ns
t_{BSYO}	CBRQ*↓ or BUSY*↓ to BUSY*↑ delay	—	12	μs
t_{LCKH}	LOCK* hold time from command*↓	100		ns
t_{LCKS}	LOCK* to command setup time	100		ns
t_{LOCK}	LOCK* width		12	μs

before the bus master activates the read command. The bus slave accesses the addressed data, drives the data lines, and activates XACK* after providing a minimum of 0 ns (t_{DXL}) setup to XACK*. t_{XACK} is defined as the time from command going active until the bus slave activates XACK*. Next the bus master inactivates the command after waiting a minimum of 20 ns (t_{CMPH}) and must hold the address valid for a minimum of 50 ns (t_{AH}). The bus slave must return the data and XACK* lines to a three-state condition in a minimum of 0 ns and a maximum of 65 ns (t_{DHR} and t_{XAH}). The bus master must guarantee that the command is active a minimum of 100 ns (t_{CMD}).

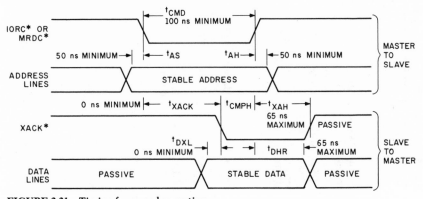

FIGURE 2-21 Timing for a read operation.

TABLE 2-4 Multibus Drivers, Receivers, and Termination Requirements

Bus signals	Driver[a,b]					Receiver[b,c]				Termination[d]		
	Location	Type	I_{OL} min, mA	I_{OH} min, μA	C_O min, pF	Location	I_{IL} max, mA	I_{IH} max, μA	C_I max, pF	Location	Type	R
DAT0*–DATF* (16 lines)	Masters and slaves	TRI	16	−2000	300	Masters and slaves	−0.8	125	18	Mother board	Pull-up	2.2 kΩ
ADR0*–ADR17*, BHEN* (25 lines)	Masters	TRI	16	−2000	300	Slaves	−0.8	125	18	Mother board	Pull-up	2.2 kΩ
MRDC*, MWTC*	Masters	TRI	32	−2000	300	Slaves (memory; memory-mapped I/O)	−2	125	18	Mother board	Pull-up	1 kΩ
IORC*, IOWC*	Masters	TRI	32	−2000	300	Slaves (I/O)	−2	125	18	Mother board	Pull-up	1 kΩ
XACK*	Slaves	TRI	32	−400	300	Masters	−2	125	18	Mother board	Pull-up	510 Ω
INH1*, INH2*	Inhibiting slaves	OC	16	—	300	Inhibited slaves (RAM, PROM, ROM, memory-mapped I/O)	−2	50	18	Mother board	Pull-up	1 kΩ
BCLK*	1 place (master)	TTL	48	−3000	300	Master	−2	125	18	Mother board	To +5 V / To GND	220 Ω / 330 Ω
BREQ*	Each master	TTL	10	−200	60	Central priority module	−2	50	18	Central priority module (not req.)	Pull-up	1 kΩ

Signal	Driver location	Type	I_{OL}	I_{OH}	C_0	Driven by	I_{IL}	I_{IH}	C_1	Termination location	Termination	Resistor
BPRO*	Each master	TTL	4.0	−200	60	Next master in serial priority chain at its BPRN/	−4.0	100	18	Not req.		
BPRN*	Parallel: central priority module Serial: prev masters BPRO*	TTL	4.0	−200	60	Master	−4.0	100	18	Not req.		
LOCK*	Master	TRI	32	−2000	300	All	−2	125	18	Mother board	Pull-up	1kΩ
BUSY*, CBRQ*	All masters	OC	20	—	300	All masters	−2	50	18	Mother board	Pull-up	1 kΩ
INIT*	Master	OC	32	—	300	All	−2	50	18	Mother board	Pull-up	1 kΩ
CCLK*	1 place	TTL	48	−3000	300	Any	−2	125	18	Mother board	To +5 V To GND	220 Ω 330 Ω
INTA*	Masters	TRI	32	−2000	300	Slaves (interrupting I/O)	−2	125	18	Mother board	Pull-up	1 kΩ
INT0*–INT7* (8 lines)	Slaves	OC	16	—	300	Masters	−1.6	40	18	Mother board	Pull-up	1 kΩ

[a]Driver requirements:
I_{OH} = high-output current drive
I_{OL} = low-output current drive
C_0 = capacitance drive capability
TRI = three-state drive
OC = open-collector driver
TTL = totem-pole driver

[b]For low and high voltages specifications see Sec. 2.4.1.
[c]Receiver requirements:
I_{IH} = high-input current load
I_{IL} = low-input current load
C_1 = capacitive load
[d] ±5% ¼-W resistors.

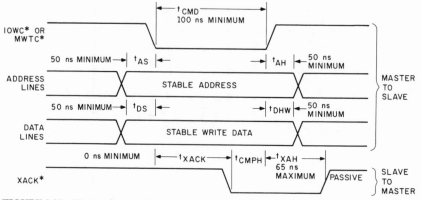

FIGURE 2-22   Timing for a write operation.

WRITE OPERATION (I/O AND MEMORY)

A write operation transfers data from the master that is controlling the system bus to a memory location or I/O device. (The timing for a write operation is shown in Fig. 2-22.) The bus master must drive the address and data lines with valid information for a minimum of 50 ns (t_{AS} and t_{DS}) before the bus master activates the write command. When the bus slave has completed storing the data in the specified address, it activates XACK*. The time from the command active to XACK* going active is the module's acknowledge time (t_{XACK}), and it must be greater than 0 ns. The bus master then removes the command after waiting 20 ns (t_{CMPH}) and holds the address and data lines valid for a minimum of 50 ns (t_{AH} and t_{DHW}). The bus slave must drive XACK* to the inactive state and put the driver in a three-state condition in less than 65 ns (t_{XAH}). It is the responsibility of the bus master to guarantee the command is active a minimum of 100 ns (t_{CMD}).

INHIBIT OPERATION

An inhibit operation may accompany any memory operation. This allows one bus slave to prevent another bus slave from driving the data and acknowledge lines. The inhibit signal may also be generated during IORC*, IOWC*, and INTA* operations but should be ignored by all bus slaves, including the module that should respond to the bus operation. Inhibit timing is shown in Fig. 2-23. The inhibiting slave must drive its inhibit lines in less than 100 ns (t_{ID}) after the bus master has a valid address on the address lines. Any bus slave that can be inhibited must be able to receive the inhibit signals and turn off its bus driver before it would normally have (when not inhibited) generated an XACK*. This implies a minimum access time of 50 ns ($t_{ID} - t_{AS}$) for any inhibited slave module, because the inhibited slave cannot generate an XACK* until it can guarantee that it has control of the bus cycle. The inhibiting bus slave must not activate XACK* until a minimum of 1500 ns (t_{XACKA}) from the active command. The inhibiting slave must remove its inhibit signals (inactive state) in less than 100 ns after the bus address has changed (t_{AIZ}).

NON-BUS-VECTORED INTERRUPTS

Non-bus-vectored (NBV) interrupts are handled on the bus master and do not require the Multibus system bus for transferring the interrupt vector address. There is no timing requirement on the system bus during NBV interrupt operations.

BUS-VECTORED INTERRUPTS

Bus-vectored (BV) interrupts are handled partly on the bus master and do require the Multibus system bus for transferring the interrupt vector address from the bus slave to the bus master. The bus master uses the INTA* command to request the vector address. The timing for BV interrupts is shown in Fig. 2-24. The first INTA* bus cycle is initiated by the bus master when the INTA* signal is activated for a minimum of 250 ns (t_{INTA}). The address and data lines are not used during the first INTA* cycle and should be ignored. The XACK* for the first interrupt cycle is self-generated by the bus master, and this can be done locally to the bus master (XACK* need not be driven). The INTA* signal

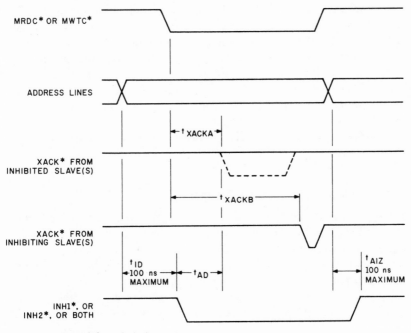

FIGURE 2-23 Inhibit AC timing.

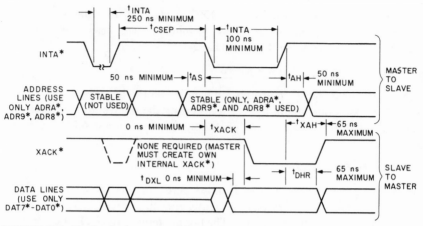

FIGURE 2-24 Timing for bus-vectored interrupts.

is driven inactive by the bus master for a minimum of 100 ns (t_{CSEP}). The bus master must maintain control of the system bus in order to guarantee that there are no intervening bus cycles.

Next, the slave interrupt controller address is put on address lines ADR8* to ADRA* (ADR8* is the least significant bit of slave interrupt controller address) by the bus master. After the address is valid for a minimum of 50 ns (t_{AS}), the second INTA* command is generated. The responding module drives the data lines (DAT0* to DAT7*) with the interrupt vector address. The least significant bit of the vector address is driven onto DAT0*. The responding module activates XACK* after the data lines have been valid for a minimum of 0 ns (t_{DXL}). The bus master then removes INTA* and holds the slave interrupt controller address a minimum of 50 ns (t_{AH}). The responding module must return the data lines and XACK* to an inactive state and put them in a three-state condition in less than 65 ns (t_{DHR} and t_{XAH}). The bus master will then execute the interrupt service routine.

2.4.6 Bus Control Exchange Timing

In this section the timing specifications for the signals required for bus control to be transferred from one bus master to another are described. The bus exchange timing is shown in Fig. 2-25.

Note that, before release of the bus (i.e., BUSY* = high), all timing requirements of any ending cycle, such as the hold times, must be met according to the Multibus specification. The same is true of taking control of the bus (i.e., driving BUSY* low). All setup and other timing parameters must be met.

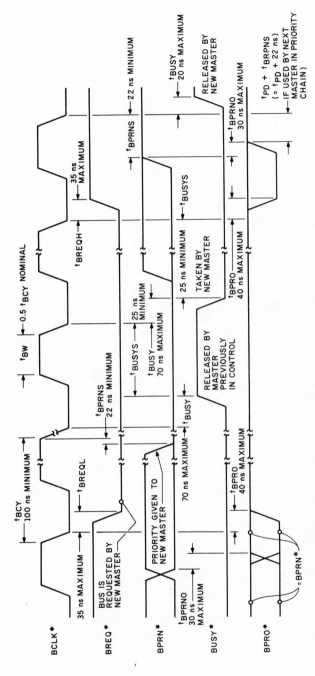

FIGURE 2-25 Bus exchange AC timing. (Note: Use t_{PD}, bus propagation delay, in all system calculations.)

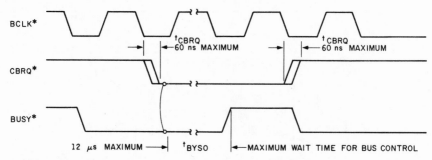

FIGURE 2-26 CBRQ* AC timing. (Note: Use t_{PD}, bus propagation delay, in all system calculations.)

COMMON-BUS REQUEST

Use of CBRQ* is optional. A requesting bus master uses CBRQ* to tell the controlling bus master that another bus master needs the bus. The timing for CBRQ* is shown in Fig. 2-26. CBRQ* is in synchrony with the falling edge of BCLK*; it can change state from 0 to 60 ns after a falling edge of BCLK* (t_{CBRQ}). Once CBRQ* is active, the bus master currently controlling the bus must give the bus up (drive BUSY* inactive) within a maximum of 12 μs (t_{BYSO}) unless it is a higher priority.

SERIAL-PRIORITY ARBITRATION

The timing specifications for serial-priority arbitration are shown in Fig. 2-27. All serial-priority arbitration signals are in synchrony with the falling edge of BCLK*.

t_{BPRO} is the maximum delay time permitted (1) from the falling edge of BCLK* to BPRO* valid or (2) from BPRN* changing state to BPRO* valid.

t_{PD} is the delay time from one bus master's BPRO* changing to the next master's BPRN* changing.

t_{BPRNS} is the setup time (22 ns maximum), the time the signal must be valid before the next falling edge of BCLK*.

The maximum number of bus masters in a system can be determined as follows. All arbitrations must occur within one BCLK* period.

$$t_{BCY} > t_{BPRO} + n(t_{PD} + t_{BPRNO}) + t_{BPRNS}$$

where the number of bus masters in the system can be $n + 2$. As an example.

$$t_{BCY} = 100 \text{ ns}$$

$$t_{BPRNO} = 30 \text{ ns}$$

$$t_{PD} = 3 \text{ ns}$$

$$t_{BPRNS} = 22 \text{ ns}$$

$$100 \text{ ns} > 30 \text{ ns} + n(3 + 30) + 22$$

$$n < \frac{100 - 30 - 22}{33}$$

$$< 1.4$$

Maximum number of masters is $n + 2 = 3$ if BCLK* = 10 MHz.

PARALLEL-PRIORITY ARBITRATION

Figure 2-28 shows the timing specifications for parallel-priority arbitration. All parallel-priority arbitration signals are in synchrony with the falling edge of BCLK*. After each falling edge, a bus master has up to 35 ns to activate BREQ* (t_{BREQL}). The parallel bus arbitration logic must generate valid BPRN*'s at least

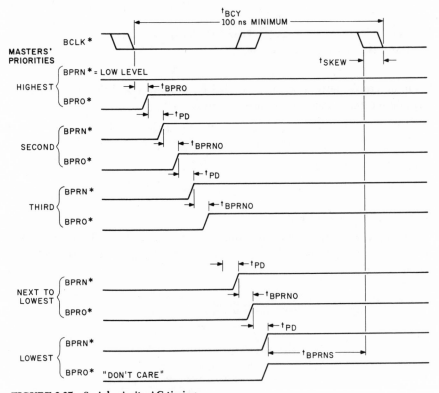

FIGURE 2-27 Serial-priority AC timing.

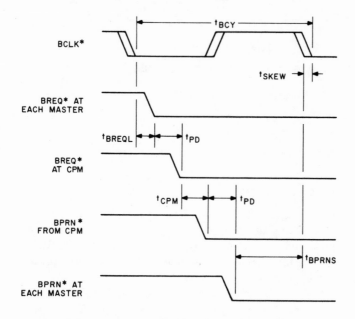

$$t_{CPM(MAX)} \leq t_{BCY\,MIN} - t_{BREQ\,MAX} - 2t_{PD\,MAX} - t_{BPRNS\,MAX} - t_{SKEW\,MAX}$$

FIGURE 2-28 Parallel-priority AC timing.

35 ns before the next falling edge of BCLK∗ (t_{BPRNS}). The time the parallel bus arbitration (t_{CMP}) logic has is calculated as follows:

$$t_{CMP} < t_{BCY} - t_{BREQ} - 2t_{PD} - t_{BPRNS} - t_{SKEW}$$
$$< 100 - 35 - 2 * 2 - 22 - 2$$

where $t_{BCY} = 100$ ns

$$t_{CMP} < 37 \text{ ns}$$

MISCELLANEOUS TIMING

The following diagrams show the timing of constant clock: (CCLK∗), Fig. 2-29; command separation (t_{CSEP}), Fig. 2-30; initialize (t_{INIT}), Fig. 2-31; and lock (LOCK∗), Fig. 2-32.

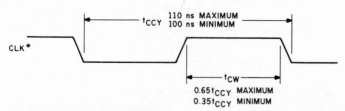

FIGURE 2-29 CCLK∗ AC timing.

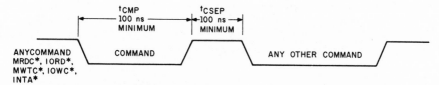

FIGURE 2-30   Command separation AC timing.

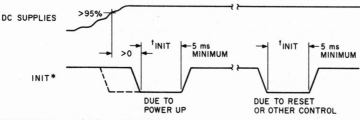

FIGURE 2-31   Initialize AC timing.

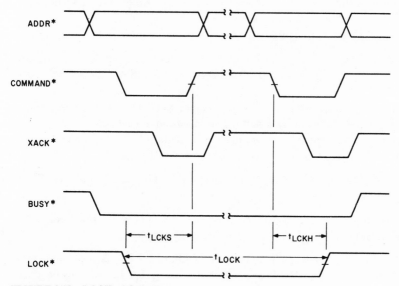

FIGURE 2-32   LOCK* AC timing.

2.4.7 Receivers, Drivers, and Terminations

In this section the driver type (TTL totem pole, open collector, and three-state), the receiver loading, and the value of the signal termination are specified. All of these specifications are listed in Table 2-4.

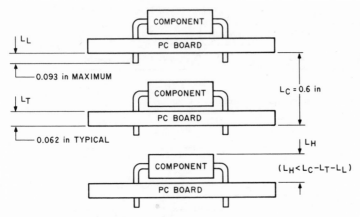

FIGURE 2-33 Board-to-board relations.

2.5 MECHANICAL CONSIDERATIONS

The Multibus specification provides all the physical and mechanical information needed in the design of Multibus-compatible modules and backplanes.

2.5.1 Board-to-Board Relations

The PCB specifications must be followed when Multibus-compatible boards are designed. Refer to Fig. 2-33 to better understand the following exercise.

1. *Board-to-board spacing L_C.* This is the center-to-center spacing of the boards when plugged into the backplane. The minimum specification is 0.6 ± 0.2 in (1.52 ± 0.05 cm). The maximum specification is limited to 18 in (45.7 cm), which is the maximum length of the backplane traces.

2. *Board thickness L_T.* The board thickness must be 0.062 ± 0.005 in (1.57 ± 0.13 mm).

3. *Component lead length L_L.* The length of the component leads below the PCB must be less than or equal to 0.093 in (2.36 mm).

4. *Component height L_H.* The maximum height of the components above the PCB is a function of the board-to-board spacing L_C. In order to be plug-compatible with all designs, $L_C = 0.60 - 0.02 = 0.58$ in (1.47 cm). The following equation is used to determine L_L:

$$L_H < L_C - L_T - L_L$$
$$< 0.58 \text{ in} - 0.067 \text{ in} - 0.093 \text{ in}$$
$$< 0.420 \text{ in } (1.06 \text{ cm}) \text{ (including board warpage)}$$

Electrically conductive components require L_H to be decreased by 0.020 to 0.040 in (0.5 to 1 mm).

2.5.2 Pin Assignments

Two connectors are required to interface to the Multibus; they plug in the backplane. They are labeled P1 (primary) and P2 (auxiliary) and have the specific signal pin assignments given in Tables 2-5 and 2-6. The P2 connector signal pin assignments are in two groups: assigned and bused. The assigned lines are as follows: ADR14*, pin 57; ADR15*, pin 58; ADR16*, pin 55; and ADR17*, pin 56. The rest of the signals are bused and used by the iLBX bus specification (see Chap. 5).

2.5.3 Connector-Naming and Pin-Numbering Standards

The connectors on the PCBs must adhere to the following standards (Fig. 2-34):

1. The connectors on the bus side of the boards will be called P1 and P2. P1 is the 86-pin main connector, and P2 is the 60-pin auxiliary connector.

2. Pins should be numbered with odd-numbered pins on the component side of the board and in ascending order when going counterclockwise around the board as shown in Fig. 2-34.

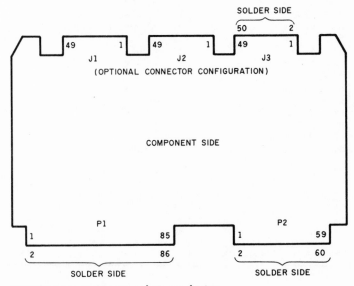

FIGURE 2-34 Connector and pin numbering.

TABLE 2-5 Multibus Pin Assignments of Bus Signals on P1 Connector

	Component side			Circuit side		
	Pin	Mnemonic	Description	Pin	Mnemonic	Description
Power supplies	1	GND	Signal GND	2	GND	Signal GND
	3	+5 V	+5 V DC	4	+5 V	+5 V DC
	5	+5 V	+ 5 V DC	6	+5 V	+5 V DC
	7	+12 V	+12 V DC	8	+12 V	+12 V DC
	9		Reserved, bused	10		Reserved, bused
	11	GND	Signal GND	12	GND	Signal GND
Bus controls	13	BCLK*	Bus clock	14	INIT*	Initialize
	15	BPRN*	Bus pri. in	16	BPRO*	Bus pri. out
	17	BUSY*	Bus busy	18	BREQ*	Bus request
	19	MRDC*	Mem read cmd	20	MWTC*	Mem write cmd
	21	IORC*	I/O read cmd	22	IOWC*	I/O write cmd
	23	XACK*	XFER acknowledge	24	INH1*	Inhibit 1 disable RAM
Bus controls and address	25	LOCK*	Lock	26	INH2*	Inhibit 2 disable ROM
	27	BHEN*	Byte high enable	28	AD10*	
	29	CBRQ*	Common bus request	30	AD11*	
	31	CCLK*	Constant clk	32	AD12*	
	33	INTA*	Interrupt acknowledge	34	AD13*	
Interrupts	35	INT6*	Parallel	36	INT7*	Parallel
	37	INT4*	interrupt	38	INT5*	interrupt
	39	INT2*	requests	40	INT3*	requests
	41	INT0*		42	INT1*	
Address	43	ADRE*	Address bus	44	ADRF*	Address bus
	45	ADRC*		46	ADRD*	
	47	ADRA*		48	ADRB*	
	49	ADR8*		50	ADR9*	
	51	ADR6*		52	ADR7*	
	53	ADR4*		54	ADR5*	
	55	ADR2*		56	ADR3*	
	57	ADR0*		58	ADR1*	
Data	59	DATE*	Data bus	60	DATF*	
	61	DATC*		62	DATD*	
	63	DATA*		64	DATB*	
	65	DAT8*		66	DAT9*	
	67	DAT6*		68	DAT7*	
	69	DAT4*		70	DAT5*	
	71	DAT2*		72	DAT3*	
	73	DAT0*		74	DAT1*	
Power supplies	75	GND	Signal GND	76	GND	Signal GND
	77		Reserved, bused	78		Reserved, bused
	79	−12 V	−12 V DC	80	−12 V	−12 V DC
	81	+5 V	+5 V DC	82	+5 V	+5 V DC
	83	+5 V	+5 V DC	84	+5 V	+5 V DC
	85	GND	Signal GND	86	GND	Signal GND

TABLE 2·6 Pin Assignments on Multibus P2 Connector

	Component side			Circuit side		
	Pin	Mnemonic	Description	Pin	Mnemonic	Description
	1		Reserved	2		Reserved
	3		Reserved	4		Reserved
	5		Reserved	6		Reserved
	7		Reserved	8		Reserved
	9		Reserved	10		Reserved
	11		Reserved	12		Reserved
	13		Reserved	14		Reserved
	15		Reserved	16		Reserved
	17		Reserved	18		Reserved
	19		Reserved	20		Reserved
	21		Reserved	22		Reserved
	23		Reserved	24		Reserved
	25		Reserved	26		Reserved
	27		Reserved	28		Reserved
	29		Reserved	30		Reserved
	31		Reserved	32		Reserved
	33		Reserved	34		Reserved
	35		Reserved	36		Reserved
	37		Reserved	38		Reserved
	39		Reserved	40		Reserved
	41		Reserved	42		Reserved
	43		Reserved	44		Reserved
	45		Reserved	46		Reserved
	47		Reserved	48		Reserved
	49		Reserved	50		Reserved
	51		Reserved	52		Reserved
	53		Reserved	54		Reserved
Address	55	ADR16*	Address bus	56	ADR17*	Address bus
	57	ADR14*		58	ADR15*	
	59		Reserved	60		Reserved

Note: Refer to the iLBX bus specification for the definition of the reserved bus lines.

3. The connectors on the non-Multibus system bus side of the board will be called J1, J2, J3, etc. An attempt should be made to number these connectors in ascending order when going clockwise around the boad as viewed from the component side.

2.5.4 Standard Outline of the PCB

Figure 2-35 is the standard outline for any Multibus-compatible board. The connectors on the non-bus edge of the PCB are not restricted as long as the dimensions of the board still meet the outline in Fig. 2-35.

2.6 LEVELS OF COMPLIANCE

The Multibus system bus supports various levels of compliance of the full specification. In this section we will discuss the variable elements of capability, the

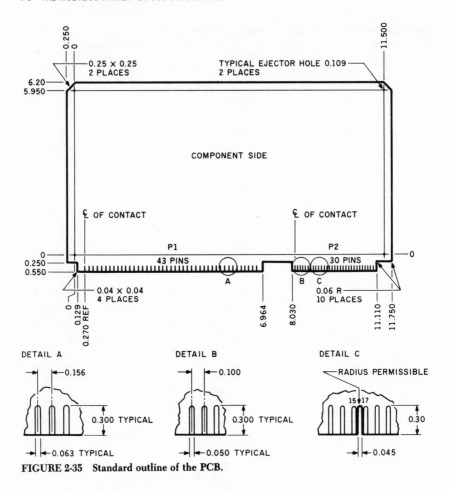

FIGURE 2-35 Standard outline of the PCB.

compliance relationship for masters and slaves, and the notation used to describe the level of compliance with the Multibus system bus.

2.6.1 Variable Elements of Capability

The Multibus system bus has flexibility built into its structure in order to permit the system designer to build different systems with boards of varying capabilities. Variations are permitted in the following areas:

1. Data path width

2. I/O address width

3. Interrupt attributes

DATA PATH

Both 8- and 16-bit data path products can operate on the Multibus system bus. All byte operations occur on the lower byte of the data path, thus allowing the 8- and 16-bit products to work together.

MEMORY ADDRESS PATH

The Multibus standard requires a 24-bit address path. In many systems a 16- or 20-bit address path may be required.

INTERRUPT ATTRIBUTES

The Multibus system bus supports various interrupt attributes. A product may support no interrupts, NBV interrupts, or BV interrupts. There are two methods of interrupt sensing: preferred level-triggered and, for historical compatibility only, edge-level-triggered.

LEVEL-TRIGGERED INTERRUPTS

The active level of the interrupt request line (INTX*) indicates an active request. Since no edge is required, several sources can be attached to a single request line. Each source must have a means of reading the interrupt request status of each of the possible interrupt sources and a programmatic means of clearing the request.

EDGE-LEVEL-TRIGGERED INTERRUPTS

The transition from the inactive (high) to the active (low) level indicates an active request if, and only if, the active level is maintained at least until it has been recognized by the bus master. This method does not support multiple sources on the same request line. Edge-level-triggered interrupts are supported for historical compatibility only and no new designs shall use it.

A bus master may support both methods or the level-triggered method. It is necessary to configure interrupt sources such that the interrupt request method corresponds to the interrupt-sensing method of the bus master. Note that a source which is compatible with level triggering is also compatible with the edge-level triggering.

2.6.2 Masters and Slaves

When constructing Multibus systems, it is not necessary that all modules have identical capabilities. One bus master may generate only 20 bits of addresses, and a slave may decode 24 bits of address. The system is functional and reliable. The only restriction is that one bus master is limited to 1M byte (20 address bits) of address space.

The system designer must evaluate the required capabilities in terms of supplied capabilities; each product will provide some set of capabilities. A transaction between two products will be restricted to use the capabilities that are supported by both products. It is the responsibility of the system designer to assure the viability of these transactions.

2.6.3 Compliance-Level Notation

The following notation allows a vendor to specify accurately a product's level of compliance with the Multibus/IEEE-796 standard. For hybrid boards, compliance levels of both the master and slave interfaces must be specified. Increasing levels of compliance imply lesser levels for data path width, memory address path width, and I/O address path width. Interrupt attributes are listed separately, because they are independent of one another. The lack of an element specification implies no capability for that element.

DATA PATH

  D8   8-bit data path

  D16   8- and 16-bit data path

MEMORY ADDRESS PATH

  M16   16-bit memory path

  M20   20-bit memory path

  M24   24-bit memory path

I/O ADDRESS PATH

  I8   8-bit I/O address path

  I16   8- or 16-bit I/O address path

INTERRUPT ATTRIBUTES

  V0   NBV interrupt requests

  V2   Two-cycle BV interrupt requests

  V3   Three-cycle BV interrupt requests

  E   Edge-level triggering only

  L   Level triggering

  EL   Level or edge-level triggering

COMPLIANCE-LEVEL MARKING

The compliance levels of a module shall be clearly marked on the PCB as well as included in the module specification.

EXAMPLES

A bus master which supported an 8- and 16-bit data path, 24 bits of memory address, 8- or 16-bit I/O address, BV (two-cycle), and NBV interrupts would be specified as follows:

Multibus compliance: Master D16 M24 I16 V02 L

A bus slave with both I/O and memory which supported an 8- and 16-bit data path, 20 bits of memory address, 8- or 16-bit I/O address, and NBV interrupts would be specified as follows:

Multibus compliance: Slave D16 M20 I16 V0 L

3

Multichannel Bus

This chapter provides the basis for a conceptual understanding of the Multichannel bus and how it extends the architecture of the Multibus system bus. Included are the logical and physical descriptions of the bus, the devices that connect to the bus, and bus-programming information. The notation used throughout this book is the same as that defined for the Multibus system bus in Sec. 2.1. The information in this chapter is based on the Intel Multichannel Bus specification (142804 Rev C). It is recomended that anyone designing on the Multichannel bus obtain the latest version from Intel Corporation.

3.1 WHY THE MULTICHANNEL BUS IS REQUIRED

As a system bus is required to perform data movement as well as processor communication or execution, or both, its overall performance decreases. In many disk-based systems there is often a large amount of data movement on the bus or there are other applications in which high-speed I/O into or out of the system is required. Often a system bus is unable to provide the necessary bandwidth for nonbuffered I/O transfers. In some cases a system bus may be capable of handling the high-speed I/O transfers while sacrificing the bandwidth required for communication or execution. This can result in overall degradation of system performance.

One way to increase the bandwidth of the system bus is to remove the high-speed real-time I/O that tends to saturate it. A typical solution is to provide a buffered DMA controller for the system as shown in Fig. 3-1. This approach creates two problems. First, a buffered DMA controller has a specialized interface for the peripheral that attaches to it. As other DMA devices are required, additional controllers must be added to the system bus. Another problem is that

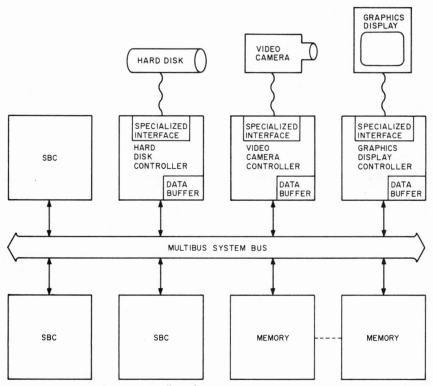

FIGURE 3-1   Typical DMA controller solution.

buffered controllers have a fixed on-board buffer size. If the buffer size requirements change, the controller also must change. Both problems affect hardware
and may affect the system software as well.

The Multichannel bus provides a standard high-speed I/O gateway to the
Multibus system bus without saturating the Multibus system with real-time
burst DMA transfers. When a standard interface is used, the Multichannel bus
shares many of the attributes of a standard system bus discussed in Chap. 1.
This bus allows multiple heterogeneous devices to be connected to it while
maintaining a standard interface. Memory as well as I/O can be connected to
allow buffers of various sizes for the DMA operations. Figure 3-2 is an example
of a Multichannel-based system. In this figure the hard disk controller, video
camera, and graphics display controller of Fig. 3-1 are combined on the Multichannel bus with the buffers. If more or different DMA devices are required,
they can be added to the Multichannel bus without affecting the system bus.
Additional memory can be added if the buffer requirements change. In both
cases the connection to the system bus remains unchanged. As with the system
bus, new VLSI can be incorporated quickly; therefore, advantage of new tech-

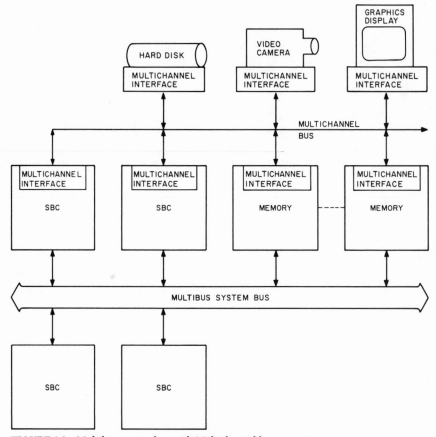

FIGURE 3-2 **Multibus system bus with Multichannel bus extension.**

nologies can be taken. The standard interface allows the system designer to take advantage of VLSI interfacing integrated circuits.

A common problem in many system applications is that the I/O devices are physically separated from the processor's system bus by relatively large distances. Normally this requires a specialized bus to be developed to communicate with these devices. The Multichannel bus has the added ability to link together I/O devices that are distributed over a distance of 50 ft (15 m) from the system bus.

3.2 LOGICAL DESCRIPTION OF THE MULTICHANNEL BUS

The Multichannel bus is a block-oriented DMA bus which, when used with the Multibus system bus, provides an architectural extension to the Multibus system bus. Figure 3-2 is a diagram of a typical Multibus system utilizing the Multi-channel bus. The key features of the Multichannel bus are:

- Standardized controlled interface

- High bandwidth

- Distributed device support over relatively long distances

- Simple data transfer technique

The bus is capable of transferring data at a maximum rate of 8M bytes per second over 50 ft (15 m) of twisted pair flat ribbon cable. The Multichannel bus can support 16 devices with 16M bytes of memory space and 16M bytes of I/O space. Data widths for the devices can be 8- and 16-bit.

The data is transferred via an asynchronous handshake between devices. Asynchronous transfers were chosen for the bus to allow communication among devices that vary in speed and distance from one another. Figure 3-3 shows an example of the Multichannel bus with several devices attached to it. In the illustration, device 1 is writing data to device 2. Device 1 signals to device 2 that data is valid after device 1 places data on the bus. Device 2 ensures that device 1 will hold the data valid until it has read the data. Once device 2 has accepted the data, it signals device 1 that it has done so. The importance of this handshake can be seen if device 1 can transfer data at 2M bytes per second and device 2 can accept data only at 1M byte per second. This interlocked handshake ensures that device 2 will receive all the data while not constraining device 1 to transfer data at that rate. If device 3 in Fig. 3-3 is capable of receiv-

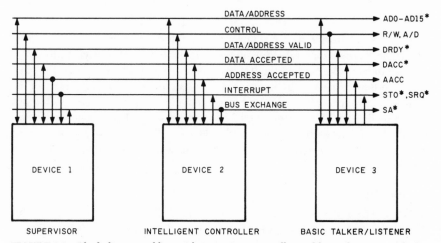

FIGURE 3-3   Block diagram of bus with supervisor, controller and basic devices attached.

ing data at a 2M bytes per second rate, device 1 could transfer at the higher rate when communicating with device 3.

3.2.1 Bus States

In order to understand the bus operation, one must first understand the device states: the mode and activity level of a device at any given time during bus operation. The bus is based on a master-slave relationship in that a master initiates the data transfer by some action on the control lines and a slave responds to this action. Referring back to Fig. 3-3, device 1 is the master and device 2 is the slave. In this example device 1 informs device 2 what type of data will be transferred and in which direction. Device 2 looks at these signal lines and decides whether it should receive or send data and when the transfer is to begin.

A master-slave approach was chosen to allow communication between devices that vary in speed and distance from one another. This approach requires a positive acknowledge interlocked transfer between devices. Its drawback is that a device must synchronize to the acknowledge.

MASTER STATE

A device is in the master state whenever it is controlling the command-action lines on the bus. The master is responsible for addressing devices and determining the length of the transfer. The Multichannel bus allows the bus mastership to be passed among the attached devices. However, only one master can be active at a time. In Fig. 3-3, device 1, the master, is responsible for addressing device 2 or 3 and controlling the data transfer. If device 2 or 3 is capable of bus mastership, device 1 may choose to move the mastership to either of the other devices.

SLAVE STATE

A device is in the slave state whenever it is monitoring the bus command-action lines. The slave is responsible for monitoring the bus for its device address. No action can be performed on the bus by a slave without direction from the master. A system can contain multiple slaves, each monitoring the bus for its address. However, only one slave can be actively transferring data on the bus at a time. In Fig. 3-3, devices 2 and 3 are the bus slaves. Each device will monitor the bus for its address being sent by device 1, the bus master. Once device 2 has been addressed for a data transfer, it will wait for the signal from device 1 to start the transfer.

ACTIVE STATE

A slave device is in the active state whenever it has been addressed for a transfer by a master. Only one slave may be active on the bus at a time. Bus masters are always active on the bus. In Fig. 3-3, device 1 is the master; therefore, it is active. Device 2, the slave, will be inactive until device 1 addresses it for a transfer operation. Once addressed, device 2 will be in the active state.

TALKER STATE

A *talker* is any device which is writing data to the bus and signaling that its data on the bus is valid. Both masters and slaves can be talkers. Referring to Fig. 3-3, the master, device 1, will be the talker during the address cycle, since only the master can write addresses on the bus. However, if the slave, device 2, is addressed to write data to the bus during a data cycle, it will become the talker. The master also can be a talker during data write transfers.

LISTENER STATE

A *listener* is any device that is reading data from the bus and signals that the data has been accepted. Both masters and slaves can be listeners. Referring to Fig. 3-3, the slave, device 2, will be the listener during the address transfer from the master, device 1. When device 2 is addressed to write data to the bus, device 2 becomes the listener. When the slave is writing data to the bus, the master is the listener. When the master is writing data to the bus, the slave is the listener.

3.2.2 Bus Devices

The Multichannel bus supports three classes of devices. Each device has a different function or responsibility on the bus. At a minimum the bus requires a supervisor type of device to control the bus and an additional device for the supervisory device to communicate with.

BASIC TALKER-LISTENER

A basic talker-listener device can write or read data to the bus but has no bus control capability. The basic devices in a system can be any combination of talker only, listener only, or talker and listener device. A basic device is a slave; therefore, its data flow is directed by a bus master. Basic talkers-listeners are addressed by a bus master, and the amount of data is controlled by a bus master. Typical basic devices are memory cards and simple I/O devices. Device 2 is the basic talker-listener for the implementation of the bus shown in Fig. 3-3. Device 2 must wait for its address from the master, device 1, and must be told whether to read or write data. In this example device 2 has no bus control capability; therefore, it will only receive the control signals.

BUS CONTROLLER

A *bus controller*, like the basic talker-listener, can read and write data to the Multichannel bus and is also capable of controlling the transfer signals and programming other devices on the bus. The bus controller appears as a slave on the bus until it is directed by the bus supervisor to assume mastership of the bus.

Normally, a bus controller is used in a system in which the supervisor cannot keep up with the data transfer rate or the system performance dictates that data be moved only once. Typical bus controllers are disk systems and high-speed I/O devices. Device 3 in Fig. 3-3 is the bus controller. When programmed by the supervisory device, device 3 appears as a slave on the bus; in this example, it is instructed to perform a transfer with the basic talker-listener device 2. When instructed, it leaves its slave status and assumes mastership of the bus. The transfer is then between devices 2 and 3.

BUS SUPERVISOR

A bus supervisor has all the properties of the bus controller and basic talker-listener. In addition, it has ultimate control of all data movement over the bus. A supervisor is always the bus master unless it passes control to a bus controller. On the Multichannel bus the supervisor is responsible for scheduling all data transfers, resolving and granting bus priority, monitoring bus status, and handling all bus interrupts. In a given Multichannel bus system there can be only one supervisor. In Fig. 3-3 the bus supervisor is device 1. In this example device 1 has control of all transfers on the bus. If device 1 requires the bus controller, device 3, to take mastership of the bus, the exchange will be under the control of device 1. Device 1 may regain bus control at any time.

At a minimum level a system would contain a supervisor, which would be the system master, and a basic talker-listener, which would be the system slave. In Fig. 3-3 the minimum system would contain the supervisor, device 1, and the basic talker-listener, device 2, which is a slave.

3.3 BUS SIGNAL DEFINITIONS

This section deals with the signals that make up the bus structure and how they are used in various bus operations.

The Multichannel bus is composed of 60 signal lines that can be broken into five classes: addresses and data, control, interrupt, data integrity, and reset. The bus does not support any power lines. Power for the devices must be supplied at the device location. There are 22 ground lines, which are used for signal return, and 8 lines that are reserved for future expansion.

3.3.1 Address-Data

The address-data (AD) group (AD0* to AD15*) consists of 16 bidirectional lines on which all address and data transfers take place. A 16-bit transfer uses all 16 lines; an 8-bit transfer uses only AD0* to AD7*. Since the bus is block-oriented, the address information is sent once for every block of data. A block of data is defined as a minimum of 1 byte to a maximum of 16M bytes. In most applications data length will be greater than 1 byte. Block data provides an increase in peformance by not wasting bus bandwidth with address information on each transfer. The multiplexed lines allow effective sharing of the same lines for address and data. This simplifies the driver, receiver, and termination of each device and reduces the width of the interconnecting cable. The control line A/D determines whether the information on the address-data lines is address or data.

3.3.2 Control

The control group is composed of five signals. Two signals, data ready (DRDY*) and data accept (DACC*), are data transfer handshake signals. One signal, address accept (AACC), is an address transfer handshake signal. Two signals, read-write (R/W) and address-data mode (A/D), are transfer control signals. The last of this group, supervisor active (SA*), is a bus control signal. In the following section these signals will be described and how they work with the bus will be explained.

ADDRESS DATA

The A/D line is driven by the current bus master to inform the slave devices whether the information on the AD lines is address or data. This line is monitored by each slave so it can actively monitor the bus for its address. When the A/D line is high, address information is placed on the bus by the master. When the A/D line goes low, this informs the addressed (active) slave that the information sent is data. When the bus is in data mode, the active slave continues to talk or listen until the A/D line goes back into the address mode. The inactive devices also must continue to monitor this line during data cycles so they can be ready for the next address cycle.

READ-WRITE

The read-write (R/W) line is driven by the current bus master to inform the slave devices the direction in which the data is flowing. The direction is always referenced to the bus master. When the R/W line is high, the master reads data from the bus as a listener and the active slave writes data as a talker. Conversely, when the R/W line is low, the master writes data to the bus as a talker and the active slave reads data as a listener. During address cycles the master places the R/W line low to inform the slaves that it is writing an address to the bus.

DATA READY

Data ready (DRDY*) is an active-low line driven by the current talking device that informs the listening device that data is valid on the AD lines. The data on the bus can be address or data, which is determined by the state of the A/D control line. It is important to note that DRDY* is used to signal that address or data is valid. Only masters drive DRDY* during address cycles, whereas any talking device drives DRDY* during data cycles. The DRDY* signal must remain active until an accept signal is received from the listening device.

ADDRESS ACCEPT

Address accept (AACC) is an active-high line driven by all slaves on the bus to inform the bus master that the address information is accepted. The AACC signal is sent by all slaves connected to the bus in response to a DRDY* when the bus is in the address mode. AACC is open collector, which allows all slaves to actively drive this line. This allows slaves of varying speeds and distances from the master to accept and assimilate the address information correctly. The disadvantage is that the address information will be accepted at the rate determined by the slowest device on the bus. This signal goes active only after the slowest device has accepted the address data.

Figure 3-4 shows an example of a Multichannel bus address cycle.

1. The master places the A/D and R/W control lines in the state signifying an address write cycle (A/D = high, R/W = low).

2. The master then places valid address information on AD0* to AD15*.

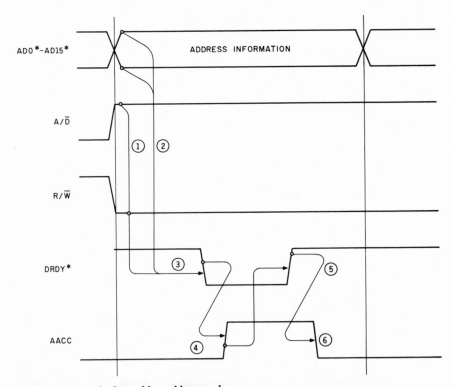

FIGURE 3-4   Multichannel bus address cycle.

3. Once this data has been allowed to propagate, the master drives DRDY*
   active.

4. The slave responds after receiving and decoding the information by driving
   AACC active.

5. The master continues to hold the DRDY* signal active and the address information valid until it receives the AACC signal. At that time it removes the
   DRDY* signal.

6. The slave, upon receiving DRDY* inactive, removes the AACC signal.

In Fig. 3-3, there are two slaves which will be driving the AACC signal. For
this example assume that device 2 is faster in response than device 3; in this
case device 2 drives the AACC signal first. Since the AACC is an open collector
device, the line remains inactive until device 3 has accepted and decoded the
information. This ensures that the address information remains valid for
device 3.

DATA ACCEPT

Data accept (DACC*) is an active-low signal driven by the active listening
device informing the talking device that it has accepted data. The DACC* signal is sent by the listening device in response to a DRDY* when the bus is in
the data mode. Only an active listening device may drive DACC*. The action
of DACC* is similar to that of AACC. The difference is that AACC is used in
address transfers and DACC is used in data transfers.

Figure 3-5 shows an example of a Multichannel bus data cycle.

1. The bus is placed in the data mode by the master driving the A/D line low.
   The data flow, as determined by the R/W line, also is set by the master.

2. The talking device places data on AD0* to AD15*.

3. After meeting the data setup time, the talking device drives DRDY* active.

4. After the listening device receives DRDY* active and reads the data, it
   drives DACC* active.

5. The data and DRDY* remain valid until the talking device receives the
   DACC* signal. At that time it removes the DRDY* signal.

6. After the listening device receives DRDY* inactive, it removes the DACC*
   signal.

SUPERVISOR ACTIVE

Supervisor active (SA*) is an active-low signal driven by the supervisor informing all devices when it has control of the bus. The signal relations for SA* are

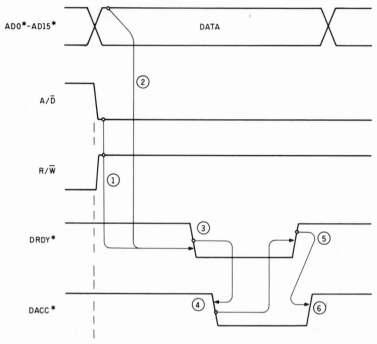

FIGURE 3-5 Multichannel bus data cycle.

shown in Fig. 3-6. A bus controller, which is programmed to be a master, must monitor this signal to know when it may take control of the bus. Once it has assumed bus mastership, it must continue to monitor this signal while it is performing a bus transaction. Under normal conditions a supervisor will allow a bus controller master to finish its transaction before regaining control of the bus. If an error occurs or a higher-priority transfer needs to take place, the supervisor can assert SA* prior to the transfer completion to take control of the bus. Once SA* has been asserted, the bus controller must turn off its bus drivers within a specified amount of time.

In Fig. 3-3, device 1, the bus supervisor, has programmed device 3 to take over the bus. Device 3 must monitor the SA* line to ensure the supervisor is no longer on the bus. If device 1 wants to regain the bus, it may assert the SA* line. It is the responsibility of device 3 to remove itself from the bus.

3.3.3 Bus Interrupt Lines

The Multichannel bus supports two bus interrupts: supervisor take over (STO*) and service request (SRQ*). Both lines are received exclusively by the supervisor and are driven by bus controllers and basic devices.

SUPERVISOR TAKE OVER

Supervisor take over (STO*) is an active-low signal driven by basic devices and bus controllers to inform the supervisor of two possible conditions: task completion and bus error. A bus controller which has mastership of the bus uses STO* to inform the supervisor that it has completed its current task. The STO* signal is also used whenever a bus error occurs. A bus error is defined as a device hardware failure (memory, disk, etc.) or a bus parity error. A device that has either of these failures asserts the STO* signal. On receipt of the STO* the supervisor will, at some time, poll and service the requesting device(s) on the bus until the STO* signal has been removed. Only the bus supervisor may act upon an STO*.

SERVICE REQUEST

Service request (SRQ*) is an active-low signal driven by a basic device or bus controller to inform the supervisor that it needs service. A supervisor may program a device to perform a task off line (e.g., a seek on a disk). The device will signal the supervisor that it is ready by asserting the SRQ* line. The service request should be used whenever service is required by a device. One designated use for the SRQ* line is a power-up configuration signal to the bus super-

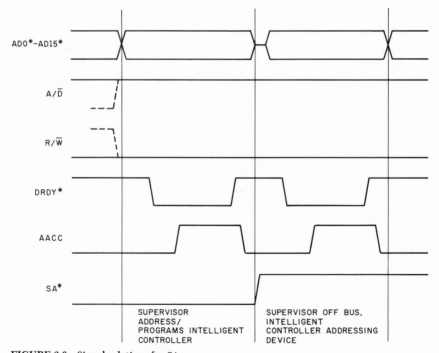

FIGURE 3-6 Signal relations for SA*.

visor. The use of this signal is covered in Sec. 3-5, "Programming Information." The supervisor has the option to mask this signal until it is ready to accept the signal. As with the STO* signal, the supervisor polls and services the requesting device(s) on the bus until the SRQ* signal has been removed.

3.3.4 Parity

The parity signal (PB*) is used to qualify the data integrity of the transfer and should be sampled by the listening device when DRDY* goes active. Parity is an active-low signal defined as follows:

1. When an odd number of AD lines are high during an address or data transfer, the parity line will be active (low).

2. When an even number of AD lines are high during an address or data transfer, the parity line will be inactive (high).

The parity signal is generated by the master for all addresses and by the talking device for all data transfers over the bus. When a listener detects a parity error, it must assert the STO* signal to the supervisor. The only exception to this rule occurs when the listener is the supervisor, in which case it will already be informed of the error.

The Multichannel bus allows certain subsets to the parity mode. The first subset is a no-parity mode. If the no-parity mode is selected, slaves must not sample parity during address transfers and listeners must not sample parity during data transfers. When a parity mode is selected, masters must generate parity during address transfers and talkers must generate parity during data transfers. Another subset is for 8-bit devices. When they are used in an 8-bit-only system, only 8-bit parity needs to be sent and received. If, however, 8- and 16-bit devices are on the same bus, the 8-bit slave must check 16-bit parity for address transfers. The 8-bit slave is only required to send and receive 8-bit parity for data transfers.

3.3.5 Reset*

The Multichannel bus supports a Reset* signal to bring the bus to a known state. The supervisor is the only device that drives Reset*, but all other devices connected to the bus receive it. After power-up, the supervisor will hold this signal low for a minimum of 5 ms. This will guarantee that all devices are in a known state and ready for the supervisor's commands. If the supervisor needs to regain control of the bus rapidly during a transfer cycle, it may choose to assert Reset* on the bus. This action will immediately stop any transaction on the bus. Current transfer and bus status data are lost when Reset* is used in this manner.

3.4 BUS TRANSFER OPERATIONS

Now that the signal lines have been defined, a functional description of each Multichannel operation is possible. The Multichannel bus supports four basic cyles: address, data, interrupt, and bus exchange. All four cycles use the basic transfer techniques shown in Figs. 3-4 and 3-5 and will be described in the following sections.

3.4.1 Address Cycle

The address cycle allows a master to activate the slave that has the resource that the master requires. There must always be an address cycle before a data cycle can start. There are two forms of addressing: the select and the deselect cycles. The select cycle tells a slave the 24-bit starting address of the data transfer, the direction of the data transfer, and the type of data transfer. The deselect cycle informs the selected slave that the data transfer cycle is completed. All addresses are transferred in two bus cycles in that two words are transferred for 16-bit devices and two bytes are transferred for 8-bit devices.

Figure 3-7 shows the signal relations for one complete address cycle.

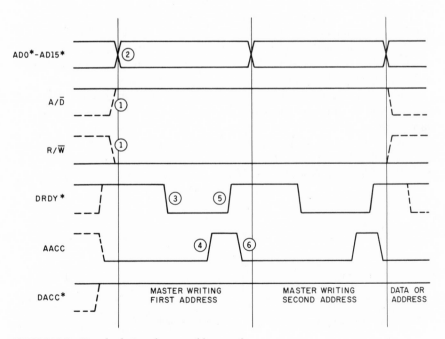

FIGURE 3-7 **Signal relations for one address cycle.**

1. The master places the A/D line high (address mode) and the R/W line low (write mode).

2. The master then places the first part of the address on AD0* to AD15*.

3. After the address is valid, the master drives DRDY* active.

4. After all the slaves accept the address, AACC goes active.

5. When the master receives AACC active, it knows that all slaves have read the address; therefore, the master removes DRDY*.

6. When the slaves receive DRDY* inactive, they remove AACC.

The second bus cycle of the address cycle occurs in the same manner as the first cycle. An address cycle is completed only after both transfers have been completed. During address cycles all slaves accept the address and drive AACC. Only after the slowest device on the bus drives AACC will the master see the signal active. This ensures proper synchronization for slow and fast devices on the bus.

The format of the address (Fig. 3-8) supports both 8- and 16-bit devices. In Fig. 3-8, the address (bits 16 to 23) = most significant byte of 24-bit memory or register address; device number = a number from 0 to 15; RES = reserved bit; M/R = memory-register address bit; R/W = read-write bit; address (bits 8 to 15) = middle byte of 24-bit memory or register address; and address (bits 0 to 7) = last significant byte of 24-bit memory or register address. The first word is composed of the high-order starting address bits (16 to 23), the device number, the memory-register (M/R) bit, and the R/W bit. The device number is the physical number that selects the slave; it is composed of 4 bits, allowing a range of device numbers between 0 and 15. Device number 15 is a special case and will be discussed in connection with the deselect cycle. The M/R bit informs the slave whether the data transfer operation will be for memory or I/O. When this bit is low, the transfer will be for memory; when it is high, the transfer will be for I/O. The R/W bit provides early status information on the direction of the data flow. A slave can decode it for advanced information on

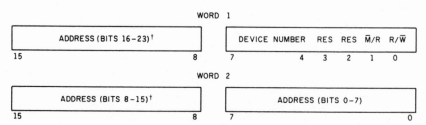

FIGURE 3-8   Address format. (Note: Bits marked † are undefined when 8-bit addressing is used.)

the direction of the data flow when the bus is placed into the data mode. When it is low, the data flow will be to the slave; when it is high, the data flow will be from the slave. The high-order address bits 16 to 23, in conjunction with word 2 address bits 0 to 15, give a 24-bit starting address.

Eight-bit devices can support either word or byte address cycles. If the device supports only byte address cycles, the starting address can only be in the range of 0 to 255 (bits 0 to 7) for both memory and I/O. An 8-bit device can support word address cycles if it requires a larger resource space while only supporting byte data transfers. In a system that supports both 8- and 16-bit devices, the 8-bit slave must check 16 bits of parity during an address cycle whether or not it supports the word address cycle.

The deselect address cycle operation follows the same sequence as the select cycle. The difference between the two is in the makeup of the address words. In the deselect cycle the device number is 15 (bits 4 to 7 of word 1 high). All other bits of the address words are zero. The deselect cycle informs all slaves that the transfer is completed. This allows inactive slaves to synchronize for the next select cycle.

3.4.2 Data Cycles

Data cycles are the transfer cycles in which data is passed between the master and the slave. The basic handshake transfer sequence is similar to that of address cycles. Data cycles differ from address cycles in that a data cycle can be composed of 1-byte to 16M-byte transfer cycles. The number of transfer cycles is determined by the master. Another difference between data and address cycles is that only the active slave is responding to the master during data cycles.

In Fig. 3-9 the bus is shown in write mode in that the master (talker) is writing data to the slave (listener).

1. The master drives the R/W line low (write mode) and the A/D line low (data mode).

2. After the bus control lines have been set, the master places the data on AD0* to AD15*.

3. Once the specified data setup time has been met, the master drives DRDY* active to inform the slave that data is valid on the bus.

4. After the slave receives DRDY* active and has read the data, the slave drives DACC* active to inform the master that it has accepted the data.

5. The master, upon receiving DACC* active, removes DRDY* and the data on AD0* to AD15*.

6. The slave, upon receiving DRDY* inactive, removes DACC*.

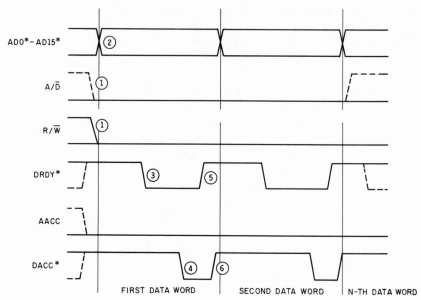

FIGURE 3-9 Bus write data cycle.

The cycle continues until the master places the bus in address mode (A/D high). The slave, upon receiving the address mode signal, stops its cycle and waits for instructions from the master.

Figure 3-10 shows a bus read sequence in that the master is reading data from the slave. This transfer sequence is similar to the bus write sequence except that now the slave is the talker and is writing data to the master, which is now the listener.

1. After the master has completed the address cycle, it places the R/W line high (read mode) and the A/D line low (data mode).

2. The slave, upon receiving the A/D line in data mode, places the data on AD0* to AD15*.

3. Once the data has met the specified setup time, the slave drives DRDY* active to inform the master that data on the bus is valid.

4. The master, upon receiving DRDY*, reads the data and drives DACC* to inform the slave that data has been accepted.

5. The slave, upon receiving DACC*, removes DRDY* and the data.

6. The master, upon receiving DRDY* inactive, removes DACC*.

The cycle continues until the master places the bus in address mode (A/D high). The slave, upon receiving the address mode signal, stops its cycle and waits for instructions from the master.

Once the bus is in data mode, the transfer sequence between the master and the slave is the same. The only difference between read and write mode is the direction of the data flow. While in data mode, all talking devices (master or slave) place data on the bus and drive DRDY*. In a similar manner, all listening devices (master or slave) read data from the bus and drive DACC*. The master has the responsibility for monitoring the number of cycles, and the slave has the responsibility for monitoring the A/D line for end of transfer.

The 8-bit data transfers are similar to the 16-bit data transfers except that the data is placed on AD0* to AD7* only. It is always the responsibility of the master to match the data width of the slave with which it is transferring data. If a 16-bit master wants to transfer data with a 8-bit slave, it must send and receive the data on AD0* to AD7* only. Also, the master must generate and check parity only for those lines. The 8-bit slave is required to generate or check parity only for AD0* to AD7* in the data mode.

3.4.3 Transfer Cycle

The basic transfer cycle is used for data transfers, bus control exchange, and interrupt handling. The transfer cycle is composed of a select address cycle, a

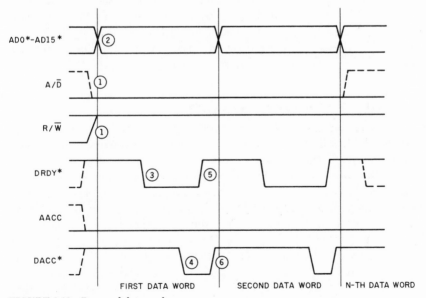

FIGURE 3-10   Bus read data cycle.

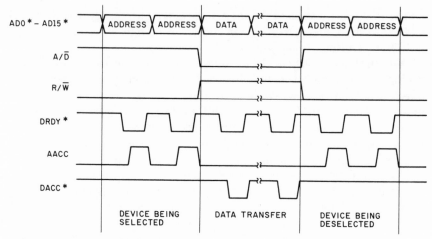

FIGURE 3-11   Complete bus transfer cycle.

data cycle of 1 byte to 16M bytes, and a deselect address cycle. Figure 3-11 shows the timing relations for one complete transfer cycle. During the select address cycle the master places the bus in the address write mode (A/D = high, R/W = low) and places the address information on the bus. After both address words have been accepted, the master places the bus in data mode (A/D = low). Depending on the data flow direction, the master will set the bus in either read or write mode. When all data has been transferred, the master will place the bus back in the address write mode. The slave, upon receiving the address mode signal, stops all current bus activity. The master completes the transfer cycle by performing the deselect address sequence.

3.4.4   Control Arbitration and Exchange

Bus control exchanging allows a supervisor to pass the bus mastership to a bus controller. Passing the control normally occurs when the supervisor cannot meet the data transfer requirements or when system performance requirements dictate that the data be moved directly to another Multichannel device without going through the supervisor. In the latter case the bus controller can access buffer memory directly and not have to move the data twice (controller to supervisor, supervisor to buffer). Control arbitration is handled by the supervisor via a system-dictated priority scheme. When a device requires service or the bus, the supervisor will grant the bus on the basis of the device's priority. This centralized method of arbitration is simple to understand and implement. Its drawback is that it is slower and less efficient than the distributed arbitration method used on the Multibus system bus. Since the Multichannel bus is primarily a data movement bus, and secondarily a multimaster bus, the centralized control was chosen.

Control exchange is handled by the SA* line and is demonstrated in Fig. 3-12. Whenever the supervisor is on the bus, it will drive SA* active. A supervisor that wishes to release the bus will program the bus controller with the required information. The bus controller must monitor the SA* line to detect when the supervisor is off the bus. Once the supervisor is off the bus, the bus controller can drive the A/D and R/W lines. The controller can now transfer with other slaves on the bus. It is the responsibility of the controller to continue to monitor the SA* line. Under normal circumstances the controller will complete its transfer cycle and inform the supervisor by driving the STO* signal active. If, however, the supervisor requires the bus prior to the transfer completion, it will drive SA* active. Upon receiving the SA* signal, the controller must relinquish the bus.

3.4.5 Interrupt Handling

STO* and SRQ* are the Multichannel bus interrupts used for signaling the bus supervisor. These signals have similar timing but their use in the system is different. Figure 3-13 shows the timing relations for STO* and SRQ*. A device that requires the attention of the bus supervisor drives either STO* or SRQ* active. Upon receiving the interrupt signal, the supervisor performs a deselect

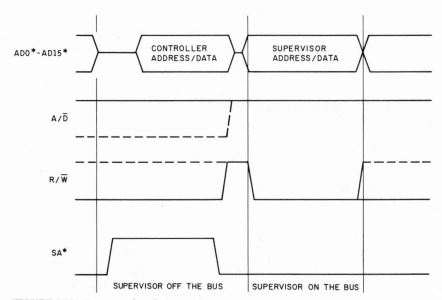

FIGURE 3-12 Bus control exchange cycle.

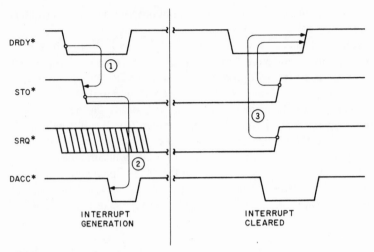

FIGURE 3-13   Bus interrupt cycle.

address cycle and begins polling the devices on the bus. When a supervisor polls, it selects each device and reads the device's appropriate interrupt register. The value in the register informs the supervisor if the device interrupted and the reason for the interrupt. Section 3.5 has detailed information on Multichannel registers and their programming. After reading the interrupt register, the supervisor deselects the device and performs some action if the device it polled generated the interrupt. The supervisor continues to poll the remaining devices until the interrupt signal has been removed from the bus. Polling priority and the supervisor's interrupt latency are dependent on system requirements and supervisor programming.

3.5   PROGRAMMING INFORMATION

The Multichannel bus contains 16M bytes of register space. The first 16 register locations (0 to 15) have been defined for Multichannel bus system usage. The remaining registers are available for user definition. In this section bus register programming, register use in device polling, bus exchanges, and interrupt handling are described.

3.5.1   Register Addressing

Multichanel register addressing is similar to Multichannel memory addressing. Referring back to Fig. 3-8, the format of the Multichannel register address is equivalent to a memory address except that M/R bit (bit 1 of word 1) is high, which indicates that the remaining 24 bits of the address cycle are a register address. A register transfer cycle follows the same flow as a transfer cycle mentioned in Sec. 3.3. Registers can be 8- or 16-bit. A 16-bit device normally has 16-bit registers, and an 8-bit device has 8-bit registers.

3.5.2 Multichannel Register Definition

To allow for system uniformity, Multichannel registers 0 to 15 are designated for system use. The system registers can be 8- or 16-bit. It is up to the programming device to know the register size. As a rule 8-bit devices do not have the functionality or flexibility of their 16-bit counterparts. The Multichannel bus registers are listed in Table 3-1. Their definitions and uses are detailed below.

STO STATUS REGISTER

The STO register is supported by all bus controllers and basic devices, and its value indicates the status of the STO* signal. The STO* signal indicates to the supervisor that a device requires assistance, and the STO register provides further definition. When a device asserts STO*, it places a nonzero value in its STO register. All other devices maintain zero values in this register space. When the supervisor reads the register on each device, it can ascertain that the device asserted STO* by a nonzero value in the register. There are two main categories for the STO register value: device error (bit 7 = high) and bus controller status (bit 7 = low). The value that can be placed in a device register may be further expanded by the user for device-specific error reporting and status reporting.

TABLE 3-1 Multichannel Bus Registers

Register number	Definition	Mode	Width
0	STO, flag, status	Read only	8 bit
1	SRQ, flag, status	Read only	8 bit
2	SRQ, mask	Write only	8 bit
3	Device command	Write only	8 bit
4	Device parameter	Write only	8 or 16 bit
5	Data address 1	Read or write	8 or 16 bit
6	Data address 2	Read or write	8 or 16 bit
7	Block length 1	Read or write	8 or 16 bit
8	Block length 2	Read or write	8 or 16 bit
9	Error address 1	Read only	8 or 16 bit
10	Error address 2	Read only	8 or 16 bit
11	Address extension	Write only	8 or 16 bit
12–15	Reserved		
16–16M bytes	User defined	Read or write	8 or 16 bit

SRQ STATUS REGISTER

The SRQ register is supported by all bus controllers and basic devices and its value indicates the status of the SRQ* signal. The SRQ* signal indicates to the supervisor that a device requires service, and the SRQ register further defines the type of service a device requires. When a device asserts SRQ*, it will place a nonzero value in its SRQ register. All other devices maintain zero values in this register space. When the supervisor reads the register on each device, it can ascertain that the device asserted the SRQ* signal by a nonzero value in the register and act upon the information provided. The Multichannel bus defines certain values for system use; it is described in Fig. 9-5.

The bus defines a power-up autoconfiguration in which the SRQ* signal and register are used. When a device is turned on, it can assert its SRQ* signal. Referring to Fig. 9-5, when bit 7 of the SRQ register value is high, the supervisor is informed that the register contains configuration information. Bits 0 and 1 further define the type of device; bit 2 defines the width of the device; and bit 3 determines whether the register contains power-up or power-down information. If bit 3 is high, the device is in power-up mode, if it is low, the device is informing the supervisor that it will be going off line. Bits 4 to 6 are always 0.

When bit 7 is low, the SRQ register contains information other than power-up configuration. The value that can be placed in the SRQ register may be futher expanded by the user for specific device requirements when bit 7 is low.

SRQ MASK REGISTER

The SRQ mask register is supported by all bus controllers and basic devices; it allows a supervisor to disable the SRQ* signal at the source device. Masking at the device allows a supervisor to set device priority in having an SRQ* service. In a system a supervisor may also elect to mask the SRQ* signal at its level and disallow any SRQ* signal from being received. Masking at the supervisor is normally performed during crucial transfer periods. To mask the SRQ* signal at a device, the supervisor writes a 1 to the device's SRQ mask register. To unmask the SRQ* signal, the supervisor writes a 0 to the SRQ mask register.

DEVICE COMMAND REGISTER

The device command register allows a supervisor to pass device specific commands to a bus controller. The value written is user-definable and may be chosen to meet system requirements. One example of device command register use is a bus takeover command. The supervisor can tell the bus controller that its registers are set and that it can take over the bus once the supervisor is off the bus. Another example is a command to an intelligent disk controller to perform an off-line buffered sector read and to signal the supervisor via the SRQ* line when the task has been completed.

DEVICE PARAMETER REGISTER

The device parameter register is used by the supervisor to pass the device number, data direction, and transfer type information to a bus controller prior to a bus takeover by the controller. The format of this register is equivalent to the first byte of the first word in the address cycle (see Fig. 3-8).

DATA ADDRESS REGISTERS

The data address register pair informs a bus controller of the starting address of the block transfer. This register pair is normally programmed by the supervisor prior to a bus takeover by the controller. The data address is composed of two 16-bit registers if on a 16-bit device yielding 32 bits of real address. For 8-bit devices the data address is composed of two 8-bit registers yielding 16 bits of real address. Data address register 1 is the most significant.

BLOCK LENGTH REGISTERS

The block length register pair informs a bus controller of the data transfer block size. This register pair is normally programmed by the supervisor prior to a bus takeover by the controller. The block length is composed of two 16-bit registers if on a 16-bit device yielding a maximum 32-bit block size. For 8-bit devices the block length is composed of two 8-bit registers yielding a maximum 16-bit block size. Block length register 1 is most significant.

ERROR ADDRESS REGISTERS

The error address register pair is read by a supervisor for the location of an error on a device. When a device generates an STO* due to an error, it will load these registers with the error address value. After the supervisor reads the STO status register, it may read the error register depending on the status register value. The error address is composed of two 16-bit registers if on a 16-bit device yielding a maximum 32-bit real error address. For 8-bit devices the error address is composed of two 8-bit registers yielding a maximum 16-bit error address. Error address register 1 is most significant.

3.5.3 Device Polling

Device polling is the method used by the supervisor to query the devices for interrupt origin. SRQ* and STO* are the two interrupts which can cause a device poll. A poll of the device occurs when the supervisor reads the SRQ status register or STO status register of the device. The timing relations shown in Fig. 3-13 are for one device. Figure 3-14 is the flow diagram of a complete bus poll. After the supervisor receives an interrupt (SRQ* or STO*), it will complete the current bus cycle and deselect the active device. The supervisor will then address and read the interrupt register of the highest-priority device. After the status register has been read by the supervisor, the device has the responsibility for removing the interrupt signal and setting its status register to zero. If the status is nonzero, the supervisor will perform some action with that device. After the action has been completed, the supervisor will test to find out whether the interrupt has been removed. If the interrupt has been removed, the poll is completed. Otherwise, the supervisor addresses and reads the interrupt status register of the next-lower-priority device. In a similar fashion, if a zero value is read and the interrupt signal is still active, the supervisor moves on to the next-lower-priority device. This cycle continues until the interrupt signal has been removed. A bus error occurs when the supervisor receives an interrupt but cannot locate the source with a poll. The handling of this class of error is system-dependent.

3.5.4 Bus Exchange Programming

Bus exchange programming occurs when the supervisor loads the bus controller's system registers for an exchange of bus mastership to the bus controller. The supervisor will load the block length registers, data address registers, device parameter register, and the device command register. When the device command register is loaded, this action informs the bus controller that all registers are loaded and the supervisor is ready to get off the bus. At this point the bus controller will monitor the SA* line for bus availability as shown in Fig. 3-12. A bus controller may be preprogrammed with the data address information, block length information, and the device parameter information. Therefore, loading of these registers may not be required. At a minimum level the device command register must be supported by the controller and loaded by the supervisor to allow for proper system synchronization.

After the controller has the bus, it will take the information (preprogrammed or loaded) and perform a transfer cycle with the directed device. On completion of the transfer, the controller will signal the supervisor via the STO* line. The value placed in the STO status register by the controller will indicate to the supervisor that the task has been completed and the bus has been released.

3.6 ELECTRICAL SPECIFICATION

In this section all the timing and loading and drive characteristics of the Multichannel bus are described.

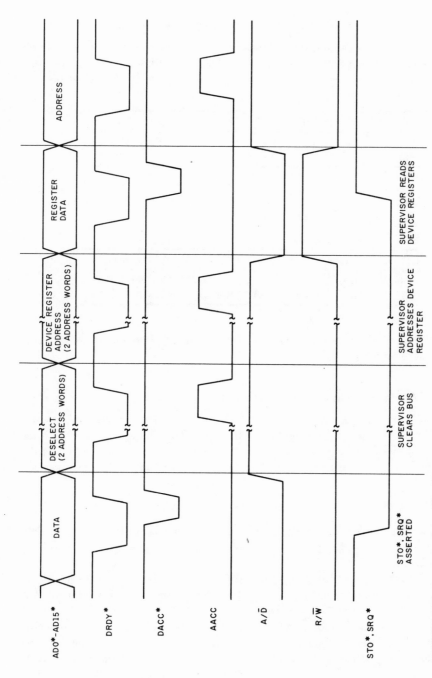

FIGURE 3-14 Supervisor bus polling sequence.

3.6.1 Logical State and Electrical Level Relations

The signal names indicate if the signals are active-high or active-low. If the signal name ends with an asterisk, the signal is active-low and has the following logical state and electrical level relations in which L = low and H = high:

Logical state	Electrical level	At receiver	At driver
0	H = TTL high	$5.25 \text{ V} \geq \text{H} \geq 2.0 \text{ V}$	$5.25 \text{ V} \geq \text{H} \geq 2.4 \text{ V}$
1	L = TTL low	$0.8 \text{ V} \geq \text{L} \geq -0.5 \text{ V}$	$0.5 \text{ V} \geq \text{L} \geq 0 \text{ V}$

If the signal name has no asterisk, the signal is active-high and has the following logical state and electrical level relations:

Logical state	Electrical level	At receiver	At driver
0	L = TTL low	$0.8 \text{ V} \geq \text{L} \geq -0.5 \text{ V}$	$0.5 \text{ V} \geq \text{L} \geq 0 \text{ V}$
1	H = TTL high	$5.25 \text{ V} \geq \text{H} \geq 2.0 \text{ V}$	$5.25 \text{ V} \geq \text{H} \geq 2.4 \text{ V}$

These specifications are based on TTL when the power source is 5 V $\pm$ 5 percent as referenced to logic GND.

3.6.2 Signal Line Characteristics

The Multichannel bus transmission medium is twisted pair flat ribbon cable which has a maximum length of 50 ft (15 m). The timing parameter t_D is the signal propagation delay per foot of flat cable. This parameter can affect the maximum transfer rate expected on the bus because of the distance between devices, and

$$t_D \text{ max} = 2 \text{ ns/ft } (6.5 \text{ ns/m})$$

Therefore, 50 ft (15 m) of cable will cause a signal delay of 100 ns and one data transfer cycle will require a minimum of 200 ns to complete the handshake operation.

Each class of signals has a particular waveshape associated with its driver-receiver characteristics. Figure 3-15 provides the signal summary for the AD, control, and support lines of the Multichannel bus.

The AD lines (AD0* to AD15*) can be at one of three levels depending on the state of the Multichannel device. When a device is driving the AD lines high, the signals are at level 1. When the bus is tri-stated with no device driving the AD lines, the signals are at level 2. When a device drives the address lines low, the signals are at level 3.

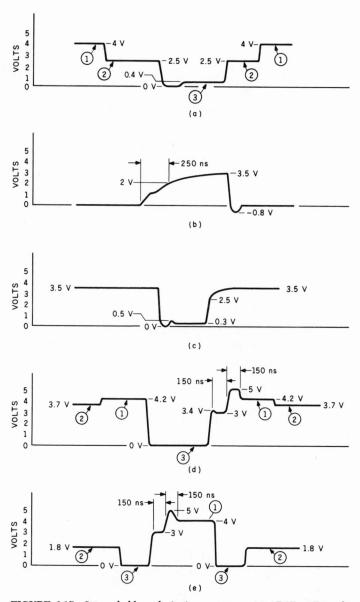

FIGURE 3-15 Setup, hold, and ringing summary: (a) AD15*–AD0*; (b) AACC; (c) DACC*, SRQ*, STO*, RESET*, SA*; (d) DRDY*, R/W, A/D, PARITY NONINVERTING; (e) DRDY*, R/W, A/D, PARITY INVERTING. (Note ① Driver on, driving high. ② Driver off. ③ Driver on, driving low.)

The signal line address accept (AACC) is an open collector driver with the typical waveform shown in Fig. 3-15. The actual pulse width for a given implementation will vary with the voltage level at which a master sees AACC active and the master's AACC active–to–DRDY* inactive time (t_6). Figure 3-15 shows the typical time to a TTL input threshold and the maximum voltage the signal can obtain.

The remaining open collector signal lines (DACC*, SRQ*, STO*, RESET* and SA*) have the typical waveforms given in Fig. 3-15. The signals have a maximum high level of 3.5 V and a minimum low level of 0.0 V. The maximum overshoot when the signal goes from a high to a low level is 0.5 V.

The differential lines (DRDY*, R/W, A/D, PARITY) have the inverting and noninverting signal waveforms shown in Fig. 3-15. The resultant signal is the difference between the two signal levels. The separation between the two signals should be no less than 1.8 V. When the drivers are off (level 2), the signal separation guarantees the level of the resultant control signal. When the noninverting signal is at level 1, the inverting signal is at level 3. Conversely, when the noninverting signal is at level 3, the inverting signal is at level 1.

3.6.3 Bus Power Specification

The Multichannel bus does not supply any power lines; therefore, every device that connects to the bus must supply its own power. The bus does supply 22 signal return grounds for all devices to use.

3.6.4 Environment

All bus specifications must be met while the environment is within the following limits:

Temperature	0 to 55°C (32° to 131°F); free moving air across the modules (200 LFM is recommended)
Humidity	90% max relative (noncondensing)
Shock	30g of force 11 ms in duration three times in three planes
Vibration	Sweeping from 10 to 55 Hz and back to 10 Hz at a distance of 0.01 in (0.25 mm) peak to peak lasting 3 min in each of three planes

3.6.5 Bus Timing

All the timing specifications of the Multichannel bus are described in this section; they are summarized in Table 3-2. Timing diagrams have been included to show the signal timing relations.

TABLE 3-2 Multichannel Bus Timing Specifications

Ref	Parameter description	Timing		Source	Note
		min	max		
t_1	A/D line setup to leading edge of DRDY*	60		T	
t_2	A/D line hold after leading edge of AACC or DACC*	40		T	
t_3	Data mode (A/$\overline{\text{D}}$ low) and R/$\overline{\text{W}}$ setup to leading edge of DRDY*	60		M	
t_4	A/$\overline{\text{D}}$ hold after trailing edge of DRDY*	50		M	1
t_5	Leading edge of DRDY* to leading edge of AACC or DACC*	0		L	2
t_6	Leading edge of AACC or DACC* to trailing edge of DRDY*	0		T	2
t_7	Trailing edge of DRDY* to trailing edge of DACC*	0		L	2
t_8	Trailing edge of DRDY* to trailing edge of AACC	0	75	L	2
t_9	Address mode (A/$\overline{\text{D}}$ high) to leading edge of DRDY*	200		M	
t_{10}	AD15*–AD0*, DRDY* in high-impedance state to A/$\overline{\text{D}}$ low		0	M	3
t_{11}	A/$\overline{\text{D}}$ high to AD15*–AD0*, DRDY* out of high-impedance state	150		M	3
t_{12}	Trailing edge of DRDY* to leading edge of DRDY* (A/$\overline{\text{D}}$ high)	250		M	
t_{13}	AD15*–AD0*, DRDY* in high-impedance state to SA* high		0	SU	
t_{14}	Trailing edge of DRDY* to leading edge of DRDY* (A/$\overline{\text{D}}$ low)	100		T	
t_{15}	SA* low to AD15*–AD0*, DRDY* out of high-impedance state	175		SU	
t_{16}	Leading edge of DRDY* to leading edge of STO*	0		L	4
t_{17}	Leading edge of AACC or DACC* to leading edge of STO*		0	L	4
t_{18}	Address mode (A/$\overline{\text{D}}$ high) to trailing edge of STO* or SRQ*	0		SL	5
t_{19}	Trailing edge of STO* or SRQ* to trailing edge of DRDY*		0	SL	5
t_{20}	Reset pulse width	RP		SU	6
t_{21}	A/$\overline{\text{D}}$ high to AD15*–ADO*, DRDY* in high-impedance state		75	SL	3
t_{22}	A/$\overline{\text{D}}$ low to AD15*–ADO*, DRDY* out of high-impedance state	0		M	3
t_{23}	SA* high to AD15*–ADO*, DRDY* out of high-impedance state	0		SU	

TABLE 3-2 **Multichannel Bus Timing Specifications** (*Continued*)

		Timing			
Ref	Parameter description	min	max	Source	Note
t_{24}	SA* low to AD15*–AD0*, DRDY* in high-impedance state		75	SU	

- All times listed are nanoseconds unless otherwise noted.
- All signals are shown as TTL-type waveforms. (For differential line pairs, the waveform applies to the TTL driver input or receiver output.)
- T refers to the selected talker for a bus cycle.
- L refers to the, or a, selected listener for a bus cycle.
- M refers to the selected master for a bus cycle.
- SL refers to the, or a, selected slave for a bus cycle.
- SU refers to the system supervisor.

1. This timing parameter applies only when there is a message mode transition from address to data mode or from data to address mode. When the mode does not change, the "address not data" line should be held at a constant level.

2. The signals specify the basic bus cycle transfer handshake. Though specified at 0 ns minimum, there is a minimum propagation delay for each parameter relative to the cable length between the talker and the listener. This propagation delay is approximately 2 ns/ft. Because the handshake requires a three-step interlock, the minimum propagation delay is multiplied by 3 to determine the total propagation delay. Thus a talker and listener with a short cable run between them would experience very little propagation delay. However, a talker and listener separated by the maximum length of Multichannel bus cable (50 ft) would experience a total propagation delay of at least 300 ns.

3. These parameters apply in messages where the master is the listener for the data mode portion of the message.

4. These parameters apply when a parity error is detected by a listener during a bus cycle. All other assertions of the interrupt lines can be asynchronous to the bus operation.

5. These parameters apply during the bus cycle when the STO or SRQ status register of the device asserting the interrupt line is read during an STO or SRQ poll.

6. The minimum Reset pulse width is 5 ms.

ADDRESS OPERATION

An address operation is generated by the bus master and received by the bus slaves. The lines involved and the timing relations are shown in Fig. 3-16. The master places address information on the bus a minimum of 60 ns (t_1) prior to DRDY* active and sets the A/D line high (address) 200 ns (t_9) and the R/W line low (write) a minimum of 60 ns (t_3) prior to DRDY*. After the setup requirements have been met, the master drives DRDY* active. All slaves on the bus respond to the DRDY* by driving AACC active a minimum of 0 ns (t_5) after receiving DRDY*. Upon receiving AACC active (all slaves have accepted the address), the master removes DRDY* a minimum of 0 ns (t_6) and holds the address 40 ns (t_2) after receiving AACC. The slaves then remove the AACC signal a minimum of 0 ns (t_8) to a maximum of 75 ns (t_8) from DRDY* inactive. The next address sent by the master must not occur until a minimum of 250 ns (t_{12}). The address cycle time t_{12} and the AACC maximum inactive time t_8 ensure that the AACC line has settled before the next address is sent.

DATA READ OPERATION

A data read operation transfers data from the slave to the bus master controlling the bus. The lines involved and the timing relations are shown in Fig. 3-17. Once the master has completed the address cycle, it guarantees that its A/D driver is turned off a maximum of 0 ns (t_{10}) prior to setting the R/W line to read mode (R/W = high) and the A/D line to data mode (A/D = low). The selected slave, which is now the talker, may begin to drive the bus a minimum of 0 ns (t_{22}) after the bus is placed in the read data mode. The slave places data information on the bus a minimum of 60 ns (t_1) prior to DRDY* active. After the setup requirements have been met, the slave drives DRDY* active. The master responds to the DRDY* by accepting the data and driving DACC* active a minimum of 0 ns (t_5) after receiving DRDY*. Upon receiving DACC* active, the slave removes DRDY* a minimum of 0 ns (t_6) and holds the data 40 ns (t_2) after receiving DACC*. The master then removes the DACC* signal a minimum of 0 ns (t_7) from DRDY* inactive. The next data cycle can occur immediately after DACC* is removed. The minimum cycle time is 100 ns (t_{14}), which is the minimum setup and hold time for a data cycle $(t_1 + t_2)$.

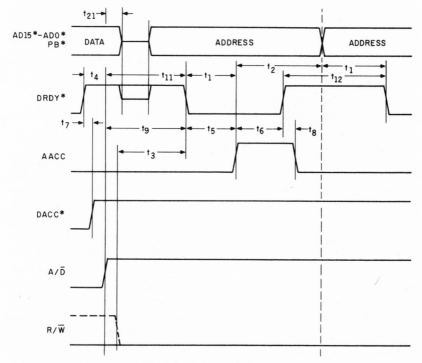

FIGURE 3-16 Address cycle timing. (Note: For differential line pairs, level denotes positive portion of differential pair.)

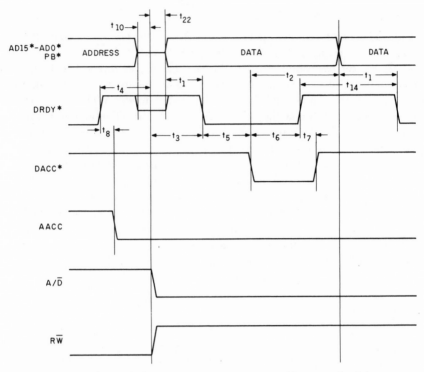

FIGURE 3-17 **Data read cycle timing.** (Note: For differential line pairs, level denotes positive portion of differential pair.)

DATA WRITE OPERATION

A data write operation transfers data from the bus master controlling the bus to the addressed slave. The lines involved and the timing relations are shown in Fig. 3-18. Once the master has completed the address cycle, it sets the R/W line to write mode (R/W = low) and the A/D line to data mode (A/D = low) a minimum of 60 ns (t_3) before driving DRDY* active. The master, which is now the talker, places data information on the bus a minimum of 60 ns (t_1) prior to DRDY* active. After the setup requirements have been met, the master drives DRDY* active. The selected slave responds to the DRDY* by accepting the data and driving DACC* active a minimum of 0 ns (t_5) after receiving DRDY*. Upon receiving DACC* active, the master removes DRDY* a minimum of 0 ns (t_6) and holds the data 40 ns (t_2) after receiving DACC*. The selected slave then removes the DACC* signal a minimum of 0 ns (t_7) from DRDY* inactive. The next data cycle can occur immediately after DACC* is removed. The minimum cycle time is 100 ns (t_{14}), which is the minimum setup and hold time for a data cycle ($t_1 + t_2$).

BUS EXCHANGE OPERATION

The bus exchange operation occurs when the supervisor passes bus control over to a bus controller and again when it regains control. The lines involved and the timing relations are shown in Fig. 3-19. When ready to release the bus, the supervisor guarantees that its A/D and control drivers are turned off a maximum of 0 ns (t_{13}) prior to releasing SA*. The selected master may begin to drive the bus a minimum of 0 ns (t_{23}) after receiving SA* inactive. When the supervisor is ready to regain control of the bus, it will drive SA* active. The supervisor must also guarantee that it will not drive the A/D and control lines a minimum of 175 ns (t_{15}) after it drives SA* active. The selected master must be off the bus a maximum of 60 ns (t_{24}) after receiving SA* active.

INTERRUPT OPERATION

Interrupt operations include both STO* and SRQ* timing. Since STO* is used to indicate bus errors as well as device status, additional timing constraints are placed on STO* for transfer error reporting. Figure 3-20 shows the timing rela-

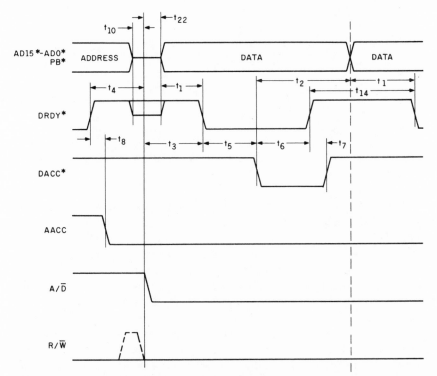

FIGURE 3-18 Data write cycle timing. (Note: For differential line pairs, level denotes positive portion of differential pair.)

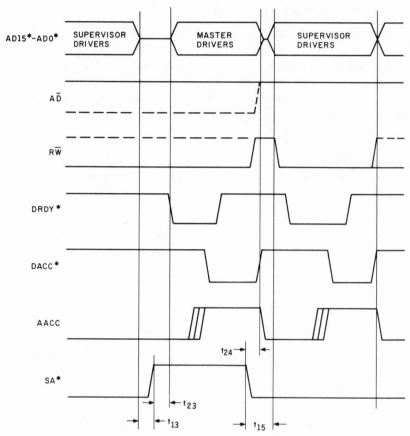

FIGURE 3-19 Bus exchange timing. (Note: For differential line pairs, level denotes positive portion of differential pair.)

tions for STO* as a transfer error signal. In the diagram the current data cycle is the cycle that error occurred in. The device that detects the transfer error asserts STO* a minimum of 0 ns (t_{16}) after receiving DRDY* active. AACC or DACC* is driven active a minimum of 0 ns (t_{17}) after STO* is asserted. The SRQ* signal is removed by reading the device's SRQ register. The SRQ* signal may be removed a minimum of 0 ns (t_{18}) after the device is selected and the bus is placed in data mode, but it must be removed a maximum of 0 ns (t_{19}) prior to the register read DRDY* going inactive. Figure 3-21 shows the timing relations of STO* and SRQ* when used other than parity error. In this case a device may place STO* or SRQ* active anytime on the bus. The SRQ* and STO* signals are removed by reading the device's interrupt register. The signals may be removed a minimum of 0 ns (t_{18}) after the device is selected and the bus is placed in data mode, but they they must be removed a maximum of 0 ns (t_{19}) prior to the register read DRDY* going inactive.

3.6.6 Receivers, Drivers, and Terminations

In this section the driver type, the receiver loading, and the signal termination requirements are defined. The driver-receiver direct-current (DC) specifications are listed in Table 3-3. Figure 3-22 is a diagram of the three bus driver-receiver configurations supported on the bus. It should be noted that all open collector lines should be received by hysteresis–Schmitt trigger devices, such as

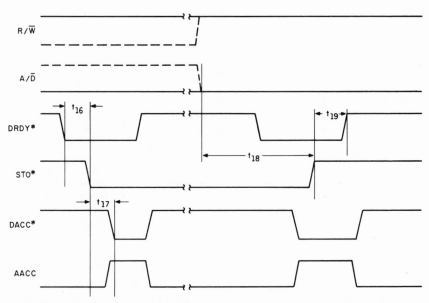

FIGURE 3-20 Transfer error interrupt timing. (Note: For differential line pairs, level denotes positive portion of differential pair.)

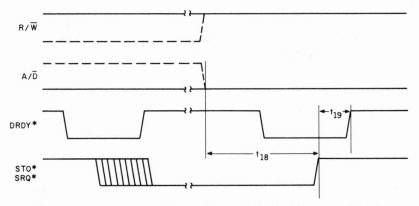

FIGURE 3-21 Status interrupt timing. (Note: For differential line pairs, level denotes positive portion of differential pair.)

TABLE 3-3 Multichannel Bus DC Specification

Signal name	Driver type	Termination[a] Ω	Minimum driver requirements, mA			Maximum receiver requirements, mA		
			High	Low	Load cap, pF	High	Low	Load cap, pF
AD15–0*	Tristate	110	−5	48	300	0.2	0.8	15
SA*	Open coll	110/220	N.A.[b]	48	300	0.4	0.6	15
Reset*	Open coll	110/220	N.A.	48	300	0.4	0.6	15
AACC	Open coll	1000/2000	N.A.	48	300	0.4	0.6	15
DACC*	Open coll	110/220	N.A.	48	300	0.4	0.6	15
SRQ*	Open coll	110/220	N.A.	48	300	0.4	0.6	15
STO*	Open coll	110/220	N.A.	48	300	0.4	0.6	15
R/$\overline{W}$	Dif, noninv	220/470	−20	40	300	0.5	0.5	15
R/$\overline{W}$/	Dif, inv	470/220	−20	40	300	0.5	0.5	15
A/$\overline{D}$	Dif, noninv	220/470	−20	40	300	0.5	0.5	15
A/$\overline{D}$/	Dif, inv	470/220	−20	40	300	0.5	0.5	15
PB*	Dif, noninv	220/470	−20	40	N.A.	0.5	0.5	N.A.
PB*/	Dif, inv	470/220	−20	40	N.A.	0.5	0.5	N.A.
DRDY*	Dif, noninv	220/470	−20	40	N.A.	0.5	0.5	N.A.
DRDY*/	Dif, inv	470/220	−20	40	N.A.	0.5	0.5	N.A.

[a]Termination provided only at the physical ends of the interconnect cable. Where the positive termination (pull-up) resistance is different from the negative termination (pull-down) resistance, the positive termination resistance is listed first.

[b]N.A. = not applicable.

the 74LS14, that have a minimum $V_{T+} - V_{T-}$ of 0.4 V. Figure 3-23 is the bus termination schematic diagram for both ends of the cable. This is the only termination on the cable, and it can be supplied by the devices or by special termination modules.

3.7 MECHANICAL CONSIDERATIONS

In this section all the physical and mechanical considerations that a designer requires for proper Multichannel bus implementation are defined. In the following sections the Multichannel bus mechanical requirments are set forth.

3.7.1 Cable Specification

A 60-conductor flat ribbon cable is the recommended bus data transmission medium. The cable has the following chracteristics:

Impedance   95 to 105 Ω nominal

Capacitance   22 pF/ft (72.18 pF/m) nominal

Propagation delay 1.7 ns/ft (5.58 ns/m) nominal

Length   50 ft (15 m) max

Multichannel implementation recommends twisted and flat cable over distances greater than 5 ft (1.5 m) or in noisy environments. For extremely noisy or harsh environments, jacketed and shielded flat ribbon cables are recommended. Table 3-4 supplies the complete bus cable specification and vendor listing.

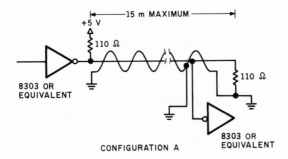

CONFIGURATION A

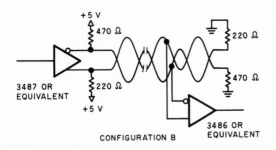

CONFIGURATION B

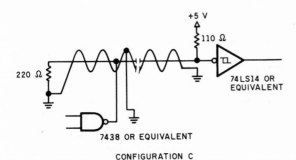

CONFIGURATION C

FIGURE 3-22 Bus driver-receiver configurations.

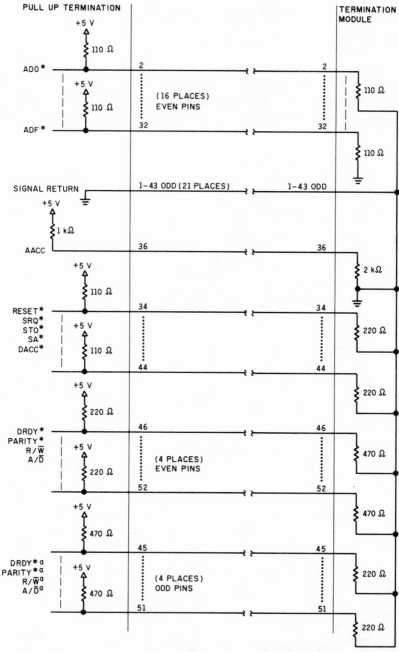

FIGURE 3-23   Bus termination configuration. (Note: ªInverted output differential driver.)

TABLE 3.4 Cable Specification and Vendor Listing

Physical properties	
Conductors	28 AWG, 7/36 strand, tinned copper
Conductor insulation	0.010-in wall, nominal
Conductor spacing, twisted pair	0.10 in, nominal
Conductor spacing, flat	0.050 in, ± 10%
Cable thickness, flat	0.042 in, nominal
Temperature rating	80°C
Electrical properties	
Impedance (nominal)	105 Ω ± 10%
Propagation velocity (nominal)	1.7 ns/ft
Capacitance (nominal)	22 pF/ft
Insulation requirements	
Voltage rating (minimum)	100 V DC
Insulation resistance (minimum)	1×10^{10} Ω

MULTICHANNEL-BUS-COMPATIBLE CABLE

Vendor	Type	Vendor number	Conductors
Belden	Plain flat ribbon	9L28060	60
Belden	Twisted pair ribbon	9V28060	60
Belden	Insulated flat ribbon	9L28260	60
Spectrastrip	Plain flat ribbon	455-240-60	60
Spectrastrip	Twisted pair ribbon	455-248-60	60
Spectrastrip	Insulated flat ribbon	151-2830-060	60

MULTICHANNEL-BUS-COMPATIBLE CONNECTORS

Vendor	Type	Vendor number	Pins
Berg	Male, header	65823-103	60
Berg	Female, mass-terminated	65949-960	60
3M	Male, header	3372-1302	60
3M	Female, mass-terminated	3334-6000	60

3.7.2 Connector-Receptacle Specification

A 60-pin connector (3M part number 3372-1302 or equivalent) is used on all devices that connect to the Multichannel bus. The mating receptacle (3M part number 3334-6000 or equivalent) is mass-terminated on the flat ribbon cable. Figure 3-24 is an outline drawing of the connector and the pin-numbering convention. A list of compatible connectors is given in Table 3-4.

3.7.3 Multichannel Bus Pin Assignments

The pin assignments for the Multichannel bus are listed in Table 3-5.

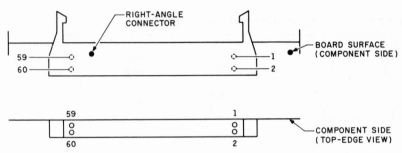

FIGURE 3-24 Connector outline and pin numbering convention.

3.7.4 Bus Termination

The terminating resistors required for the Multichannel bus can be placed on the devices or handled by special terminating modules. The bus specification does not place any restriction on the method of cable termination. The only requirement is that the bus be terminated by the pull-up resistors at one end of the cable, pull-down resistors at the other end of the cable, and no other termination resistors.

3.8 LEVELS OF COMPLIANCE

The Multichannel bus supports various levels of compliance of the full specification. In this section the variable elements of capability and the notation used to describe the level of compliance are discussed.

3.8.1 Variable Elements of Capability

The Multichannel bus has, built into its structure, flexibility which allows the system designer to build different systems with boards of varying capabilities. Variation in the following areas is permitted:

- Data path width

- Address path width

- Parity support

- Interrupt register support

DATA PATH

Both 8- and 16-bit data path products can operate on the Multichannel bus. All byte operations occur on the lower byte of the A/D bus (AD0* to AD7*), which allows 8- and 16-bit products to work together.

ADDRESS PATH

Both 8- and 16-bit address path products can operate on the Multichannel bus.
For the 8-bit address path both address words are transferred on the lower byte
of the A/D bus (AD0* to AD7*). The 8-bit address path devices support only
8 bits of memory and I/O address. The 16-bit address path devices support 24
bits of memory and I/O address.

PARITY

The Multichannel bus supports both a parity mode and a no-parity mode. If a
parity mode is selected, then, at a minimum, all talkers must generate parity.

TABLE 3-5   Multichannel Bus Pin Assignments

Lower row			Upper row		
Pin	Mnemonic	Signal name	Pin	Mnemonic	Signal name
1	GND	Ground	2	AD0*	A/D line 0
3	GND	Ground	4	AD1*	A/D line 1
5	GND	Ground	6	AD2*	A/D line 2
7	GND	Ground	8	AD3*	A/D line 3
9	GND	Ground	10	AD4*	A/D line 4
11	GND	Ground	12	AD5*	A/D line 5
13	GND	Ground	14	AD6*	A/D line 6
15	GND	Ground	16	AD7*	A/D line 7
17	GND	Ground	18	AD8*	A/D line 8
19	GND	Ground	20	AD9*	A/D line 9
21	GND	Ground	22	AD10*	A/D line 10
23	GND	Ground	24	AD11*	A/D line 11
25	GND	Ground	26	AD12*	A/D line 12
27	GND	Ground	28	AD13*	A/D line 13
29	GND	Ground	30	AD14*	A/D line 14
31	GND	Ground	32	AD15*	A/D line 15
33	GND	Ground	34	RESET*	Reset
35	GND	Ground	36	AACC	Address mode accept
37	GND	Ground	38	SRQ*	Service request
39	GND	Ground	40	STO*	Supervisor take over
41	GND	Ground	42	DACC*	Data mode accept
43	GND	Ground	44	SA*	Supervisor active
45	PB*/	Parity bit (inv.)	46	PB*	Parity bit
47	R/$\overline{\text{W}}$/	Read not write (inv.)	48	R/$\overline{\text{W}}$	Read not write
49	A/$\overline{\text{D}}$/	Address not data (inv.)	50	A/$\overline{\text{D}}$	Address not data
51	DRDY*/	Data ready (inv.)	52	DRDY*	Data ready
53	RES	Reserved	54	RES	Reserved
55	RES	Reserved	56	RES	Reserved
57	RES	Reserved	58	RES	Reserved
59	RES	Reserved	60	RES	Reserved

When the no-parity mode is selected, then, at a minimum, all listeners on the bus must not check parity. When parity mode is selected, an 8-bit device in a 8- and 16-bit system must check parity for all 16 bits.

INTERRUPT REGISTER

Whenever a device supports the interrupts SRQ* and STO*, it must also support the associated registers. A device may support one, both, or neither of these registers.

3.8.2 Compliance-Level Notation

The following notation allows a vendor to succinctly and accurately specify a product's level of compliance with the Multichannel bus standard. The omission of an element specification implies no capability for that element.

DEVICE TYPE

    SUP   Supervisor

    CON   Controller

    BD   Basic device

DATA PATH

    D8   8-bit data path

    D16   8- and 16-bit data path

ADDRESS PATH

    A8   8-bit address path

    A16   16-bit address path

PARITY

    P8   8-bit parity generated and checked

    P16   16-bit parity generated and checked

INTERRUPT SUPPORT

    SRQ   SRQ interrupt, register-supported

    STO   STO interrupt, register-supported

COMPLIANCE-LEVEL MARKING

The compliance level of a module must be clearly stated in the module specification and may be marked on the PCB.

EXAMPLES

A basic device with 8-bit data and address that supports 16-bit parity and the STO interrupt would be specified as follows:

Multichannel bus compliance BD D8 A8 P16 STO

An intelligent controller with 16-bit address and data width which supports SRQ and STO interrupts but does not support parity would be specified as follows:

Multichannel bus compliance CON D16 A16 STO SRQ

3.9 SUMMARY

Since the Multichannel bus is an integral part of the Multibus family, it can architecturally enhance any Multibus system design. It can extend the range of the Multibus system bus in terms of performance and physical distribution. It has the bandwidth to handle most high-speed data movement applications while providing a straightforward interface. If the user has partitioned the system so that the high-speed data requirements can be moved to the Multichannel bus, the design can take full advantage of the Multibus family.

4

iSBX I/O Bus

This chapter provides the basis for a conceptual understanding of the iSBX/
IEEE-P595 bus and describes how the bus extends the architecture of the Multibus system bus. Included are the logical and physical descriptions of the bus
and the devices that connect to the bus. Also, a detailed look is taken at the
electrical and mechanical specifications. The notation used throughout this book
is the same as that defined in the Multibus/IEEE-796 functional description in
Sec. 2-1. The information in this chapter was based on the Intel iSBX Bus Specification (14686-002) dated March 1981 and the Proposed IEEE Standard Specification IEEE P595 I/O Expansion Bus. It is recommended that anyone designing with the iSBX bus obtain the latest versions of these specifications from Intel
Corporation.

4.1 WHY THE ISBX BUS IS REQUIRED

Engineers designing systems around board-level computers historically have
chosen between large and small boards. Large boards, such as the Multibus
boards, reduce the space and also the number of boards required for a complete
system. But the addition of small amounts of capability, such as a few I/O lines,
to the system necessitates another large board, which might be overkill for the
application. Smaller boards provide greater flexibility in customizing a system,
but their disadvantage is that even a simple system requires several boards and
connectors, which add unnecessarily to the cost of the system.

Advances in semiconductor technology also favor a smaller-board approach.
The ever-increasing circuit densities of new integrated circuits (ICs) mean that
more capabilities can be provided on a single computer board. This increased
computing power opens up new applications which may require different I/O

capabilities, specialized processing, or customized I/O devices. The board-level designer needs the flexibility to customize a system without using large boards.

The iSBX concept, together with Multibus-compatible boards, provides the advantages of boards of both sizes. A combination of the two sizes permits the system designer to configure precisely the single-board computers (SBC) for individual applications at a lower cost. Given the larger size, the SBC can support the microprocessor, the memory, some general-purpose I/O, and the iSBX Multimodule[1] board. The iSBX Multimodule board is a small I/O expansion board that provides the SBC with application-specific I/O, such as an IEEE-488 controller or analog input or output channels. These small Multimodule boards enable the users to buy the exact I/O capabilities required for their systems. System size and cost are thereby kept at a minimum.

The iSBX concept provides the following benefits to the system designer:

1. *Low cost.* The ability to expand the I/O capability of an SBC incrementally lets the user add only the function the application requires. This lowers the cost of functional expansion.

2. *Simple upgradability.* The on-board addition of totally new capabilities to SBCs may be done discretely. This increases the SBC functional capability and permits new iSBX Multimodules designed with state-of-the-art VLSI to be used on previously designed SBCs.

3. *Increased performance.* The iSBX Multimodule board, like other local on-board components, communicates directly with the host board microprocessor and provides maximum performance. This on-board expansion can also increase system performance. The available Multibus bandwidth is increased by reducing system bus traffic to standard Multibus-compatible expansion boards that have been replaced.

4. *Compatibility.* All future 8- and 16-bit SBCs with the iSBX interface can use iSBX Multimodules designed previously or in the future.

5. *Low power.* The smaller boards require minimal power, which generates less heat than Multibus-size boards. This also reduces the system power supply needs, which lowers the total system cost.

6. *Dedicated connector.* The iSBX connector is a highly reliable connector specifically designed for this application.

4.2 LOGICAL DESCRIPTION OF THE iSBX BUS

The iSBX concept provides 8- and 16-bit I/O flexibility to any SBC or board-product line. It does so by providing a universal I/O interface on the baseboard

---

[1]Multimodule is a trademark of Intel Corporation, Santa Clara, California.

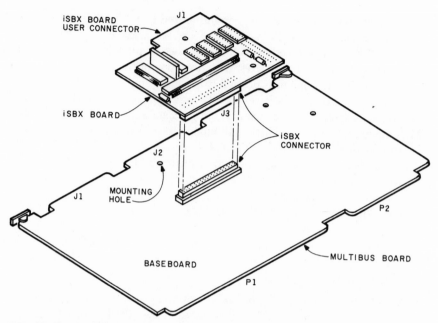

FIGURE 4-1   iSBX Multimodule board concept.

as shown in Fig. 4-1. This universal interface is a general-purpose I/O expansion bus, called the iSBX bus, and it is used to connect the baseboard to small boards. These small boards are called iSBX Multimodule boards or Multimodule boards (Fig. 4-2). Their function is to convert the iSBX bus into a customized I/O interface. A diagram of a typical SBC which utilizes the iSBX interface is shown in Fig. 4-3.

The primary function of the iSBX bus is to provide a path for I/O mapped data between the host board and the Multimodule board. The key features of the iSBX bus are summarized below.

- Low-cost I/O expansion.

- A standardized controlled local I/O expansion interface.

- Low overhead cost on baseboard.

- Both 8- and 16-bit data transfers are supported.

- Both interlocked and noninterlocked transfers are supported.

4.2.1 Bus Devices

The basic elements in an iSBX system are the baseboard and the iSBX Multimodule boards (Fig. 4-1). Figure 4-4 shows an SBC with iSBX bus support.

FIGURE 4-2   Multibus-compatible boards with iSBX bus support and iSBX Multimodule boards.

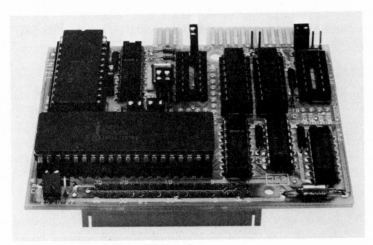

FIGURE 4-3   iSBX Multimodule board.

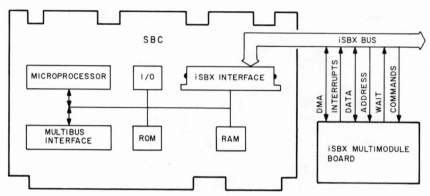

FIGURE 4-4   Block diagram of SBC with iSBX bus support.

BASEBOARD

The baseboard provides an electrical and mechanical interface for the iSBX Multimodule boards. The electrical interface provides the communication link between the two elements. The baseboard is the master of that link; it controls the address, chip selects, and command signals. The baseboard also provides the mechanical interface for Multimodule boards. The single-wide Multimodule board is mounted to the baseboard in two locations (Fig. 4-2): at the top of the Multimodule board by a nylon screw and spacer assembly and at the bottom of the board by the iSBX connector, which was designed specifically for this application.

There are two classes of baseboards: those with direct memory access (DMA) support and those without. Baseboards designed with DMA controllers can support the DMA aspects of the iSBX bus interface. These boards, in conjunction with an iSBX Multimodule board, can perform direct I/O–to–memory or memory–to–I/O operations. Baseboards without DMA support use a subset of the bus specification and do not use that aspect of the Multimodule board's capabilities.

iSBX MULTIMODULE BOARDS

iSBX Multimodule boards are small, specialized I/O boards which plug into the iSBX interface on the baseboard (Fig. 4-2). These modules convert the iSBX bus interface to a defined specialized I/O interface. The iSBX bus specification defines two standard PCB form factors: single-wide (2.5 × 3.7 in; 6.35 × 9.4 cm) and double-wide (2.5 × 7.5 in; 6.35 × 18.8 cm). These two form factors allow for a broad range in circuit complexity. A typical single-wide iSBX Multimodule board requires less than 10 percent of the PCB area (the iSBX connector and one mounting hole) to support the interface; the rest of the space is available for application circuitry. An example of an iSBX Multimodule is a serial channel controller (Fig. 4-3). This Multimodule board converts the iSBX bus interface into an RS-232 or RS-422 serial communication channel.

4.2.2   8- and 16-Bit Compatibility; Bus Device Notation

The iSBX bus specification supports both 8- and 16-bit data transfers. Baseboards with 8-bit data paths can support only 8-bit iSBX Multimodule boards. All 8-bit baseboards support the 8/8 bit mode (the baseboard is an 8-bit system, the first 8 in the 8/8 bit mode, and the baseboard can support 8-bit iSBX Multimodule boards, the second 8 in the 8/8 bit mode) of the iSBX specification. Baseboards with 16-bit data paths can be designed to support only 8-bit iSBX Multimodule boards or both 8- and 16-bit iSBX Multimodule boards. A 16-bit baseboard designed to accommodate only 8-bit iSBX Multimodule boards supports the 16/8 bit mode of the bus specification. A 16-bit baseboard designed to accommodate 16-bit iSBX Multimodules supports the 16/16 bit mode. A baseboard that supports the 16/16 bit mode must also support the 16/8 bit mode; that is, it supports both 8- and 16-bit iSBX Multimodule boards. The different modes for iSBX-compatible systems are summarized in the following table.

Mode	Description
8/8	An 8-bit baseboard that supports 8-bit iSBX Multimodule boards
16/8	A 16-bit baseboard that supports 8-bit iSBX Multimodule boards
16/16	A 16-bit baseboard that supports 8- and 16-bit iSBX Multimodule boards

4.3   BUS SIGNAL DEFINITIONS

In this section the iSBX bus signals are described. Also described is how the basic operations occur over the iSBX bus. The iSBX bus is composed of 44 signal lines for the 16/16 bit mode and 36 signal lines for the 8/8 and 16/8 bit modes. These lines can be broken into several classes: address and chip select (five signal lines), data (eight signal lines for the 8/8 and 16/8 bit modes and 16 signal lines for the 16/16 bit mode), control (9), interrupts (2), option (2), and power (8). The different classes are explained in the following sections.

4.3.1   Address and Chip Select Lines

The address and chip select lines can be divided into two groups:

Class	Signal	Function
Address	MA2–MA0	Address lines (2–0)
Chip selects	MCS1*, MCS0*	Chip select lines (1–0)

The baseboard provides the decode logic for the iSBX interface. The logic generates the chip selects for the iSBX Multimodule boards and passes on the least significant portion of the I/O address to the Multimodule board. The board decodes all but the lower-order bits of the I/O address in generating the two iSBX Multimodule board chip selects (MCS1* and MCS0*). In 8-bit baseboard systems supporting the 8/8 bit mode of the bus specification, the baseboard assigns two blocks of eight I/O port addresses for each iSBX interface it provides. In 16-bit baseboard systems supporting the 16/8 or 16/16 bit mode, the baseboard assigns two blocks of 16 I/O port addresses for each of its iSBX interfaces. The I/O addresses reserved by the baseboard for each iSBX interface it provides are summarized in Table 4-1. Note that the 8-bit and 16-bit baseboard systems reserve different addresses and that the address assignments are required by Intel's iSBX Bus Specification. The IEEE-P595 Bus Specification only recommends these addresses.

ADDRESS

The three address lines MA2 to MA0 carry the least significant portion of the binary address of the I/O device location that the baseboard is referencing; MA0 is the least significant bit of the address. The address lines are positive true input lines to the Multimodule board. In 8-bit baseboard systems the MA2 to MA0 are mapped directly to the three least significant address bits of the microprocessor. In 16-bit baseboard systems (e.g., one based on an 8086 microprocessor), MA2 to MA0 are mapped to address bit 3 through address bit 1 on the baseboard, since address bit 0 is used in the chip select generation.

The iSBX bus supports both byte and word addressing (Fig. 4-5). A byte (8 bits) location is the smallest addressable unit of storage. There are two types of byte address locations, an even-byte address (address 0 of the baseboard is inactive) and an odd-byte address (address 0 of the baseboard is active). Two consecutive byte locations form a word. The iSBX bus in 16/16 bit mode can transfer a word if the first byte location of the word is an even-byte address (an even-word address). If the first byte location of the word is an odd-byte address (an odd-word address), the baseboard must perform two byte accesses and assemble the word.

TABLE 4·1 Baseboard I/O Addressing Assignments for iSBX Bus (Hexadecimal Notation)

iSBX Multimodule connector no.	Chip select	8-bit baseboard address (8/8 bit mode)	16-bit baseboard address (16/8 bit mode)	16-bit baseboard address (16/16 bit mode)
iSBX 1	MCS0*	F0–F7	0A0–0AF	0A0,2,4,6,8,A,C,E
	MCS1*	F8–FF	0B0–0BF	0A1,3,5,7,9,B,D,F
iSBX 2	MCS0*	C0–C7	080–08F	0A0,2,4,6,8,A,C,E
	MCS1*	C8–CF	090–09F	081,3,5,7,9,B,D,F
iSBX 3	MCS0*	B0–B7	060–06F	060,2,4,6,8,A,C,E
	MCS1*	B8–BF	070–07F	061,3,5,7,9,B,D,F

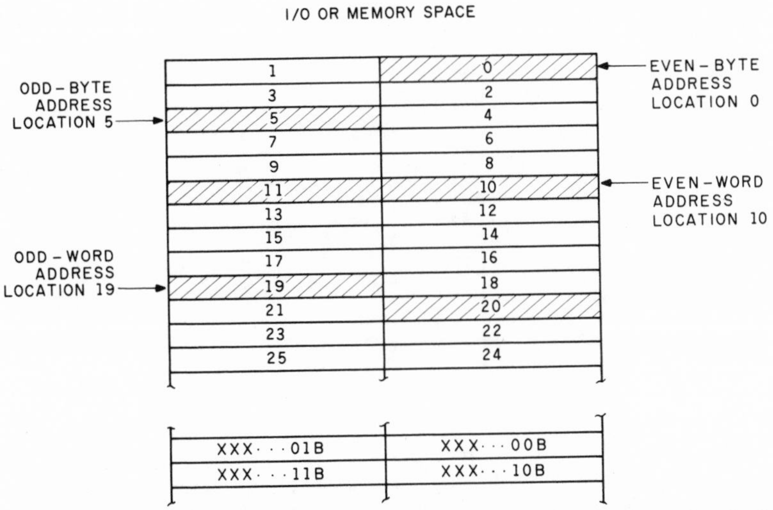

I/O OR MEMORY SPACE

FIGURE 4-5 Memory and I/O Address Mapping. (Note: Bus master must break odd-word address access into two byte accesses and reform the word.)

CHIP SELECT LINES

In 8-bit systems, the negative true input lines MCS1* and MCS0* to the iSBX Multimodule board are the result of the baseboard decode logic. This logic decodes the appropriate local bus address bits into the iSBX Multimodule chip select lines, as defined in Fig. 4-6. The chip select signals, along with the I/O command signals, enable communication with the iSBX Multimodule boards.

In 16-bit systems, the chip select signals optionally have two definitions: one for the 16/8 bit mode and one for the 16/16 bit mode. These options are selectable by the user for each interface provided on the baseboard, depending on the data path width of the iSBX board that is installed.

The 16/8 bit mode is used when a 16-bit baseboard must interface with an 8-bit iSBX board. The chip select lines serve the same function as in an 8-bit baseboard with different I/O address assignments. The 16-bit baseboard uses the lower data byte (MD7 to MD0) of the 16-bit word to communicate with the Multimodule board. The upper data byte (MD15 to MD8) is not defined and should not be used. Only even I/O port addresses are used (Table 4-1). This requires the baseboard to reserve 32 I/O port addresses. The 16 even ports are used, leaving the 16 odd ports unused.

The 16/16 bit mode is used when a 16-bit baseboard must interface with a 16-bit iSBX Multimodule board. The baseboard uses all 16 data lines to communicate with the iSBX Multimodule board. In this mode, the chip select terms are also used to control low-byte, high-byte, and word transfers as well as address decoding. The MCS0* is used for low-byte (even-byte) transfers;

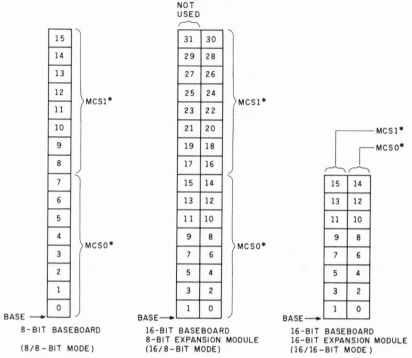

FIGURE 4-6 iSBX baseboard chip select assignments.

MCS1* is used for high-byte (odd-byte) transfers; and both MCS0* and MCS1* are used for even word data transfers.

Figure 4-7 shows a portion of the logic equations and possible circuit for part of MCS1* and MCS0* generation in a 16-bit baseboard system. In this example, the baseboard has Intel's iAPX[2] 80286 16-bit advanced microprocessor. The baseboard logic generates four signals which are used to generate the two iSBX chip selects. The chip select 1* and chip select 2* signals indicate that the baseboard is addressing an I/O address in the range of 0C0H to 0CFH (hexadecimal) and 0B0H to 0BFH, respectively. Address 0* is the least significant address bit. When active, it indicates that an even-byte transfer is requested. An active BHEN* (byte high enable) indicates an odd-byte transfer is being requested. In the 16/8 bit mode the MCS1* and MCS2* terms are simply the chip select 1* and chip select 2* terms, respectively, without modification and have no data flow control terms in them. In the 16/16 bit mode the MCS1* and MCS2* terms include data flow control. The MCS0* term includes the address 0 term which controls the lower byte (the even byte). Thus, chip select 0* is logically ANDed

---

[2]iAPX is a trademark of Intel Corporation, Santa Clara, California.

with address 0* to produce MCS0*. The MCS1* term includes the high-byte control (odd-byte) term BHEN*. Thus, chip select 0* is logically ANDed with BHEN* to produce MCS1*. If the baseboard addresses I/O address 0C3H, then chip select 0* will be active and the address odd (address 0* is active). This will result in an active MCS1*.

4.3.2 Data Lines

The data lines MD15 to MD0 are used to transmit information to or receive it from the iSBX ports on the iSBX Multimodule board. There are 16 bidirectional

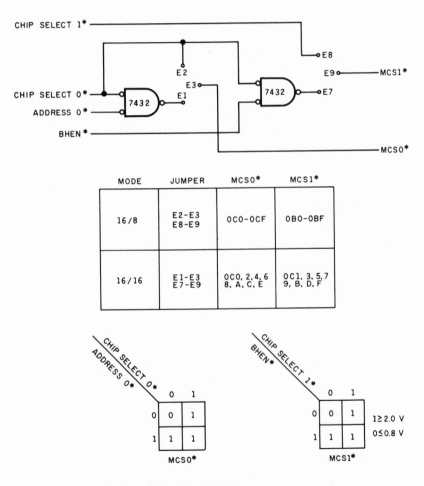

CHIP SELECT 0* = 0C0 - 0CF (HEX)
CHIP SELECT 1* = 0B0 - 0BF (HEX)

FIGURE 4-7   iSBX baseboard clip select logic (hexadecimal notation used).

positive true data lines MD15 to MD0. MD0 is the least significant bit for all data transfers except odd-byte transfers in the 16/16 bit mode, in which case MD8 is the least significant bit of the byte. Eight-bit baseboards permit only 8-bit data transfers and therefore can support only 8-bit iSBX boards. Sixteen-bit baseboards can support both 8- and 16-bit data transfers and therefore can support both 8- and 16-bit iSBX Multimodule boards. All of the data transfer types are shown in Fig. 4-8 and are labeled 1 to 5. 16/16 bit mode baseboards support three types of data transfer: (1) even-byte transfers on MD7 to MD0, (2) odd-byte transfers on MD15 to MD8, and (3) word-data transfers on MD15 to MD0. 16/8 bit mode baseboards support only one type of data transfer, the (1) even-byte transfers on MD7 to MD0. An 8/8 bit mode baseboard can support both (4) even-byte transfers and (5) odd-byte transfers on MD7 to MD0.

In 16/16 bit mode systems, the two chip select lines also control the data flow. The data flow is summarized in Fig. 4-9. Even-byte transfers require an active MCS0* (low); odd-byte transfers require an active MCS1* (low); word transfers require that both MCS0* and MCS1* be active (low). An even-word transfer is, in effect, an even-byte and an odd-byte transfer at the same time. There are two consecutive byte addresses for each word; the even-byte address (MCS0* = low) corresponds to the word data bits MD7 to MD0. Conversely, the odd-byte address, which is the word address + 1 (MCS1* = low), corresponds to the word data bits MD15 to MD8.

4.3.3 Control Lines

The control lines define the data transfer protocol on the iSBX bus. The control lines can be broken down into four basic groups.

Class	Signal	Function
Commands	IORD*	I/O read command
	IOWRT*	I/O write command
System control	MWAIT*	Extend command until done
	MPST*	iSBX board present
DMA	MDRQT	DMA request
	MDACK*	DMA acknowledge
	TDMA	Terminate DMA
Utilities	MCLK	iSBX clock
	RESET	Initialize

COMMAND LINES

The command lines IORD* and IOWRT* are negative true signals controlled by the baseboard and are inputs used to request an operation of an iSBX Mul-

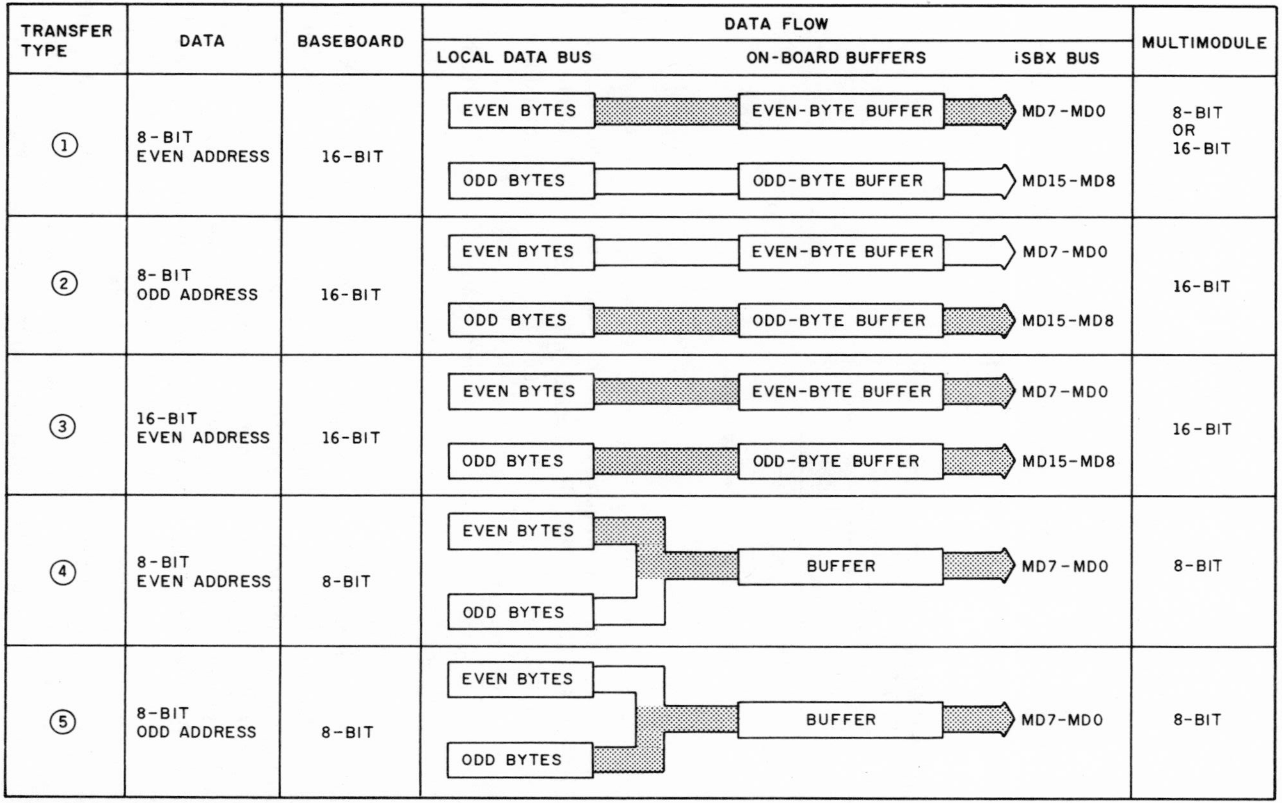

TRANSFER TYPE	DATA	BASEBOARD	DATA FLOW			MULTIMODULE
			LOCAL DATA BUS	ON-BOARD BUFFERS	iSBX BUS	
①	8-BIT EVEN ADDRESS	16-BIT	EVEN BYTES / ODD BYTES	EVEN-BYTE BUFFER / ODD-BYTE BUFFER	MD7-MD0 / MD15-MD8	8-BIT OR 16-BIT
②	8-BIT ODD ADDRESS	16-BIT	EVEN BYTES / ODD BYTES	EVEN-BYTE BUFFER / ODD-BYTE BUFFER	MD7-MD0 / MD15-MD8	16-BIT
③	16-BIT EVEN ADDRESS	16-BIT	EVEN BYTES / ODD BYTES	EVEN-BYTE BUFFER / ODD-BYTE BUFFER	MD7-MD0 / MD15-MD8	16-BIT
④	8-BIT EVEN ADDRESS	8-BIT	EVEN BYTES / ODD BYTES	BUFFER	MD7-MD0	8-BIT
⑤	8-BIT ODD ADDRESS	8-BIT	EVEN BYTES / ODD BYTES	BUFFER	MD7-MD0	8-BIT

FIGURE 4-8 Data transfer types.

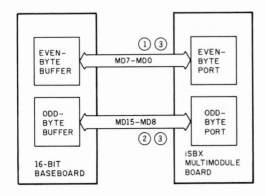

TRANSFER TYPE	DATA TRANSFER	MCS0*	MCS1*
①	8-BIT EVEN ADDRESS	LOW	HIGH
②	8-BIT ODD ADDRESS	HIGH	LOW
③	16-BIT EVEN ADDRESS	LOW	LOW

FIGURE 4-9 iSBX bus data flow control (16/16 and 16/8 bit modes).

timodule board. There are two commands, each with its unique signal on the bus. An active command indicates to the iSBX board that the address and chip select lines are valid and that the selected (MCS* active) iSBX Multimodule board should perform the specified operation. The I/O read command is used by the baseboard to request that data be sent from the iSBX Multimodule I/O port to the baseboard. Conversely, an I/O write command is used by the baseboard to send data from the baseboard to the iSBX Multimodule I/O port.

MULTIMODULE WAIT

Multimodule wait (MWAIT*) is a negative true signal used by the iSBX Multimodule board to extend the current data transfer cycle. The extension is accomplished by putting the microprocessor on the baseboard in a wait state and thereby providing additional time for the iSBX Multimodule board to perform the requested operation. The MWAIT* signal is generated by the iSBX Multimodule board from address and chip select information only. When the iSBX Multimodule has completed the requested operation, it drives MWAIT* inactive. This permits the microprocessor on the baseboard to continue. The interlocking mechanism permits iSBX Multimodule boards of different speeds to be on the bus. The interlocked command protocol can be summarized as follows: First the baseboard generates valid address and chip select(s); then the iSBX Multimodule board can cause the baseboard to wait—extend its current data cycle by activating MWAIT*. The iSBX Multimodule board controls the amount of time that it needs to wait. After it has waited long enough to perform the requested operation, it responds with an inactive MWAIT*, which permits the baseboard to continue.

The iSBX bus uses a negative type of acknowledgment method. It assumes that all operations will occur at the baseboard's maximum speed unless told to wait. The baseboard starts an operation, and it is the responsibility of the iSBX Multimodule board to tell the baseboard to wait if more time is needed to perform the operation. The MWAIT* signal is normally in the no-wait condition, which permits the baseboard to continue at maximum speed. The advantages of a negative type of acknowledgment method are low overhead and no special circuitry for time-out (the state when a nonexistent location is accessed). A positive acknowledgment method, which is used on Multibus systems, requires the bus slave module to generate a response before continuing. The advantages of a positive acknowledgment method are the independent timings of the master and the slave of two communicating units. The slave unit is not required to generate a wait signal in a fixed amount of time, and future baseboards with faster microprocessors will not need added extra circuitry to guarantee the wait timing.

MULTIMODULE PRESENT

Multimodule present (MPST*) is a negative true signal driven low by an iSBX Multimodule board to inform the baseboard that an iSBX board is installed. This interface signal goes to the baseboard decode logic. If the Multimodule is not installed, the address space normally reserved for the Multimodule board I/O ports can be used on system bus slave boards. This is important when designing a new board with the iSBX interface that also has to be backward-compatible with an older product. When the MPST* signal is in the inactive state, the iSBX I/O port locations will be decoded to be off board (not present on the board) and the SBC will go to the system bus to find them; it will appear as if there were no iSBX interface on the SBC. If the Multimodule is installed, then the I/O decode logic is activated to respond to the iSBX I/O port addresses as onboard resources and route the requests to the Multimodule I/O port. This signal is not needed for new products, since the iSBX addresses will be reserved for future expansion anyway.

4.3.4 Direct Memory Access

The DMA lines control the communication link between the DMA controller on the baseboard and the iSBX Multimodule board. Use of the DMA lines is optional, because not all baseboards provide DMA channels and not all iSBX Multimodule boards are capable of supporting a DMA transfer.

MULTIMODULE DMA REQUEST

Multimodule DMA request (MDRQT) is an active-high output signal from the iSBX Multimodule board to the baseboard's DMA controller. MDRQT is asserted when a request that a DMA cycle be initiated is made.

MULTIMODULE DMA ACKNOWLEDGE

Multimodule DMA acknowledge (MDACK*) is an active-low input signal to the iSBX Multimodule board from the baseboard DMA controller. MDACK* acknowledges that the requested DMA cycle has been granted.

TERMINATE DMA

Terminate DMA (TDMA) is a static bidirectional line. The direction is determined by configuration. Once configured, TDMA can operate in only one direction. In the output mode TDMA is used by the iSBX Multimodule board to terminate DMA activity of the DMA controller. In the input mode TDMA is used by the DMA controller to terminate requests from the iSBX Multimodule board.

4.3.5 Miscellaneous Signals

INITIALIZE LINE

The initialize line (RESET) is an active-high input line to the iSBX Multimodule board generated by the baseboard to put the iSBX Multimodule board into a known internal state.

MULTIMODULE CLOCK LINE

The Multimodule clock line (MCLK) is an input line to the iSBX Multimodule board. It is a timing signal. The 10-MHz ($+0$, -10 percent) frequency can vary from baseboard to baseboard. The clock is asynchronous with all other iSBX Multimodule bus signals. The MCLK requirements are the same as the constant clock (CCLK*) requirements of the Multibus specification.

MULTIMODULE INTERRUPT REQUEST LINES

The Multimodule interrupt request lines (MINTR0 and MINTR1) are active-high output lines from the iSBX Multimodule board; they are used to inform the baseboard that it needs service. This permits the baseboard to initiate a function on an iSBX Multimodule and start executing another task while it is waiting for the iSBX Multimodule to complete its task. Once it has completed the task, it will notify the baseboard by requesting a service interrupt.

OPTION LINES

The option lines are user-defined signals. They are connected to wire-wrap posts on the baseboards. They can be used, as an example, as extra interrupt request lines or custom signals to pass information between the baseboard and the iSBX Multimodule board.

POWER LINES

Three voltages and a ground are provided on the iSBX bus. The three voltages are $+5$, $+12$, and -12 V. There are three pins each for the $+5$ V and ground, and there is one pin each for $+12$ and -12 V.

4.4 BUS OPERATION OVERVIEW

Now that the definitions of the signal lines are understood, a functional description of each iSBX bus operation can be undertaken. The iSBX bus supports I/O read, I/O write, DMA, and interrupt operations.

4.4.1 I/O Read Operations

There are two types of I/O read operations that a baseboard and an iSBX Multimodule board can perform: a full-speed I/O read and an interlocked I/O read. Once the baseboard initiates the read operation, the iSBX Multimodule board determines which of the two read operations is performed.

FULL-SPEED I/O READ OPERATION

The full-speed I/O read operation is a noninterlocked data transfer, and it has strict timing requirements. The Multimodule board is not required to generate any acknowledgment indicating that the requested operation is completed. Figure 4-10 is a timing diagram of a full-speed I/O read operation. The following sequence is shown in Fig. 4-10:

1. The baseboard places the address on the address lines and generates a valid chip select for the iSBX Multimodule board. It waits until the address and chip select setup times (the time for the iSBX Multimodule board to decode the information) are met.

2. The transfer is initiated by activating the I/O read command (IORD*) signal. The iSBX Multimodule board must generate valid data on the data lines from the addressed I/O port in less than 250 ns.

3. The baseboard then strobes in the data and terminates the read cycle by deactivating the I/O read command.

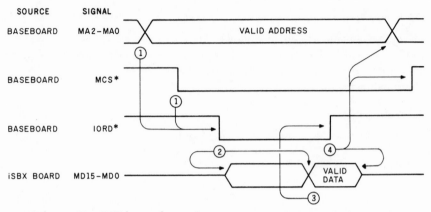

FIGURE 4-10 Fast iSBX bus read operation.

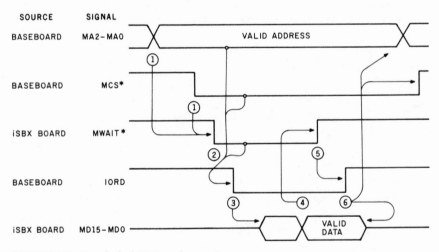

FIGURE 4-11 Interlocked iSBX read operation.

4. After a small delay, the address lines may become invalid and the chip select lines may be driven inactive.

INTERLOCKED I/O READ OPERATION

The second type of I/O read operation is an interlocked operation. The Multimodule wait (MWAIT*) is used by the iSBX Multimodule board to extend the read cycle. This permits the iSBX Multimodule board to control the access time. Figure 4-11 is a timing diagram of an interlocked I/O read operation. The following sequence is shown:

1. The baseboard places the address on the address lines and generates a valid chip select for the iSBX Multimodule board, just as in a full-speed I/O read operation.

2. The iSBX Multimodule board then activates the MWAIT* signal, which in turn removes the ready input to the microprocessor on the baseboard, and causes it to go into a wait state.

3. Before going into its wait state, the microprocessor on the baseboard provides the address and chip select setup times and initiates the transfer by activating the I/O read command (IORD*).

4. The iSBX Multimodule board will drive the MWAIT* signal inactive when valid read data is on the data bus. This in turn takes the microprocessor out of its wait state and permits the operation to continue.

5. The baseboard strobes in the data and terminates the data transfer cycle by putting the IORD* signal in the inactive state.

6. After a small delay, the address lines can go invalid and the chip select lines may be driven inactive.

4.4.2 I/O Write Operations

There are two types of write operations that a baseboard and iSBX Multimodule board can perform: a full-speed I/O write and an interlocked I/O write. Once the baseboard initiates the write operation, the iSBX Multimodule board determines which of the two types of I/O write operations is to be performed.

FULL-SPEED I/O WRITE OPERATION

The full-speed I/O write is a noninterlocked operation. No acknowledgment is required. Figure 4-12 is a timing diagram of a full-speed I/O write operation. The following sequence is shown:

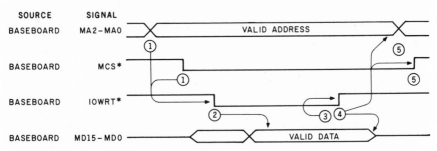

FIGURE 4-12 Fast iSBX bus write operation.

1. The baseboard places the address on the address lines and generates a valid chip select for the iSBX Multimodule board.

2. The baseboard waits until the address and chip select setup times are met, and then the transfer is initiated by activating the I/O write command (IOWRT*) signal.

3. The iSBX Multimodule board must store the data on the data lines into the addressed I/O port in less than 300 ns, of which the data will be valid a minimum of 250 ns. This means that the data can be invalid at the beginning of the write cycle.

4. When the operation is completed, the baseboard terminates the data transfer cycle by driving IOWRT* inactive.

5. After a small delay, the address and data lines may become invalid and the chip select lines may be driven inactive.

INTERLOCKED I/O WRITE OPERATION

The second I/O write operation is an interlocked operation. The MWAIT* is used by the iSBX Multimodule board to control its own access time. Figure 4-13 is a timing diagram of an interlocked I/O write operation. The following sequence is shown:

1. The baseboard places the address on the address lines and generates a valid chip select for the iSBX Multimodule board, just as in a full-speed I/O write operation.

2. The iSBX Multimodule board then activates the MWAIT* signal, which in turn removes the ready input to the microprocessor on the baseboard and causes it to go into a wait state.

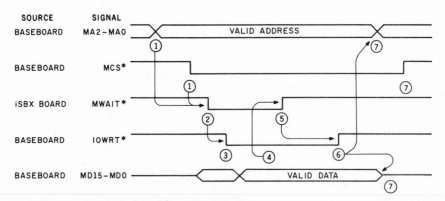

FIGURE 4-13 Interlocked iSBX bus write operation.

3. Before going into its wait state, the microprocessor on the baseboard provides the address and chip select times and initiates the transfer by activating IOWRT*.

4. The data lines will then become valid.

5. The microprocessor stays in a wait condition until the data is stored in the addressed I/O port location. The iSBX Multimodule board then drives the MWAIT* signal inactive and the microprocessor exits its wait state and continues executing its code.

6. The baseboard then terminates the data transfer cycle by putting the IOWRT* signal in the inactive state.

7. After a small delay, the address and data lines can go invalid and the chip select lines may be driven inactive.

4.4.3 Direct Memory Access Operations

Direct memory access is a means of exchanging blocks of data between an iSBX Multimodule port and system memory. The block of data typically is a series of consecutive memory locations. The process is initiated by executing software that sets up the DMA controller and iSBX Multimodule board. The software determines the direction of the data movement (memory to iSBX Multimodule board or vice versa), the starting address of the memory block (where the data is or where it is to be put), and the length of the block of data. Once started, the data transfers are made automatically under the control of the hardware DMA controller as demanded by the iSBX Multimodule board. The DMA process can transfer data in one of two ways: single data transfers done one at a time on a cycle-steal basis or strings of single data transfers done consecutively in a burst mode.

An iSBX Multimodule system can support DMA operations when the baseboard has a DMA controller and the iSBX Multimodule board can support a DMA mode. Figure 4-14 is a block diagram of an SBC with a DMA controller and iSBX bus support. The DMA controller is on the same local bus as the microprocessor. The local bus can be controlled by only one device at a time; most of the time, it is controlled by the microprocessor. When DMA activity is requested, the DMA controller requests control of the local bus. The control, once granted, will result in a temporary halt of all other activities on the local buses for the duration of the iSBX Multimodule board's request for DMA service. This is known as cycle stealing. Except for theft of the local bus, the DMA activity should not interfere with normal microprocessor operation. This can cause the interrupt latency time (the time from receiving an interrupt to the time the service routine begins to be executed) to increase, because the microprocessor must wait until it can regain control of the local bus.

Figure 4-15 is a timing diagram of a DMA read operation. Data is transferred from the iSBX Multimodule port to system memory. The following sequence is shown in Fig. 4-15. (The software has already set up the hardware for the DMA transfer.)

1. The DMA read cycle is initiated when the iSBX Multimodule board activates its Multimodule DMA request (MDRQT) signal. The baseboard uses MDRQT to activate the DMA controller, which requests control of the local and iSBX buses from the microprocessor.

2. Once the DMA controller gains control of the local buses, it notifies the requesting iSBX Multimodule board by activating the Multimodule DMA acknowledge (MDACK*) signal. The iSBX Multimodule board uses MDACK* as its chip select. The address (MA2 to MA0) signals are ignored, and chip select (MCS1* to MCS0*) signals must be high.

3. The DMA controller then initiates the transfer by activating the IORD* signal. At this point, the iSBX Multimodule board can perform a full-speed I/O read or an interlocked I/O read operation. Figure 4-15 shows a full-speed operation.

4. If the iSBX Multimodule board is not ready for the next DMA cycle, it must drive MDRQT inactive and thereby notify the DMA controller to wait for the next DMA cycle.

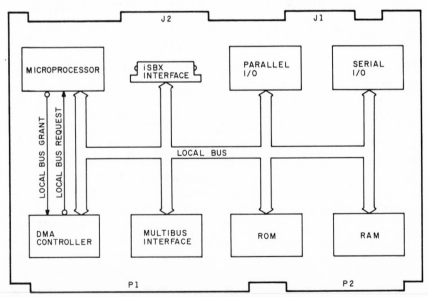

FIGURE 4-14   Block diagram of an SBC with a DMA controller.

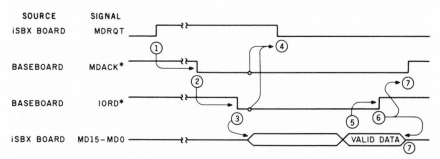

FIGURE 4-15 iSBX bus DMA full-speed read operation.

5. The iSBX Multimodule board must generate valid data on the data lines from its DMA port in less than 250 ns after the falling (high to low) edge of IORD*.

6. The DMA controller saves the data, or the data is stored in a memory location directly, and it then terminates the current DMA read cycle by driving the IORD* signal inactive.

7. After a small delay, the MDACK* signal may be driven inactive. The DMA controller would then release the baseboard buses back to the microprocessor.

In cycle stealing, the iSBX Multimodule board ceases to request DMA service after each data transfer and requests service again when ready. The terminate DMA (TDMA) signal can be used by the baseboard to notify the iSBX Multimodule board, or vice versa, to stop the DMA transfers in the event of an error condition.

If the MDRQT signal is not driven inactive, the DMA controller will continue to perform another DMA read cycle. This series of high-speed continuous DMA data transfers, called burst mode, is used when data must be moved as quickly as possible. Burst mode is faster because the DMA controller does not arbitrate for the local buses for each data transfer cycle. It arbitrates once for the first data transfer cycle and does not release the local buses until the block of data has been transferred.

4.4.4 Interrupt Operations

Figure 4-16 is a timing diagram of an interrupt operation. The following sequence is shown:

1. The iSBX Multimodule board initiates an interrupt operation by activating one of the Multimodule interrupt request (MINTR0 and MINTR1) signals.

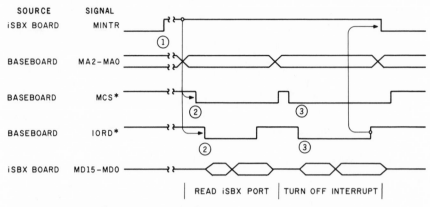

FIGURE 4-16   iSBX bus interrupt operation.

This signal is routed to the interrupt controller on the baseboard. When the interrupt controller detects an active interrupt request, it notifies the microprocessor, which causes the program currently being executed to be automatically suspended. The state of the microprocessor is saved, and the program execution control is transferred to the Multimodule board interrupt service routine.

2. The service routine will perform the required operations, such as an I/O read operation, to the iSBX Multimodule board.

3. The service routine must also cause the MINTR1 or MINTR0 signal to be driven inactive.

In summary, from its point of view, the iSBX Multimodule board initiates an interrupt operation by activating an interrupt request signal (MINTR1 or MINTR0) and removes the interrupt when the baseboard notifies it to do so.

4.5   DETAILED ELECTRICAL DESCRIPTION

In this section all the timing and loading and drive specifications of the iSBX bus are described.

4.5.1   Logical State and Electrical Level Relations

Signal names indicate whether the signals are active-high or active-low. If the signal name is followed by an asterisk, the signal is active-low and has the following logical state and electrical level relations, in which H = high and L = low:

Logical state	Electrical level	At receiver	At driver
0	H = TTL high state	5.25 V ≥ H ≥ 2.0 V	5.25 V ≥ H ≥ 2.4 V
1	L = TTL low state	0.8 V ≥ L ≥ −0.5 V	0.5 V ≥ L ≥ 0 V

If the signal name is not followed by an asterisk, the signal is active-high and has the following logical level and electrical state relations:

Logical state	Electrical level	At receiver	At driver
0	L = TTL low state	0.8 V ≥ L ≥ −0.5 V	0.5 V ≥ L ≥ 0 V
1	H = TTL high state	5.25 V ≥ H ≥ 2.0 V	5.25 V ≥ H ≥ 2.4 V

These specifications are based on TTL when the power source is 5 V ± 5 percent referenced to GND.

4.5.2 Signal Line Characteristics

The rise and fall times of all signals on the bus must not exceed the following limits. (This is not part of the specification but is a good practice to follow.)

	Totem pole	Three-state
Rise time, ns	10	10
Fall time, ns	10	10

The settling time for all commands, Multimodule clock and interrupt request lines after a transition, is zero. The ringing on these lines cannot go beyond the noise immunity levels. These control signals are used to determine the state of the bus, and ringing beyond the noise immunity levels could cause system failures. Address, chip select, MWAIT*, and data lines can ring beyond the noise immunity levels; the only requirement is that they be stable for their setup times. The setup, hold, and signal ringing are summarized in Fig. 4-17.

4.5.3 Bus Power Specification

All power supply voltages are ±5 percent at the iSBX bus interface.

Minimum voltage, V	Nominal voltage, V	Maximum voltage, V	Maximum current, A
+4.75	+5.0	+5.25	3.0
+11.4	+12.0	+12.6	1.0
−12.6	−12.0	−11.4	1.0
—	GND	—	6.0

Note: Per iSBX bus interface on the baseboard.

4.5.4 Temperature and Humidity Limits

All bus parameters and specifications must be met within the following temperature and humidity limits:

Temperature 0 to 55°C (32 to 131°F); free moving air across iSBX Multimodules and baseboard (200 LFM recommended)

Humidity 0 to 90% maximum relative (no condensation); 25 to 40°C (77 to 104°F)

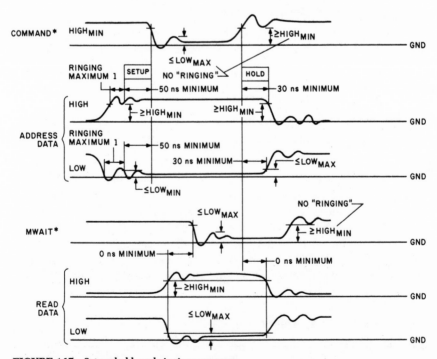

FIGURE 4-17 Setup, hold, and ringing summary.

Shock[3]   30g of force 11 ms in duration three times in three different
                  planes (recommendation only)

Vibration[3]   Sweeping from 10 to 50 Hz and back to 10 Hz at a distance
                  of 0.010 in (0.025 mm) peak-to-peak lasting 15 min in each
                  plane.

4.5.5 Storage

Temperature -40 to 70°C (-48 to 158°F)

Humidity   5 to 95% maximum relative (no condensation)

Shock[3]   30g (recommendation only)

Vibration[3]   1.0g

4.5.6 Bus Timing

In this section all the detailed timing specifications on the iSBX bus are
described; they are summarized in Table 4-2. For clarity, the timing diagrams
in this section show only minimum or maximum values required for each
parameter. The bus timing specification summary table should be referred to
for complete minimum and maximum information. The timing diagrams show
how all of the parameters are defined in relation to the signals involved. All
timing is measured at 0.8 V for a low and 2.0 V for a high with full loading
capacitance C_L.

READ OPERATION

A read operation transfers data from the iSBX Multimodule port to the microprocessor on the baseboard. The lines involved and the timing specifications are
shown in Fig. 4-18. The baseboard must first drive the address lines, MA2 to
MA0, with a valid address in a minimum of 50 ns (t_1) and a valid chip select,
MCS1* or MCS0*, in a minimum of 25 ns (t_7) before the IORD* signal goes
active.

If the read cycle is a full-speed (noninterlocked) type of data transfer, the
iSBX Multimodule board must access the addressed port data and drive the data
lines with valid data in less than 250 ns (t_4). The I/O read command must be
active in a minimum of 300 ns (t_3).

If the read cycle is an interlocked type of data transfer, the iSBX Multimode
has a maximum of 75 ns (t_{19}) to drive MWAIT* low. The iSBX Multimodule
board must complete the operation by driving the data lines with the accessed
port data in a maximum of 4 ms (t_{17}). There must be a setup time of at least 0
ns (t_{24}) of valid data before MWAIT* can be driven high.

[3]Intel iSBX specification only

TABLE 4-2 iSBX Bus Timing Specification Summary

Symbol	Parameter	Minimum	Maximum
t_1	Address stable before read	50 ns	—
t_2	Address table after read	30 ns	—
t_3	Read pulse width	300 ns	—
$t_4{}^b$	Data valid from read	0	250 ns
t_5	Data float after read	0	150 ns
t_6	Time between read and/or write	—	c
t_7	CS stable before CMD	25 ns	—
t_8	CS stable after CMD	30 ns	—
t_9	Power-up reset pulse width	50 ms	—
t_{10}	Address stable before write	50 ns	—
t_{11}	Address stable after write	30 ns	—
t_{12}	Write pulse width	300 ns	—
$t_{13}{}^b$	Data valid to write	250 ns	—
t_{14}	Data valid after write	30 ns	—
t_{15}	MCLK cycle	100 ns	110 ns
t_{16}	MCLK width	35 ns	65 ns
$t_{17}{}^a$	MWAIT* pulse width	0	4 ms
t_{18}	Power-on reset pulse width	50 μs	—
t_{19}	MCS* to MWAIT* valid	0	75
t_{20}	MDACK * set up to I/O CMD	25	—
t_{21}	MDACK *hold after CMD	30	—
$t_{22}{}^d$	CMD or TDMA to MDRQT removed	—	150 ns
t_{23}	TDMA pulse width	300 ns	—
$t_{24}{}^a$	MWAIT* to valid read data	—	0
$t_{25}{}^a$	MWAIT* to WRT CMD	0	—
t_{26}	MDRQT inactive to TDMA	0	—

[a]Required only if WAIT* is activated.

[b]If MWAIT* is not activated.

[c]To be specified by each iSBX Multimodule board.

[d]Required in cycle-steal mode and for last operation in burst mode.

In both read operations, the data is strobed in by the baseboard and the command is driven high. The iSBX Multimodule board must put the data lines in a three-state condition (the lines are floating with no devices driving them) in less than 150 ns (t_5). The baseboard must hold the chip select line active for a minimum of 25 ns (t_8) and the address line a minimum of 30 ns (t_2).

WRITE OPERATION

A write operation transfers data from the baseboard to the iSBX Multimodule port. Timing for a write operation is shown in Fig. 4-19. The baseboard initiates the write operation by driving the address lines with a valid address in a min-

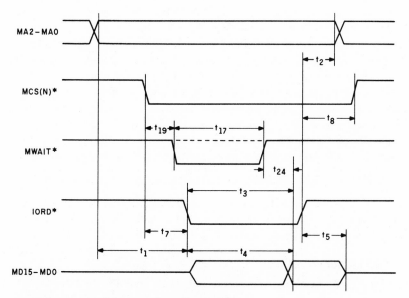

FIGURE 4-18 Read data transfer cycle timing.

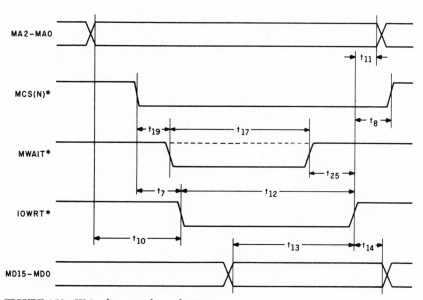

FIGURE 4-19 Write data transfer cycle timing.

imum of 50 ns (t_{10}) and activates a chip select line (MCS1* or MCS0*) in a minimum of 25 ns (t_7) before the IORD* signal is driven active.

If the write operation is a full-speed type of data transfer (noninterlocked), the command will remain active a minimum of 300 ns (t_{12}) and the data will be valid a minimum of 250 ns (t_{13}) before the IORD* is driven inactive. The iSBX Multimodule must store the data in the addressed port during this time.

If the write operation is an interlocked type of data transfer, the iSBX Multimodule must drive MWAIT* active (low) in less than 75 ns (t_{19}). The iSBX Multimodule board must complete the write operation in less than 4 ms (t_{17}). Once the data is stored in the addressed port, the MWAIT* signal is driven inactive (high). The baseboard can drive IORD* inactive (high) in a minimum of 0 ns (t_{25}).

In both cases, once the IORD* signal is driven inactive, the baseboard must hold the data valid for a minimum of 30 ns (t_{14}), the address for a minimum of 30 ns (t_{11}), and the chip select line for a minimum of 30 ns (t_8).

DIRECT MEMORY ACCESS OPERATION

Timing for a DMA operation is shown in Fig. 4-20. An iSBX Multimodule initiates a DMA cycle by activating its MDRQT signal. Once the DMA controller on the baseboard gains control of the baseboard's local bus, it activates MDACK*. The DMA controller must wait a minimum of 25 ns (t_{20}) before the iSBX bus command goes active. The iSBX Multimodule board must remove MDRQT (go inactive) in a maximum of 150 ns (t_{22}) to guarantee the DMA controller will not go into burst mode. The Multimodule board can perform an interlocked or noninterlocked type of data transfer. Once the data operation is complete and the command is driven inactive, the MDACK* signal must be held a minimum of 25 ns (t_{21}). If the TDMA signal is used, it must be held active a minimum of 300 ns (t_{23}).

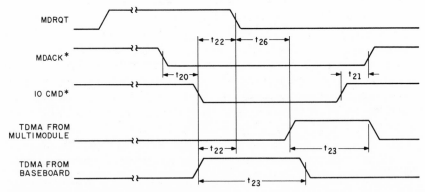

FIGURE 4-20   DMA data transfer cycle timing.

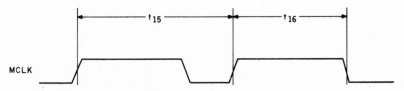

FIGURE 4-21   iSBX bus Multimodule clock timing.

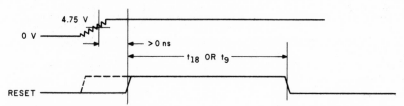

FIGURE 4-22   Reset timing.

MISCELLANEOUS TIMING

Figure 4-21 is a diagram of the timing of the Multimodule clock (MCLK), and Fig. 4-22 is a timing diagram of initialization (RESET).

4.5.7   Receivers, Drivers, and DC Specifications

In this section the driver type (TTL totem pole or three-state), the receiver loading, and the driver capabilities are specified. All these specifications are listed in Table 4-3.

4.6   BASEBOARD LAYOUT CONSIDERATIONS

The placement of the baseboard iSBX connector is user-defined. The only requirement is the placement of the mounting holes relative to the iSBX connector as shown in Fig. 4-23. However, it is recommended that the connector instead be placed as shown in Fig. 4-24, which puts the iSBX Multimodule board user I/O connector (top of the iSBX Multimodule board) at the same height as the baseboard I/O connector. It also provides enough room for installing three single-wide or one single- and one double-wide Multimodule boards. In addition, it should be noted that an iSBX Multimodule board should not be placed over a microprocessor-type chip, because that would prevent the use of any in-circuit emulator (ICE[4]) modules. Placement over ROMs and other socketed parts also should be avoided.

[4]ICE is a trademark of the Intel Corporation, Santa Clara, California.

TABLE 4·3 ISBX Bus Input and Output Specification Summary

Bus signal name	Type[a] drive	I_{OL} min, mA	At V_{OL} max, V	I_{OH} min, μA	At V_{OH} min, V	C_0 min, pF
OUTPUT[b]						
MD0–MD15	TRI	1.6	0.5	−300	2.4	130
MINTR0-1	TTL	2.0	0.5	−100	2.4	40
MDRQT	TTL	1.6	0.5	− 50	2.4	40
MWAIT*	TTL	1.6	0.5	− 50	2.4	40
OPT1-2c	TTL	2.0	0.5	− 50	2.4	40
TDMA	TTL	1.6	0.5	− 50	2.4	40
MPST*	TTL	2.0	0.5	−100	2.4	40

Bus signal name	Type[a] receiver	I_{IL} max, mA	At V_{IN} max,[d] V	I_{IH} max, μA	At V_{IN} max,[d] V	C_1 max, pF
INPUT[b,e]						
MD0–MD15	TRI	−0.45	0.4	70	2.4	40
MA0–MA2	TTL	−0.5	0.4	70	2.4	40
MCS0*–MCS1*	TTL	−4.0	0.4	100	2.4	40
RESET	TTL	−2.1	0.4	100	2.4	40
MDACK*	TTL	−1.0	0.4	100	2.4	40
IORD*–IOWRT*	TTL	−1.0	0.4	100	2.4	40
MCLK	TTL	−2.4	0.4	100	2.4	40
TDMA	TTL	−1.0	0.4	100	2.4	40
OPT1–OPT2c	TTL	−2.0	0.4	100	2.4	40

[a]TTL = standard totem pole output. TRI = three-state.

[b]Per iSBX Multimodule I/O board.

[c]These are recommended specifications. These lines are user-defined, so it is the responsibility of the user to ensure adequate drive.

[d]Test conditions.

[e]All inputs: V_{IL} max = 0.8 V; V_{IH} min = 2.0 V.

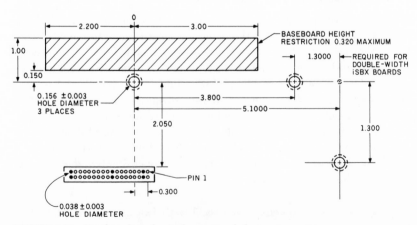

FIGURE 4-23 Baseboard mechanical mounting hole requirements.

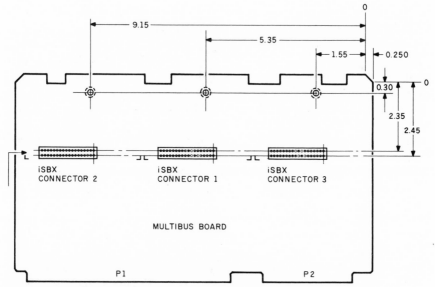

FIGURE 4-24 Baseboard layout considerations.

The length of the traces that go to the iSBX interface should be kept as short as possible to minimize the ringing and cross-talk effects. The power distribution to the iSBX interface also is very important. The power and ground traces should be as wide as possible and have on them as much copper as can be obtained, and the path from the power pins on the Multibus P1 connectors to the iSBX connector should be as short as possible. There should also be 0.1-μF capacitors on all power lines as close to the interface as possible.

4.7 MECHANICAL CONSIDERATIONS

The iSBX bus specification sets forth all the physical and mechanical considerations involved in the design of iSBX bus–compatible modules and baseboard interfaces.

4.7.1 iSBX Connector

The mechanical goals of the iSBX connector are to:

- Provide a very reliable electrical interconnection
- Remain operational during worst-case environmental conditions (temperature, shock, and vibration)
- Provide a reliable mechanical interface
- Support both 8- and 16-bit baseboards

In order to meet the above goals, the unique iSBX connector was created. Reliability was a major design requirement; each electrical and mechanical specification has a built-in safety margin. The connector has specially designed features that assure high quality. An example is protection of all the pins so that handling the connector during manufacturing or use will not damage the pins. The connector has a closed and sealed self-aligning design, which protects the interconnection and lessens the possibility of corrosion in harsh environments. The pins are made of a high-grade copper alloy and are gold-plated. They provide a very reliable low-resistance connection (0.01 Ω max at 3 A) for over 200 insertions. The connectors are also keyed to ensure that the iSBX Multimodule boards are installed properly, thereby avoiding damage due to installation errors. Screwdriver slots are designed in to aid in unmating the connector pair safely.

The iSBX connector body is made of a glass-reinforced nylon (or equivalent) material which was specifically chosen to guarantee a minimum of 200 cycles of mating and unmating. The maximum mating force is 20 lb (44 kg), and the unmating force is between 5 and 30 lb (11 and 66 kg). The connector functions under severe shock and vibration stresses: it can withstand a $50g$ shock for 11 ms and a $50g$ vibration from 1 to 65 Hz with ± 0.04-in (1-mm) vibration displacement.

There are two types of iSBX connectors: a 36- and a 44-pin version. The 36-pin connector is used for 8-bit iSBX Multimodule boards (Fig. 4-25), and the 44-pin connector is used for 16-bit iSBX Multimodule boards (Fig. 4-26). Compatibility of 8- and 16-bit systems was achieved with a unique mechanical design. The 16/16 bit mode of the bus specification requires the addition of eight lines. These eight interconnections were added, but with a 0.2-in (5-mm) gap between pins 38 and 39. The gap permits the shorter 8-bit connector to fit on the longer 16-bit connector (Fig. 4-27).

4.7.2 Pin Assignments

The signal pin assignments for both 36- and 44-pin connectors of the iSBX bus are shown in Table 4-4. As can be seen in the table, 36 lines are used for the 8/8 and 16/8 bit modes and an extra 8 lines are added for interfacing to the 16/16 bit mode. Figure 4-28 shows the pin-numbering method used on the iSBX connector.

4.7.3 iSBX Multimodule Board Height Requirements

Figure 4-29 shows the iSBX Multimodule board height requirements. The total board height, in inches (millimeters), minus the iSBX connector is:

TABLE 4-4 Pin Assignments of Bus Signals on the iSBX/IEEE-P959 Connector

Pin[a]	Mnemonic	Description	Pin[a]	Mnemonic	Description
43	MD8	MDATA bit 8	44	MD9	MDATA bit 9
41	MD10	MDATA bit 10	42	MD11	MDATA bit 11
39	MD12	MDATA bit 12	40	MD13	MDATA bit 13
37	MD14	MDATA bit 14	38	MD15	MDATA bit 15
35	GND	Signal ground	36	+5V	+5 V
33	MD0	MDATA bit 0	34	MDRQT	M DMA request
31	MD1	MDATA bit1	32	MDACK*	M DMA acknowledge
29	MD2	MDATA bit 2	30	OPT0	Option 0
27	MD3	MDATA bit 3	28	OPT1	Option 1
25	MD4	MDATA bit 4	26	TDMA	Terminate DMA
23	MD5	MDATA bit 5	24		Reserved[b]
21	MD6	MDATA bit 6	22	MCS0*	M chip select 0
19	MD7	MDATA bit 7	20	MCS1*	M chip select 1
17	GND	Signal ground	18	+5V	+5 V
15	IORD*	I/O read cmd	16	MWAIT*	M wait
13	IOWRT*	I/O write cmd	14	MINTR0	M interrupt 0
11	MA0	M address 0	12	MINTR1	M interrupt 1
9	MA1	M address 1	10		Reserved[b]
7	MA2	M address 2	8	MPST*	iSBX multimodule board present
5	RESET	Reset	6	MCLK	M clock
3	GND	Signal ground	4	+5V	+5 V
1	+12V	+12 V	2	−12V	−12 V

[a]Pins 37 to 44 are used only on 16/16-bit mode systems.

[b]All undefined pins are reserved for future use.

Maximum component height	0.400 (10.16)
Maximum PCB thickness	0.070 (1.78)
Maximum component lead length	<u>0.080 (2.03)</u>
	0.550 (13.97)

The total board height, in inches (millimeters), with the iSBX connector is:

Maximum component height	0.400 (10.16)
Maximum PCB thickness	0.070 (1.78)
Maximum male iSBX connector height	<u>0.357 (9.07)</u>
	0.827 (21.01)

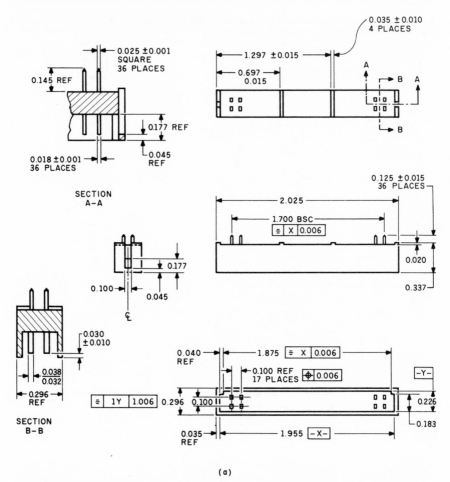

FIGURE 4-25 36-pin iSBX connector dimensions: (a) 36-pin male connector; (b) 36-pin female connector. (Note: All dimensions are in inches, and unless otherwise specified tolerances are 0.xxρ01, 0.xxxρ005.)

Figure 4-30 shows all component height requirements associated with the iSBX system. The total height in inches (millimeters) of a baseboard and iSBX Multimodule board is:

Maximum component lead length	0.090 (2.28)
Baseboard PCB thickness	0.070 (1.78)
iSBX connector pair height	0.540 (13.72)

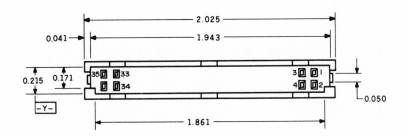

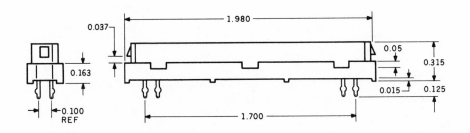

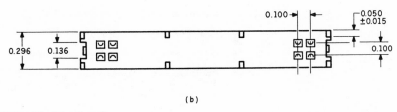

(b)

FIGURE 4-25 *(Continued)*

iSBX Multimodule board PCB thickness	0.070	(1.78)
iSBX Multimodule component height	0.400 (10.16)	
	1.170 (29.72)	

Because iSBX Multimodule board component leads protrude 0.090 in (2.28 mm) max from the solder side, the baseboard must not have any components higher than 0.400 in (10.16 mm) max under the iSBX Multimodule board.

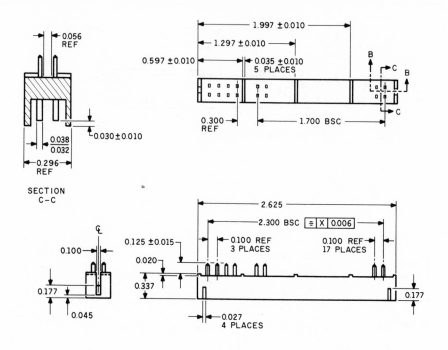

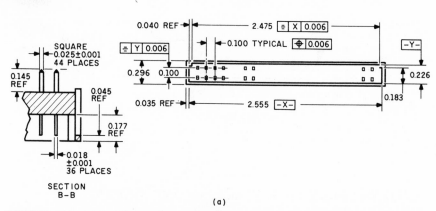

SECTION
B-B

(a)

FIGURE 4-26 44-pin iSBX connector dimensions: (a) 44-pin male connector; (b) 44-pin female connector. (Note: All dimensions are in inches, and unless otherwise specified tolerances are 0.xxρ01, 0.xxxρ005.)

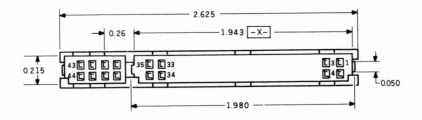

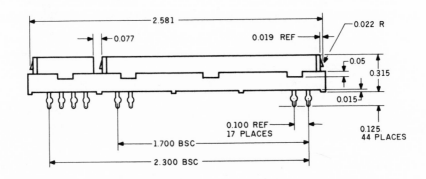

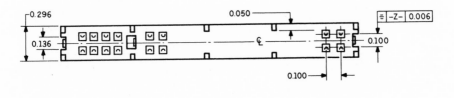

(b)

FIGURE 4-26 *(Continued)*

4.7.4 iSBX Multimodule Board Outlines

The iSBX Multimodule board has two standard board outlines and one variation, as shown in Figs. 4-31 to 4-33.

4.7.5 iSBX Multimodule Board User I/O Connector Outlines

The top edge of the iSBX Multimodule board can be defined by the designer.
Figures 4-34 to 4-36 show the suggested top edge connector dimensions for the
most common designs.

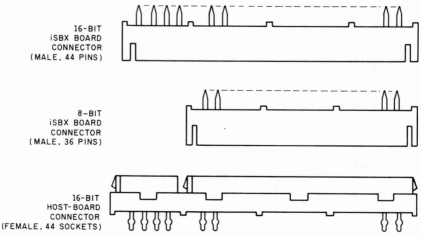

16-BIT
iSBX BOARD
CONNECTOR
(MALE, 44 PINS)

8-BIT
iSBX BOARD
CONNECTOR
(MALE, 36 PINS)

16-BIT
HOST-BOARD
CONNECTOR
(FEMALE, 44 SOCKETS)

FIGURE 4-27   8- and 16-Bit iSBX connector compatibility.

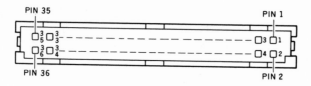

FEMALE CONNECTOR, 36-PIN, TOP VIEW

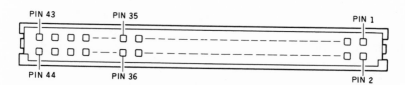

FEMALE CONNECTOR, 44-PIN, BOTTOM VIEW

FIGURE 4-28   iSBX pin connector numbering.

4.8   LEVELS OF COMPLIANCE

The iSBX bus supports various levels of compliance with the full specification. In this section we discuss the variable elements of capability, the compliance relations for baseboards and iSBX Multimodule boards, and the notation used to describe the level of compliance with the iSBX bus.

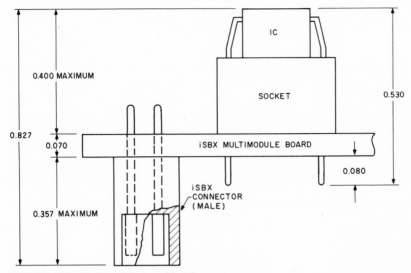

FIGURE 4-29 Multimodule board height requirements.

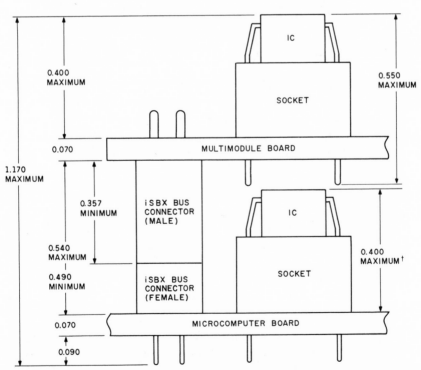

FIGURE 4-30 Baseboard and Multimodule board height requirements. †See Fig. 4-23 for additional restrictions.

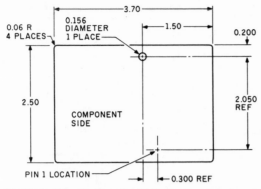

FIGURE 4-31 Single-wide iSBX Multimodule board dimensions. (Note: All dimensions are in inches, and unless otherwise specified tolerances are 0.xxρ01, 0.xxxρ 005.)

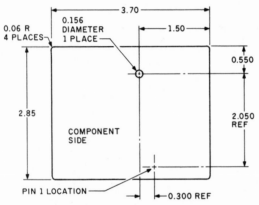

FIGURE 4-32 Single-wide (variation) board dimensions. (Note: All dimensions are in inches, and unless otherwise specified tolerances are 0.xxρ01, 0.xxxρ005.)

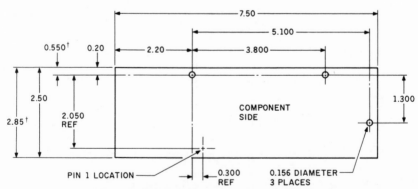

FIGURE 4-33 Double-wide iSBX Multimodule board dimensions. (Note: All dimensions are in inches, and unless otherwise specified tolerances are 0.xxρ01, 0.xxxρ005.)
†Double-wide (variation) board dimensions.

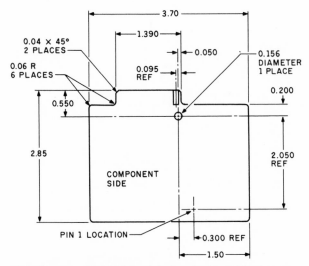

FIGURE 4-34 iSBX Multimodule board with 13/26-pin connector dimensions. (Note: All dimensions are in inches, and unless otherwise specified tolerances are 0.xxρ01, 0.xxxρ005.)

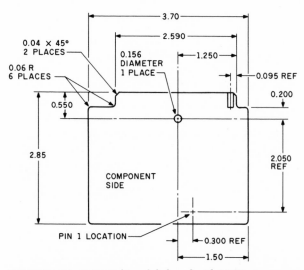

FIGURE 4-35 iSBX Multimodule board with 25/50-pin connector dimensions. (Note: All dimensions are in inches, and unless otherwise specified tolerances are 0.xxρ01, 0.xxxρ005.)

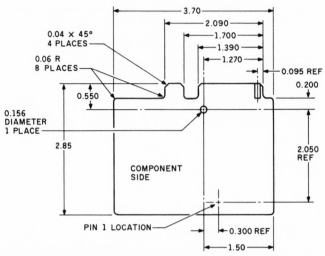

FIGURE 4-36 **iSBX Multimodule board with 13/26- and 20/40-pin connector dimensions. (Note: All dimensions are in inches, and unless otherwise specified tolerances are 0.xxρ01, 0.xxxρ005.)**

4.8.1 Variable Elements of Capability

The iSBX bus has flexibility built into its structure to permit the board designer to build different systems with modules of varying capabilities. It permits variations in the following areas:

1. Data path width

2. DMA support

3. Asynchronous transfer control (no MWAIT*)

DATA PATH

Both 8- and 16-bit data path products can operate on the iSBX bus. Baseboards with 16-bit data paths can support 8-bit only or both 8- and 16-bit iSBX Multimodule boards. 8-bit baseboards can support only 8-bit iSBX Multimodules.

DMA SUPPORT

DMA support is optional on both baseboards and iSBX Multimodule boards. Both elements must support DMA in order to perform DMA activity.

INTERLOCKED OPERATION

The support of MWAIT* is optional on both the baseboards and iSBX Multimodule boards. Both elements must support MWAIT* in order to perform asynchronous data transfers. Typically, baseboards will almost always support the interlocked operation, and some iSBX Multimodules do not require MWAIT*. This option allows the use of low-cost single-chip microcontroller devices that do not support a ready function.

4.8.2   Baseboards and iSBX Multimodule Boards

In the construction of systems with iSBX Multimodules, it is not necessary for all iSBX bus modules to have identical capabilities. For example, a baseboard which does not support DMA can be combined with an iSBX Multimodule board that does support DMA. The system is functional and reliable, and the only restriction is that no DMA operations can occur. It does only standard read and write operations.

The system designer must evaluate the required capabilities of the system and compare them with the capabilities of the particular products selected. Each product will provide some set of capabilities. A transaction between a baseboard and an iSBX Multimodule board must be restricted to use the capability which both products support. It is the responsibility of the system designer to assure the viability of the operations.

4.8.3   Compliance-Level Notation

The following notation allows a vendor to succinctly and accurately specify a product's level of compliance with the iSBX bus specification. Increasing the levels of compliance subsumes the lesser levels for data path. The lack of an element specification implies no capability for that element.

DATA PATH

D8   8-bit iSBX Multimodule board.

D16   16-bit iSBX Multimodule board.

D8/8   8-bit baseboard that can support an 8-bit iSBX Multimodule board.

D16/8   16-bit baseboard that can support only an 8-bit iSBX Multimodule board.

D16/16   16-bit baseboard than can support both 8- and 16-bit iSBX Multimodule boards.

DMA SUPPORT

DMA   Baseboard or iSBX Multimodule board that can support DMA operations.

INTERLOCKED OPERATION

F   Baseboard that does not support interlocked operations. This requires all operations to be full speed.

I   Expansion module that requires interlocked operations. This requires the baseboard to support operations that use MWAIT*.

COMPLIANCE-LEVEL MARKING

The compliance levels of a module shall be documented in all product specifications and optionally marked on the PCB.

EXAMPLES

A 16-bit baseboard that supports both 8- and 16-bit iSBX Multimodule boards, has DMA capabilities, and provides interlocked operations would be specified as follows:

iSBX bus baseboard D16/16 I DMA

An 8-bit baseboard that supports interlocked operations but does not support DMA would be specified as follows:

iSBX bus baseboard D8 I

5

iLBX Bus

This chapter provides the basis for a conceptual understanding of the iLBX bus and how it serves as an execution extension of the Multibus system bus. Included are the logical and physical descriptions of the iLBX bus and the devices that connect to the bus. The notation throughout this book is the same as that defined for the Multibus system bus in Sec. 2.1. The information in this chapter is based on the Intel iLBX Bus Specification (145695 Rev. A). It is recommended that anyone designing on the iLBX bus obtain the latest version of the specification from Intel Corporation.

5.1 WHY THE iLBX BUS IS REQUIRED

When the system bus supports more than one microprocessor, the available bandwidth for each microprocessor decreases as additional microprocessors are added to the bus. There are two basic methods of handling the bandwidth reduction. The typical approach is to ensure that the bandwidth of the bus is sufficient to handle all the microprocessors and peripherals expected to be attached to the bus. The single-bus approach is demonstrated in Fig. 5-1. The problem with this approach is that the bus will not allow the system to migrate when faster microprocessor and/or peripheral technologies are available or when additional microprocessors are added to the system. As microprocessors are added, each must arbitrate for the bus to get at its resources. The overall effect is a relative degradation of the system performance. Therefore, the bus becomes obsolete very quickly. This can be clearly demonstrated on the Multibus system bus. An 8-MHz central processing unit (CPU) executing and moving data on the Multibus system bus utilizes almost the entire bandwidth of the bus. If a second CPU is added, only 20 percent increase in overall system performance is realized, because a large amount of CPU time is wasted while the second CPU waits to acquire the bus. If a third CPU is added, virtually no additional system performance is obtained, because the third CPU wastes all of its time arbitrating for the system bus and never reaches its resources.

The second method of increasing bus bandwidth is to remove the heavy data traffic from the system bus. Data movement from or to high-speed I/O devices and code execution are the two major sources that saturate the system bus. The Multichannel bus (discussed in Chap. 3) can remove the high-speed I/O requirements from the system bus. The iLBX can remove the execution requirements for each microprocessor from the system bus when the on-board memory resources are insufficient.

The iLBX bus provides a standard memory extension bus for each Multibus system bus SBC. The iLBX bus helps prevent saturation of the system bus by removing all or most execution requirements from the system bus. This is done by allowing each SBC to extend its memory resources and thereby create a virtual single-board computer, which reduces the requirement to use global memory resources on the system bus. Figure 5-2 shows a typical Multibus system utilizing the iLBX bus. In this illustration SBC 1 is executing code on its iLBX bus and SBC 2 also is executing code on its iLBX bus. The global memory on the system bus is used for data passing and interprocessor communication.

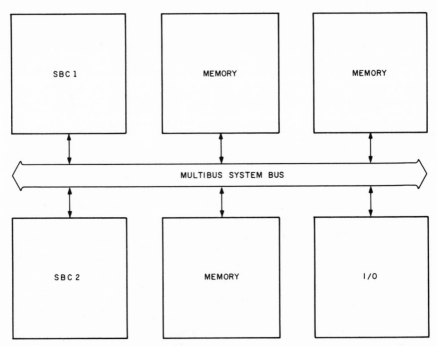

FIGURE 5-1   Single-bus system architecture.

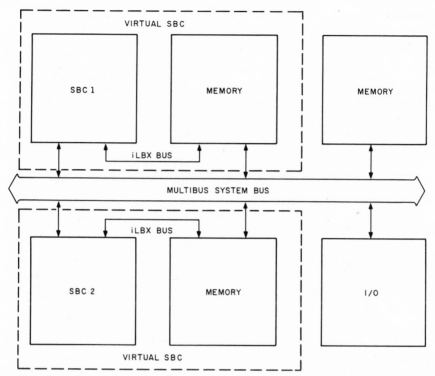

FIGURE 5-2   iLBX bus system architecture.

The iLBX bus allows connection of up to four memory boards, yielding a total local expansion address space to 16M bytes. The iLBX bus is unique in that it allows a tighter timing exchange between the SBC and the memory resources while maintaining a standard interface.

5.2   LOGICAL DESCRIPTION OF THE iLBX BUS

The iLBX bus is a standardized execution bus which, when used with the Multibus system bus, provides an architectural extension of the Multibus system bus. A diagram of a typical Multibus bus system utilizing the iLBX bus is shown in Fig. 5-2. The key features of the iLBX bus are:

• Standardized controlled interface

• 16M-byte local memory expansion

• 8- or 16-bit data transfers

- Primary and secondary master support

- Mechanical fit with existing Multibus system bus chassis and backplanes

The maximum transfer rate for the bus is 9.5M bytes per second for 8-bit data transfers and 19M bytes per second for 16-bit data transfers. The bus supports two to five devices and has a total address space of 16M bytes.

The bus uses a master-slave data transfer approach in that the master initiates address and command information for the data transfer and the slave responds to this information. One of the five devices that the bus supports must be the master. One to four slaves can be added to the bus depending on system memory requirements. Figure 5-3 shows an example of the iLBX bus with several slave memory devices attached to it.

The master initiates the transfer by placing address-status information on the bus and generating an address valid signal. If the master is writing data, it will then place data on the bus and generate a data valid signal. The addressed slave responds to the data valid signal by generating an acknowledge signal (to the master) after it has received the data. If the master was reading data from the slave, the addressed slave will generate the acknowledge after it has placed valid data on the bus. This is the same type of asynchronous interlocked transfer scheme that is used by the Multibus system bus and the Multichannel bus. The asynchronous handshake between the master and the slave allows devices of varying speeds to coexist on the same bus. Slave memory device 1 in Fig. 5-3 can have a slower or faster access time with respect to slave memory device 2 and still accurately transfer data with the master.

5.2.1 Bus Devices

The bus supports three device categories as follows:

- Primary master

- Secondary master

- Slave

In the following section the requirements and attributes of each device are explained. The system requirements of these devices also will be explored.

PRIMARY MASTER

The primary master is responsible for controlling all transfers over the iLBX bus and controlling the secondary master's access to the bus. The iLBX bus must contain one and only one primary master. In Fig. 5-3 the primary master is shown driving the address, status, and control lines to the slave devices. During

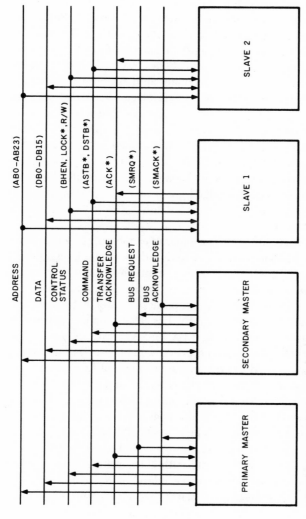

FIGURE 5-3 iLBX bus system implementation.

173

a read data transfer the slaves are driving the data lines, and during a write data transfer the primary master is driving the data lines.

The primary master drives all address, status, and command lines for iLBX bus data transfers. The bus supports a simple bus exchange mechanism for one additional master called a secondary master. To support this simple bus exchange capability, the primary master must monitor the bus request signal from a secondary master and drive the bus grant acknowledge signal when it is ready to give up the bus. The primary master must also supply the termination for the required iLBX bus signal lines. A typical primary master is a Multibus system bus iSBC that also contains an iLBX bus interface.

An allowed subset of the bus is a primary master that does not support a secondary master. In this case the master is called a limited primary master. Normally a limited primary master is chosen for a system to lower the cost. By not supporting a secondary master, the limited primary master can replace three-state drivers with normal TTL and also simplify its control logic. The limited primary master does not monitor the bus request signals, nor does it drive the bus grant acknowledge signal.

SECONDARY MASTER

In many applications the primary master cannot supply all the functions or the data movement bandwidth required. For these applications a secondary master is used. An example of a secondary master is a hard disk controller that is allowed access to the memory resources on the iLBX bus. The secondary master has the same control features as a primary master but cannot access the bus until the primary master gives it the bus. The secondary master's purpose is to provide alternate access to the iLBX bus. As its name implies, the secondary master must totally rely on the primary master for bus access. The primary master is not required to give up the bus until all its requirements have been met. A drawback to the secondary master is that it prevents the primary master from using the bus once it is given control of the bus. If a secondary master has a high utilization of the iLBX bus, it may prevent the bus from meeting its primary requirement, which is high bandwidth execution.

The iLBX bus specification limits the bus to one optional secondary master. The limit of two masters simplifies the bus arbitration to a basic centralized request-grant scheme. When the secondary master requires the bus (Fig. 5-3), it asserts the bus request line. When the primary master is ready to give up the bus, it asserts the bus grant acknowledge signal. The secondary master may keep the bus while it continues to assert the bus request signal. Once it removes the bus request signal, it must turn off all bus drivers. When the secondary master controls the bus, it must actively drive all the signal lines (except the data lines on a data read and the bus grant acknowledge line) until it releases the bus to the primary master. The secondary master must not provide any termination to the iLBX bus lines.

SLAVE

Slave devices have the memory resources that the primary and secondary master require. The iLBX bus supports a maximum of four slave devices with a combined addressable space of 16M bytes.

The slave monitors the address lines for a valid address and, depending on the control lines, will either read data from the bus and place the data in the addressed memory location or write data to the bus from the addressed memory location. The bus utilizes a positive acknowledge interlocked handshake between the master and the slave. When the master is performing a data read operation, the slave will drive the acknowledge line when it places valid data on the bus, thereby permitting it to control the access time. That is, when the master is performing a write operation, the slave will drive the acknowledge line when it has placed the data into its memory. A typical slave implementation is shown in Fig. 5-3. The slave is responsible for driving the acknowledge line for each accessed data operation and driving the data lines during an accessed read operation.

5.3 BUS SIGNAL DEFINITION

In this section the signals that make up the iLBX bus structure and how they are used to perform the various data transfer operations are described.

There are 56 signal lines for the 8- and 16-bit data operations. They can be broken down into five classes: address, data, control, command, and bus access. The bus does not supply any power lines. Power for the devices must come from the Multibus system bus. There are seven signal return ground lines. The bus also has one reserve line for 8- and 16-bit data interfaces. All of the iLBX bus signals are listed in Table 5-6.

5.3.1 Address Lines

The bus contains 24 positive-true address lines, AB23 to AB0, which allow a maximum address space to 16M bytes. All 24 lines must be driven by the active master in some manner during a transfer cycle. The lines are decoded by each of the slave devices to determine if the requested resource is in its area, and they provide the address to access a unique location on the slave.

Figure 5-4 shows a basic data transfer cycle, which begins when the master places the address on the bus. After the address is valid, the master informs the slaves of the valid address by driving the address strobe signal.

Since the address information does not remain valid during the entire transfer cycle, the slave should latch the address with the falling edge of the address strobe signal. Allowing the master the capability of removing the address prior

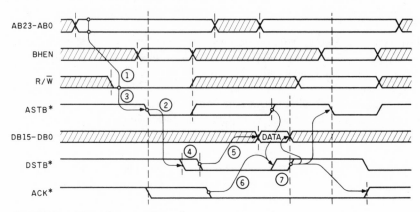

FIGURE 5-4 Write data transfer cycle.

to cycle completion provides the means for address pipelining. The master may place the address of the next cycle on the bus during the current cycle to allow the slave additional time to decode the address information.

5.3.2 Data Lines

The iLBX data lines, DB15 to DB0, provide a positive-true data path between the master and the addressed slave. All 8- and 16-bit data transfers between the master and the slave use only the data lines DB15 to DB0 for the data transfer. The 16-bit-width iLBX interfaces use all 16 lines, and 8-bit-width iLBX interfaces use only DB7 to DB0. During a write operation the master is driving the data lines and the slave is receiving the data lines. During a read operation the slave is driving the data lines and the master is receiving the data lines. The timing relations for 8- and 16-bit data transfers are shown in Fig. 5-4.

It is important to note that, in contrast to the Multibus system bus, the iLBX bus cannot simultaneously support different interface widths. As discussed in Chap. 2, the Multibus system bus has a swap byte interface. The swap byte interface allows 8-bit-width interfaces to transfer data with 16-bit-width interfaces. With the swap byte the data is always placed on the low-order data byte by the 8-bit CPU. The iLBX bus can support 8- or 16-bit-width interfaces only. This implies that if an 8-bit CPU, such as an 8088, is required to transfer data with a 16-bit-width interface device, the 8-bit CPU must simulate the 16-bit interface. The 8-bit CPU would be required to transfer data on the high byte (DB15 to DB8) for odd addresses and the low byte (DB7 to DB0) for even addresses. As will be seen in later sections, signal lines are available to make this type of transfer possible. Chapter 10 offers guidelines for designing mixed-device interfaces.

5.3.3 Transfer Parity

Transfer parity (TPAR*) provides a means of detecting transfer integrity violations. The support of this signal is optional. When it is used, it operates as an additional data line with the same timing requirements as the data lines. The iLBX bus uses odd parity defined as follows: When there is an even number of 1 bits in the transfer data, the transmitting device drives the TPAR* signal low.

The decision to use parity in a system depends on the cost versus the application requirements. If the parity option is selected, then all boards in the system must support parity. Parity support adds cost and performance overhead to the iLBX interface.

5.3.4 Control Status Lines

The iLBX bus has three control status lines that are driven by the master to support the data transfer. The read-write (R/W) line informs the slave of the direction of the data flow. The byte high enable line (BHEN) is used to inform the slave on which part of the data bus the data will be transferred and the length of the transfer. In the following sections the uses of these signals are described.

READ-WRITE

The bus master performing the data transfer controls the direction of the data flow with the R/W signal. When the master is writing data to the bus and the slave is receiving data, the master will drive the R/W line low. When the master drives the R/W line high, the master will be reading the data lines and the slave will be driving data on the data lines.

Timing for the R/W line and the address lines is similar in that the signal does not remain valid throughout the transfer cycle. Figure 5-4 shows the relations of R/W to the other bus signals. After driving the address and control lines valid, the master will generate the address strobe signal. The slaves should latch the state of R/W with the falling edge of the address strobe.

BYTE HIGH ENABLE

The byte high enable (BHEN) signal is an active-high line driven by the master and used on 16-bit interfaces for data transfer size control and alignment. For 8-bit interfaces the BHEN signal is not used, and all data is transferred on DB7 to DB0. Table 5-1 shows the byte and word alignments used on the iLBX bus. When active, the BHEN signal informs the slave to send or receive data on the high-order data byte (DB15 to DB8).

Table 5-2 is a list of the 16-bit interface data transfer combinations. For the 16-bit interface, the BHEN line is decoded with the address line AB0 informing the slave whether the data transfer will be on the low byte (DB7 to DB0), high byte (DB15 to DB8), or word transfer (DB15 to DB0). BHEN must be latched

TABLE 5·1 Byte, Word, and Double-Boundary Definition; 16-Bit Data Frame

Boundaries	Element identifier	
Bit	15 to 8	7 to 0
Byte	Byte 1	Byte 0
16-bit word	Word	

TABLE 5·2 Boundary Selection

	Signal and level	
Segment	BHEN	AB0
Byte 1	High	High
Byte 0	Low	Low
Reserved	Low	High
Word	High	Low

with the address strobe in the same manner as the R/W line. It is important to note that the iLBX bus does not support a swap byte, such as the Multibus system swap byte. The effect of a "no swap byte" transfer mode forces all interface widths to be the same. The interface widths for all the bus modules must be either 8 or 16 bits.

The BHEN does not remain valid for the entire transfer cycle and therefore must be latched with address strobe by the slave in the same manner as the R/W line. Figure 5-4 shows the timing relations of these signals to address strobe.

5.3.5 Command Lines

The iLBX bus has three command lines to control the transfer data cycle. Two signals, address strobe and data strobe, are driven by the master to initiate and control the cycle. Acknowledge, which is driven by the slave, acknowledges and terminates the cycle. These signals are defined in the following section.

ADDRESS STROBE

Address strobe (ASTB*) is an active-low signal driven by the master to initiate a transfer cycle and to inform the slave that valid address and control status are on the bus lines. Since address and status do not remain valid for the entire transfer cycle, the slaves also use the falling edge of ASTB* to latch the address and control status information.

Figure 5-4 shows the timing relations for an iLBX bus transfer cycle.

1. The master places the address and control status on the bus.

2. After meeting the specified setup time for address and control status, the master drives the ASTB* signal low. Upon receiving the active ASTB* signal, the slave, if it is the selected slave, latches the information and begins the cycle. If a slave is not selected, it will wait for the next ASTB*, which signals the start of a new cycle.

DATA STROBE

Data strobe (DSTB*) is an active-low line driven by the master to set up the actual transfer of data. The signal is also used by the master to indicate the end of the transfer cycle. The DSTB* signal, when used in conjunction with the R/W signal, indicates the direction of data flow to the slave. The definition of DSTB* varies slightly depending on the direction of the data transfer from master to slave (write) or from slave to master (read).

During a write operation the master informs the slave that valid data will be on the bus by driving the DSTB* signal low. Figure 5-4 is an example of a write operation. In this figure the active bus master places address and control status information on the bus in the manner described for the address strobe operation above.

3. To inform the slave that the cycle is a write cycle, the master places the R/W control status line into the write mode prior to issuing the ASTB* signal.

4. After meeting the required setup and hold times for the address, the active master indicates that valid data will be on the bus by driving the DSTB* line low.

5. The master then drives valid data on the data lines a specified time after it drives DSTB* low. The selected slave samples the data after detecting the falling edge of the DSTB* signal and waiting the specified setup time.

During the read operation the master informs the slave that it can place data on the data bus by driving the DSTB* signal low. A read operation is shown in Fig. 5-5. In a read operation the master places address and control status on the bus in a manner similar to that of the write operation. The main difference is that the R/W status signal now indicates a read cycle to the slave.

3. To inform the slave that the cycle is a read cycle, the master places the R/W control status line into the read mode prior to issuing the ASTB* signal.

4. After the master has met the specified setup and hold times, the master drives the DSTB* signal low.

5. The slave then drives the bus with its data.

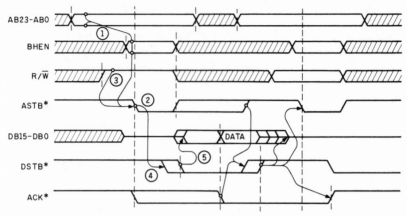

FIGURE 5-5   Read data transfer cycle.

ACKNOWLEDGE

The selected slave drives the acknowledge (ACK*) signal to inform the master that the current cycle can be completed. The ACK* signal timing requirements can vary with different master-slave combinations.

There are three basic acknowledge types: (1) acknowledge before data strobe, (2) acknowledge after data strobe, but prior to data valid or accepted, and (3) acknowledge after data strobe and when data is valid or accepted. Acknowledge types 1 and 2 are called advanced acknowledge in that the slave issues the ACK* signal before the slave accepts data or places valid data on the bus. This type of acknowledge takes advantage of a microprocessor's delay from the time of receiving acknowledge to the time of sampling or removing data. The first type of acknowledge requires a very tight timing relationship between the master and the slave. The second type of acknowledge relaxes some of the restrictions placed on the first type. The third type of acknowledge does not place any special timing restrictions on the master or the slave. The third type of acknowledge is equivalent to the Multibus system bus XACK* signal.

Since the iLBX bus is an execution bus, it allows for flexible acknowledge timing to gain increases in performance. Although the restrictions decrease through the three types of acknowledge, so does the performance. Type 1 acknowledge offers the best and type 3 the lowest system performance. A type 1 acknowledge requires a trade-off of a narrow range of compatible boards and a more difficult design for increased performance. The type 1 acknowledge is inflexible with regard to slaves with varying memory speeds or changes in microprocessor clock frequency. The type 3 acknowledge provides the full range of board compatibility for simple system upgrade and a simple design with relaxed timing constraints, rather than optimum performance.

Figures 5-4 and 5-5 show basic acknowledge sequences for write and read operations, respectively. In these figures the slave is using the type 2 acknowledge.

4. After the master has completed the address portion of the transfer cycle, it issues a DSTB* to the bus.

5. In doing so, it drives data on the data lines.

6. The slave, upon receiving the DSTB* signal, generates the ACK* signal to the master.

7. After receiving the ACK* signal, the master removes the data and the DSTB* signal, which signals the end of the cycle.

Since this is a type 2 acknowledge, the slave must ensure that its acknowledge timing relative to the DSTB* strobe meets the timing requirements of the master. Specifically, the slave must ensure that, when it issues the ACK* signal, the master will continue to hold data valid on a write so that the slave can complete the cycle. During a read cycle the slave's acknowledge timing must meet the master's timing requirement for input data. If the acknowledge sequence were a type 3, the slave would assert the ACK* signal only when data was valid on a read cycle and was accepted on a write cycle. Early type 1 and 2 acknowledges allow for overlap in the data synchronization times of master and slaves. The penalty for the early acknowledge is the requirement that a user, during system design and integration, understand and modify the master-slave timing relationship.

To optimize system performance, a slave device should provide a means of varying its acknowledge timing to match the master timing. In a primary- and secondary-master system the type 1 and type 2 advanced acknowledge timing must satisfy both master timing requirements. Acknowledge timing during read and write cycles with multiple masters is covered in Chap. 9.

5.3.6   Bus Access Control Lines

The iLBX bus provides two signals to allow a secondary master access to the bus. Secondary-master request is driven by the secondary master when it requires access to the bus. Secondary-master acknowledge is driven by the primary master to grant the bus to the secondary master. Lock, the third control signal, allows a primary and secondary master on the iLBX bus to restrict Multibus system bus access to a slave board with dual-port memory.

LOCK

Lock (LOCK*) is a signal that is driven by the active master to restrict access to a dual-ported RAM that is connected to the iLBX bus and the Multibus system bus. The master ensures the memory port direction is toward the iLBX bus

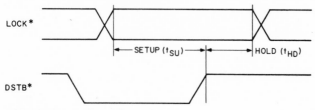

FIGURE 5-6   Lock transfer cycle.

by driving the lock signal low. By locking the memory port to the iLBX side, the master ensures that common data will not be disturbed between accesses, which is important when semaphore exchanges are performed in a multiple microprocessor system. By locking the bus, the master prevents the dual-ported memory from being busy. This guarantees access time to the slave memory, which can be important in the support of real-time burst transfers.

The timing relations for the lock signal are shown in Fig. 5-6. The master begins a transfer cycle in a normal manner. If the master desires to lock subsequent data cycles to the given data cycle, it must drive LOCK active prior to the removal of DSTB*. This ensures that the following data cycle will be locked. The slave will remain locked while the master continues to drive the lock signal low. To ensure the next cycle will not be locked, the master must remove the lock signal after ASTB* active and prior to DSTB* inactive in the last locked cycle.

Care should be taken when implementing lock on both the iLBX bus and the Multibus system bus, because a deadlock situation can occur. The problem arises when a locked transfer crosses physical memory boundaries on both buses. The sequence is as follows: A Multibus bus master is performing a locked transfer that crosses the boundary into a dual-port memory that is currently locked by the iLBX bus master. Simultaneously, the iLBX bus master is performing a locked transfer which crosses the boundary into the dual-port memory that is occupied by the Multibus bus master. When this situation occurs, neither master can get to its resource and a deadlock follows. One way to avoid the deadlock is to allow the slave memory to unlock when a physical boundary is left. This can cause the corruption of data on the slave memory. Slaves can be designed to optionally select either lock mode and thereby allow the system environment to dictate which form of lock recognition to use. In either case software may be required to prevent system failure.

SECONDARY-MASTER REQUEST

The secondary master uses the secondary-master request (SMRQ*) line to request the bus from the primary master. The primary master grants control of the bus by sending a secondary-master acknowledge (SMACK*) signal to the secondary master. Once the secondary master has control of the bus, it can maintain control by continuing to drive the SMRQ* signal. Once the secondary master completes its bus operation, it removes the SMRQ* signal. At this point the primary master can regain control of the bus.

SECONDARY-MASTER ACKNOWLEDGE

The primary master informs the secondary master that the bus can be used by driving the SMACK* signal low. The master uses this signal in response to a secondary-master request. The master is responsible for keeping SMACK* active while the secondary master continues to drive SMRQ* active. Once the secondary master removes the SMRQ* signal, the master can remove the SMACK* signal.

Figure 5-7 shows the timing relations of these two signals.

1. When the primary master receives the SMRQ* signal, it continues to perform its operation until it is ready to release the bus.

2. When the primary master is ready to release the bus, it drives SMACK* low. The master must ensure that its drivers are three-stated a maximum time after driving SMACK*.

3. The secondary master, after receiving the SMACK* signal, drives the bus address data and control lines after a specified minimum time.

4. Once the secondary master has the bus, it can retain control until it removes the SMRQ* signal. The secondary master must ensure that its address, data, and control lines are three-stated when it releases the SMRQ* signal.

5. The primary master responds by removing the SMACK* signal and driving the bus address, data, and control lines.

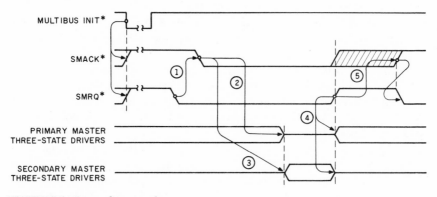

FIGURE 5-7 Bus exchange cycle.

5.4 BUS OPERATION OVERVIEW

The operation protocol for the iLBX bus has four main parts:

- Write data operation

- Read data operation

- Bus time-out operation

- Bus transfer operation

Each primary master, secondary master, and slave uses or participates in one or more of these operations. In the following section these operations and the device participation in each operation are described.

5.4.1. Write Data Operation

The active master (either primary or secondary) is responsible for initiating the write cycle. The cycle is initiated when the master places the address of the location to which it wishes to write data on address lines AB23 to AB0 and drives ASTB* active. The master must meet the minimum address setup time prior to driving ASTB*. Upon receiving the ASTB* signal, the selected slave latches the address information. The master also places the R/W signal into the write mode (R/W = low) prior to ASTB*.

At this point the slave can react to the cycle in one of three different ways. Figure 5-8a to c shows the three timing relations for the slave's ACK* response. Figure 5-8c is the timing relation for when the slave generates the ACK* (type 3 acknowledge) signal after it places the data into the memory location. In this case the master initiates the cycle as described above. When the master is ready to transfer data, it drives the DSTB* signal active. The master must then ensure that data will be valid on the data lines, DB15 to DB0, a maximum of 35 ns after DSTB*. The slave in Fig. 5-8c will not drive ACK* until it has accepted the data. Once the master receives ACK*, it will remove the DSTB* signal and thereby inform the slave that the cycle has ended.

Figure 5-8b is the timing relation when the slave acknowledges the write cycle prior to placing the data into its memory (type 2 acknowledge). The cycle is similar to the normal acknowledge described above up to the generation of the DSTB* signal. When the slave receives the DSTB* signal, it generates the ACK* signal prior to completing the write cycle on board. This type of cycle must be statically configured between the master and the slave, and the point at which the ACK* signal is sent will vary with the master-slave combination. For this cycle to occur, the slave must ensure that, after sending ACK*, the master will keep data and DSTB* valid for the minimum time required for the

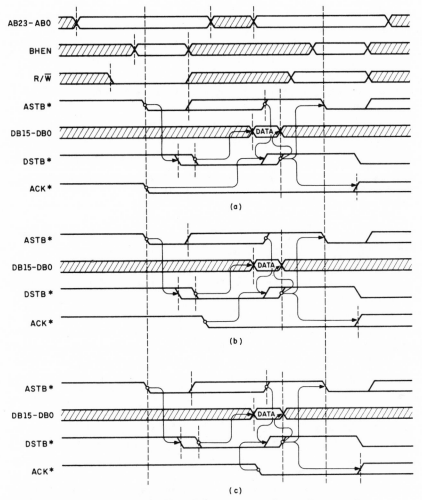

FIGURE 5-8   Write cycles with acknowledge: (a) type 1; (b) type 2; (c) type 3.

slave to complete the cycle successfully. To configure this system, the user must have a good understanding of the master-slave timing relationship of the system.

Figure 5-8a is the timing relation when the slave acknowledges prior to the master issuing the DSTB* signal (type 1 acknowledge). This cycle is initiated in a manner similar to that of the cycles described above. After ASTB* is sent by the master, this cycle differs from the cycles described above. In this cycle the slave may generate the ACK* signal any time after receiving the ASTB* signal. To use this early acknowledge cycle, the master must guarantee that data and DSTB* are valid some time after ASTB*. The slave must guarantee that it can complete the write cycle with the data hold times of an early acknowledge cycle. This early acknowledge cycle requires an extremely tight relationship between master and slave. It also provides the best performance of the three cycles. Configuring a system of this type must be done with extreme care. The user must closely examine the master and slave timing requirements before configuring the system.

When early acknowledge systems with both primary and secondary masters are configured, both timings must be taken into consideration. As a rule, the early ACK* signal from the slave must meet the timing requirements of the fastest master. The requirements for the iLBX system configurations with primary and secondary masters and with advanced acknowledge are covered in Chap. 9.

5.4.2 Read Data Operation

The read cycle is very similar to the write cycle except that the master is now reading (receiving) data from the memory resource. The active master (either primary or secondary) is responsible for initiating the read cycle. The cycle is initiated when the master places the address of the location from which it wishes to read data on address lines AB23 to AB0 and drives ASTB* active. The master must meet the minimum address setup time prior to driving ASTB*. Upon receiving the ASTB* signal, the selected slave latches the address information. The master also places the R/W signal into the read mode (R/W = high) prior to ASTB*.

In a manner similar to that of the write cycle, the slave can react to the read cycle in one of three different ways. Figure 5-9a to c shows the three timing relations for the slave's ACK* response. Figure 5-9c is the timing relation when the slave generates the ACK* signal after it places valid data on the data bus (type 3 acknowledge). The master initiates the cycle as described above. When the master is ready to receive data, it drives the DSTB* signal active. Upon receiving DSTB*, the active slave may turn on its data buffers to the bus. The slave in Fig. 5-9c will not drive ACK* until it has placed valid data on the bus. Once the master receives ACK*, it will remove the DSTB* signal and thereby inform the slave that it has accepted the data and that the cycle has ended.

Figure 5-9b is the timing relation when the slave acknowledges the read cycle prior to placing the data on the data bus (type 2 acknowledge). The cycle is similar to that of the normal acknowledge described above up to the generation of the DSTB* signal. Once the slave receives the DSTB* signal, it can generate the ACK* signal prior to data valid on the data bus. This type of cycle must be statically configured between the master and the slave, and the point at which the ACK* signal is sent will vary with the master-slave combination. For this cycle to occur, the slave must ensure that, after sending ACK*, the

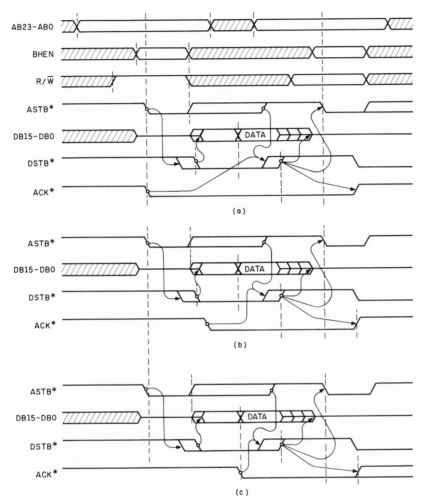

FIGURE 5-9   Read cycles with acknowledge: (a) type 1; (b) type 2; (c) type 3.

master will not require the data until the slave's data is valid. Normally the master's hardware reference manual will specify the time required for data valid from its DSTB* signal. Once data has been accepted by the master, the cycle ends in the same manner as the normal acknowledge read cycle. To configure this system, the user must have a good understanding of the master-slave timing relationship of the system.

Figure 5-9a is the timing relation when the slave acknowledges before the master issues the DSTB* signal (type 1 acknowledge). This cycle is initiated in a manner similar to that of the cycles described above. After ASTB* is sent by the master, this cycle varies from the others. In this cycle the slave may generate the ACK* signal any time after receiving the ASTB* signal. To use this early acknowledge cycle, the master must guarantee that DSTB* is valid some maximum time after ASTB*. The slave must guarantee that the master will not require the data until its data is valid. As in the other cycles, the slave can not place data on the data bus until it receives DSTB*. This early acknowledge cycle requires an extremely tight relationship between the master and the slave. It also provides the best performance of the three cycles. This type of system must be configured with extreme care. The user must closely examine the master and slave timing requirements before configuring the system.

When early acknowledge systems with both primary and secondary masters are configured, both timings must be taken into consideration. As a rule, the early ACK* signal from the slave must meet the timing requirements of the fastest master. The requirements for the iLBX system configurations with primary and secondary masters and with advanced acknowledge are covered in Chap. 9.

5.4.3 Bus Time-Out Operation

An iLBX bus time-out allows a read or write cycle to terminate without receiving an acknowledge from a slave device. Bus time-out is used to prevent the bus from locking up whenever a resource does not respond to the address the master places on the bus. Generation of the time-out is the responsibility of the active bus master. The time-out duration is a minimum of 1 ms from ASTB* going active. This cycle is demonstrated in Fig. 5-10. After the master generates the address and the ASTB* signal, it generates the DSTB* as in a normal cycle. After waiting a minimum of 1 ms from the ASTB* signal for the acknowledge, the master terminates the cycle by removing the DSTB* signal.

Normally a time-out is generated either when there is no resource at the address the master placed on the bus or when the resource is unable to respond before the master generates the time-out. A dual-port memory slave that is

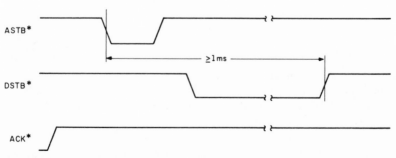

FIGURE 5-10 Bus time-out cycle.

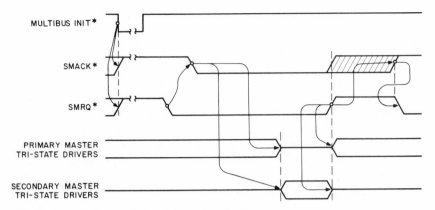

FIGURE 5-11   SMRQ∗ and SMACK∗ timing relations.

locked to the Multibus system bus may prevent the slave from responding before time-out occurs. In either case it is up to the master to ascertain if a time-out has occurred and, if so, the manner in which it was handled. The slave must be able to handle a premature end of cycle if it could not respond prior to the master generating the time-out.

5.4.4   Bus Exchange Operation

A bus exchange allows a secondary master to request and take over the bus from a primary master. A maximum of two masters (one primary and one secondary) may share the iLBX bus. The iLBX bus uses an asynchronous request-acknowledge process to pass control between the two masters. The control signal lines for the bus arbitration are SMRQ∗ and SMACK∗.

The primary master is responsible for controlling the secondary-master bus access. The primary master monitors the SMRQ∗ line and generates the SMACK∗ when it is ready to give up the bus. The secondary master drives the SMRQ∗ signal when it wants the bus and receives the SMACK∗ signal from the master. After power-up initialization, the master has control of the bus. Figure 5-11 shows the timing relations for a bus exchange.

In Fig. 5-11, the secondary master requests the bus by driving the SMRQ∗ signal low. The SMRQ∗ signal is asynchronous to the read or write cycles; therefore, it can go low whenever a secondary master requires the bus. After the primary master receives the SMRQ∗ signal, it can release the bus at any time. The decision of when to release the bus rests solely with the primary master, and there is no maximum time limit on the primary master. When the primary master is ready to release the bus, it drives SMACK∗ low. This indicates to the secondary master that the primary master will be off the bus some maximum time after it generated SMACK∗.

Once the secondary master has waited the maximum time, it may take control of the bus. The secondary master performs transfer cycles in the same manner as a primary master. The secondary master may retain bus control for one or more cycles. Control is retained as long as the secondary master continues to drive SMRQ∗. This allows the secondary master to perform multiple data transfers without returning bus control to the primary master. After the secondary master completes its data transfer(s), it returns the bus to the primary master by removing the SMRQ∗ signal. The secondary master must ensure that all of its bus drivers are three-stated prior to removing the SMRQ∗ signal. Once the master detects the removal of the SMRQ∗ signal, it removes the SMACK∗ signal and begins to drive the bus. After releasing control of the iLBX bus, the secondary master must detect the SMACK∗ signal going inactive before it can request the bus again by issuing another SMRQ∗ signal.

Since there can be only two masters on a bus, the arbitration circuitry is very simple. In many applications a microprocessor's HOLD/HOLDA lines can provide the arbitration with minimal overhead. Additional circuits can be added to provide more flexibility and performance. Board-level designs and trade-offs are covered in Chap. 10.

5.5 DETAILED ELECTRICAL DESCRIPTION

5.5.1 Logical State and Electrical Level Relations

The signal names indicate whether the signals are active-high or active-low. If the signal name ends with a asterisk, the signal is active-low, and has the following logical state and electrical level relations, in which H = high and L = low:

Logical state	Electrical level	At receiver	At driver
0	H = TTL high	$5.25 \text{ V} \geq \text{H} \geq 2.0 \text{ V}$	$5.25 \text{ V} \geq \text{H} \geq 2.4 \text{ V}$
1	L = TTL low	$0.8 \text{ V} \geq \text{L} \geq -0.5 \text{ V}$	$0.5 \text{ V} \geq \text{L} \geq 0 \text{ V}$

If the signal name has no asterisk, the signal is active-high and has the following logical state and electrical level relations:

Logical state	Electrical level	At receiver	At driver
0	L = TTL low	$0.8 \text{ V} \geq \text{L} \geq -0.5 \text{ V}$	$0.5 \text{ V} \geq \text{L} \geq 0 \text{ V}$
1	H = TTL high	$5.25 \text{ V} \geq \text{H} \geq 2.0 \text{ V}$	$5.25 \text{ V} \geq \text{H} \geq 2.4 \text{ V}$

These specifications are based on TTL when the power source is 5 V $\pm$ 5 percent as referenced to logic ground.

5.5.2 Signal Characteristics

The iLBX bus transmission medium is 60-conductor flat ribbon cable with a maximum length of 4 in (10.16 cm). Because of the short length of the bus, signal termination other than signal pull-up resistors is not required. To meet the low bus noise requirements, the rise and fall times of all signals on the bus must not exceed the following requirements:

	Totem pole	Three-state
Rise time, ns	10	10
Fall time, ns	10	10

The settling time for all command and bus control signals after a transition is zero. On these lines the ringing cannot go beyond the noise immunity levels. These signals are used to determine the state of the bus, and ringing beyond the noise immunity levels can cause system failures. Address, data, and status may ring beyond the noise immunity levels provided they settle out below the noise level to meet the specified signal setup time. Setup, hold, and ringing are summarized in Fig. 5-12.

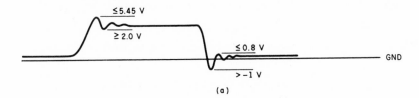

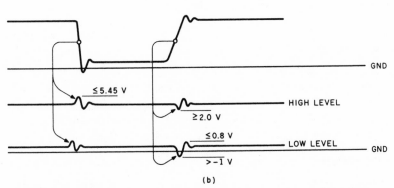

FIGURE 5-12   Setup, hold, and ringing summary: (a) Ringing due to line reflection; (b) line-to-line coupling.

The high-impedance termination of the iLBX bus reduces the need for high-current drivers such as 74S240s and 74S38s. Care should be taken when selecting the bus interface drivers for a design. Excessive current from the Schottky-type drivers can create unwanted system noise which may result in system failures. The basic rule is to use LS drivers for the bus unless signal delays require the use of S drivers. Also, to keep system noise to a minimum, the signal stub lengths on the boards should be as short as possible and not exceed 2 in (5.08 cm) in length.

5.5.3 Bus Power Specification

The iLBX bus interface does not support power signals. Power for the bus interface circuitry must come from the Multibus system bus power signals.

5.5.4 Temperature and Humidity Limits

All bus parameters and specifications must be met within the following environmental limits:

Temperature	0 to 55°C (32 to 131°F); free moving air across the iSBC board (200 LFM recommended)
Humidity	5% to 90% maximum relative (noncondensing); 25 to 40°C (77 to 104°F)
Shock	30g force for 11 ms duration three times in three different planes.
Vibration	Sweeping from 10 to 50 Hz and back to 10 Hz at a distance of 0.010 in (0.025 mm) peak-to-peak lasting 15 min in each plane.
Storage temperature	40 to 70°C (-40 to 104°F)

5.5.5 Bus Timing

In this section all the detailed timing specifications for the iLBX bus are described. They are summarized in Table 5-3. The timing diagrams show only the minimum or maximum values required for each parameter; they define the parameters in relation to the signals involved. All timing is measured at 0.8 V for low and 2.0 V for high with a specified loading capacitance C_L.

READ OPERATION

A read operation transfers data from a slave to a primary or secondary master. The signal lines involved and the timing specifications are shown in Fig. 5-13.

TABLE 5-3 AC Timing Summary[2]

Ref	Parameter description	Timing		Source	Note
		Minimum	Maximum		
t_1	ASTB* duration (width)	25		M	
t_2	Address setup to leading edge of ASTB*	40		M	
t_3	Address hold after leading edge of ASTB*	40		M	
t_4	BHEN setup to leading edge of ASTB*	30		M	
t_5	BHEN hold after leading edge of ASTB*	30		M	
t_6	$R/\overline{W}$ setup to leading edge of ASTB*	20		M	
t_7	R/W hold after leading edge of ASTB*	25		M	
t_8	Trailing edge of ASTB* to trailing edge of DSTB*	10		M	
t_9	Trailing edge of DSTB* to leading edge of ASTB*	25		M	
t_{10}	DSTB* duration (width)	50		M	
t_{11}	Leading edge of ASTB* to leading edge of DSTB*	0	95	M	1
t_{12}	ACK* hold after trailing edge of DSTB*	0	45	S	2
t_{13}	Leading edge of ACK* to read data valid	0	t_{acc}	S	3
t_{14}	Read data hold time after trailing edge of DSTB*	0	45	S	
t_{15}	Leading edge of ACK* to trailing edge of DSTB*	80		M	
t_{16}	Leading edge of DSTB* to read data valid	0		S	
t_{17}	Leading edge of ASTB* to write data alid		80	M	1
t_{18}	Leading edge of DSTB* to write data valid		45	M	
t_{19}	Write data hold time after trailing edge of DSTB*	20		M	
t_{20}	Leading edge of ASTB* to first sample of ACK* line	$45 - t_9$		M	6
t_{21}	LOCK* setup to trailing edge of DSTB*	15		M	
t_{22}	LOCK* Hold after trailing edge of DSTB*	15		M	
t_{23}	SMACK* low to three-state drivers in high-impedance state		35	PM	
t_{24}	SMACK* low to three-state drivers out of high-impedance state	35		SM	
t_{25}	SMRQ* high to three-state drivers in high-impedance state		0	SM	

TABLE 5·3 (*Continued*)

Ref	Parameter description	Timing		Source	Note
		Minimum	Maximum		
t_{26}	SMRQ* high to three-state drivers out of high-impedance state	0		PM	5
t_{27}	SMRQ* high to SMACK* high	0		PM	
t_{28}	SMRQ* low to SMACK* low	0		PM	
t_{29}	SMACK* high to SMRQ* low	0		SM	
t_{30}	Leading edge of ASTB* to trailing edge of DSTB* (abort)	1 ms		M	7
t_{31}	Write data active after trailing edge of DSTB*	45		M	4

- All times listed are nanoseconds unless otherwise noted.
- TPAR* timing is the same as DB15 to DB0.
- M refers to the currently active bus master.
- S refers to the currently selected slave device.
- PM refers to the primary master.
- SM refers to the secondary master.

1. Board designs can implement either of two transfer rates, optimized and nonoptimized, based on the degree of close coupling desired between the master and slave devices. Two factors determine the coupling and the degree of optimization realized when the iLBX bus is implemented: the acknowledge acceptance time of the master device and the range of variability in the slave device to preacknowledge the data transfer. A master device designed for optimized operations must meet both the t_{11} and t_{17} maximum times for the write operations and the t_{11} maximum time for the read operations. When the master devices meet the required times, the slave device is allowed to drive the acknowledge line low any time after the leading edge of the address strobe. A master device that does not meet the maximum write time requirements, by default, transfers data by using the nonoptimized timing, and the slave device must wait for the leading edge of the data strobe before driving the acknowledge line low. See note 3 for the slave device timing restrictions.

2. The selected slave device must stop driving the acknowledge line low immediately upon detection of the trailing edge of the data strobe. The 45-ns maximum holdover time listed for the acknowledge signal allows for the assumed input-to-output delay for the acknowledge driver of 15 ns and the typical pull-up charge time through a 330-Ω resistor required to bring the acknowledge signal from 0.2 to 2.4 V DC, assuming a worst-case capacitive load of 5 pF.

3. The slave device should be provided with variable timing capabilities for driving the acknowledge line low. For write operations, the slave device can drive the acknowledge line low anytime after the leading edge of the address strobe signal subject to the limitations listed in note 1. For read operations, the slave device can preacknowledge the data transfer by driving the acknowledge line low before it provides valid data on the data lines. Preacknowledgement is subject ot the limitations listed in note 1. The amount of variability provided should range from 0.0 ns (data valid when the slave drives the acknowledge line low) to the maximum access time of the slave's memory resources (t_{acc}). If the board designer chooses not to provide variable timing, the slave device must have data valid at the time it drives the acknowledge line low.

4. The minimum t_{31} guarantees that a master does not start to drive the data bus (write cycle) until the slave has stopped driving the data bus (preceding read cycle).

5. The t_{26} timing does not apply during system initialization (for example, when the primary master receives the Multibus interface initialization.

6. The t_9 time used for computing t_{20} is the actual t_9 time of the master. The t_{20} time can range from 0 to 20 ns.

7. The minimum operation abort time is 1 ms.

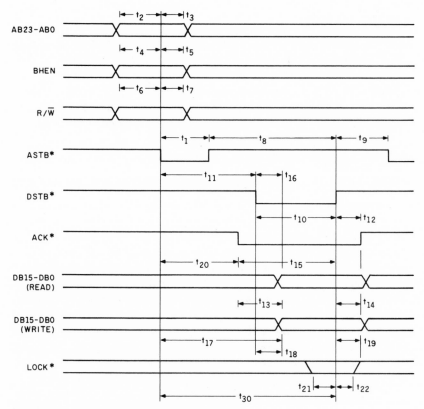

FIGURE 5-13 Read, write, and lock AC timing.

The master places valid address a minimum of 40 ns (t_2), BHEN a minimum of 30 ns (t_4), and R/W status a minimum of 20 ns (t_6) prior to the falling edge of ASTB*. After the falling edge of ASTB* the master must maintain the address information a minimum of 40 ns (t_3), the BHEN signal 40 ns (t_5), and the R/W signal 25 ns (t_7). The master must also guarantee that ASTB* remain low a minimum of 25 ns (t_1).

Once the address portion of the cycle has been completed, the slave may drive the ACK* line active prior to receiving the DSTB* signal active if early acknowledge is used or drive ACK* when DSTB* is driven by the master. If the early acknowledge is used, the master must guarantee that DSTB* will go low a maximum of 95 ns (t_{11}) from ASTB* falling edge. This will ensure that the access time will include all the slave's buffer delays. In either case the slave may not drive the data bus until 0 ns (t_{16}) after DSTB* active. The slave's data must be valid on the bus for a minimum of 0 ns to a maximum of t_{acc} after acknowledge (t_{13}). The 0-ns minimum implies that data is valid when ACK* is generated, while the t_{acc} maximum is the earliest acknowledg allowed (that is, the maximum access time of the slave board from ASTB*).

After an active ACK* is received, the master must keep DSTB* active for a minimum of 80 ns (t_{15}). Once the master removes the DSTB* signal, the slave must hold the data valid a minimum of 0 ns to a maximum of 45 ns (t_{14}) from DSTB* inactive. In a similar fashion the slave must remove the ACK* signal after DSTB* goes inactive a minimum of 0 ns to a maximum of 45 ns (t_{12}). The times t_{12} and t_{14} prevent buffer fights or a false acknowledge on the following cycle.

WRITE OPERATION

A write operation transfers data from a primary or secondary master to a slave. The signal lines involved and the timing specifications are shown in Fig. 5-13. The address portion of a write cycle is equivalent to a read cycle. The master places valid address a minimum of 40 ns (t_2), BHEN a minimum of 30 ns (t_4), and R/W status a minimum of 20 ns (t_6) prior to the falling edge of ASTB*. After the falling edge of ASTB* the master must maintain the address information a minimum of 40 ns (t_3), the BHEN signal 30 ns (t_5), and the R/W signal 25 ns (t_7). The master must also guarantee that ASTB* will remain low a minimum of 25 ns (t_1).

Once the address portion of the cycle has been completed, the slave may drive the ACK* line active prior to the DSTB* going active if a type 1 acknowledge is used or drive ACK* active when DSTB* is driven active by the master for a type 2 or 3 acknowledge. If the early acknowledge is used, the master must guarantee that DSTB* will go low a maximum of 95 ns (t_{11}) from ASTB* falling edge and that data will be valid a maximum of 80 ns (t_{17}) after ASTB* active. In a normal or advanced acknowledge cycle the master must guarantee that data is valid 45 ns (t_{18}) after DSTB* active.

After an active ACK* is received, the master must keep DSTB* active for a minimum of 80 ns (t_{15}). Once the master removes the DSTB* signal, it must hold the data valid a minimum of 20 ns (t_{19}) from DSTB* inactive. In a similar fashion the slave must remove the ACK* signal after DSTB* goes inactive a minimum of 0 ns to a maximum of 45 ns (t_{12}). The time t_{12} prevents a false acknowledge on the following cycle.

LOCK OPERATION

The lock cycle, which is used to prevent dual-port access from the Multibus system bus side, can be used on either the read or the write cycle. The signal lines involved and the timing specifications are shown in Fig. 5-13. A master starts a read or write cycle in a normal manner as described above. If the master desires to lock the next access to a slave resource, it must drive the lock signal active 15 ns (t_{21}) prior to DSTB* going inactive. The master may keep lock active for as many cycles as necessary, but it must hold the lock signal active a minimum of 15 ns (t_{22}) after DSTB* goes inactive. To guarantee that a cycle will not be locked, the master must remove lock 15 ns (t_{21}) prior to DSTB* going inactive and hold the lock signal inactive 15 ns (t_{22}) after DSTB* goes inactive.

BUS EXCHANGE OPERATION

A bus exchange operation allows a secondary master to request and obtain the bus from the primary master. The signal lines involved and the timing specifications are shown in Fig. 5-14. The request is initiated by the secondary master driving the SMRQ* signal active. The request is made asynchronously to any data transfers occurring on the bus. The primary master responds by driving SMACK* active a minimum of 0 ns (t_{26}) after receiving SMRQ*. The primary master must be off the bus a maximum of 35 ns (t_{23}) after driving SMACK* low. The secondary master must wait a minimum of 35 ns (t_{24}) after receiving SMACK* low before it can drive the bus. Once the secondary master has the bus, it may continue to keep the bus provided that SMRQ* remains active. When the secondary master has completed its transfer(s), it must ensure that the bus drivers are off a maximum of 0 ns (t_{25}) from driving SMRQ* inactive. The primary master may remove the SMACK* signal 0 ns (t_{27}) and drive the bus a minimum of 0 ns (t_{26}) from receiving SMRQ* inactive. The secondary master may request the bus again a minimum of 0 ns (t_{29}) after SMACK* goes inactive.

5.5.6 Receivers, Drivers, and DC Specifications

In this section the driver type (TTL totem pole, three-state, or open collector), the receiver loading, and the driver capabilities are specified. The specifications are listed in Table 5-4.

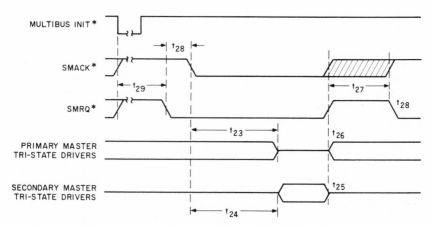

FIGURE 5-14 Primary and secondary master bus exchange AC timing.

TABLE 5-4 DC Loading Summary

Signal name	Driver type	DC termination[a] (to +5 V DC)	Minimum driver requirements			Maximum receiver requirements		
			High, mA	Low, mA	Load cap, pF	High, mA	Low, mA	Load cap, pF
DB15–0	Three-state	10 kΩ	0.6	9	75	0.15	2	18
TPAR*	Three-state	10 kΩ	0.6	9	75	0.15	2	18
AB23–0	Three-state	None	0.4	20	120	0.10	5	30
R/$\overline{\text{W}}$	Three-state	None	0.2	8	75	0.05	2	18
BHEN	Three-state	None	0.2	8	75	0.05	2	18
LOCK*	Three-state	None	0.2	8	75	0.05	2	18
SMRQ*	TTL	10 kΩ	0.05	2	20	0.05	2	18
SMACK*	TTL	None	0.05	2	20	0.05	2	18
ASTB*	Three-state	10 kΩ[b]	0.2	9	75	0.05	2	18
DSTB*	Three-state	10 kΩ[b]	0.2	9	75	0.05	2	18
ACK*	Open coll.	330 Ω	N.A.	20	45	0.05	2	18

[a]All terminators are located on the primary master unless otherwise noted.

[b]Additional AC terminations for ASTB* and DSTB* lines are required on each slave device. Each terminator is a series RC (100-Ω, 10-pF) network between the signal line and ground. The location of the termination network should be as close as possible to the receiver component input.

5.6 MECHANICAL CONSIDERATIONS

The Intel iLBX Bus Specification defines all the physical and mechanical considerations required to design iLBX-compatible boards or implement the iLBX bus in a system. In the following sections such requirements as form factor, connectors, and pin-numbering conventions are described.

5.6.1 Bus Connector Considerations

The bus signals are available at the P2 edge connector of the Multibus system bus form factor. The iLBX bus uses a mass-terminated flat ribbon cable as the interconnect medium between boards. The medium was chosen to provide a flexible and low-cost backplane that can be easily retrofitted into existing system designs. The flat ribbon allows variable spacing between boards that connect to the iLBX bus. Since there are many Multibus bus–compatible backplanes with board-to-board spacing ranging from 0.6 to 1 in (1.52 to 2.54 cm), the flat cable lessens the need for multiple PCB backplane solutions. Vendors that produce iLBX-compatible cable and connectors are listed in Table 5-5.

BUS CABLE

The bus interconnect cable uses 28-AWG, 60-conductor, flat ribbon cable for both 8- and 16-bit interfaces. The maximum length for the 60-conductor cable is 4 in (10.16 cm). The following are the general cable specifications:

TABLE 5-5 iLBX-Compatible Cable and Connector Vendor List

Vendor	Vendor part no.	Conductors or pins
	iLBX BUS–COMPATIBLE CABLE	
T & B Ansley	171-60	60
T & B Ansley	173-60	60
3M	3365/60	60
3M	3306/60	60
Berg	76164-060	60
Belden	9L28060	60
Spectrastrip	455-240-60	60
	iLBX BUS–COMPATIBLE RECEPTACLES	
Kelam	RF30-2803-5	60
T & B Ansley	A3020 (609-6026 modified)	60

Impedance	$100\ \Omega\ \pm 10\%$
Propagation velocity	2.0 ns/ft (6.56 ns/m) max
Capacitance	15 pF/ft (49.2 pF/m) max
Voltage rating	100 V DC min
Insulation resistance	$1 \times 10^{10}\ \Omega$ min

BUS CONNECTORS

The bus interconnect uses 60-pin mass-terminating female receptacles for 8- and 16-bit iLBX bus interfaces. The female receptacle must have a key block compatible with the keyslot specification for the iLBX bus P2 connector.

BUS CABLE ASSEMBLY

The cable assembly can have two to five female edge receptables mass-terminated at the flat ribbon cable. The receptable spacing may vary with the number of boards and the board-to-board spacing. The only restriction on it is that the length of the cable assembly cannot exceed 4 in (10.16 cm). Figure 5-15 shows an example of an iLBX bus interface cable assembly. For mechanical reliability and system integrity the connectors must be fastened to the card cage–backplane assembly.

5.6.2 Form Factor Considerations

Since the iLBX bus normally coexists on a Multibus system bus board, many of the mechanical requirements of the Multibus system bus apply to the iLBX bus.

The board-to-board spacing, board thickness, component lead length, and component height are equivalent to the Multibus system bus specification. Refer to the Intel Multibus Specification or Chap. 2 for general mechanical specifications.

CONNECTOR LOCATION AND BOARD OUTLINE

The 8- or 16-bit iLBX bus interface resides on the Multibus system bus form factor P2 connector. The bus signals on the P2 connector are in compliance with the IEEE 796 specification and supersede the Multibus system bus P2 definition. The four high-order address bits (ADR14* to ADR17*) of the Multibus specification are retained on P2. The battery backup and front-panel control signals have been moved to an auxiliary connector, P3. The auxiliary connector definition is covered in the following section. The Multibus system bus P1 connector definition is unchanged and is not affected by the iLBX bus definition. Figure 5-16 illustrates the standard board outline, as defined by the Multibus bus specification, modified for the iLBX bus. The 8- and 16-bit iLBX bus implementations use the standard P2 connector as defined by the Multibus system bus specification.

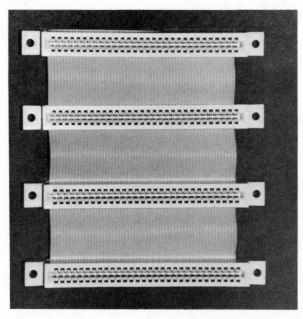

(a)

FIGURE 5-15   iLBX bus interface cable assembly.

PIN-NUMBERING CONVENTION

The iLBX bus pin-numbering convention is the same as the Multibus system bus pin-numbering convention. Figure 5-17 illustrates the iLBX bus P2 pin-numbering convention. It should be noted that the iLBX bus address and data lines are in decimal. The four high-order Multibus address lines that reside on the P2 connector retain the hexidecimal numbering.

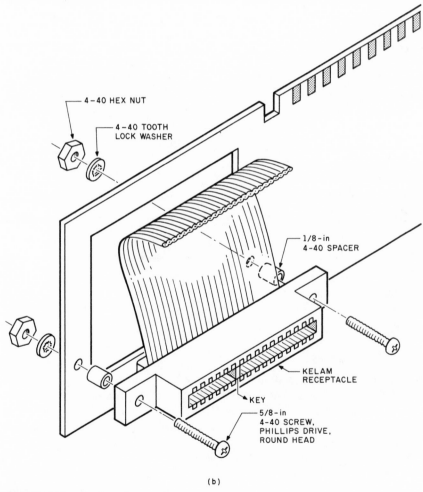

(b)

FIGURE 5-15 *(Continued)*

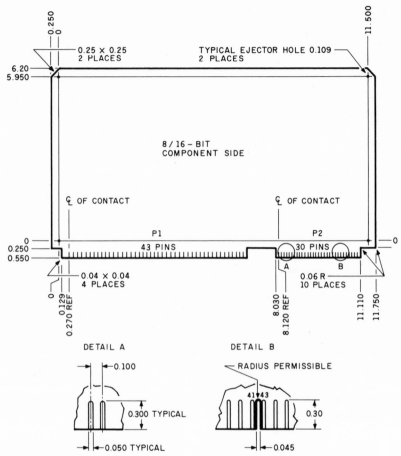

FIGURE 5-16 Standard board outline.

PIN ASSIGNMENTS

The 8- or 16-bit configuration uses the standard form factor 60-pin P2 edge connector and occupies 56 of the 60 signals. The iLBX pin assignments for both 8- and 16-bit interfaces are listed in Table 5-6. The four Multibus system bus high-order address lines (pins 55 to 58) retain the standard Multibus system bus function and location.

CONNECTOR KEYSLOT

The iLBX bus specification contains a keyslot to prevent plugging iLBX bus–compatible boards into P2 connectors with Multibus system bus battery backup and front-panel control signals. All iLBX-compatible boards must utilize this keyslot, which is located between P2 pins 41 and 43. Figure 5-16 shows the location and dimensional specification of the P2 iLBX keyslot.

BATTERY BACKUP AND FRONT-PANEL CONNECTOR

In order to provide room for the iLBX bus on P2, the Multibus system bus battery backup and front-panel control signals were moved to an auxiliary connector. The auxiliary connector (P3) is a right-angle pin connector which mounts at the top of the board. The 14 signals assigned to the P3 connector are divided into two groups: battery backup (pins 1 to 6) and front-panel control (pins 7 to 14). The subset of the P3 connector allows iLBX boards to implement either subset or the entire connector. For example, a primary master iSBC board with no battery backup requirements may only use the front-panel control portion, whereas a slave memory device needs only to implement the battery backup portion.

Figure 5-18 illustrates the allowed area for P3 placement on a Multibus bus form factor. The P3 connector must be located within the specified area to keep the interconnecting cable lengths to a minimum. Figure 5-19 illustrates the P3 connector height, spacing, and pin location requirements. The P3 pin assignments are listed in Table 5-7. The signal lines on the P3 connector are standard Multibus system bus signals; they are fully defined in the Intel Multibus specification.

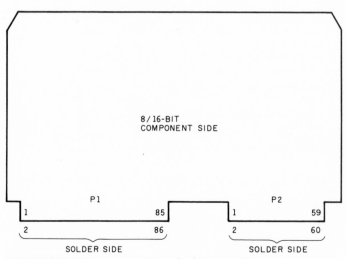

FIGURE 5-17   P2 connector pin-numbering convention.

TABLE 5·6 ILBX P2 Pin Assignments (Decimal Notation except Multibus Address)

Component side			Solder side		
Pin	Signal	Signal name	Pin	Signal	Signal name
1	DB0	Data line 0	2	DB1	Data line 1
3	DB2	Data line 2	4	DB3	Data line 3
5	DB4	Data line 4	6	DB5	Data line 5
7	DB6	Data Line 6	8	DB7	Data line 7
9	GND	Ground	10	DB8	Data line 8
11	DB9	Data line 9	12	DB10	Data line 10
13	DB11	Data line 11	14	DB12	Data line 12
15	DB13	Data line 13	16	DB14	Data line 14
17	DB15	Data line 15	18	GND	Ground
19	AB0	Address line 0	20	AB1	Address line 1
21	AB2	Address line 2	22	AB3	Address line 3
23	AB4	Address line 4	24	AB5	Address line 5
25	AB6	Address line 6	26	AB7	Address line 7
27	GND	Ground	28	AB8	Address line 8
29	AB9	Address line 9	30	AB10	Address line 10
31	AB11	Address line 11	32	AB12	Address line 12
33	AB13	Address line 13	34	AB14	Address line 14
35	AB15	Address line 15	36	GND	Ground
37	AB16	Address line 16	38	AB17	Address line 17
39	AB18	Address line 18	40	AB19	Address line 19
41	AB20	Address line 20	42	AB21	Address line 21
43	AB22	Address line 22	44	AB23	Address line 23
45	GND	Ground	46	ACK*	Slave acknowledge
47	BHEN	Byte high enable	48	R/$\overline{\text{W}}$	Read not write
49	ASTB*	Address strobe	50	DSTB*	Data strobe
51	SMRQ*	Secondary master request	52	SMACK*	Secondary master acknowledge
53	LOCK*	Access lock	54	GND	Ground
55	ADR16*	Multibus address extension line 22	56	ADR17*	Multibus address extension line 23
57	ADR14*	Mutlibus address extension line 20	58	ADR15*	Multibus address extension line 21
59		Reserved	60	TPAR*	Transfer parity

5.7 LEVELS OF COMPLIANCE

The iLBX bus supports various levels of compliance of the full specification. In this section we will discuss the variable elements of compatibility, the compliance relations for interfaces, and the notation used to describe the level of compliance of the iLBX bus–compatible board.

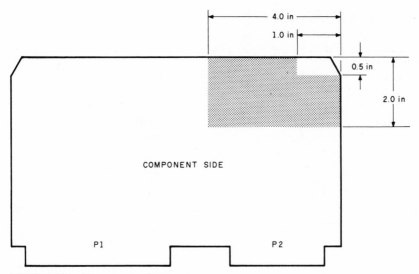

FIGURE 5-18 P3 connector placement area.

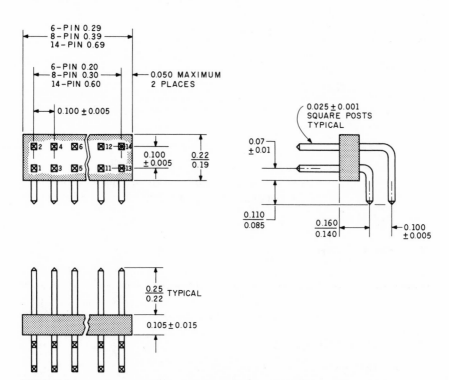

FIGURE 5-19 P3 connector dimensions. Materials and finishes: Insulator—glass-filled polyester or equivalent; Contact—phosphor bronze; Finish—0.000020-in minimum gold over 0.000050-in minimum nickel plate.

TABLE 5·7   iLBX P3 Pin Assignments

Lower Row			Upper Row		
Pin	Mnemonic	Signal name	Pin	Mnemonic	Signal name
1	+5	+5 V DC battery	2	GND	Ground
3	+5	+5 V DC battery	4	GND	Ground
5	MPRO*	Memory protect	6	NVE*	Non-volatile enable
7	ALE	Address latch enable	8	GND	Ground
9	ARES*	Reset switch	10	GND	Ground
11	INT	Front-panel INT	12	RE	Reserved
13	PFSN*	Power fail sense	14	PFIN*	Power fail interrupt

5.7.1   Variable Elements of Compatibility

The iLBX bus has, built into its structure, flexibility that permits the board designer to build different systems with modules of varying capability. It permits variations in the following areas:

1. Device type

2. Data path width

3. Parity support

DEVICE TYPE

The iLBX bus supports four device types that have varying degrees of capability. Primary masters, secondary masters, limited primary masters, and slaves can coexist on a bus implementation. Also, some iLBX bus–compatible devices may support multiple-device implementations.

DATA PATH WIDTH

The iLBX bus supports devices with 8- and 16-bit data widths. The bus requires that an implementation contain homogeneous device widths. Therefore, an 8-bit device may communicate only with other 8-bit devices. If an 8-bit CPU wishes to communicate with a 16-bit iLBX bus interface, it must emulate a 16-bit interface. A single device may support multiple data width interfaces.

PARITY SUPPORT

Parity support is optional for primary masters, secondary masters, and slave devices. If the parity option is chosen, then all transmitting devices must support parity. Similarly, if the parity option is not chosen, the receiving devices must not check parity.

5.7.2 Compliance-Level Notation

The following notation allows a vendor to specify a product's level of compliance succinctly and accurately with the iLBX bus specification. Increasing the levels of compliance subsumes the lesser levels for data path. The lack of an element specification implies no capability for that element.

DEVICE TYPE

PM   Primary master

SM   Secondary master

LPM   Limited primary master

SL   Slave

DATA WIDTH

D8   8-bit interface width

D16   16-bit interface width

PARITY

P   Parity supported by device

COMPLIANCE LEVEL MARKING

The compliance level of a module must be clearly documented in the module specification and may be clearly marked on the PCB.

EXAMPLES

A primary master that can communicate with 8- or 16-bit interface widths will be marked as follows:

iLBX bus PM D8 D16

A 16-bit interface width slave that supports parity will be marked as follows:

iLBX bus SL D16 P

A 16-bit interface width primary master that can also operate as a secondary master will be marked as follows:

iLBX bus PM SM D16

5.8   SUMMARY

As an integral part of the Multibus family, the iLBX bus provides another architectural enhancement to a Multibus system design. When a system is properly
partitioned, the iLBX bus can extend and increase the system performance by
removing the microprocessor execution requirements from the Multibus system
bus.

PART 2

The Multibus Family Architectures

6

◀━━━━▶

Single-Board
Computers

This chapter provides the basis for a conceptual understanding of single-board computers (SBCs) and the motivations for using them. The effects of SBCs on the system structure, as well as the performance effects of SBCs, are examined. Included is an example of designing a system on the Multibus system bus by using SBCs.

6.1 DEFINITION OF A SINGLE-BOARD COMPUTER

Simply stated, an SBC is a basic computer system that is totally self-contained on a single-printed-circuit board (PCB) which takes full advantage of very large scale integration (VLSI) technology. A typical SBC consists of a microprocessor, read-only memory (ROM) sockets, random-access memory (RAM), a parallel input/output (I/O) interface, a serial communication interface, priority interrupt logic, and programmable timers. A standard system bus interface is usually included to offer compatibility with expansion memory boards, digital and analog I/O expansion boards, peripheral controllers, and other SBCs.

The concept of an SBC came about because of the advances in the semiconductor industry which provided increasing capabilities in lower chip count and at lower costs. The evolution of the electronics used to build computer systems has also had a major impact on the design methodology used to implement the systems. In the 1950s diode-transistor logic (DTL) and resistor-transistor logic (RTL) were the current technologies. In a typical design methodology during that period the system design task was divided into four subtasks or phases: circuit design, functional unit design, subsystem design, and system integration as shown in Fig. 6-1. If a new computer system was desired, the system designer would start with the system requirements and divide them into their smallest pieces. Each of the pieces would be designed by first building the circuitry blocks, such as counters, adders, and multiplexers, from basic DTL and RTL elements such as AND and NAND gates. That was the circuit design phase. Then the circuitry blocks were used to create functional units, such as a memory controller, an interrupt controller, and an accumulator logic unit. That was the functional unit design phase. The functional units typically required that multiple boards be implemented. Each board was a custom design and could be used only in that computer system. The functional modules were then incorporated into a subsystem, such as a CPU or memory subsystem, during the subsystem design phase. The subsystems were racks of boards and, in some cases, different boxes. The final step in the design methodology was the system integration phase, in which all of the subsystems were integrated into a single product: a complete computer system.

The use of a computer in a product was very expensive. Large design engineering staffs and complex manufacturing areas were needed to assemble, test, and integrate the final product. The heavy expense in personnel, capital, and product cost greatly limited the scope of problems that could be economically addressed by using computers. However, the product lifespan was long because the computer technology used to implement the system was advancing slowly. Lifespans of 5 to 10 years were long enough to get an acceptable return on investment. The large investment of engineering and manufacturing time and capital resulted in large profits with minimal maintenance costs.

The integrated circuits introduced in the 1960s saved the designer a great deal of time and effort in the area of circuit design; they almost eliminated the circuit design phase of the methodology (Fig. 6-1). Subsystems that had previously required three or four boards could be redesigned on one or two boards. Circuitry such as an up and down synchronous counter, which had required five or six small-scale integration (SSI) transistor-transistor logic (TTL) devices to implement it, could be replaced with one medium-scale integration (MSI) TTL device. This made the designer's task simpler, which in turn reduced the design and debug time. Incorporating a computer into a product was now less costly. The use of in-house-designed computers in a product required a computer design engineering staff to design the functional units, a manufacturing area with the ability to build many complex—at least in those days—boards,

1950s	RTL	BUILD CIRCUITS	BUILD CPU	BUILD SUBSYSTEM	INTEGRATE SYSTEM
1960s	IC	–	BUILD CPU	BUILD SUBSYSTEM	INTEGRATE SYSTEM
1970s	MICROPROCESSOR	–	–	BUILD SUBSYSTEM	INTEGRATE SYSTEM
1980s	SBC	–	–	–	INTEGRATE SYSTEM

FIGURE 6-1 Evolution of design methodology.

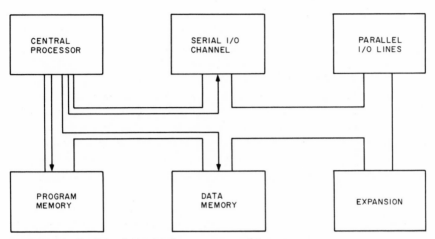

FIGURE 6-2 Traditional common-bus computer architecture.

and, finally, the ability to integrate and test the units as a system. These computer systems were very general machines, and they were customized by programming them to perform a particular task. The programming had to be in machine language. The cost of incorporating a computer system in a product was declining: the design time was shorter, and the cost of the computer itself was lower because of the lower component count and lower costs. The decline in cost of using a computer system in the end product increased the number of ways in which computers could be economically used.

The most popular system bus architecture was the common- or shared-bus approach (Fig. 6-2). The common-bus architecture provided modular memory and I/O expansion in support of a single central processing unit (CPU). The CPU on the common bus was treated like any other subsystem, but the bus was designed to support a particular CPU subsystem. The CPU was the central element in the system, since every CPU operation required access to other subsystems through the common bus. An I/O instruction, as an example, required the CPU to use the system bus twice to fetch the instruction and operand from memory, and then a third system bus cycle was used to transmit the data to the I/O port. The system bus was in constant use by the CPU and therefore the overall system performance was critically dependent on the system bus responsiveness. The timing and control lines of the common bus had to be tailored to the signals and timing of a specific CPU or family of CPUs. The system bus architecture was almost an extension of the CPU itself.

In the 1970s the first microprocessor, Intel Corporation's 4-bit 4004, became available. Many 8-bit microprocessors, such as Intel's 8008, 8080, and 8085, Motorola's 6800, and Zilog's Z80, followed. They made it possible to avoid the issue of the CPU design altogether. As component technologies matured, industry standards were created. These standards started with the dual in-line packaging and logic design families such as TTL. Then standard pin-out configurations for commonly used components were established. Higher-level standards, such as signal levels and protocols for communications, also were developed. The 8080, 8085, and Z80 microprocessors became industry standards because of their wide use in providing standard bus interfaces for peripheral devices and standard microprocessor instruction sets. High-level languages for microprocessors such as PL/M and BASIC were provided on the 8080, 8085, and Z80 instruction set. The system designer now concentrated on building subsystems ar.d then integrating them. The software had grown in importance, in terms of investment of time and energy and value added by the company, to the point of equaling the hardware investment.

Now, in order to incorporate a microcomputer in a product, a design engineer with microprocessor experience was needed. There was still the requirement to manufacture circuit boards, though of lesser complexity, and to integrate them into an end product and test them. Both the circuit design and functional unit design phases could be almost eliminated (Fig. 6-1). The standardization of the microprocessors supported the production of very friendly assembly languages and a few high-level languages which made the software task easier. But at the same time, the microprocessors became more and more powerful. This made possible the solution of very complex problems. But, in turn, solving complex problems required that the software programs become more complex in scope, and bigger. The common-bus architecture was still the most commonly used approach to designing systems because the system bus was again an extension of the CPU bus, which now was a microprocessor.

The 1970s and early 1980s saw the production of large-scale integrated (LSI) and very large scale integrated (VLSI) components such as 8- and 16-bit microprocessors, universal synchronous-asynchronous receiver-transmitters (USARTs), parallel I/O ports, and memories. These semiconductor technology advances made it possible to increase the functional density of the microcomputer subassemblies and to drastically reduce their cost and at the same time increase their reliability. It became possible to integrate on a single circuit board all of the basic elements of the common-bus computer architecture (Fig. 6-3). This resulted in the first SBC architecture. Instead of a box containing a minimum configuration of a CPU board, memory boards, and I/O boards, there are families of SBCs that provide the same capabilities. Two examples of commercially available SBCs are Intel's iSBC 86/30 board, which provides a high-performance 16-bit microprocessor, an RS-232-compatible serial channel, three 8-bit parallel I/O ports, 128K bytes of RAM and sockets for up to 64K bytes of erasable programmable read-only memory (EPROM), and National Semiconductor's BLC 80/316 board, which has a Z80A microprocessor, 64K bytes of RAM, three 8-bit parallel I/O ports, an RS-232-compatible serial channel, and up to 8K bytes of EPROM.

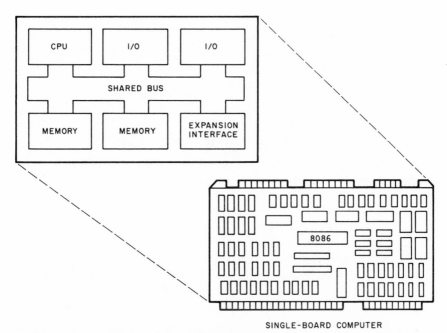

SINGLE-BOARD COMPUTER

FIGURE 6-3 **The SBC evolution—a first-generation architecture. LSI technology made it possible to pack the basic elements of a computer onto a single PC board.**

The mid-1980s produced even more complex VLSI configurations. Devices with over 200,000 transistors are available; they allow almost a complete computer to be designed on a single chip. There are highly integrated microprocessors with a faster and more powerful CPU, a clock generator, high-speed direct memory access (DMA) channels, a programmable interrupt controller, three programmable 16-bit timers, programmable memory and peripheral chip select logic, a programmable wait state generator, and a local bus controller. The designer simply adds the peripherals and memory needed for the particular application and has a complete computer system.

The SBC solves the overall computer design problem. By utilizing an SBC, it is possible, when designing a computer system by using SBCs, to go directly to the integration phase and almost entirely bypass the circuit design, board debugging, and subsystem building phases (Fig. 6-1). The requirements of integrating a processor into a product are now very different from those of the 1960s. A design engineer is still required to integrate the system, but the emphasis is now in the area of applications engineering. Manufacturing support is no longer required for the microcomputer portion of the product; it is needed only for system integration and test. Programming support has evolved to provide the microprocessor user with high-level languages such as PL/M, FORTRAN,

COBOL subsets, C, PASCAL, and BASIC. As technology has progressed, the degree of difficulty and the resources required to create a computer-based solution to solve an application need have changed drastically. The costs have declined to the point of opening up many new application areas ranging from controlling elevators and building environments to word processing and computer-aided design.

6.1.1 Trends in and Motivations for Using an SBC

The emerging trends in SBCs are in two basic directions. The first is toward higher levels of functional density, throughput, and versatility in a single, ready-to-use unit. Each year sees the introduction of SBCs with greater capability at a relatively constant cost. As an example of the trend, an SBC initially introduced with 4K bytes of RAM would be replaced two years later by one with 16K bytes of RAM and two years after that by one with 64K bytes of RAM. Each new generation provided more and more memory on the same PCB area. The second trend in SBCs is for a fixed capability to be offered at lower and lower costs over time. Each new generation of SBC provides the same capabilities implemented with fewer components and in a more cost-effective manner. As an example, the original SBC might be implemented on a four-layer PCB and require 100 integrated circuits (ICs), whereas the next generation might be implemented on a two-layer PCB and require only 60 ICs and at a lower cost.

Both trends are illustrated in Fig. 6-4 by three generations of Intel Corporation SBCs. The first generation is the iSBC 86/12A, an SBC with a 5-MHz 8086 microprocessor. Two years after its introduction came two new Intel SBCs. The iSBC 86/05 provided about the same capabilities as the iSBC 86/12A but at a lower cost. The iSBC 86/14, an iSBC 86/12A look-alike, provided increased

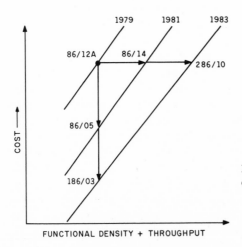

FIGURE 6-4 SBC cost-versus-capability evolution.

memory capacity and increased throughput. Two years later, Intel introduced two new SBCs, the iSBC 186/03 and the iSBC 286/10. The iSBC 186/03 provided about the same capabilities as the iSBC 86/05 but at a lower cost, and the iSBC 286/10 provided greater memory capacity and throughput than the iSBC 86/14 at about the same cost. After two generations of SBCs, an SBC user could purchase the iSBC 286/10, which was 10 times faster, provided greater reliability with memory protection, and had 16 times more address space than the iSBC 86/12A, with which it had software compatibility, at about the same cost as the iSBC 86/12A at its introduction. An SBC user who does not require more capability but does require lower cost could purchase the SBC 186/03 at about half the cost of the iSBC 86/12A.

The effect of these trends has been to bring microprocessor power to low- and medium-volume applications in which microprocessors were not previously cost-effective. There are several reasons for the widespread use of microprocessors. A general-purpose system component, such as an SBC, has enabled many companies to use the same SBC design in several different applications. This has the advantage of high-volume usage across product lines, as in the component environment, without SBC modification except for new software in the EPROMs and the reconfiguration of some SBC hardware options. The flexibility derives from the general-purpose nature of the SBC. Another reason for the success of SBCs at low to medium volume is sheer cost efficiency, since very few development dollars need to be amortized over a small volume of product.

As SBC technologies matured, industry standards for system components were created or have evolved. One of the industrial standards that has evolved is the Multibus/IEEE-796 system bus specification. It defines very clearly the bus form factor, the signal line definitions, and the electrical specifications and gives design examples. Other industry standards that have evolved or are in the process of evolving are the iSBX/IEEE-P595 local I/O expansion bus, the iLBX local memory expansion bus, and the Multichannel high-speed DMA cable bus. Together, these four structures comprise the Multibus family, which provides the system designer with maximum flexibility in designing a microcomputer system and provides the user with the advantages of standardized interfaces. Another advantage of the Multibus family of standards is the growing support by multiple vendors that supply compatible board-level products. There are over 120 Multibus family vendors and over 2000 Multibus, iSBX, iLBX, and Multichannel products. The result is a very competitive market that offers the user high-quality products at low prices. Multiple sources of some Multibus family products also have appeared in the marketplace, and they have eliminated the need to use and the risk of using sole-source products.

Multibus-compatible SBCs available today have an impressive range of capabilities and features that reflect their diversity of application. The performance and functions of these SBCs are intimately related to the performance and functions of the components used to build them. The Multibus system bus is microprocessor-independent, and most of the industry's microprocessor components have been designed to operate on it. There are available SBCs with all of the industry standard microprocessors: Intel's 8080, 8085, 8088, 8086, 80186 and 80286, Motorola's 6800 and 68000; Zilog's Z80, and National Semiconductor's 800. The growing popularity of the Multibus structure has encouraged the semiconductor industry to supply Multibus-compatible VLSI devices, which prolongs the lifespan of the Multibus system bus. There are available off-the-shelf SBCs ranging from very low cost versions with 8-bit microprocessors, 1K byte of RAM, four sockets for EPROMs, and some user I/O all the way up to high-performance SBCs with 16-bit microprocessors with complete operating system support and performance comparable with that of minicomputers.

Intel Corporation introduced the first 8-bit SBC, the iSBC 80/10, on the Multibus system bus in 1976, and today the 8-bit SBC still dominates the marketplace. SBCs with 8-bit microprocessors are durable, simple, reliable, and very economical. A typical 8-bit SBC is half as expensive as its 16-bit SBC counterpart. Now in their fourth and fifth generations, the 8-bit SBCs are proven, reliable designs that permit projects to proceed without delays. In 1982 more than forty-five different 8-bit SBCs were offered by more than twenty vendors; they spanned a broad range of performance and price. All those SBCs were compatible with the industry standard Multibus system bus and supported by an extensive array of Multibus-compatible memory, I/O, peripheral, and communication boards. This wide choice of SBCs permitted the system designer to select an off-the-shelf SBC with capabilities that very closely fitted the application needs. Some 8-bit SBCs were made by multiple vendors. For example, National Semiconductor's BLC 80/10 was slot-compatible with Intel's iSBC 80/10.

The maturity of the 8-bit SBC product line is reflected in the wide range of support of proven standard operating systems and application languages. Another indication of 8-bit market maturity is the number of application-specific SBCs available, such as communication controllers, analog I/O controllers, and machine controllers. An example of a dedicated 8-bit design is Intel's iSBC 569 Intelligent Digital Controller board, which provides up to four microprocessors to share the digital I/O signal processing. The central-control microprocessor is an 8085, and the remaining three microprocessors are MCS-8041/8741's Universal Peripheral Interface (UPI-41) devices. This permits the I/O processing algorithm to be tailored to application requirements by programming the UPI-41 microprocessors. The devices off-load the 8085 microprocessor from time-consuming tasks such as pulse counting, event sensing, and parallel or serial digital I/O data formatting. Another example of a dedicated 8-bit SBC is Intel's iSBC 88/45 Advanced Data Communications Processor board, which provides three HDLC/SDLC half-full duplex communication channels that support RS-232C (including modem support), CCITT V.24, or RS-422A/449 interfaces. The board is powered by an 8-MHz 8088 with 16K bytes of dual-ported RAM and up to 128K bytes of EPROM. There is an on-board DMA controller that supports up to 800-kBd (kilobaud) operations. Two iSBX bus connectors are included for user I/O expansion.

The first Multibus-compatible 16-bit SBC, the iSBC 86/12, was introduced by Intel Corporation in 1978. SBCs built with 16-bit microprocessors span a wide range of price, performance, and memory capacity that is generally above that of 8-bit SBCs. The 16-bit SBC is not as mature as the 8-bit SBC, but it is maturing rapidly. Today most 16-bit SBCs are second- or third-generation designs. After only 4 years from the introduction of the first 16-bit SBC, in 1984 there were over 40 different commercially available 16-bit SBCs offered by over 30 vendors. Most of those vendors were offering only one product, which reflects the fact that the 16-bit SBC business was still in the early phase of its life cycle. In the coming years the 16-bit SBC user will have many vendors with a large selection of SBCs and support products to choose from. There are already second sources of 16-bit SBCs. National Semiconductor Corporation provided the industry with the first second-source 16-bit SBC when it introduced its BLC 86/ 12, which is equivalent to Intel's iSBC 86/12. Software support also is growing rapidly, and very extensive operating systems and application languages are available.

6.1.2 SBCs: What Level of Integration Should You Buy?

The success of the SBC concept and the Multibus system bus has led to the introduction of a very wide range of standard off-the-shelf SBC products. The SBC user has a choice of the level of completion or integration that is purchased. Should it be at the lowest level, that of components, and leave all of the design and manufacturing to be done, or should it be at a higher level? The four levels of integration available are components, SBC boards, packaged systems, and turnkey systems (Fig. 6-5). Buying at the lowest level reduces the purchase costs and maximizes the value added to the product by the company's engineering, manufacturing, and marketing groups. It does not, however, necessarily maximize the return on investment of the project because of the high amortized costs of the design and manufacturing start-up expenses. The alternative is to start at a higher level of integration and concentrate the value added in the later stages of the process. This approach results in larger purchase costs, but the design and manufacturing start-up investment and development time are reduced. Somewhere along the continuum of levels of integration, the profits will be maximized for your application.

The two major cost elements to consider, in trying to locate the best point on the continuum, are in the areas of design and manufacture. The design costs include development, evaluation, test, manufacturing, quality, and product engineering and documentation and prototype costs—all the costs of converting an idea into a set of documents that the manufacturing area can use. The manufacturing costs include materials, direct and indirect labor, overhead, test, scrap and warranty costs—all the costs of taking the engineering documentation and converting it into real products. A medium-complexity SBC costs from $200,000 to $300,000 to develop. If this total is amortized over 300 boards, the cost per board is $670 to $1000. Over 1000 boards it is $200 to $300, and over 3000 boards it is $70 to $100. A product lifespan of 2 years is not unreasonable with VLSI technology moving so rapidly. Therefore, volume is a very important parameter in final board costs.

Some other areas of concern are time-to-market pressures, lack of qualified personnel, and capital equipment costs. The urgent need to meet competition with a better, more cost-effective product is decreasing the time-to-market window and increasing pressure on the product development team. This shortened design cycle makes luxuries like chip-level designs for low and medium volume or individual system implementations impractical. As a result of the increased time-to-market pressure, more and more system designers are turning to standard off-the-shelf boards. In this approach fewer technically trained personnel and less capital equipment are needed to develop a product.

Another important consideration is to understand what the true added value is. Traditionally, value added was seen as consisting largely of design and manufacturing skills; the assumption was that microcomputer hardware is the major factor in the value added portion of the product. This view supported custom-

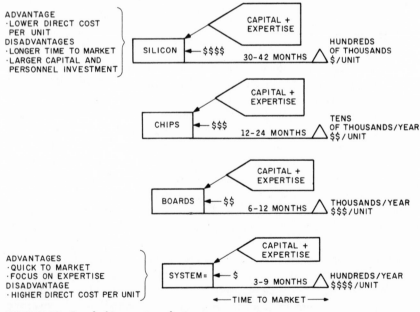

FIGURE 6-5 Level of integration of microprocessor systems.

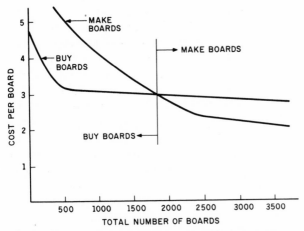

FIGURE 6-6 Board make-versus-buy comparison. (Note: Cost is in thousands of dollars for Multibus size boards, and in hundreds of dollars for iSBX size boards.)

ized boards that were optimized for specific products. Major redesigns were accepted because of the very high volume and long-life products. However, the perspective of value added has changed. Application expertise has grown in importance because software has become the major factor in the value added. If the success of the project does not require a unique computer design, the use of standard off-the-shelf SBCs frees engineering development resources for use on other project opportunities.

At what level of volume does it pay to stop buying finished boards and start building them? A typical make-versus-buy comparison graph for a medium-complexity SBC is shown in Fig. 6-6. The crossover point is a function of the cost structure to develop a new board-level product, but typically it is about 2000 to 3000 units a year. Beyond that point, the fixed-cost overhead tends to dominate the material and direct labor costs of a product. Above it the amortized overhead costs become a small percentage of the total product costs. However, time-to-market pressures may still be an overriding factor in the make-versus-buy decision.

6.2 SBC ARCHITECTURES

The architecture of computer systems has evolved because of the advances of VLSI technology and the introduction of SBCs. Integrating the memory and I/O onto the CPU board reduces the CPU's dependence on the system bus. The Multibus architecture was designed specifically to take advantage of VLSI and SBC technology advances. It uses multiple independent buses in one microcomputer system. Each SBC has access to a mixture of the basic computer resources by using its local or on-board bus. The local bus definition of an SBC can be changed with each generation of microprocessor to provide an optimum operating environment.

6.2.1 First-Generation Architecture

The architecture of a first-generation SBC is shown in Fig. 6-3. It was used on Intel's iSBC 80/10 and iSBC 80/20, National Semiconductor's BLC-80/05, and Zendex Corporation's ZX-80/15. The on-board bus connects the microprocessor with a limited amount of local memory and I/O. The Multibus system bus is used for expansion of memory and I/O. Each SBC retains its own most commonly used resources on its own internal bus. Operations on these local resources occur totally on the individual board and require no use of the Multibus system bus. This reduces the number of requests to use the Multibus system bus, since the system bus will be used only when a resource that is not on the SBC is needed. The local versus global (on-board versus off-board) distinction rests on the value of the physical address referenced. If the requested resource lies within the address range of on-board memory of I/O (a local reference), no system bus request is made. Only when the address references a global or off-board memory or I/O location is a Multibus system bus request initiated.

This type of SBC architecture permits future VLSI to be integrated into the system quickly and easily. In a Multibus-based system any of the boards in the system can be upgraded with a new design incorporating the latest VLSI without affecting the other boards in the system. The new design can change the local bus to optimize bus performance with each new generation of VLSI, and the Multibus system bus interface provides the tie with the other boards in the system.

One potential disadvantage of this type of SBC architecture is that the resources on the local bus can be accessed only by the local microprocessor. No other Multibus master, such as an SBC, can access a resource that is local to another SBC. This type of SBC architecture is desired if the system design calls for a resource to be protected from any Multibus access, which is the case for most I/O devices. However, memory typically doesn't need to be protected in this manner. If, for example, a disk controller has been requested to move data from a disk file to a local SBC's memory, the disk controller must first move the data into global memory and then have the SBC move the data from global memory into its local memory. That wastes system bus bandwidth, and moving the data twice slows the system down. Further, the approach requires global memory in the system which may not have been needed and so adds unnecessary expense.

First-generation SBC architecture can be modified to avoid this problem as shown in Fig. 6-7. The architecture simply merges two independent board designs, that of the CPU board and a memory board, onto a single board. The two functions are packaged together on one PCB. This architectural modification was used on Intel's Model 225 Intellec Series II/85 Microcomputer Development System CPU board and Zendex Corporation's ZX-85 SBC. The memory is connected directly to the Multibus system bus, which makes the memory a global resource. Since the SBC does not have local RAM, the microprocessor on the SBC must use the Multibus system bus to access the RAM. The architecture is basically of the common-bus type, and all bus masters must utilize the Multibus system bus to fetch instructions or data from the memory. Another bus master can access the global memory that is physically on the SBC by gaining control of the Multibus system bus and performing a memory read or write cycle.

The disadvantage of the modified SBC architecture is the same as that of any other common-bus architecture: the common system bus can rapidly become the bottleneck of the system and limit the overall system throughput. All the microprocessor's activities must use the system bus, which is slower than if the resource were local. The system performance is reduced in two ways: (1) Since the memory is global, each access must arbitrate for the system bus and go

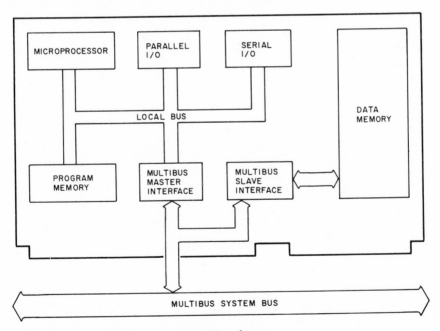

FIGURE 6-7 A modified first-generation SBC architeture.

through two sets of buffers. An advanced acknowledge can not be used. The result is a 20 to 50 percent reduction in performance. (2) The system bus bandwidth is used for execution of the program code. Fast DMA transfers can easily approach the full bandwidth of the system bus during block transfers, so that all other masters must be idled for extended periods. Such performance constraints can severely limit total system performance. Also, this common-bus approach requires one additional complete Multibus interface, or 10 percent of the PCB area, and the system performance is slower. However, one less board is needed in the system.

6.2.2 Second-Generation Architecture—Dual-Port Memory

Dual-port architecture (Fig. 6-8) has the performance advantages of local memory resources and eliminates the inaccessibility of those resources. Many second-generation SBCs, such as Intel's iSBC 86/30 and iSBC 286/10 and National Semiconductor's BLC-86/12, have been built with this architecture, which is organized around a three-bus hierarchy: the on-board bus, where the microprocessor, ROM, and I/O are connected; the dual-port bus, where the RAM is connected; and the Multibus system bus, where the other system global resources are connected (Fig. 6-9). Each bus in the hierarchy can communicate only between itself and an adjacent bus, and each bus can operate independently of the others. The microprocessor can use its local I/O or ROM resources while

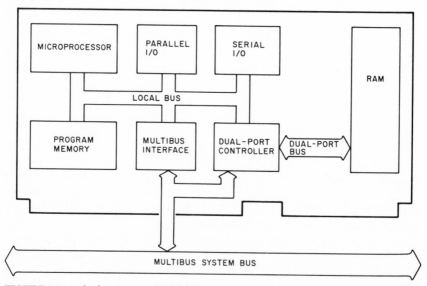

FIGURE 6-8 A dual-port memory architecture.

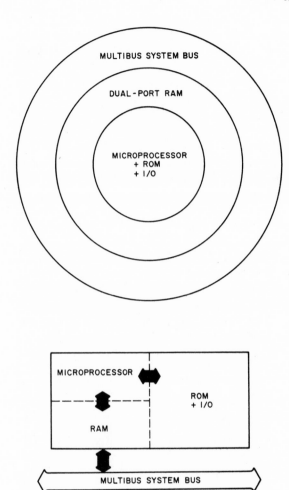

FIGURE 6-9 Dual-port architecture hierarchy.

another master on the Multibus system bus is accessing RAM that is connected to the dual-port bus. The microprocessor on this SBC can also access the RAM connected to the dual-port bus while the Multibus system bus is being used by another bus master. The SBC can be designed to optimize the microprocessor-to-RAM interface and operate at maximum speeds as long as the dual-port memory is not busy servicing a Multibus request.

The disadvantage of dual-port architecture is the hardware overhead required to implement the dual port, which consists of additional address and data buffers and some logic used to control the access of the dual-ported memory. In a 16-bit SBC design, the dual-port overhead is about 10 percent. The overhead can be reduced to about 5 percent with future VLSI support and even more by integrating into one or two VLSI devices the Multibus interface logic and the dual-port logic.

Another approach to implementing a dual-port architecture with multiple boards is to design an SBC by using a first-generation architecture (Fig. 6-3) and include an iLBX interface. This SBC and a dual-ported memory board together form a virtual SBC with dual-ported memory. An example of the configuration is shown in Fig. 6-10. The memory on the expansion board appears to the microprocessor as if it were a local resource, since the Multibus system bus is not used. The system bus bandwidth is preserved, and the memory access is fast because the iLBX bus was designed for high-speed memory accesses. The memory on the expansion board is also a global resource accessible by any Multibus master. A board set in which this type of architecture is implemented consists of Intel's iSBC 186/03, an SBC with an 8-MHz iAPX 80186 microprocessor, and Intel's iSBC 012CX, a 512K-byte dual-ported memory board. By this approach a very high degree of modularity of memory size is provided. The dual-ported memory board can be as small as 128K bytes of high-speed RAM and as large as 2M bytes. The iLBX bus supports up to four expansion memory boards that make from 128K bytes to 8M bytes of RAM available to the microprocessor on the SBC and the Multibus system bus.

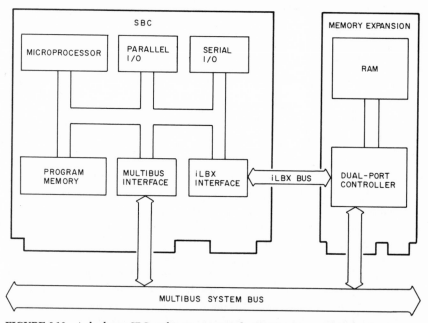

FIGURE 6-10   A dual-port SBC architecture using the iLBX memory expansion bus.

6.2.3 I/O Expansion

In the early days, all SBCs had general-purpose I/O capabilities to fit a wide range of applications. VLSI technology was in its infancy, and state-of-the art components provided the basic computer resources required in most applications. SBCs were made by various companies, and they differed primarily in the quantity of RAM and EPROM. The I/O was fairly consistent: 24 to 48 parallel I/O lines and one RS-232-compatible serial communication channel. Most of the new VLSI devices that were being developed in the semiconductor industry were microprocessors, EPROM, RAM, and some very basic I/O devices such as interrupt controllers and timers. New SBCs were designed each time a memory component or microprocessor was introduced, but not each time a new VLSI I/O device was introduced.

Things have changed significantly since the early days of SBCs. Now SBCs provide solutions for a wide range of specialized applications by taking advantage of VLSI technology that puts tremendous capability on a single chip of silicon. There is now VLSI to interface to a wide range of peripherals such as CRTs, general-purpose interface bus (GPIB) compatible interfaces, floppy disks, hard disks, tape drives, and printers. The selection of the I/O portion of the SBC makes the task of designing a general-purpose SBC more complicated. An SBC user can purchase standard board products that solve a specific I/O application. Two such examples are Heurikon Corporation's MLZ-90A, which includes as its I/O a floppy disk controller and a hard disk and tape interface, and Intel Corporation's iSBC 88/40, which provides 16 differential or 32 single-ended analog input channels. However, making the I/O portion of an SBC application specific has two effects. The specialized I/O permits the SBC to solve a specific problem and provides a single-board solution. But the specialized I/O also makes the SBC less general-purpose. The SBC can be used in fewer applications within a company, with resulting lower volumes and higher costs.

The iSBX bus was created to provide a general-purpose solution for complex application-specific problems, take advantage of new VLSI technology, and use general-purpose low-cost SBCs. It permits the addition of specialized VLSI capability to a general-purpose SBC while maintaining the SBC's cost-effectiveness for many types of applications. The SBC can be designed for a wide range of applications with general-purpose I/O. The iSBX bus permits specialized I/O modules, iSBX Multimodule boards, to be economically added to the baseboard to create an application-specific SBC. The iSBX bus makes it possible to apply new VLSI technology to an SBC without the need for redesigning that SBC. Both new and old SBCs, which support the iSBX bus interface, can be configured with new iSBX Multimodule boards that incorporate the latest VLSI device.

As an example, a general-purpose baseboard can be designed (Fig. 6-11) with a high-speed 16-bit microprocessor, a high-speed math coprocessor, two DMA

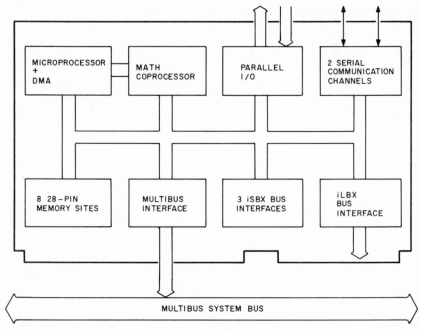

FIGURE 6-11   A block diagram of a general-purpose SBC.

channels, eight 28-pin sites which support up to 256K bytes of ROM or 128K bytes of RAM, some parallel I/O, two serial channels, and three iSBX connectors. Off-board expansion is provided via the Multibus system bus, the iSBX bus, and the iLBX bus interfaces. This general-purpose SBC can be customized to be a measurement-and-control SBC by installing an off-the-shelf eight-channel analog-to-digital converter iSBC Multimodule and a 16-channel analog input channel iSBX Multimodule. The number of channels for each application determines the number and mix of iSBX Multimodules used. The same SBC can be configured to be a communication controller by installing a two-channel serial I/O iSBX Multimodule board. Up to eight serial channels, two channels from the SBC, and six channels from three iSBX Multimodule boards can be supported.

Another advantage that the iSBX concept provides is new economy of design for I/O expansion. In the past, a Multibus-compatible board was required for any I/O expansion or added capability—a full-size Multibus board which may have provided more board area and cost than was necessary. The designer typically added capability with this extra PCB area, which increased the board cost. It is not cost-effective on a full-size Multibus board to provide only 24 I/O lines because the cost of the board and bus interface logic is greater than the cost of the added capability. The iSBX Multimodule board comes in two small sizes (9.25 and 18.75 in^2; 59.70 and 121.0 cm^2). The system designer has three form factors to choose from (Fig. 6-12) to get the most cost-effective solution: a Multibus board, a single-wide iSBX Multimodule board, and a double-wide iSBX Multimodule board. This provides for incremental I/O expansion to meet the cost and capability goals of the project.

With multiple iSBX connectors on a baseboard, a true SBC solution is possible. That eliminates the cost of cabling, connectors, chassis, and card cage. Removing the extra components also increases the system reliability, since there are fewer things to fail. The longevity of the SBC design is extended, because new VLSI technology can be quickly and easily added via the iSBX interface. There is also a wide range of off-the-shelf iSBX Multimodule boards from simply parallel and serial I/O expansion to floppy disk and video display control-

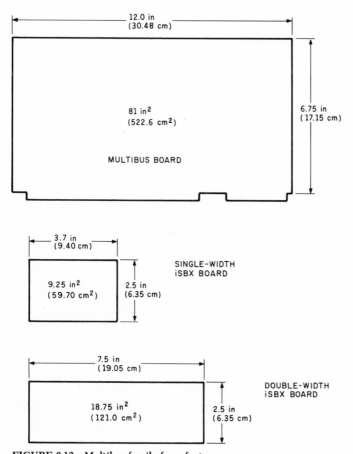

FIGURE 6-12 Multibus family form factors.

lers. Some Multimodules are produced by more than one manufacturer, which assures availability when the product goes into production.

For I/O expansion that requires more PCB area than an iSBX Multimodule board has, the Multibus system bus provides a standard board size of 81 in^2 (522.6 cm^2). The larger size permits the board designer more flexibility. Some typical Multibus I/O expansion boards are 72 parallel I/O lines, 8 serial communication channels, 48 optically isolated I/O lines, and 16 differential nonisolated inputs with a 12-bit analog-to-digital converter and two 12-bit digital-to-analog converters. These I/O expansion boards interface directly with any bus master via the Multibus system bus.

The maximum data rate into and out of these Multibus I/O expansion boards is limited by the Multibus structure. The Multibus can support up to 5 megawords per second, but the fastest DMA controller on the Multibus today is about one megaword per second. If more bandwidth is required, the Multichannel bus could be used to connect high-speed I/O devices directly to the system memory and support speeds of up to 4 megawords per second. The interface costs of the Multichannel are higher than the cost of the Multibus, but the realized performance is higher and the Multichannel bus can extend up to 50 ft (15 m) versus 18 in (45.7 cm) for the Multibus system bus.

6.2.4 Memory Expansion

There are three ways to expand the memory capacity of an SBC. The first is by using a memory Multimodule (Fig. 6-13); the second is by using the Multibus system bus and a Multibus memory expansion board; and the third is by using the iLBX bus and an iLBX memory expansion board. Each of the three methods provides different amounts of memory, performance, and cost.

The memory Multimodule board provides simple, low-cost expansion of the memory complement available on a particular SBC. Each memory Multimodule is designed to operate only on specific SBCs. A typical memory Multimodule consists of only memory devices. The local memory capacity is doubled, since the memory devices on the memory Multimodule are exactly the same devices as on the baseboard. Examples of different memory Multimodules are Intel's iSBC 300A, a 32K-byte RAM Multimodule implemented with sixteen 16K-byte dynamic RAM devices, and the iSBC 304, a 128K-byte RAM Multimodule implemented with sixteen 64K-byte dynamic RAM devices.

Any SBC that supports 16K- or 64K-byte dynamic RAM devices can be designed to support one of the above memory Multimodules. The baseboard provides the address decode logic and chip select signal. The expansion memory appears to the local microprocessor as on-board or local memory and therefore can be accessed as quickly as the existing baseboard memory. The memory Multimodule is mounted on the SBC, and pins that extend from the Multimodule board mate with sockets. The Multimodule is secured with nylon

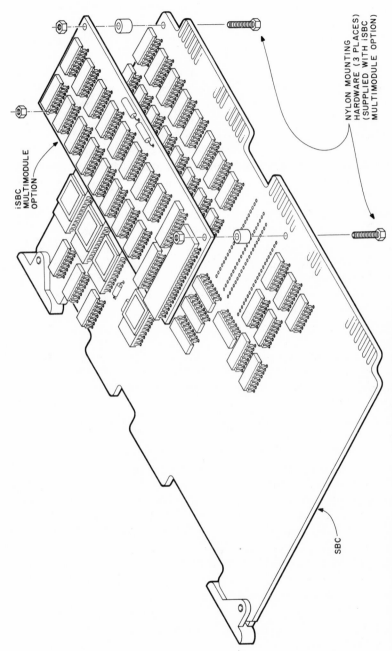

NYLON MOUNTING
HARDWARE (3 PLACES)
(SUPPLIED WITH iSBC
MULTIMODULE OPTION)

iSBC
MULTIMODULE
OPTION

SBC

FIGURE 6-13 Installation of memory multimodule on SBC baseboard.

231

screws, spacers, and nuts to ensure the mechanical security of the assembly. The memory Multimodule approach is the least expensive method of memory expansion, in terms of material cost, board area, power, and card cage slot space, but its capacity is very limited.

The second method of SBC memory expansion, via the Multibus system bus to a memory board, provides the system with global memory and is the least expensive method of memory expansion for large (more than 128K bytes) amounts of memory. The Multibus memory expansion market is very competitive. Over twenty vendors provide slot-compatible boards, ranging from 32K bytes to 512K bytes, with parity or ECC options. The disadvantage of this Multibus memory expansion is that performance with the SBC is two to three times slower than with local memory. Intel's iSBC 86/05 can operate out of its local memory with no wait states. When accessing memory on the Multibus system bus, the microprocessor typically inserts six to seven wait states. This takes a four-clock-cycle fetch and makes it a 10- to 11-cycle fetch, or two times slower.

The third method of SBC memory expansion is via the iLBX bus to a memory board. The memory can be expanded in a very modular manner by using up to four memory expansion boards. An SBC can be configured to have anywhere from 128K bytes to 2M bytes of memory by using 64K-byte dynamic RAMS, and 8M bytes of memory can be obtained by using 256K-byte dynamic RAMS. This approach eliminates the Multibus memory board's performance disadvantage. The iLBX bus was specifically designed to provide a very high speed path between the microprocessor and the memory. The bus is dedicated to one SBC and need not be arbitrated for each time it is used. It also supports advanced acknowledges for improved performance. The disadvantage of this approach is the extra expense of another interface.

6.3 A SIMPLE DESIGN USING SBCs

Digital controllers of industrial equipment are rapidly replacing older analog technology controllers. The new digital controllers provide more capabilities and higher reliability at a lower cost. In this example we will design a digital controller of an agitated heating tank as shown in Fig. 6-14. The controller will control two functions of the tank: (1) maintain the level in the tank and (2) maintain a specified temperature of the liquid.

The first step in designing the system is to break the problem into logically modular subproblems. Each of the subproblems should be as independent of the others as possible to minimize communication and interactions. The tank controller can be divided into two control loops that must be maintained (Fig. 6-15). The first control loop maintains the level in the tank, which can be influenced by the temperature of the liquid, the output flow rate, and the input flow pressure. The second control loop maintains the temperature of the liquid in

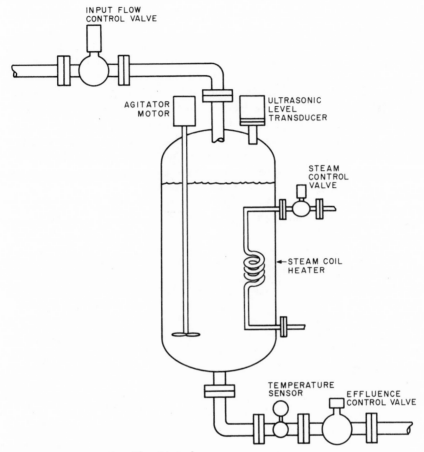

INPUT FLOW
CONTROL VALVE

AGITATOR
MOTOR

ULTRASONIC
LEVEL
TRANSDUCER

STEAM
CONTROL
VALVE

STEAM COIL
HEATER

TEMPERATURE
SENSOR

EFFLUENCE
CONTROL VALVE

FIGURE 6-14 An agitated heating tank.

the tank, which can be influenced by the input flow temperature, the ambient temperature, and the steam temperature.

A block diagram of the tank controller functions is shown in Fig. 6-16. The control algorithm will produce an output signal which is a function of the error signal; that is, the lower the level of the tank, the more the input flow control valve is turned on. The feedback variables, the ultrasonic level transducer, and the temperature sensor are sampled and compared with the set points, the desired temperature and level, to obtain the error signal. The output signal is used to drive the control elements, the input flow control valve, and the steam control valve. The low-pass filters are used to smooth the input and output transactions. The software algorithms will perform as many functions as possible to minimize the hardware product cost; they will provide the low-pass filter, the control algorithm, and data logging. The hardware will perform the rest of the functions in the block diagram.

The hardware requirements for the tank controller are analog input channels to read the feedback variables, analog output signals to govern the control elements, a serial communication channel to establish a connection with a system or factory controller, some parallel I/O to read manual set points and to control some local status indicators. The data log function can be obtained by sending the information to the system controller or by storing the information in bubble memory. The bubble memory provides mass storage that is nonvolatile and is highly reliable under harsh environments that floppy disk storage can not tolerate. The microprocessor must also have high-speed-mathematics capabilities to execute the control algorithm and low-pass filtering.

The hardware implementation of the tank controller (Fig. 6-17) is centered around the general-purpose SBC (Fig. 6-11) discussed earlier. The SBC base-

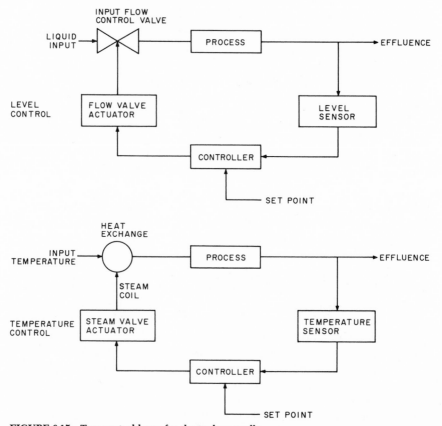

FIGURE 6-15 Two control loops for the tank controller.

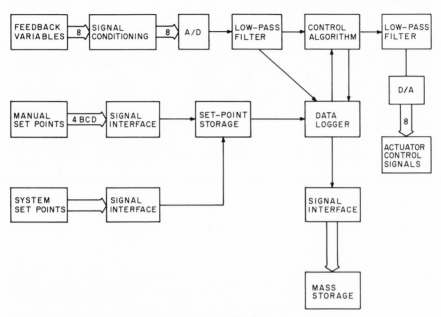

FIGURE 6-16 Block diagram of the tank controller functions.

board provides the microprocessor and the high-speed-mathematics coprocessor which executes the control algorithms, the low-pass filter, and the data log functions. The EPROM memory on the SBC is used to store the control program, and the RAM is used for data storage. The parallel I/O is used to monitor the manual set points and control the local display lights, and one of the two serial channels connects the tank controller with the system controller. Three iSBC Multimodules must be added to complete the required hardware capabilities. The first iSBX Multimodule board is an analog input Multimodule used to monitor the ultrasonic-level transducer and the temperature sensor. The second iSBX Multimodule board is a digital-to-analog converter Multimodule used to operate the input flow and steam control valves. The third iSBX Multimodule board is a bubble memory Multimodule used to store the set-point information and tank status (data logging).

6.4 SUMMARY

A single-board computer (SBC) is a single printed-circuit board with a self-contained basic computer on it. It is an outgrowth of the advance the semiconductor industry is making in providing complex functions at lower and lower cost and chip count. The SBC concept has become very popular, and an array of compatible products, all based on the Multibus system bus, have been made

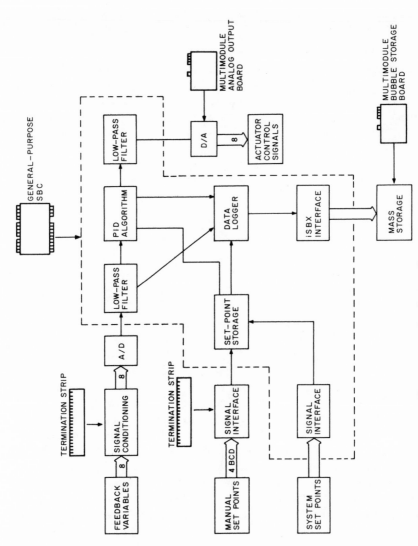

FIGURE 6-17 Hardware implementation of tank controller

available by many different board-level vendors. Both 8- and 16-bit SBCs have evolved, and they provide a wide range of price and performance choices.

The initial SBC architecture was a straightforward extension of the common-bus architecture used by most minicomputers and first-generation microprocessor systems. It defined two buses: the local, or on-board, bus and the system expansion, or Multibus system, bus. The local bus connected all of the resources on the SBC together. If expansion of those resources was needed, the Multibus system bus was used to connect multiple boards together. The local bus was free to change from design to design, whereas the Multibus system bus remained constant to provide a solid board-level interconnect structure.

The disadvantage of that architecture was that local resources, and RAM in particular, were not accessible from the system bus. That led to the creation of a second-generation SBC architecture, that of a three-bus design: the local bus, the dual-port memory bus, and the Multibus system bus. The local bus and the Multibus system bus are used in the same manner as in the first-generation SBC designs. The dual-ported memory provides access to the RAM on the SBC from two different sources: the local microprocessor and any Multibus master. The RAM appears to be local to the microprocessor in that the access to it is faster than to Multibus memory. The dual-ported RAM is also a global resource, since other bus masters can access it. The second-generation SBC architecture provides a single-board solution with performance equal to that of first-generation architecture implementation and also provides global RAM access.

The SBC makes many price-performance expansion options available when additional resources are needed. I/O can be expanded with low-cost iSBX Multimodule boards. If more capacity is required, a Multibus-compatible board can be used. If more throughput is needed, the Multichannel cable bus can be used. There are also many price-performance memory expansion options. The lowest-cost and lowest-capacity expansion is with memory Multimodule boards, which provide memory expansion for dedicated SBC boards. More capacity can be obtained with Multibus memory boards, a very complete family which provides modular expansion at very competitive prices. The highest-performance memory expansion is with iLBX bus–compatible memory boards. SBC and memory boards that support the iLBX bus provide very high performance modular expansion but at a price higher than that of the Multibus expansion option.

7

Multiprocessing with Microprocessors

This chapter provides the basis for a conceptual understanding of a multiprocessor system and the motivations for using it. The effects of a multiprocessor system on the system structure and the performance effects are examined. Included is an example of how to design a multiprocessor system on the Multibus system bus.

7.1 DEFINITION OF A MULTIPLE-PROCESSOR SYSTEM

Not all multiple-microprocessor systems are multiprocessor systems. An example of a multiple-microprocessor system that is not multiprocessing is a uniprocessor system with an intelligent disk controller that uses a microprocessor to control and manage the disk. In this example there are two microprocessors: one is general-purpose, and the other (the microprocessor on the disk controller) is dedicated to a fixed task, basically performing logic replacement, and is not available to the system user. There are many similarities between multiple-microprocessor systems and multiprocessor systems, since both have the same basic purpose: the support of simultaneous operation in the system. The distinctions are often not clearly visible, as is illustrated by the frequent misuse of the term "multiprocessor."

Putting together systems with multiple microprocessors can result in a spectrum of capabilities which depends upon the system architecture. As can be seen in Fig. 7-1, this spectrum starts at one end with nonstop computing, moves through multiprocessing and multicomputing, and ends up with locally distributed processing. There are three important variables that help define the different classes of multiple-microprocessor systems in the spectrum. They are the degree of coupling between the microprocessors in the system (the degree to

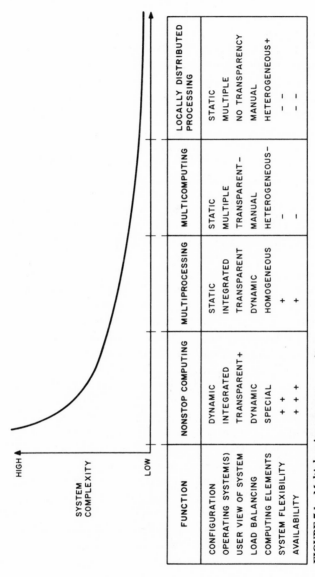

FUNCTION	NONSTOP COMPUTING	MULTIPROCESSING	MULTICOMPUTING	LOCALLY DISTRIBUTED PROCESSING
CONFIGURATION	DYNAMIC	STATIC	STATIC	STATIC
OPERATING SYSTEM(S)	INTEGRATED	INTEGRATED	MULTIPLE	MULTIPLE
USER VIEW OF SYSTEM	TRANSPARENT +	TRANSPARENT	TRANSPARENT –	NO TRANSPARENCY
LOAD BALANCING	DYNAMIC	DYNAMIC	MANUAL	MANUAL
COMPUTING ELEMENTS	SPECIAL	HOMOGENEOUS	HETEROGENEOUS –	HETEROGENEOUS +
SYSTEM FLEXIBILITY	+ +	+	–	– –
AVAILABILITY	+ + +	+	–	– –

SYSTEM COMPLEXITY HIGH LOW

FIGURE 7-1 Multiple microprocessor spectrum.

which one microprocessor needs to know about the other microprocessors), the method of allocation of tasks, and the characteristics of the system modules.

Systems which employ nonstop or fault-tolerant technologies provide very large mean time between failure (MTBF) of the order of 400 to 500 years. This high level of reliability will enable nearly any user to completely eliminate or sharply reduce the cost of computer failure due to maintenance and lost business resulting from a down computer. A nonstop computer system ensures continuous and correct operation, even in the event of a hardware failure anywhere in the system, without delays and human intervention. Hardware failures are automatically detected and diagnosed. Transient errors are corrected and the system continues. Hard errors are logged, the system operator is notified, and the bad component is disabled. All the microprocessors in the system are tightly coupled with highly integrated complex hardware and software.

To the right on the multiple-microprocessor spectrum is multiprocessing (Fig. 7-2). Further to the right on the spectrum are microprocessor systems that are less and less integrated: the individual microprocessors in the system require less knowledge of the others, and system architecture is more and more visible to the user. Another aspect of moving to the right on the spectrum is lower system complexity and therefore cost. A multiprocessor system uses a single integrated operating system to allocate tasks and system resources dynamically. The microprocessors are tightly coupled and homogeneous; they all have exactly the same environment and can execute programs equally. Multiprocessing is explored in greater detail later in this chapter.

Next on the spectrum is multicomputing (Fig. 7-3), which provides less coupling between the microprocessors. The microprocessors in a multicomputing system can be heterogeneous: they can have different architectures, and the resources available to them can be different. An example of a heterogeneous system is one built with Intel's iAPX 80286 and National's NCS 16032, which together perform a particular task. Multicomputing requires predetermined system partitioning and mainly uses dedicated hardware and software. The system load must be balanced during the development of the system and therefore cannot be dynamically balanced in real time. This isolation of tasks permits simplified development and debugging of the specific executives on each of the microprocessors. A multicomputing architecture is less complex and has lower risk of implementation than a multiprocessing architecture. Multicomputing architectures are discussed in more detail in Chap. 8.

The last element on the multiple-microprocessor spectrum is the locally distributed processing (LDP) shown in Fig. 7-4. Here the processing elements are very loosely coupled and the user is aware of the different elements in the system. There is very little program interaction between the processors, although the processors may share read/write (R/W) memory to pass information. Systems consist of numerous independent heterogeneous process modules for specific application tasks. Each of the microprocessors is able to access its own

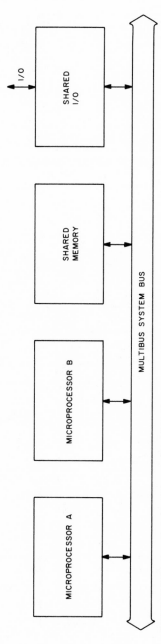

FIGURE 7-2 A multiprocessing configuration.

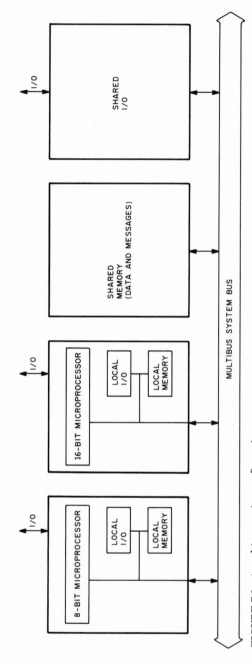

FIGURE 7-3 A multicomputing configuration.

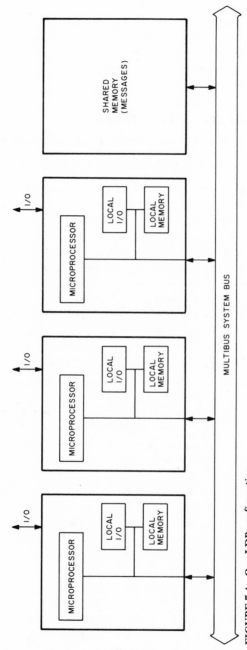

FIGURE 7-4　One LDP configuration.

memory without any contention from the other process modules, which results in as much concurrency or parallelism as possible. These modules, however, have limited communication capabilities with one another, and the communication path is typically through shared nonmemory resources. They may be capable of minimal reconfiguration in the event of a microprocessor failure.

7.2 WHAT IS A MULTIPROCESSOR COMPUTER?

An important difference between multiple-computer systems and multiprocessors is based on the extent to which common resources are shared. A multiple-microprocessor system consists of two or more separate and discrete computers that can communicate, whereas a multiprocessor is a single computer with multiple processing units. The *American National Standard Vocabulary for Information Processing* defines a multiprocessor as "a computer employing two or more processing units under integrated control." The "integrated control" part of the definition is extremely important, since a multiprocessor must have a single integrated operating system. Two additional concepts need to be added to the quoted definition. They are sharing and interaction (degree of coupling), which are among the basic capabilities a multiprocessor must have.

From a hardware point of view, a multiprocessor must have the capability for direct sharing of all system resources by all processors, including dedicated resources such as mathematics, direct memory access (DMA), other special processing units, and the sharing of I/O devices with all microprocessor and memory combinations (Fig. 7-2). Sharing in this context means that the memory or I/O device should be addressable (accessible) by all microprocessors or bus masters; merely linking together a number of microprocessors or computer systems does not result in a multiprocessing system. There may be some qualification on the sharing of all resources of a particular type. One exception to the sharing concept in a multiprocessor system is the idea of special memory. The special memory is partitioned to create some private memory for each of the processors for initialization and error recovery activity. The basic concept of total sharing is still valid in the general sense.

The degree of interaction (the level at which one microprocessor can act on or with another) is a key distinction between a multiple-microprocessor system and a multiprocessor system. In multiple-microprocessor systems the physical unit of interaction is usually the complete file or data set; in a multiprocessor system the level of interaction allowed is more flexible. In fact, any of the microprocessors in a multiprocessor system must be allowed to access even the smallest physical unit, such as a byte in memory. Interaction is possible with all forms of data: files, data sets, and even data elements. From an operating system point of view, interaction must be possible between complete jobs, tasks, and individual job steps.

Another criterion for multiprocessing is that the microprocessors making up the system should not be highly specialized. I/O channels, intelligent dedicated I/O controllers, and similar specialized processing units often share main memory with the central microprocessors, but such configurations do not fit within the notion of a pure multiprocessing system. Also, a microprocessor should be capable of independent processing.

It is the combination of these concepts of integrated control, sharing, and interaction at all levels that completely characterizes the hardware and software required to provide a true multiprocessor system. The following is a summary of the characteristics of a multiprocessor system:

- A multiprocessor contains two or more homogeneous processors of comparable capability.

- All processors share access to global (common) memory. Some private (local) memory is allowed.

- All processors share access to I/O channels, DMA controllers, control units, and I/O devices.

- The entire system is controlled by one integrated operating system that provides interaction between processors and their programs at the job, task, data set, and data element levels.

- Each of the processors can do significant computation individually and interact with the other processors at all levels for both hardware and software.

- The processors are not highly specialized.

7.3 MOTIVATION FOR MULTIPROCESSING

System designers historically have preferred multiprocessing over uniprocessing as a solution to computer system needs when an increase in system performance over that which a uniprocessor system could provide was required. As microprocessor costs continue to fall, the use of microprocessors in many types of multiprocessing systems will increase. The characteristics of the system most affected by a multiprocessing architecture are:

- Throughput
- Reliability
- Availability
- Flexibility
- VLSI revolution

7.3.1 Throughput

Computation speed has increased by orders of magnitude since the early 1970s. The major share of the increase in speed has come from the microprocessor system silicon. Figure 7-5 demonstrates the effective performance of a few industry-standard microprocessors over time. Speed increases in the silicon itself, in the future, will become harder to achieve and will have more effect on system structure than ever before. The basic speed of the system components will not increase at the same rate as in the past. Because of basic physical laws, the silicon is quickly approaching the upper limit of the speed at which a digital computer can transfer information. However, system performance requirements continue to grow. If increased speed is required, the system architecture must be changed to make better use of the system components.

The multiprocessor architecture is used to achieve high performance in a number of ways. All of the ways share the theme of parallelism of computer programs which can be exploited by delegating different tasks or functions to separate processors. Given a single job which taxes the resources of the fastest microcomputers available, it may be possible to split that job up into a number of subtasks (or processes), run each on a different processor, and thereby reduce the overall execution time. Weather forecasting is a good example of parallelism working well, because the forecast algorithms use matrix multiplication which can be done simultaneously. Unfortunately, determining which parts of a program can be run in parallel is very difficult. Significant advances in the automatic decomposition of sequential programs into parallel executable tasks are

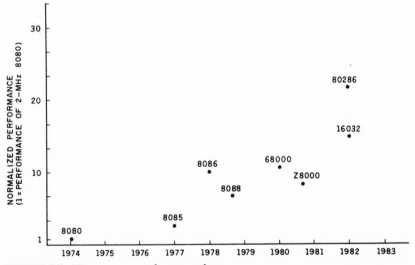

FIGURE 7-5 Microprocessr performance chart.

needed before the benefits of parallel processing of a single program can stand as the primary reason for using multiprocessing systems.

Another aspect of increased throughput is efficient utilization of the computer system. Given that the fastest microprocessor cannot handle the job stream, the multiprocessor architecture seems like a good idea. The classical example is a system that needs to process six jobs. Three of the jobs are I/O-bound (the jobs are mostly waiting for an I/O operation to be completed), and the other three jobs are processor-bound (the microprocessor is running continuously). If these two groups of jobs were put separately on two uniprocessing systems, their throughput would not be optimized. However, on a multiprocessing system the jobs would get done much better because the microprocessors would always be busy starting I/O operations or computing. Using two processors as a multiprocessor is usually better than configuring the two as uniprocessor systems and partitioning the workload between them in a dynamic load environment. That is true because in a multiprocessor system the sharing of hardware resources and processor time tends to smooth out effects that are due to random variations in job characteristics. In the above example, two microprocessors are used to execute the six jobs; ideally, the system throughput should have doubled. However, it is important to note that system performance is not a linear function of the number of processors, because there are contention problems in both the hardware and software.

The concurrency concept can be extended to include operating system functions. A uniprocessor must switch operating states to perform operating system functions. A system can be partitioned, as an example, in such a way that all the peripheral operations are executed on the operating system processing units (Fig. 7-6). The concurrent execution of user programs and operating system programs can be extended to include the concurrent execution of multiple-user programs (multiprogramming). The idea of multiprogramming is to process a number of independent jobs on single or multiple microprocessors and control a number of I/O devices in an overlapped or concurrent fashion. In the latter case, the turnaround time should be considerably lower. An operating system supporting multiprogramming permits programs to be developed separately in smaller and simpler tasks. There can be no interaction between the different software tasks. A multiprogramming system gives the software being executed the appearance of many machines but uses just one. A multiprogramming operating system has to manage the program division by keeping track of the status of each program and the requirements of each application and maintaining the correct priority.

Another method of increasing concurrency in the execution of the software is multitasking. It is very similar to multiprogramming, but an interaction is allowed to take place between the different software tasks. A form of task-to-task communication is permitted. An executive is written to manage tasks, priorities, and intertask communication. The result is sharing of the micropro-

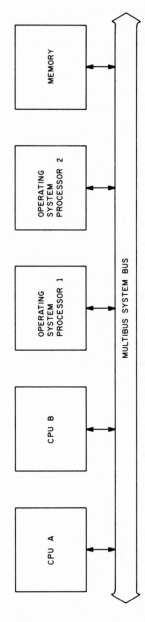

FIGURE 7-6 A partitioned multiprocessor configuration.

248

cessor I/O to increase efficiency and system throughput. Although multiprogramming and multitasking can be accomplished in a uniprocessor system, in high-performance systems additional main processors are used to enhance the capability for true multiprogramming. The multiprocessor configuration shown in Fig. 7-6 is not multiprocessing in the purest sense because the operating system processors are dedicated to a particular task. However, the implementation of this type of system is less difficult and is a good stepping stone to obtaining true general-purpose multiprocessing.

7.3.2 Reliability and Availability

In many industrial control applications of computer systems a failure can have a dramatic effect on the safety of the people working with the computer controller equipment. A failure can damage the equipment or materials being processed (which could result in the loss of millions of dollars). If a uniprocessor system is used, a failure is catastrophic; whereas if a multiprocessor is used, the remaining processors are potentially available and can work undisturbed to yield what is called gracefully degraded service. Redundancy is one of the most effective tools for improving the realiability of a computer system; multiprocessors have been used to create highly reliable systems. Multiprocessor systems can provide a wide range of reliability and availability. The *reliability* of a system is the probability that the system will continue to run useful computations without a failure over a given length of time. The *availability* of a system is the probability that a system will be available to run useful computations.

The most basic multiprocessor systems have inherent redundancy in the processing portion of the design, in that there is more than one processing unit. Failure in one of the processor units can be noncritical—the system can continue processing with the remaining hardware at a reduced rate. The task on that processor may be lost, but the rest of the system can continue to operate. Some operational capability may be retained, provided the system can first detect and then reconfigure itself to operate without the failed unit. This type of multiprocessor architecture increases the availability of the system; but since a task can be lost, there is no improvement in system reliability. The hardware and software can, however, be designed to support restarting the task of a failed processor on another processor and continue from a point close to the point at which the failure occurred. This method is very software-intensive.

Another approach to getting better reliability and availability is a dual-processor system in which one processor supports the system operations and the other is in standby mode. If the primary processor fails, the standby processor is called on to take over the processing responsibilities. Typically the standby processor will shadow the primary processor by tracking or duplicating the latter's operations. The objective is a takeover without loss of information. In this context availability is defined to be the ability to provide service; the computer system does what it is supposed to do even after a component in the system fails. If a system is built with only one dual-processor pair, it would not be a multiprocessor system. It would, however, be a multiple-processor system. The main difficulty in this scheme is the detection of a failure in the primary processor.

Even higher reliability and availability in system designs can be obtained by increasing the number of processors in the system and letting them vote on the answers. All the processors perform the same tasks and then compare answers. If any differences are found, the answer in the majority is taken as the correct one. This approach is used when very high reliability or a very long MTBF is required. The method also provides very high availability. The user does not see any effect of a failure in the hardware, since the system automatically compensates for the failure. Only if two failures occur can the system completely fail. Since a single failure will not interrupt operation, overall reliability depends on the speed with which the repairs can be made before another hardware failure occurs.

In fault-tolerant computing, redundancy, voting, and isolation are essential. Replicated hardware and software ensure that the redundant modules will continue to operate correctly if a failure occurs in one module. The outputs of the modules are compared simultaneously. If the answers disagree, the majority modules will outvote the faulty module to maintain the validity of the output data. For working modules to be able to outvote a faulty module, a minimum of three modules must perform the same function. Reliability could be enhanced by implementing increased redundancy with voting modules additional to those needed for triple redundancy, but at an increase in system cost. Although communication between them is required, replicated modules must be isolated so that a mulfunctioning unit will not affect the performance of the other modules.

7.3.3 Flexibility

Flexibility is a measure of the ease with which a system configuration can be altered. Multiprocessor systems are by their nature flexible and expandable; additional modules can be added incrementally and conveniently. The systems can be customized to specific applications or grow incrementally in the field to meet the ever-changing computer demands of a particular customer. Another aspect of flexibility is the ability of a system to reconfigure itself either dynamically under the control of the operating system or statically under the control of the system operator at initialization time (when the machine is first turned on or after a failure has been detected).

7.3.4 VLSI Revolution

With each new generation of microprocessors, using microprocessors in a multiprocessor configuration provides the potential for better price-performance advantages. Multiple microprocessors can provide higher system throughput, better system reliability and availability, improved real-time response, and the possiblity of modular expansion. Advances in semiconductor technology have inverted the cost of the central processor, the system memory, and I/O boards with the higher cost of the peripherals, making the computing power relatively cheap. Today, to design for maximum efficiency and economy, the system designer must keep the expensive peripherals busy. In computation-bound applications (in which the microprocessor execution is the limiting factor) the least expensive resource in the system is limiting the overall system performance. Microprocessors built into multiprocessing systems can serve to answer this need.

7.3.5 Software Is Still a Problem

One of the major bottlenecks of decentralized multiprocessors is the lack of suitable operating systems. Since several processes must be coordinated, overhead grows. This tends to complicate the operating system very much, and it is possible that the addition of processors may increase instead of decrease the average time per computation.

Reliability is not only a hardware issue; it is also a software problem. If the operating system works incorrectly, an unreliable computer system results. The operating systems should be written in a high-level language instead of in assembly language, which is difficult to understand and maintain. Structure programming must be used to produce code that is more legible, better documented, and easier to check out. The operating system should be built on a small kernel with multiple layers of extensions on top of it in order to enhance reliability.

7.4 MULTIPROCESSOR ARCHITECTURES ON THE MULTIBUS STRUCTURE

The Multibus structure provides the simplest and least complex type of multiprocessor interconnection scheme, a time-shared common bus which provides common communication paths connecting all of the functional units. This arrangement can be used to assemble most basic multiprocessor systems (Fig. 7-7). The Multibus interconnection system is totally passive; it has no active components such as switches or amplifiers. Transfers operations are controlled completely by the Multibus interface on the bus master and bus slave units by using time-sharing techniques. A bus master initiates a transfer by first deter-

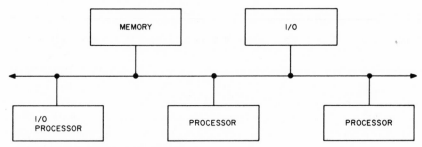

FIGURE 7-7 Time-shared common bus.

mining the availability of the bus, gaining control of the bus, initiating the transfer, waiting for the bus slave to respond, and releasing control of the system bus once the bus cycle is completed.

Multiprocessor systems based on the Multibus structure have a high degree of modularity. Hardware changes can be made by simply adding or removing bus masters or bus slaves. All that is required to modify the system configuration is to physically attach or detach the bus unit. The Multibus masters in the system are required to know what other modules are present and also their internal addresses, but that requirement is basically a software issue. The quantity and type of functional modules are transparent to the Multibus interconnection scheme. The scheme is very reliable because of its low complexity, and its cost is relatively low because each bus module has a single interface point. However, it does introduce a single critical component in the system that can cause a system failure as a result of a malfunction in any of the bus interface circuits.

Another aspect of this simple approach to building a multiprocessor system is the system software implication. The complexity of system software is most likely to be proportional to the complexity of the hardware. As the software becomes more complex, it runs slower. The entire difference in performance between a high-capacity hardware system with complex system software and a simple medium-capacity alternative with a less complex operating system may vanish.

The benefits of simplicity and low cost do not come free. Limitations to overall system performance result from having only one path for all transfers. The total overall transfer rate within the system is limited by the bandwidth and speed of this single path, the Multibus system bus. Interconnection techniques that overcome this weakness, such as crossbar buses or multiport memories, add to the complexity and cost of the system. This limitation does confine Multibus-based systems to smaller configurations.

Another possible limitation to the single time-shared bus is the single critical path it provides for all system elements. A failure of any bus interface brings the entire system down. This makes the reliability of the bus and its interfaces a very important factor in the system design. The Multibus system bus has been designed with reliability in mind, and given suitable choices of interface technology and careful implementation of the bus interface circuitry, the limitation of possible susceptibility to failure can be eliminated.

7.4.1 A Simple Multiprocessor Architecture

The simplest multiprocessor architecture that can be built on the Multibus structure is shown in Fig. 7-8. The primary reason for using this hardware configuration is its greater performance than a single processor system can deliver. More performance can be obtained by simply adding more microprocessors. However, the addition of extra microprocessors (and necessary memory and I/O) does not result in a linear increase in performance. Microprocessors tend to have a very high bus utilization (the percentage of the instruction cycle that the system bus is required to access the instruction from memory divided by the time it takes to fetch and execute that instruction) ranging from 50 to 60 percent on an 8080 to 60 to 70 percent on a 6800. The 16-bit microprocessors have even higher burst bus utilization factors; the 80286 and 68000 are in the 80 to 90 percent range. Because of this high bus utilization, the system bus can be saturated very quickly by only a few microprocessors. Adding more microprocessors would not improve the system performance; it would have the opposite effect of reducing the system performance because of increased contention on and latency to the system bus. There are two ways to solve the bus contention problem, both of which center around reducing the required bandwidth of each of the microprocessors on the system bus. The first is to add a cache memory front end, and the second is to partition the system to have processor-memory pairs called functional units. The goal of each method is to reduce the demand on the system bus.

7.4.2 A Cached Memory Architecture

The goal of a cache-based architecture is to provide a microprocessor with the effect of having high-speed memory even though the system main memory is

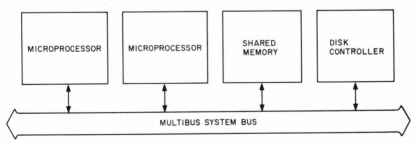

FIGURE 7-8   A simple multiprocessor architecture.

slow. Figure 7-9 exemplifies a main and cache memory system in which a high-speed intelligent memory, the cache memory, is between the microprocessor and the slower system memory. The microprocessor appears to have very fast system memory because the purpose of a cache memory is to always have the information requested by the microprocessor. At any given time, the cache memory contains as many instructions and data words as the microprocessor currently needs. New information, as it is needed, is brought from main memory to the cache memory, where it displaces old information. The cache memory is transparent to the programmer and can appear between any two levels in the memory hierarchy.

As microprocessors get faster, their bus utilization will continue to increase and cycle times will continue to decrease. The result will be a need for faster memory systems. A large-capacity memory system which is cheap and reliable can best be implemented by using a dynamic RAM memory system with error-correction code (ECC) or error-correcting circuitry. A memory system with ECC provides high reliability through detection and correction of single-bit errors. The term ECC refers to a data-encryption scheme that attaches a number of ECC check bits to every memory location (six for 16-bit words). The check bits are used to verify that the data in the memory has not changed since it was written.

In terms of access and cycle times, dynamic memory and its controller technology will always be slower than the microprocessors. A cache memory between the microprocessor and its dynamic RAM memory system will make the cache memory system access time seem fast. The modularity of the memory in cache-based systems is excellent. The memory is easily expandable, and the expanded memory can be easily shared by all microprocessors in the system, since all the main memory can be part of a central pool.

Cache-based systems work well if (1) executing programs tend to reuse instructions and data and (2) programs tend to use instructions and data which are stored near recently used instructions and data. The first property, reuse, means that once information is fetched from main memory to cache memory, subsequent accesses to it are at fast cache-memory speed because the data is already in the cache memory. The second property, locality, means that if a request to main memory is satisfied by bringing into cache memory a block of information larger than is immediately needed, the additional information is likely to be needed soon, and its presence in cache will save references to the main memory.

Cache designs in multiprocessor systems can be very complex and have many variables which affect the cache architecture performance and therefore the system performance. Only a brief overview of cache designs will be given here. Special consideration must be given by a designer to solving classical cache problems such as data coherence (cache data and main memory data becoming

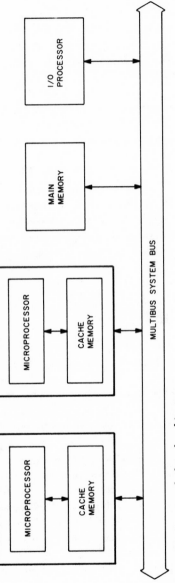

FIGURE 7-9 A cache-based architecture.

different because another device changes main memory without having all caches updated) and locked bus operations (guaranteed exclusive access to a memory location).

Two major parameters in a cache design are cache capacity and the speed or rate at which the cache can be filled. The cache capacity is the number of memory blocks that can be resident in the cache at any given time. The rate at which the cache can be filled is the data transfer rate of the cache–system memory combination.

Selection of the appropriate cache system parameters can have a dramatic impact on system performance. Performance can be roughly estimated with a simple model which predicts the performance of a single microprocessor in the system as a function of its effective access time from the memory system. The cache hit ratio (CHR) is the probability that an addressed word is in the cache memory; *actual* is the effective microprocessor performance or the total time necessary to fetch and execute an instruction from main memory. A microprocessor's actual performance is a function of the wait states, which are governed by the effective access time of the memory system. A no-wait-state performance results in *actual* = 1; infinite-wait-state performance results in *actual* = 0. Table 7-1 shows the actual-versus-wait states of an 8086 microprocessor. The performance of a cache-based microprocessor can be predicted as follows:

$$\text{Performance factor} = \text{CHR} + (1 - \text{CHR})(1/actual)$$

and

$$\text{Performance} = 1/\text{performance factor}$$

CHR can vary between 0 and 1, where 0 means the cache memory never has the data the microprocessor needs and must go to main or system memory for each request. Thus, the cache architecture has no effect on system performance and the microprocessor will operate at its actual performance level. A 1 means the cache always has the data the microprocessor needs and is therefore running at maximum performance. The effect of the CHR on the performance of an 8086-based system, as a function of the wait states required to execute from the main memory, is shown in Fig. 7-10. This figure shows that if the CHR can be maintained above 0.90, the difference between a one-wait-state and a five-wait-state performance is reduced to less than 7 percent, at a CHR of 0.8 the difference is about 10 percent; and at a CHR of 0 the difference is about 40 percent. The cache architecture can improve the effective access time of main memory by two to three times as long as the CHR can be kept above 0.95. The designer must trade off cache memory cost (bigger cache memory sizes produce higher CHRs) and system throughput.

Another measure of performance is the effective access time of the memory

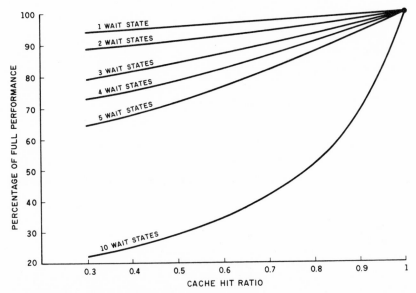

FIGURE 7-10   8086 performance in a cached system.

system as seen by the microprocessor. Effective access time is the average of all access times, which can be determined as follows:

Effective access time = CHR × cache access time
$$+ (1 - \text{CHR}) \times \text{main memory access time}$$

The CHR is a complex function of the cache design parameters and the application program behavior. Trade-offs must be based on the cost-performance goals of each project. Program behavior is the most difficult data to obtain. Historically it has been derived by tracing typical programs and then simulating different cache models with the above data and implicitly getting CHR.

7.4.3   A Functional Partitioned Multiprocessor Architecture

Another approach to reducing the system bus bandwidth requirements is to partition the system into functional units (Fig. 7-11). Each functional unit can perform any of the system functions or tasks. All of the resources required to perform any system task are located on the functional units (such as a math coprocessor or a DMA controller) or are shared (such as disk I/O). All of the functional units must be homogeneous; that is, they must be identical. The units must have the same amounts of ROM, RAM, and local I/O and have equal

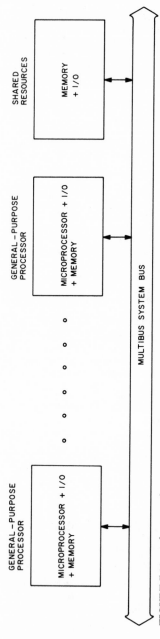

FIGURE 7-11 A functional partitioned multiprocessor architecture.

access to all shared resources so that any functional unit can perform any of the tasks the system executes. This reduces the use of the Multibus system bus to data movement and signaling between processing elements (interprocessor communications). There is a single ready list from which all the functional units get their task assignments.

The type of architecture described above provides very high system throughput. Performance of each of the individual functional units is basically independent of the number of functional units in the system. Once the task is loaded into its memory, the functional unit can operate at its maximum rate, since all the resources needed are local. The most important resource in terms of performance is local memory that the microprocessor can immediately access. The local memory eliminates contention in the system and speeds up each memory access. Typically in a functional unit architecture, the overall system throughput will be limited by I/O throughput, not by the microprocessor throughput. The goal is to maximize the local or on-board activity and minimize the system bus activity.

Since the goal is to maximize local or on-board resource usage, the role of the Multibus system bus changes. In any multiple-microprocessor system, the system bus can be used in three different ways: as an execution bus, as a data movement bus, and as an interprocessor message-passing bus. For typical programs the bandwidth required on the system bus, in order of need, is for execution, data movement, and message passing. The bandwidth requirements for each of the different ways in which the bus can be used are functions of the particular environment the system is in. In the simple time-shared common-bus architecture, all the microprocessors execute all their code over the system bus. In the time-shared common-bus configuration, the Multibus structure is used primarily as an execution bus. The system bus is used to move data and pass messages, but a high percentage of time the system bus is used as an execution bus. In the cache-based architecture the goal is to eliminate execution on the system bus and so increase the available bandwidth of the system bus. The Multibus structure is used primarily to move data and can be called a data movement bus. In a functional unit–based architecture the goal is to eliminate execution and greatly reduce the data movement in the system, and thereby increase the available bandwidth of the system bus. The Multibus structure is used primarily to pass messages to the different functional units in the system and can be called a message bus.

System throughput is typically defined as the number of instructions executed per second by the system. This number, in a multiprocessor system, is usually limited by the throughput or bandwidth of the system bus. The functional unit architecture trades off cost to minimize the required system bus bandwidth and maximize performance of each of the functional units. The major cost comes in having multiple sets of memory and multiple copies of the operating system. The memory in the system cannot be pooled because all of the memory must be local to each functional unit. The system must be statically configured in such a way that each functional unit has the worst-case memory needs—the configuration of programs that requires the most memory at the same time. This type of architecture takes advantage of inexpensive VLSI to keep the expensive peripherals busy.

The functional unit architecture is based on the concept that all the resources required by a functional unit can be local or shared. Some of the resources, such as memory and mathematics, must be local, which means they must be integrated onto the SBC. The size of the SBC PCB is fixed by the Multibus specification; the number of devices that fit on a single board is therefore limited. If a system needed a functional unit with more memory than could fit on standard Multibus-size boards, it could not be implemented. The iLBX bus was designed to solve that problem. This bus allows an SBC to expand its local memory without using the Multibus system bus. It provides a tightly coupled, high-bandwidth connection between the microprocessor and its memory (Fig. 7-12). Each of these units is, in effect, a complete microprocessor system supporting all the

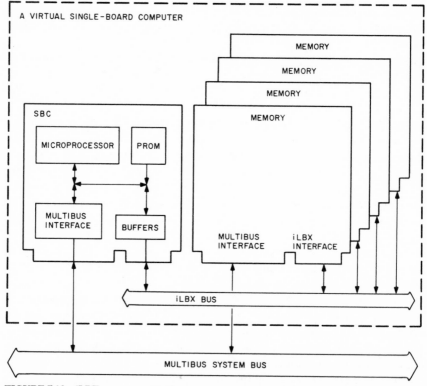

FIGURE 7-12 iLBX memory extension.

memory the microprocessor needs. The iLBX structure permits the architectural benefits of the SBC concept to be preserved.

The iLBX bus supports up to four memory boards. With 512K-byte ECC memory boards, a functional unit can have over 2M bytes of local memory. The expansion memory boards can be dual-ported, with one port connected to the iLBX bus and the other to the Multibus. An SBC and dual-ported iLBX memory board configuration provides all the advantages of having local high-speed memory, as well as the advantages of having a shared memory. This type of configuration also uncouples the microprocessor design from the memory design. When new memory devices become available, a new memory board can be designed without affecting the microprocessor board design.

7.5 SYSTEM BUS REQUIREMENTS FOR MULTIPROCESSOR SYSTEMS

The structure that connects all the system resources together is the Multibus system bus, which is also called the system bus. The basic requirements on the structure to support multiprocessing and sharing of resources are to:

- Share system resources such as memory and I/O

- Provide an interprocessor signaling mechanism

- Provide an efficient bus-arbitration scheme

7.5.1 Shared System Resources

A shared resource is part of the system which is required by more than one of the system bus masters and therefore is a possible source of contention. The Multibus structure provides the capacity for any system bus master to (1) control and transfer data to and from any memory location, (2) pass bus control or ownership to another bus master (such as a microprocessor, DMA, or I/O channel controller module), and (3) access any memory location. Typical shared resources are the Multibus backplane, memory and I/O, programs, data buffers, data files, queues, and run-time variables.

7.5.2 An Interprocessor Signaling Mechanism

To ensure the integrity of data that is shared while being accessed by one microprocessor, there must be a hardware lock that can be used to prevent another microprocessor from accessing the data while it is being used. This lock permits a microprocessor to perform multiple operations on a memory location and be guaranteed that no other processor will be able to access the memory. On top of this lock function, semaphores or test-and-set flags can be built in memory. Conflicts over shared resources can be resolved via the semaphore procedure.

The requesting microprocessor tests the status of the semaphore by reading a memory location, which is simply a resource-busy indicator. If busy (the memory location contents are all 1's), the requester must wait. If not busy (the memory location contents are all 0's), the sempahore is set to busy by writing all 1's in the memory during the access to the resource and then reset when finished. The lock function permits the microprocessor to perform a read-modify-write operation as if it were one instruction, even though it is actually two separate operations, a read and then a write.

Another method of interprocessor signaling is the use of interrupts. Each microprocessor must have the capability to signal or interrupt another to request that a task be done or to inform that a task is completed. The Multibus supports a limited number of interrupt lines. Each external device is preassigned to individual processors via hard-wired interrupt lines.

7.5.3 An Efficient Bus-Arbitration Scheme

Arbitration entails the use of the bus control logic to accept requests from bus masters, perform the arbitration, and inform the bus masters of its decision. The Multibus system bus provides two basic methods of arbitration: serial, which is a decentralized arbitration method (the arbitration logic is distributed throughout the bus masters), and parallel, which is a centralized arbitration method (the arbitration logic is a self-contained hardware module). Both are discussed in detail in Chap. 2.

7.6 THREE MULTIPROCESSOR IMPLEMENTATIONS

In the Multibus environment—a time-shared common bus—there are three basic architectures that support multiprocessing: a single time-shared bus, a single time-shared bus with a cache front end, and functional units. Each microprocessor's system bus usage in a multiprocessor system can be broken down into three basic areas: the need to execute code, the need to move data, and the need to communicate with other processors. The system architecture will determine what requirements are put on the system bus structure(s). Some common attributes of all multiprocessing systems that are built into the Multibus system bus are discussed here before we go into the details of some particular multiprocessor architectures.

Interprocessor communication can be implemented by using global memory and interrupts. All interrupts in the system are predetermined. Each interrupt level on the Multibus system bus must have only one sender and one receiver. There are eight interrupt lines on the Multibus system bus, and therefore only eight interrupt sender-receiver pairs can be made. A common I/O device would need as many interrupts as there are processor boards.

Memory-mapped hardware is used to translate virtual addresses into addresses in physical memory. The private memory on each of the processor boards is used during initialization to identify itself and set up the translation hardware. In a multiprocessing environment, precise memory requirements for a group of concurrently executing programs can be difficult to predict. As a result, programs and data must be able to move to make more room for additional programs. The memory map facilitates dynamic variation of physical locations during program execution without any need to change the programs that are running. The memory map hardware can be external to the microprocessor implemented with TTL, or it can be incorporated in the microprocessor. The software, in conjunction with the microprocessor, can perform the memory-mapping function. To do so, extensive use is made of indirect addressing through pointers in the microprocessor registers. Some microprocessors that support this type of software memory mapping are Zilog's Z80, Signetic's 2650, and Intel's 8086, 80186 and 80286.

We will now discuss the different needs of three Multibus system bus–based multiprocessor architectures.

7.6.1 Single Time-Sharing Bus System

Figure 7-13 is a block diagram of a multiprocessor system on the Multibus system bus. Each processor unit consists of a microprocessor, the bus interface logic, some private memory, and an interrupt controller. The main memory is accessible by all bus masters and therefore is considered global memory. I/O is also considered to be global if it is accessible by all bus masters.

The performance improvements in the system are the result of the parallel execution of the different microprocessors in the system. The fetching of instructions and data is sequential because it occurs over the common system bus. Therefore, a key to system performance is the microprocessor bus utilization and transfer rate versus system bus transfer rate. The system bus can yield, at best, 100 percent. Realistically taking into account arbitration and bus transfer times, the number is reduced to 80 to 90 percent. In the case of two 8086 microprocessors, the bus utilization required to operate both microprocessors at full speed would be about 150 percent, which is not possible. As seen in Fig. 7-14, the addition of a second microprocessor results in a 50 percent overall system improvement; the third microprocessor actually provides a negative performance increase of 10 percent. The addition of this third microprocessor puts a higher demand on the system bus than the system can handle, and so the bus becomes saturated in supporting two microprocessors.

The bus utilization factor is not directly proportional to system performance on an 8086 because of the system's unique architectural enhancements. The internal functions of the 8086 are divided into two major functional areas: an

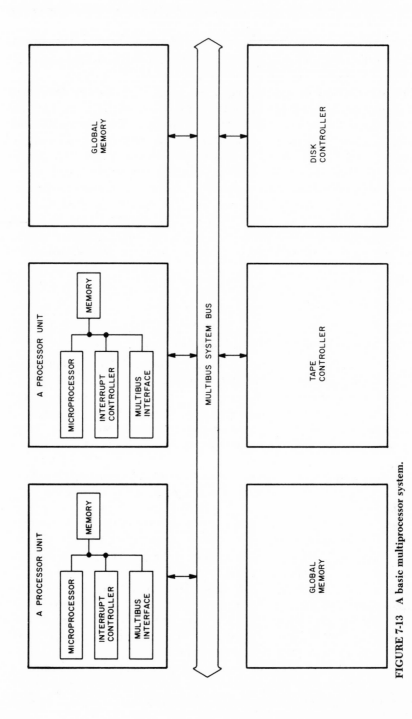

FIGURE 7-13   A basic multiprocessor system.

execution and control unit (EU) and a bus interface unit (BIU), as shown in Fig. 7-15. The EU performs all the basic processing functions, accepts prefetched instructions from the BIU, and returns address requests. The purpose of the BIU is to maximize bus bandwidth utilization, which the BIU does by prefetching instructions and then queuing them up for the EU to use. Hence the EU need not wait for completion of a bus cycle before taking in a new instruction. The independent BIU and EU permit the fetch of one instruction to occur at the same time a previously fetched instruction is being executed. This parallel action has a smoothing effect between bus-bound and execution-bound instructions. Table 7-1 shows the performance of an 8086 as a function of the number of wait states the memory system needs. If the memory system needs one wait state, the overall system performance is reduced by only 8 percent even though the fetch cycle is 20 percent longer.

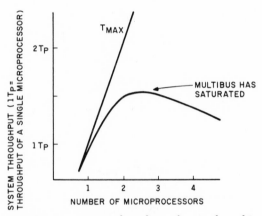

FIGURE 7-14 System throughput of a simple multi-processor system.

TABLE 7-1 8086 Performance versus Number of Wait States

Number of wait states	% of 0 wait state performance[a]
0	100
1	92
2	84
3	74
4	65
5	57
10	17

[a]Executing a typical program.

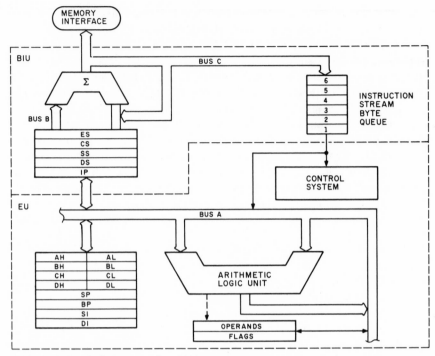

FIGURE 7-15   Block diagram of an 8086 microprocessor.

7.6.2 Single Time-Sharing Bus System with Cache

Figure 7-16 is a high-level block diagram of a processor board with cache memory located between the processor and the Multibus system bus. The block diagram consists of a microprocessor, a cache memory, a dual-ported cache controller which also fully supports the Multibus interface, some local I/O for diagnostics, and some local memory for initialization and diagnostics. The cache memory is built with fast static RAM, which can provide a basic capacity ranging from 4K bytes to 64K bytes by using today's static RAM technology. The size of the cache memory will depend on the environment of the multiprocessor system and will require simulations for its determination. It has the biggest effect on the CHR; the larger the cache memory, the closer to 1 the CHR gets. Cache memory is fast but expensive, so a cost-performance trade-off must be made.

The effective access time from the cache memory must be equal to or better than the microprocessor's no-wait state needs in order to get maximum performance out of the system. To achieve a high CHR, prefetch techniques must be used; when a miss is encountered on an access to the cache memory, an entire block will be replenished to it. If increased system confidence is needed, parity can be used in the cache array to provide memory error detection with an interrupt to the operating system if an error should occur.

The block size is another variable that needs to be customized for a particular environment. The larger the block size, the higher the chances that the cache memory will have requests already present. But large block transfers use up the system bandwidth, which needs to be conserved. Large block sizes can also result in moving data which is not needed, and that also is wasteful.

The cache memory is dual-ported with one port to the microprocessor and the other to the Multibus system bus. A synchronous time slice arbitration technique can be used to guarantee access times to the microprocessor. The memory is fast enough to appear to each side of the dual port as a dedicated resource. This means that the memory access speed must be better than twice as fast as needed to get no-wait performance. If the microprocessor makes a memory request just after a Multibus cycle has started, the cache memory can service the Multibus cycle, and then the microprocessor request, without slowing up the microprocessor. The Multibus side of the dual-port memory must latch up the requested information and wait for the Multibus master to complete the operation. This permits microprocessor execution at full speed even while the cache is being replenished.

The problem of data coherence must be solved in cache-based multiprocessing systems or in cache-based uniprocessor systems with DMA activities. Unless special safeguards are taken, cached copies of main memory data will not remain identical either because local write operations to cache memory have

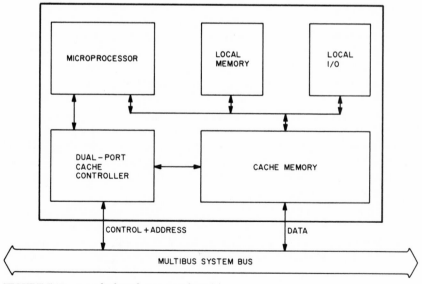

FIGURE 7-16 A cache-based processor board.

not been trasnferred back to main memory or because an update at main memory has taken place and a new copy of the updated block has not been forwarded to the cache memory in the system.

One solution to data coherence is based on a single concept, that of a primary copy of data which is always in main memory. The system policy to assure data coherence is as follows: Updates (writes) can be made only to a primary copy (main memory). The primary copy can be cached for read-only operations, and any write operation must cause all cache memories with a copy of that location to be invalidated. The microprocessor board performing the write need not invalidate its cache but must wait for main memory to be written into before continuing. The dual-ported cache controller must monitor Multibus write operations in order to invalidate its locally cached copies of recently updated central memory blocks. The invalidation process can be merged with the microprocessors' accesses of the cache memory without reducing performance. All write operations by a microprocessor will update both the local cache memory and the central memory of the microprocessor. This procedure is known as write through.

Locked bus operations also must be supported. The system policy to solve this problem can be as follows: Before any microprocessor can access a memory location when its lock signal is active, it must first wait to gain control of the Multibus system bus; and when the lock signal on the system bus is active, all microprocessors in the system may not access any memory. Thus in a read, modify, and write operation, the system would be frozen at the start of the read and all cache memories would be updated or invalidated during the write portion of the cycle.

The performance of the system is highly dependent on the rate of cache memory replenishment, which needs to be higher than the microprocessor execution rate. That is, the cache memory must be able to fill faster than the microprocessor can access it (assuming sequential accesses). Taking into account memory system cycle times, Multibus arbitration times, and bus surrender delays, a conventional type of transaction (arbitrate; request data from memory; wait for an acknowledgment; surrender system bus) could be inadequate. A block move of data from the memory system to the cache is what is needed, since it requires only one system bus arbitration and one bus surrender cycle per block transfer. The Multibus protocols do not define a block move capability, so one must be creative in designing the cache controller and memory system interface while maintaining Multibus compatibility.

Since the cache controller will transfer blocks of sequentially addressed information, it would be useful for the memory system to have the ability to access the next (the current address plus 1) memory location in anticipation of the next memory request. If the two addresses match (the next Multibus cycle and the preceding memory address plus 1), the memory can acknowledge the transfer almost immediately. Memory operations can now be overlapped with data delivery time, since the memory knows (or attempts to know) the next address in advance. Resulting transfer rates two to three times higher could be realized. This implementation is, in effect, a memory board with a front-end cache memory of one-word depth. A more general but higher-cost solution would be to design a memory board with a cache front end that has a 2K- to 4K-byte cache memory. The access time of cache resident data could be less than 100 ns.

7.6.3   Functionally Partitioned Single Time-Sharing Bus System

Another approach, the use of functional units, combines the time-sharing bus for all shared accesses and dedicated buses (the local on-board bus and the iLBX memory expansion bus) for all local accesses. The system (Fig. 7-17) consists of multiple functional units that can be divided into two groups based on the types of tasks they will perform. Group 1 are application units (AU), which will execute all the user application code, and group 2 is the system unit (SU), which will execute all the operating system I/O code. The system unit provides full operating system support for tasks running on it and provides some operating system functions for the application units. The application units contain the minimum amount of operating system software required to support the applications it is executing.

The rest of the system consists of global memory and global I/O—devices such as disk drives and tape drives. A closer look at the AU or SU reveals a self-contained computer system, which has all of the processing power and memory required to do any of the tasks of the computer system. Each of these functional units will be built with the same set of boards: a processor board and up to four memory boards. The processor board consists of the microprocessor, an interrupt controller, timers, ROM sockets, a Multibus interface, and an iLBX interface. The memory board is a dual-port design with one port interfacing to the Multibus system bus so other bus masters can access the memory. The other port interfaces to the iLBX bus, thereby providing a private high-speed access path between the micoprocessor and its memory.

The performance of a functionally partitioned system is approximately proportional to the number of microprocessors in the system. Recall that the number one architectural goal of the functional unit configuration is to maximize on-board execution and to use the Multibus system bus only for data movement and interprocessor communication. There are some shared tables in global memory for the operating system, which permits the functional units to operate almost independently of each other. The only time conflicts occur is when a shared resource such as the Multibus or the system unit is used. A system with mostly local resources also has an added benefit in that the global I/O will be transferred over the Multibus faster, since there will be less contention for the system bus.

The operating system for this type of multiprocessor system will be complex. It must manage all the processors in a cooperative manner, since communication between the processes is taking place. It is apparent that confusion may

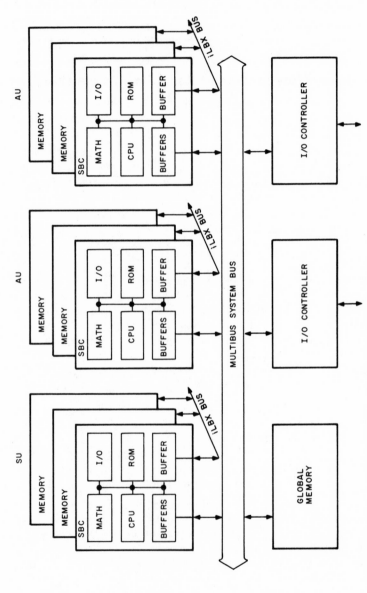

FIGURE 7-17 Functionally partitioned single-time-shared bus sysem.

270

result if two or more processes attempt to access and update a shared resource such as memory or disk storage at the same time. A global mutual exclusion scheme is necessary to guarantee that shared resources can be managed properly. This permits a process to reserve and release common resources without confusion. Device drivers must be written to allow multiple processors to access the I/O controllers. This requirement has implications for short- and medium-term scheduling and allocation of the shared resource.

7.7 SUMMARY

Multiprocessor systems are being developed because they provide several increased system capabilities, which include increases in performance, reliability, availability, and flexibility. Performance of single-microprocessor systems appears to be approaching limits imposed by the laws of electrical propagation delays. An alternative to improving the overall system performance is to use new system organizations which take advantage of multiple low-cost microprocessors. The low cost of microprocessors also significantly reduces the incremental cost/performance ratio of multiprocessor systems. The availability of uniprocessor systems is solely dependent on the availability of the individual modules that make up the system. A multiprocessor system can be used to provide a fail-safe capability to reconfigure itself dynamically in the event of an element failure. By design, the system is very flexible; it provides a very effective way to handle unpredictable loads, because each task can be dynamically allocated to any of the N processing modules in the system.

Three multiprocessor implementations built on top of the Multibus system bus have been evaluated: a single time-sharing bus system, a single time-sharing bus system with cache, and a functionally partitioned single time-sharing bus system. Of the three, the single time-sharing bus system was found to be the least complex to implement but was very limited because of the limited bandwidth of the Multibus system bus. With today's 16-bit microprocessors, only two microprocessors could be used. One way to reduce the processor modules' bus bandwidth demands is to put a cache memory in between the microprocessor and the system bus, as was done in the example of the single time-sharing bus system with cache. This type of multiprocessing provides more expansion capability. It supports three or four processor modules, but the implementation cost and the hardware design complexity are considerably higher. The third alternative, a functionally partitioned single time-sharing bus system, takes advantage of VLSI technology and provides dedicated local environments for each of the processor modules, called functional modules. A partitioned system permits each of the processor modules to operate at maximum speed independently of the system work load except when using common resources such as I/O. The hardware design complexity is similar to that of the single time-sharing bus design and provides better performance than the single time-sharing bus with cache. The major disadvantage of the functionally partitioned approach is that the memory usage is higher than in the other two approaches.

REFERENCES

Comtre Corporation: *Multiprocessors and Parallel Processing* (New York: John Wiley & Sons, Inc., 1974).

Siewiorek, Daniel P., C. Gordon Bell, and Allen Newell: *Computer Structures: Principles and Examples* (New York: McGraw-Hill Book Company, 1982).

Stone, Harold S., T. Chen, M. Flynn, S. Fuller, W. Lane, H. Loomis, Jr., W. McKeeman, K. Magleby, R. Matick, and T. Whitney: *Introduction to Computer Architecture* (Chicago: Science Research Associates, Inc., 1975).

8

Multicomputing
with Microprocessors

This chapter provides the basis for a conceptual understanding of multicomputing architectures and the motivations for using them. The effects of a multicomputing system on the system structure and the performance effects are examined. Also given in this chapter is an example of how to design a multicomputing system on the Multibus system bus.

8.1 DEFINITION OF A MULTICOMPUTING SYSTEM

As microprocessor costs continue to fall and the design aids to integrate microprocessors into systems continues to improve, these compact, powerful processing elements are being incorporated into many types of multiple-processor systems that provide higher system throughput or higher system availability, or both. A spectrum of multiple-microprocessor capabilities is described in Sec. 7.1. One point on that spectrum is multicomputing (Fig. 8.1). A multicomputing architecture is a top-down design philosophy that is based on a functional partitioning of the solution of a particular problem into a number of smaller and simpler subparts. Each of these subparts is divided into a separate well-defined functional module. Each of the functional modules performs a dedicated set of functionally bounded tasks, such as control of individual machines in automated factory environments and the control of various sensors and actuators in process control environments. The modules have well-defined interfaces to the other functional modules. These interfaces should be very solid and should become standard within the company or be industry standard.

Module interfaces are the key to success of a multicomputing design, since the designer deals with only the tasks of the functional module and the standard interface, and not with the entire problem. The module is designed, tested, and verified against the interface standard before it is integrated into the larger sys-

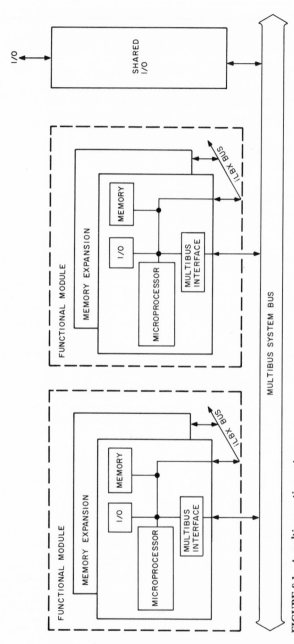

FIGURE 8-1 A multicomputing system.

tem. The interface standard must be very stable and should undergo very little change during the development of the project, because changes to the standard cause many problems with updating and retesting the modules that interface to it. A standard must be designed to absorb new VLSI quickly and easily, be technically usable, and be long-lived. If it is to become an industrial standard, it must also be adopted by a standards body, such as the Institute of Electrical and Electronics Engineers (IEEE), and be supported by multiple vendors.

Examples of electrical interface standards which were designed for easy incorporation of VLSI technology are the Multibus/IEEE-796 system bus, the iSBX/IEEE-P959 local I/O expansion bus, and the Multichannel high-speed DMA cable bus. Examples of software interface standards designed with VLSI technology in mind are the IEEE-P754 floating-point standard and Intel's iMMX[1] 800 Message Exchange Software, which permits two loosely coupled processors to communicate with each other.

A multicomputing system is built by using multiple microprocessors each of which has a dedicated task or function. The integration of the software and hardware into a single unit is called a functional module. Each of the functional modules needs to be as autonomous as possible. It can then be implemented independently of the other functional modules and can be optimized for specific requirements. Communication and sharing among functional modules is limited by the independent nature of the modules. Predetermined partitioning (static allocation) allows very simple, specialized executives to be developed for individual microprocessors. However, it requires that the system load or job balancing among the different functional modules be done during the development of the system. Therefore, the system can not be dynamically balanced in real time as a multiprocessing system can be. The isolation of each of the functional module's tasks permits simplified development and debugging of the specific executives on each of the microprocessors. These executives also can be extremely efficient. Some typical functions that can be partitioned easily into functional modules are mass storage, data processing, communications, and real-time control of machinery or the I/O portion of an operating system.

Increased performance of a multicomputing system is based on the concurrent execution of unrelated events. In contrast, for performance increases multiprocessors rely on parallelism, the processing of all bits of a word or multiple parts of a single program simultaneously. An example of a multicomputing system in the process control area is a testing system. It is divided into two basic parts, test and control. Each of the test functional modules is dedicated to testing a particular module or assembly. The control functional module is used to coordinate the testing, monitor the test results, and perform data logging as

---

[1]iMMX is a trademark of Intel Corporation, Santa Clara, California.

required. Each of these modules is independent of the other. If one of the test modules failed, it could be taken off-line and the rest of the system would continue to operate. If the control module failed, each of the test modules could become an independent test station. The test monitoring and data logging would be lost, but the factory could continue to operate. As capacity in the test area increases, more test modules can be added and have a minimal effect on the rest of the system.

From a hardware point of view, a functional module must have the capability of sharing some but not all of the system resources with the other functional modules, DMA controllers, and special processing units. The shared resources are called global resources. Each functional module has a set of resources which are local or private to it and can be accessed only by it. A typical functional module (Fig. 8-1) consists of a microprocessor, its control circuitry, RAM, programmable read-only memory (PROM) sockets, some dedicated I/O, and a Multibus interface. The Multibus interface provides the interprocessor gateway into and out of the functional module. Interprocessor communication is typically performed via shared memory. The shared memory, if it is dual-ported, can be located on the functional module or in global memory.

A very important attribute of multicomputing systems is the ability to support heterogeneous processing elements effectively. Such elements have dissimilar attributes such as different microprocessor architectures, address spaces, available resources, and resource management policies. The wide range of VLSIs available today allows the designer to specialize a particular function in a microcomputer system and pick the best cost and performance trade-offs for that function. The multicomputing architecture is the glue that permits all the functional modules to be put together to perform the overall system function.

Multicomputing architectures also buffer the system from a particular type of VLSI. The functional modules are as autonomous as possible and are loosely coupled in contrast to multiprocessors, which require very tight interaction between processing elements. Each functional module sees only the system interface of the other modules and not the implementation behind it. One implementation can be replaced by another which uses a different microprocessor, and this will have no effect on the rest of the system. The reimplementation is localized on that functional module. This permits each application to successfully use the right microprocessor for a particular task or function, which balances the required price-performance trade-offs in a profitable manner.

In summary, a multicomputing system can be defined as a system which efficiently realizes concurrent programming concepts in a multiple-microprocessor machine. The machine is constructed from a federation of self-contained, nearly autonomous microprocessor modules, each with its own RAM, PROM, and dedicated I/O, that cooperate to achieve the solution of a particular problem. The system is based on a distributed control strategy through a high-level operating system that unifies and integrates the control of the logically distributed functional modules. Each of the functional modules has a unique local executive or operating system which operates asynchronously with respect to the other modules. Communication is effected through shared memory.

8.2 MOTIVATION FOR MULTICOMPUTING

As applications become more complex and more application code is written in high-level languages, a much higher demand is placed on the computer system to offer ever-increasing price-performance ranges. The design must be upward-compatible with future VLSIs so there is a clear migration path from today's design to tomorrow's higher-performance version. To meet this need, computer systems have gone to multiple loosely coupled microprocessors, or what is called a multicomputing architecture. Implementing multicomputing systems can be very difficult for both hardware and software relative to what a uniprocessing system would require, but it is significantly easier than implementing a multiprocessor system. The benefits of multicomputing clearly outweigh the risks in most multiple-microprocessor applications. Multicomputing provides most of the benefits of multiprocessors but is structured to be easier and less costly to implement. The benefits of a multicomputing architecture are:

- Increased throughput and reduced response time

- Modular design

- Design simplicity

- Extensibility and modular expansion

- Quick incorporation of new VLSI

- Standard interfaces

Of course, not all application problems can be solved by taking advantage of multicomputing architectures. A uniprocessor solution should be considered first because of its lower cost and less complex design. Careful design practices are rquired to realize a given cost and performance specification. The constraints of interprocessor synchronization and communication reduce the effective power of the microprocessors; this overhead can limit the total throughput as additional functional modules are created. Selection of the microprocessors, the allocation of functions to them, the organization of the data structures, and the system control strategy are important design issues which affect cost and performance.

Now we will examine the benefits of designing with a multicomputing architecture.

8.2.1 Increased Throughput and Reduced Response Time

In the past the speed of a computer system has been increased by developing faster primitive logic elements and utilizing concurrency, which takes advantage of the fact that many computations can be so configured as to allow several parts of the computation to be done at the same time. Faster primitive logic elements result in the construction of larger, faster central processors and memories, which can suffer from problems of cost, complexity, and reliability. The continuing decline in microprocessor costs will significantly reduce the incremental cost/performance ratios and make the use of concurrency to increase system speed an increasingly attractive alternative over large uniprocessing designs. Multicomputing architectures are designed to take advantage of that trend.

Concurrency can be introduced in a computer system at different levels: individual bits, single operations, subtasks, or entire tasks. The successive levels of concurrency involve higher levels of complexity in the concurrent functions. VLSI microprocessors make task-level concurrency increasingly attractive because microprocessors are inexpensive and are able to carry out very complex functions. This type of concurrency is central to the multicomputing approach to computation. The approach is best applied to problems that lend themselves to decomposition into a set of relatively independent tasks with little need for global information or synchronization. If a problem meets these requirements, maximum task-level concurrency can be achieved. Individual tasks can be assigned to separate functional modules, and the functional modules can execute the tasks without much intercommunication.

Each functional module in the multicomputing system can be independently upgraded by replacing it with a new functional module which incorporates the newest and fastest microprocessors as new technology becomes available and the system throughput requirements increase. The semiconductor industry can design and fabricate new and faster devices every two to four years. This is usually quicker than a new complex multiprocessor system can be built. A multicomputing architecture supports system upgrades easily and quickly because the functional module is partitioned. Therefore, only a subset of the total problem need be reimplemented, which minimizes the effort. The interface of the functional module is well defined, making the reimplementation straightforward. A functional module can also be reimplemented to lower its cost by using new highly integrated VLSI components. New products can get to the marketplace quicker and with less risk. The development time and expenses are minimized because the implemented system is a mix of old, proven designs and new, higher-performing or lower-cost designs.

PERFORMANCE IN REAL-TIME SYSTEMS

Many real-time control systems have feedback loops between the computer and the outside environment. The data is sensed by the computer; some computations are made; and the results generate some actions which affect the outside environment. The new environmental data is fed back to the computer through its sensors. Real-time digital control systems are designed to regularly sense conditions of the controlled process and respond with signals to actuators that control the processes. Also, real-time system designs typically allow static partitioning and allocation, which makes real-time control systems a perfect fit for a multicomputing architecture.

Real-time situations often demand a time response from sensing an event to taking some action which is very critical. Performance is measured more in terms of response time than throughput. Another real-time requirement is the ability to handle bursts of events, which may require a large and immediate increase in processing throughput over normal conditions. Local intelligence usually can meet such response requirements more easily than a centralized system can.

It is very difficult to write an operating system that handles real-time requirements and human interface requirements at the same time, since these two sets of requirements have opposing effects on the operating system. The real-time operating systems must be small and fast and have limited functions, more like an executive than a complete operating system. In contrast, the human interface is required to be friendly to the user; that is, it must be very easy to use and very forgiving of mistakes. The interaction is very flexible, and the operating system tells the user what is needed instead of just displaying go–no-go status. The friendlier the human interface, the more elaborate the code must be and the slower the real-time response of the system will be.

Many real-time control systems are now being used by operators with little or no computer training who demand a friendly, intelligent interface with the system. This function can be most economically provided by logically distributed intelligence dedicated to being friendly. The system can be divided into two basic parts: the real-time modules and the human interface modules. The real-time modules can be fast and simple and have small executives controlling them. The human interface module can have a large quantity of memory and a complex operating system that is very friendly (to the operator). The system components can be optimized for both parts of the applications.

In summary, the basic nature of multicomputing systems is to divide a problem into a number of subproblems. Each of the subproblems can be attacked with its own microprocessor. This dedication of hardware permits the response time and throughput of each of the subproblems to be as fast as possible. The independence of each of the subproblems permits the easy upgrading of the hardware with future VLSI technology of a particular functional module without affecting the other functional modules in the system.

8.2.2 Module Design and Design Simplicity

The multicomputing architecture forces the designer to use modular design methods. By partitioning the system in a functional manner and assigning individual modules to particular tasks, hardware and software designs of large, complex systems are simplified, productivity is increased, and the debugging phase of the project is facilitated. This modular approach can also be used to allow system expansibility with little or no cost burden added to a base product.

The designer starts a typical design by defining the system by its requirements; the system must be described or represented in terms of its function and performance. This ensures that all of the important aspects of the system design will be based on the specifications and requirements of the system. Once the functions to be performed are defined, the design is partitioned into a set of logical blocks each of which is a functional module. Together the functional modules have the capability of performing all of the desired system functions. Once they have been selected, the interfaces between them must be identified. The interfaces define what resources must be shared, if the modules must synchronize information, and what performance is required. A functional simulation can then be carried out to determine if the functional design is capable of producing the desired results. Once satisfied that the functional description is correct, the designer can develop block diagrams which show how each of the various hardware and software modules go together in the system.

Next, suitable standard interfaces are selected or new interface standards are based on the interface requirements previously established. New interfaces should be avoided if at all possible because the design will lose all the benefits of using industry-standard products that support the standard interface in the design. Among those benefits is the use of products of multiple vendors that provide connectability and portability between different designs. Development time and cost are reduced because the interface is already developed, tested, and verified. (This is discussed in more detail in Sec. 1.2.) In the future, when upgrades are needed, the system designer will have the option of building a new functional module in-house or purchasing a functional module that supports that standard from an outside vendor. The silicon itself will be evolving to connect directly with industry-standard interfaces, which will make the functional modules even less costly.

Once the system is partitioned and the interfaces are defined, the system must be built. The system structure is developed to formally establish the control relations between the functional modules. The structure can then be breadboarded, or a prototype can be designed. This process of decomposing and refining the design can be repeated on each of the functional modules. This takes the design into smaller and smaller blocks until the entire system is implemented. Each of the functional modules can be individually tested and refined. Once the individual modules are complete, they can be merged with other functional modules, where they can be tested and refined. This process is continued until the entire system is completed.

The approach used to design multicomputing systems enforces a modular or structured design approach to building systems. This approach leads to systems that are more comprehensible, easier to debug, more reliable and flexible, and quicker to prove correct than large monolithic designs. The modular problem decomposition strategy offers greater conceptual clarity from the point of view of the system designer. It also enables better evaluation of overall system performance and assesement of the contributions and interactions of the individual functional modules. Large uniprocessor systems are typically very difficult to debug and prove correct, partly because of a lack of modularity. Also, it is easier to incorporate future advances in VLSI and other technologies in these functional modules because of the well-defined interfaces. The designer need only design a functional module that meets the hardware and software interface standards in order to provide a new, higher-performing system.

Separating the design into functional modules helps to simplify the entire design task. It is easier to solve five small problems than one large one, which may be overwhelming. In large monolithic designs, coupling between subsystems is generally much tighter than coupling between functional modules. Any change in a subsystem can ripple through the entire system and cause the design task to grow exponentially. The structuring of the design to maintain independence of the functional modules is the key to success of the multicomputing approach.

A modular extensible structure is extremely appealing in terms of cost for today's highly programmable multifunctioned VLSI component technology. A single hardware design can support many different interfaces such as Intel's 8274 Multiprotocol serial controller (MPSC), which supports two complete serial channels that can be programmed to operate as an asynchronous, a byte synchronous, or a bit synchronous communication channel. Minimizing the number of hardware module types and allowing them to be used repetitively results in a very attractive cost structure. Each functional module can be customized with software and standard add-on modules, such as iSBX Multimodule boards, to give it a particular set of capabilities. This approach also minimizes service costs, because there are fewer board products to learn and the number of items to be put in inventory also is minimized.

The SBC user can purchase off-the-shelf hardware and software modules to produce a specific functional module. One example is a serial network architecture (SNA) network controller which is made by putting Xicom Technologies Corporation's SNA MicroNode[2] software package on Intel's iSBC 88/45 Advanced Data Communications Processor board. Together these products

[2]MicroNode is a trademark of Xicom Technologies Corporation, Larkspur, California.

form an SNA functional module which provides a low-cost, high-performance interface to IBM SNA/SDLC communications networks.

8.2.3 Flexibility and Modular Expansion

Flexibility is a measure of the ease with which a system configuration can be changed. Modular expansion is a measure of the degree of compactness and isolation of system elements that can be added to or taken off. A highly flexible system is usually highly modular, whereas a highly modular system may not be very flexible. Many systems today are capable of modular expansion of most of the system hardware, but they lack the software flexibility necessary to incorporate additional or new system elements effectively. Multicomputing systems can easily provide modular expansion, which permits the tuning of potential processing power to meet the demands of a particular task by incremental addition or deletion of functional modules. Multicomputers permit the design to be generic for a set of basic problems; functional and capacity extensions can be used to accommodate particular applications without redesigning the basic system. This capability allows a smooth transition to be made in the size of the computer system when there is a need to handle larger or specialized problems. It is also possible to alter the configuration of the functional module tasks in response to changing problem demands or requirements. Multicomputers typically are not capable of real-time (by the operating system) flexibility and modular expansion, but they are easily modified during a system redesign to provide entirely new capabilities.

8.2.4 Incorporating New VLSI Quickly with Standard Interfaces

One of the biggest problems that faces a system designer today is keeping up with VLSI technology. Each year sees the introduction of new devices that are cheaper and faster and have higher reliability than their predecessors. The functional density and interface difficulty are increasing at a similar rate. This avalanche of technology can strain products and the individual's ability to assimilate its effects. The strain can threaten products and entire companies; products can become obsolete before they reach the marketplace.

The multicomputing architecture was designed to handle the rapidly changing technology. It is based on partitioning a problem among multiple microprocessor modules. The system designer needs to have a goal of making each of the hardware and software interfaces between the modules an industry standard in order to minimize the design effort and take advantage of a proven interface. Each functional module becomes a building block for the system. This permits the system, in the future, to take advantage of new products that were designed to that interface standard. Take as an example a multicomputing system that was designed with one of its functional modules based on Intel's iSBC 86/12A or National Semiconductor's BLC 86/12, an SBC with local PROM, I/O, 32K to 64K bytes of dual-ported RAM, and a 5-MHz 8086 microprocessor. If more performance is needed from it, this functional module can be replaced with Intel's iSBC 86/14, a totally compatible upgrade of the iSBC 86/12A with an 8-MHz 8086. If more performance is needed later, Intel's iSBC 286/10 can be installed; it is an iSBC 86/12 look-alike which uses an 8-MHz iAPX 80286 microprocessor. The iSBC 286/10 provides performance two to four times better than that of the iSBC 86/14. Moreover, the performance of this functional module can be increased four to eight times over that of the original iSBC 86/12 with the iSBC 286/10 without making major changes to the overall system. The required changes were localized to one functional module, and the other functional modules in the system were not affected. This permits the system to be upgraded quickly and easily. That in turn, improves the competitive position in the marketplace since, quickly and easily, the product can be the first with the newest, highest-performing technology.

8.3 MULTICOMPUTING ARCHITECTURES WITH THE MULTIBUS FAMILY

In this section we will see how multicomputing architectures can be used in the effective design of systems with the Multibus family of structures.

The Multibus family supports many levels of hardware system expansion capabilities, which provides the system designer with a wide range of cost-performance solutions based on industry-standard interfaces. The interfaces provide open, flexible, and upgradable designs through:

- Expansion by adding Multibus/IEEE-796–compatible boards

- Expansion of on-board memory capability by using the iLBX bus

- Low-cost, incremental I/O expansion by using iSBX/IEEE-P959 bus–compatible boards

- Expansion of high-speed I/O capabilities by using the Multichannel cable bus

Recall that the multicomputing architecture is based on a modular partitioning of a problem into a set of smaller, more manageable problems. This partitioning requires that the hardware and software also be modular and configurable. The Multibus/IEEE-796 system bus is the foundation of the Multibus family; it provides a modular system expansion capability that the other family members build upon. The system bus supports multiple 8- and 16-bit functional modules. The address range supported is up to 16M bytes, and data transfer rates of up to 5 megatransfers per second can be obtained. The system bus interconnection scheme is transparent to the tasks on and the quantity of the functional modules. The Multibus structure provides a very reliable interconnection scheme owing to its relatively low complexity. Its cost also is relatively low as a percent of the total board cost because of the VLSI device support that is available. The entire Multibus interface portion of the board design can be implemented by using less than 10 percent of the board area, which leaves 90 percent of the board for implementing the required board function.

Multibus-based multicomputing systems have a high degree of modularity. The hardware configuration can be changed by simply adding or removing functional modules. Each functional module must be self-contained; that is, all of the memory and local I/O resources required to perform the assigned task are local to that functional module and must not use the system bus for expansion of the module's local resources. The iLBX memory expansion bus permits the functional module to expand its memory capacity beyond what could be physically placed on the board. The memory capacity can be changed by adding memory boards to or removing them from the iLBX bus. This structure results in the creation of a logical or virtual SBC; the memory associated with that functional module appears as if it were all on-board or local memory (Fig. 8-2). In a multicomputing system there can be multiple independent iLBX buses and each functional module can control its own iLBX bus.

The functional module's local I/O can also be supplemented simply by using low-cost iSBX Multimodule boards. The functional module can be configured precisely by choosing the appropriate iSBX Multimodule board to satisfy the individual application needs at a lower cost than using a full Multibus expansion I/O board. Since the resource is local to the functional module, the Multibus interface is available for other system activities such as sending messages and data movement.

Today many applications require the ability to process data at very high rates. This means that data must flow into and out of the system at similarly high rates, and that necessitates the connection of numerous high-speed I/O devices to the system. This real-time activity can saturate the system bus. Even if the system bus does not become completely saturated, the bandwidth required for other bus functions such as execution and communication will be sacrificed and the result will be an overall degradation of system performance. One way to avoid this problem is to remove the real-time high-speed I/O from the system bus. The Multichannel bus provides a standard high-speed I/O gateway which can be connected to the system memory without using the system bus. This permits the data to be moved directly between the memory and the high-speed I/O device. The Multibus bandwidth thereby saved frees the Multibus system bus for other activities (Fig. 8-3).

In summary, high-performance multicomputing systems are based on concurrent execution of events. The Multibus family supports concurrency by permitting multiple operations on multiple functional modules simultaneously. Each of the functional modules has its local high-performance bus structures that support the independent program execution. For applications that require

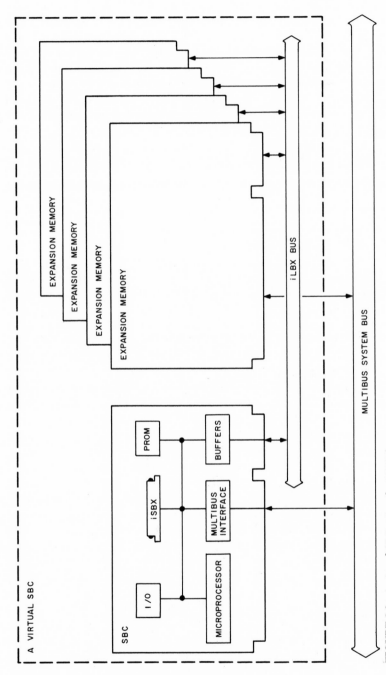

FIGURE 8-2 A virtual SBC using the iLBX bus.

285

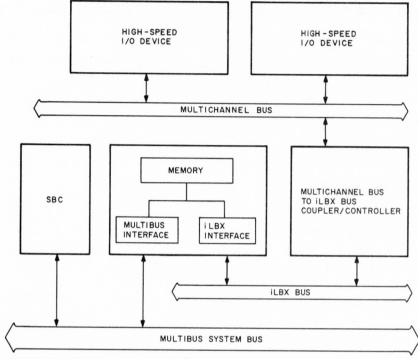

FIGURE 8-3 Multichannel bus to memory architecture.

more memory than can fit on a single SBC, the iLBX bus provides a private high-speed microprocessor-to-memory data path to memory expansion modules. Since the iLBX bus is local to the SBC, there is no contention for the memory bus, which provides a guaranteed microprocessor-to-memory bandwidth. This bandwidth is independent of the number of functional modules in the system, since each module has a dedicated iLBX bus. The performance of a functional module can be guaranteed independently of the system configuration. The concept of using independent dedicated bus structures to increase system performance is available in the I/O portion of an SBC design with the iSBX and Multichannel buses.

8.3.1 How to Use a System Bus in a Multicomputing Architecture

The Multibus system bus can have up to three major functions in a system architecture. They are (1) interprocessor communication, (2) block data movement, and (3) execution of the instructions and operand fetching done by the microprocessor. The goal in the multicomputing architecture is to use only the first two major functions in order to preserve as much system bandwidth as possible.

INTERPROCESSOR COMMUNICATION

In multicomputing systems there is a need for the different functional modules to be able to signal each other the occurrences of certain events. This signaling requires that, on demand, the microprocessor be preempted from the current task, save its internal state, and begin executing a different task. The most commonly used way to do that is to use interrupts.

Interrupts can be sent between functional modules in two ways: directly via Multibus interrupt lines or by defining a special memory location that will generate an interrupt to the local microprocessor when another bus master writes data into that memory location. The direct interrupt approach provides a path on the Multibus system bus by using dedicated interrupt lines. The source of the interrupt consumes a single line. A functional module that resides on the system bus can recognize the signal and service the interrupt. Since the source is fixed, the servicing module knows from the line level where the request is from. This eliminates the need for the requesting module to add an identification tag to the service request. The Multibus structure allows up to eight interrupt lines. This limit on the number of interrupt lines can cause difficulty in larger systems: it leads to the sharing of interrupt lines, which causes software difficulties. There is also a performance impact, since all microprocessors that share the interrupt lines are interrupted even if the signal is not destined for them.

Another approach is to design into the hardware a memory or I/O location that is uniquely associated with a functional module. The hardware would be located on the functional module and would generate an interrupt to the local microprocessor each time some data was written into its special memory or I/O location. The local microporcessor would then service the request and turn off the interrupt. This method permits functional modules to generate and recognize multiple interrupt addresses. The address recognition is by the hardware, which means that each functional module is interrupted only to service requests sent to it. Another advantage of this method is that it allows information to be passed with the interrupt. This means that interrupt information such as a return address or a pointer to a task control block can be passed on the interprocessor communication mechanism. The major disadvantage to this approach is the additional cost of the hardware to provide the address recognition and interrupt capabilities.

BLOCK DATA MOVEMENT

Block data movement involves moving the contents of continuous memory location from one functional module environment to another. One method of performing block transfers is to use direct memory access (DMA) hardware, which is designed to move blocks of data between memory or I/O ports very quickly. Some of the newer microprocessors provide DMA integrated into the microprocessor chip or DMA with very efficient string move instructions. Block movement is particularly applicable to dealing with functional modules that manage moderate-size blocks of data such as mass-storage devices, graphics, and voice generation.

EXECUTION OF CODE

The first application of the Multibus system bus, when it was introduced in 1975, was to connect an Intel 8080 microprocessor to its memory and I/O devices. All of the microprocessor's instructions and operand fetches were performed over the system bus. The Multibus system bus was used primarily as an execution bus. The bandwidth or transfer rate of a system bus, generally over time, becomes the limiting factor in the overall system performance in systems that use the system bus as an execution bus. Of the three major system bus functions (interprocessor communication, block data movement, and code execution), the code execution function is the most demanding of the system bus. Every system has a fixed transfer rate that is designed into it. Over time, as microprocessors become faster and faster, systems that use the system bus for execution will become system bus bandwidth–limited. If a system has a goal to use two or three generations of new microprocessors over its life span, its architecture must not use the system bus for execution.

In summary, one of the goals of a multicomputing architecture is to partition each of the functional modules so that it is an independent microcomputer minisystem. This results in preserving the system bandwidth. Of the three system bus functions listed above, only the first two, interprocessor communication and block movement, are required. All execution is local to that functional module and does not use the system bus. This minimizes the use of the system bus and provides bandwidth headroom growth for future system upgrades.

8.4 A SIMPLE MULTICOMPUTING SYSTEM EXAMPLE

A fire and security system is one application area into which a multicomputing architecture fits nicely. The system monitors multiple sensors for door and window openings and smoke detectors, and also provides an operator control interface. The fire and security system is a fully distributed multiple processing system composed of completely asynchronous, nearly autonomous modules. The architecture allows for almost limitless extensibility without special reprogramming of the entire system. This section gives an example of how the fire and security system might be implemented by using a multicomputing architecture and the Multibus family structures.

8.4.1 Designing the System

The first step in designing the system is to break the problem into logically modular subproblems. Each subproblem is a region of highly interactive control whose relations with the other subproblems are much less interactive. The architecture consists of a set of asynchronously communicating subproblems or tasks. Figure 8-4 is a functional flow diagram that represents the fire and security system. The system can be divided into four functions—monitoring the smoke detectors, temperature, and window and door positions throughout the building—and a supervisor that is in charge of the overall system. Each function is nearly independent of the others. The monitor functions must read each of the sensors at least once a second and report to the supervisor once a minute that the building is in a normal condition. The supervisor function receives status information from the monitor functions and displays it to the operator(s). If an abnormal condition occurs, the system must alert the operator, update the operator display, and if a fire is detected, call the fire department.

The block diagram of the fire and security system is shown in Fig. 8-5. The problem can be broken down into two basic functions: (1) the real-time I/O module and (2) the human interface module. The real-time I/O module has limited intelligence which scans the smoke detectors, the temperature transductors, and the window and door position indicators. The module has the ability to enable and disable a sensor line and perform self-test functions. The human interface module supports a color graphics operator console and a hardcopy device and provides the following functions: log events, provide the operator with a graphic display of building status, generate hard copy of reports of system events, and provide an automatic interface to fire department.

Three of the four functions are real time in nature and can be done by one hardware unit, the real-time I/O functional module. Figure 8-6 is a block diagram of the real-time I/O module hardware. Both the smoke detectors and the door limit switches are converted to standard TTL signals via the conditioning strips. The SBC selected provides 48 TTL I/O lines. Additional I/O can be added via an iSBX Multimodule, which provides 24 I/O lines. A baseboard can be designed to handle up to three iSBX Multimodule boards. If two iSBX Multimodule boards are used, 48 I/O lines can be added to the baseboard's 48 to generate a total of 96. The third iSBX connector is needed to provide eight analog inputs for converting the temperature sensors to a digital reading. Additional analog inputs can be installed via the iSBX Multimodule connectors if fewer digital I/O lines are needed. This gives the basic design the flexibility to be customized for each of the different building installations with minimal cost overhead.

The last of the four functions, the human interface, can best be handled on a separate functional module (Fig. 8-7). The same baseboard can be used as was used with the real-time I/O module but with different iSBX Multimodules

290

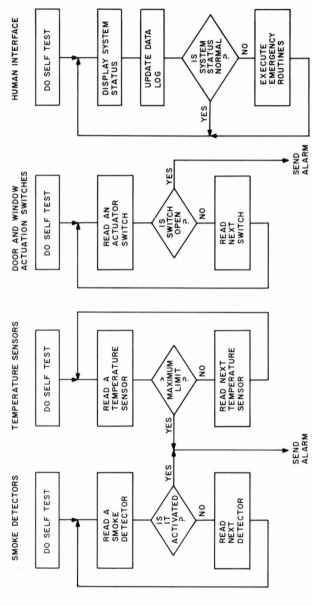

FIGURE 8-4 A functional flow diagram of the fire and security system.

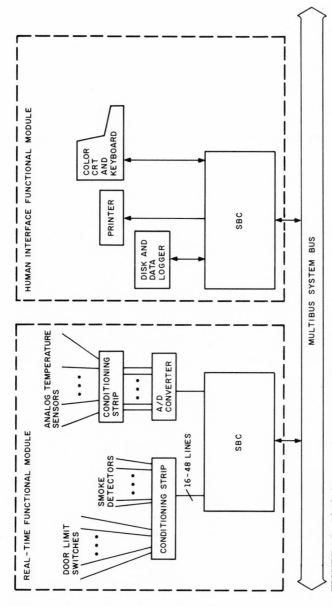

FIGURE 8-5 Block diagram of fire and security system.

291

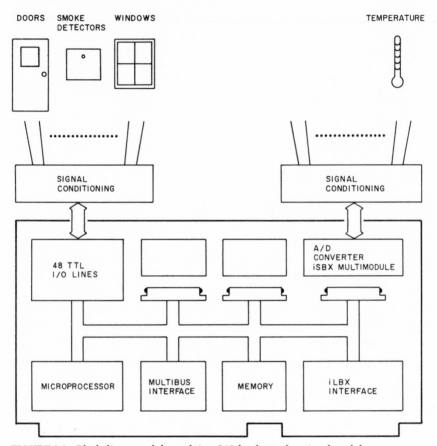

FIGURE 8-6 Block diagram of the real-time I/O hardware functional module.

mounted on it. The disk storage can be handled with a floppy disk Multimodule board that can support up to four 8-in floppy disks or four 5¼-in floppy disks. A color graphic Multimodule can support the visual display and the keyboard. The hard-copy printer can be driven with the standard parallel port on the SBC.

The SBC provides up to eight 28-pin sites, which support many different types of 28-pin memory devices such as PROMs, ROMs, electrically erasable PROMs (EEPROMs), and byte-wide RAMs. This flexibility is made possible by the standard pin-out compatibility of the different memory devices. The 28-pin sites permit the system designer to install the precise amount of memory as well as the required type—PROM, EEPROM, RAM. The same baseboard can be used in different applications, and in each application the required type and amount of memory can be installed. If the application requires more memory than can be installed on the baseboard, the iLBX interface can be used to expand the memory of the SBC to other boards without using the Multibus system bus. This permits the human interface module to have large amounts of RAM if needed. Operating systems with very friendly interfaces typically require large amounts of RAM (more than 100K bytes) to implement the friendliness.

Once the problem has been partitioned, the requirements for interconnection of the modules must be identified. How much communication capability is necessary depends upon the frequency and speed with which information must be exchanged between the individual functional modules. The greater the concentration of local function, the lower the demand on the interconnection. The message traffic is typically a large number of very small messages that need to be processed very quickly. This means that the overhead of sending and receiving messages in the hardware and software must be small and fast.

The software that performs the intermodule communication can be simplified if the relation between the functional modules can be based on a transaction-processing method. The method requires that the system operate by functions or tasks requesting and receiving actions from the other modules. For example, one functional module invokes action on the part of another functional module by sending a command with some data or a message. Command and data are placed in a queue in memory. The queues are formed between

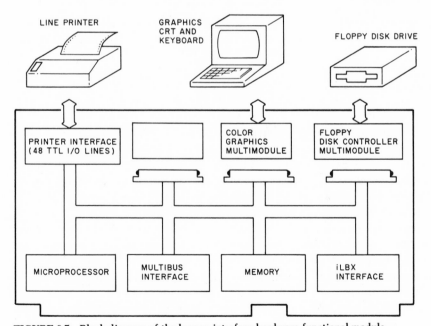

FIGURE 8-7 Block diagram of the human interface hardware functional module.

the functional module's tasks. They facilitate pipelining of commands and increase the functional module's independence. Without queues the sender of a message would have to wait until the receiver could take the message. If the queue becomes full, the sender must wait until the receiver has freed enough queue space. The queue size must be so adjusted that a sender rarely waits.

The recipient functional module must first ask for a message. If a message is not present, the functional module waits. If a message is present, the functional module services the command and returns a reply describing the results. All of the functional modules must be cooperative; that is, all of the functional modules must work together toward the common end. If one of the modules does not follow the communication protocol, the system can not operate correctly.

The message-passing protocol must provide a uniform interface for all the functional modules independently by the type of microprocessor and the software executive that is controlling it. The protocol must also provide a reliable, variable-length message transfer mechanism between the functional modules. There should be no constraints on the message sizes. The message software needs to inform the user task of the status of an attempted message delivery. This provides the user with great flexibility to react and guarantee the reliable delivery of messages between tasks on different functional modules. This type of cooperative intermodule communication fits very well into a multicomputing system.

A standard message-passing protocol that meets the above requirements is the Multibus interprocessor protocol (MIP) specification, which was developed by Intel Corporation. MIP specifies a standard method for processes executing on different Multibus-compatible SBCs. The protocol allows both 8- and 16-bit microprocessors to communicate by passing data between one another in a reliable, controlled manner. Intel has converted the MIP specification into a product called iMMX 800, a software implementation of MIP. It provides intertask communication through shared memory of different functional modules and executes different tasks within different executives.

In the fire and security system example, the software interface to each of the individual functions was so defined that another functional module can simply send a formatted command message with a return address to it. The message is put in a queue in global memory or in its own dual-ported memory. Each function waits for messages to arrive, services them, and returns the results. If the human interface needs to know the status of the smoke detectors, it sends a status type of command message to the real-time module and awaits a reply with the smoke detector's status. If the temperature reading goes beyond a set limit and the real-time module determines that a fire may have started, it sends a command message to the human interface module reporting the condition. The human interface module will alert the operator, call the fire department, and activate the building alarm system. Then the human interface module sends a message back to the real-time module that appropriate action has been taken. The interaction can be made simple and straightforward while maintaining flexibility.

Multicomputing architectures are based on having a reliable communication mechanism. Otherwise, messages could be lost and the system made unreliable. The Multibus structure provides a very reliable communication path. All system bus transfers incorporate a handshake methodology which requires both the sending module and the receiving module to be actively involved. The sending module can not complete the transfer without the receiving module's acknowledging that it received the data. This bus protocol is used for each byte transferred. Additional details on Multibus bus cycles can be obtained in Chap. 2.

8.4.2 Adding High-Speed I/O

An option to the fire and security system is a surveillance camera which can display different areas of the building and alert the operator if anything moves in a specified area. The surveillance option can be incorporated into a functional module and easily added to the system.

Figure 8-8 is a functional representation of the surveillance option. A frame of data is read from a camera and the data is processed. The high-resolution graphics display unit is updated, and the frame just processed is compared with the preceding frame from the camera. If there is no difference, a frame of data is transferred from the next camera and the operation is repeated. If there is a difference, the area that is different on the graphics display is marked and the operator is alerted.

Figure 8-9 is a block diagram of the surveillance functional module, which consists of three hardware modules: the surveillance controller unit (SCU), the video camera reader unit (VCRU), and a large RAM board. The three units are connected together via the iLBX bus, which provides a high-speed, private data path. The SCU initiates a surveillance operation by requesting the VCRU to select a particular camera and transfer one frame of data into the RAM board. The VCRU will request the iLBX bus from the SCU. Once the VCRU is granted access to the iLBX bus, it will directly access one frame or scan of data that represents the image seen by the camera. When the task has been completed, the VCRU returns control of the iLBX bus to the SCU and notifies it of the completion. The SCU then processes the data to correct for minor camera movements. The SCU updates the high-resolution graphics display with the current frame of data. This frame of data is then compared with the preceding frame from the same camera. If there is no difference, the SCU requests the VCRU to go on to the next camera. If there is a difference, the SCU will mark the area, update the operator display, and send a message to the supervisor to alert the operator of the situation.

In this example the display requires a high-speed interface between the SCU and the high-resolution graphics display. One approach to solving this problem is with a custom-designed I/O interface and controller. This approach is often expensive and can consume lengthy development time. Another approach to solving the problem is to use a standardized general-purpose intelligent controller with a flexible I/O bus architecture that is capable of supporting a wide range of device requirements. This approach takes advantage of a proven I/O bus structure while minimizing development time and expense by maximizing the use of an accepted, industry-standard I/O bus and permitting the use of off-the-shelf hardware.

The Multichannel bus was used between the SCU and the high-speed graphics display because it provides a very high bandwidth (up to 8M bytes per second) and sufficient physical distribution (up to 50 ft, or 15 m). The Multichannel bus provides the system with a demonstrated reliable foundation for all of the high-speed I/O transfers. The primary goal of the graphics interface is to provide a flicker-free updating capability. The updating requires a high-performance interface with a transfer rate of approximately 1M byte per second,

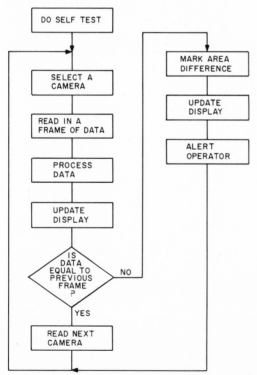

FIGURE 8-8 A functional diagram of the surveillance option.

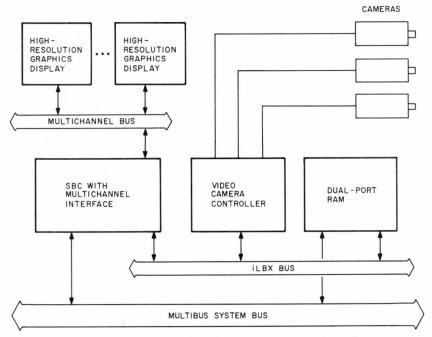

FIGURE 8-9 Block diagram of the surveillance hardware functional module.

which the Multichannel bus can easily handle. The interface must also have the capability of transferring anything from a few bytes up to 64K bytes of data. (The Multichannel can transfer up to 16M bytes per device.) Future expansion capability is built into the system, since the Multichannel bus can support up to 14 additional displays. The Multichannel bus also provides physical distribution of the displays from the multicomputer system electronics because the Multichannel bus signals are transmitted over a 60-wire flat cable. This permits the display(s) to be up to 50 ft (15 m) away from the system electronics.

In this example, it was demonstrated how a problem can be partitioned into a set of nearly independent tasks each of which is implemented separately. The system is then constructed by merging the independent tasks, and the result is a complete fire and security system. The system is modular in that the number of items monitored and controlled is expandable to meet the needs of the individual installation. The system can support modular expansion of such new capabilities as the surveillance option.

8.5 SUMMARY

The multicomputing concept is based on dividing a problem into a set of smaller, more comprehensible subproblems. The subproblems can then be solved by using independent hardware and software functional modules which in total provide the solution to the system design problems. Modularity results in structured designs which increase the comprehensibility of the system, the ease of debugging, the reliability and flexibility of the system, and the speed of verifying the correctness of the design.

Each number of the Multibus family, the Multibus system bus, and iLBX bus, the iSBX bus, and the Multichannel bus, provides the designer with all the basic tools to construct a multicomputing system. The Multibus system bus provides a reliable communication link between all the functional modules and supports a high degree of modularity. The iLBX bus provides for local memory expnasion of a functional module without affecting the traffic on the Multibus system bus. The iSBX bus permits the functional module's I/O to be customized to meet the needs of each application. I/O expansion via the iSBX bus is low in cost and can operate at local I/O speeds because the Multibus system bus is not required. And the last member of the Multibus family, the Multichannel bus, provides a standard, very high speed gateway into and out of the multicomputing-based system.

The Multibus family of buses provides the structures that support concurrent execution of tasks by multiple functional modules, which results in very high performance systems. Since each functional module operates independently of the others, the response time can be optimized for each application and the overall system throughout increased. The functional module independence also permits upgrades of individual modules without affecting the other modules in the system. The upgraded module can incorporate new VLSI technology simply by designing the new technology to meet the requirements of the standard interface. The other functional modules view this new module as if it were the old one, since both old and new support the same standard interface.

REFERENCES

Eckhouse, R. H. Jr., and L. R. Morris: *Minicomputer Systems* (Englewood Cliffs, N.J.: Prentice-Hall, Inc. 1979)

Tomek, Ivan: *Introduction to Computer Organization,* (Rockville, Md.: Computer Science Press, Inc., 1981).

PART 3

Multibus
Family
Applications

9

System Design Guidelines

This chapter provides information on building systems which use the Multibus system bus family. Included are guidelines for system integration, the use of the various Multibus family structures, levels of compliance, and common system design mistakes. The notation throughout this book is the same as that defined for the Multibus system bus, covered in Sec. 2.1.

9.1 BUILDING MULTIBUS-BASED SYSTEMS

The Multibus system bus is an industry-standard OEM bus. To allow for many types of system configurations, the boards, backplanes, and card cages have many user-selectable options. Some of the options must be configured when the system is built; others may be chosen to fit the application. When building Multibus systems, the designer must be aware of several specific areas:

- Multimaster configuration
- Memory configuration and addressing
- Interrupt configuration
- Time-out
- Bus clocks
- Levels of compliance
- Mechanical considerations

Some general considerations and guidelines in each of these areas are provided in the following sections. Included in each section are some of the common configuration mistakes to avoid.

9.1.1 Bus Arbitration Techniques

There are two basic methods for resolving a master's priority on the Multibus system bus: serial and parallel priority. Each has its advantages and disadvantages, and its use is dictated by the application. In the following section we explain the system trade-offs and common configurations.

SERIAL PRIORITY

The Multibus specification can support a maximum of 16 masters. However, the standard hardware shipped with SBC boards allows for only a maximum of three masters in a serial-priority configuration. Serial priority is the simplest to use and requires no additional hardware. Its disadvantages are the limit of three masters and the inability to handle special-priority modes such as rotating priority. If your application requires three or fewer masters (and is not expected to go beyond three masters) and does not require special modes (e.g., rotating priority), then serial priority is correct for it.

When configuring a serial-priority system, the designer must decide which master has the highest priority and which the lowest. One criterion for choosing priority should be the maximum allowable latency for a particular master to get to its Multibus resource. The designer must trade off real-time transfers versus overall system performance. For example, a system with two processor boards and a disk controller requires some consideration. If the disk's real-time transfers must guarantee access to the bus the next cycle after its bus request, then the disk should be given the highest priority. In many disk applications, the disk board tends to saturate the bus and potentially limit the processors board's execution bandwidth. Therefore, if the disk board architecture allows the disk system to delay its bus access, then the disk should be placed in the lowest-priority slot and thereby allow the processor boards to utilize the bus bandwidth. This type of configuration can increase system performance if execution-bound. The application must be reviewed for real-time transfer requirements, high bus utilization requirements, and low bus utilization. Priority is normally configured in the same order for boards with these requirements.

Once the priority order of the bus masters has been decided, the designer must choose the location of the masters with respect to the backplane and configure the serial-priority signals (daisy chain) accordingly. Specifically, the BPRO∗ signal of the higher-priority master must be connected to the BPRN∗ input of the lower-priority master. On most standard Multibus-compatible backplanes, all adjacent slots provide the daisy chain connections of BPRO∗ and BPRN∗. If adjacent slots are used, only grounding of the highest-priority master's BPRN∗ input is required. (Note: this step is required even if there is only one master in the system and that master is required to access the bus.) If adjacent slots are not used, the daisy-chained signals must be wire-wrapped on the backplane to the appropriate slots. Figure 9-1 shows an example of Intel's iSBC

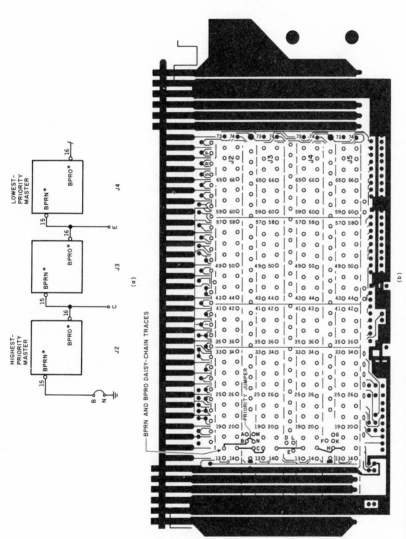

FIGURE 9-1 Serial-priority configuration example: (a) iSBC 604 schematic representation; (b) iSBC backplane configuration. (Note: Traces removed for clarity.)

604 backplane serial-priority configuration. In this example there are three masters that occupy adjacent slots J2 to J4. For this configuration only the highest-priority master in slot J2 requires its BPRN* input grounded for proper system operation. This is accomplished by jumpering stake pins B and N together on the backplane.

PARALLEL PRIORITY

Parallel priority allows the system bus to be expanded to 16 bus masters. Normally, parallel priority is chosen by a system designer when more than three masters are required for the system or when additional flexibility for priority resolving is required. The disadvantage of parallel priority is that additional circuitry is required over and above what is on the SBC boards. Various parallel-arbitration schemes are covered in Chap. 10.

When designing a system with parallel priority, the system designer must choose the parallel-priority method, the number of masters in the system, and the relative priority of the system masters. The decision on the latter is similar to that of serial priority (i.e., low latency, high bus utilization, low bus utilization). The use of special parallel-priority modes, such as rotating priority or software-selectable priority, are totally dependent on the application.

To configure the system with parallel priority, the signals BREQ* and BPRN* from each bus master must be connected to the priority-resolving circuitry. Each standard backplane available has different levels of configuration capabilities. On Intel's iSBC 604A/614A or equivalent backplanes, no parallel-priority circuitry capability is available. A system designer using this type of backplane must provide a small circuit board with the priority-resolving circuitry and must bring the BREQ* and BPRN* signals from the stake pins on the solder side of the backplane. Intel's iSBC 608/618 or equivalent backplanes provide the capability to add a basic parallel-priority circuit directly to the backplane. An added feature of these backplanes is that each slot's BREQ* and BPRN* signals are routed to the circuitry. Figure 9-2 shows an example of an iSBC 608 parallel-priority configuration. In it the four masters are placed in slots J8, J7, J2, and J1. Since the parallel-priority circuitry is provided on the iSBC 608 backplane, only the jumpering of the BREQ* and BPRN* signals for each master is required.

COMMON-BUS REQUEST

The CBRQ* signal, a bidirectional Multibus interface signal that is used in conjunction with the serial- and parallel-priority resolution schemes, improves bus access time by allowing a bus master to retain control of the Multibus interface without arbitrating for the bus on each transfer cycle. A bus master receiving the CBRQ* signal gives up the bus when a higher-priority master requests it. This occurs because of the removal of the lower-priority master's BPRN* signal. Also, depending on the CBRQ* configuration, a master that has lower priority than the master receiving CBRQ∗ can access to the bus request by driving the CBRQ∗ line active. As an example, Intel's 8289 bus arbiter chip provides many options for the various implementations of common-bus request. Table 9-1 is an explanation of the CBRQ∗ modes for the 8289 bus arbiter chip.

The system designer must decide which boards, if any, will use CBRQ∗ and the relative priority of those boards. Also, the designer must ensure that the chosen boards support the CBRQ∗ signal to meet the design requirements.

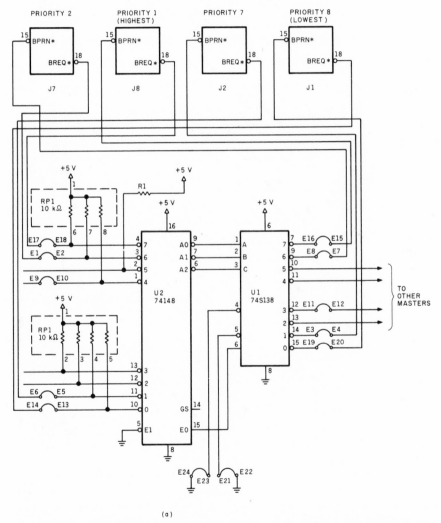

(a)

FIGURE 9-2 Parallel-priority configuration example: (a) Schematic representation; (b) iSBC 608 backplane configuration (next page). (Note: Traces removed for clarity.)

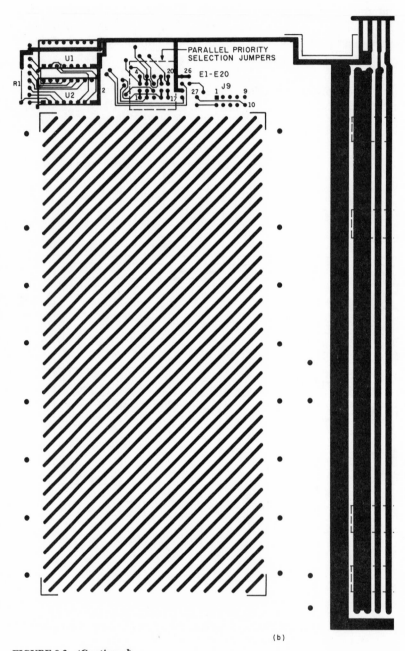

PARALLEL PRIORITY
SELECTION JUMPERS

U1

R1

U2

E1-E20

J9

(b)

FIGURE 9-2 *(Continued)*

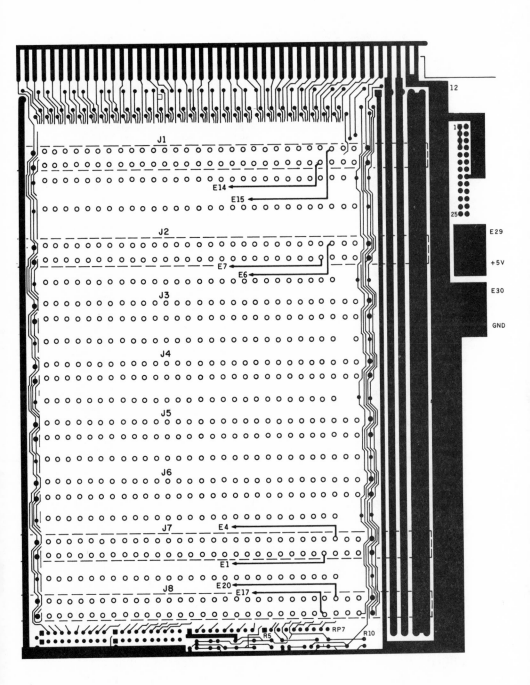

TABLE 9-1   8289 CBRQ* Modes

Interface state	CBRQ* state	ANYRQST state	Description
1	Low	Low	The bus arbiter that is controlling the Multibus interface retains control unless a higher-priority master deactivates BPRN* or the next machine cycle does not require the use of the Multibus interface. It may then be relinquished to a lower-priority device.
	High	Low	The bus arbiter that has control of the Multibus interface retains control until another bus arbiter pulls CBRQ* low. When CBRQ* goes low, the conditions are as described above.
2	Low	High	The bus arbiter that has control of the Multibus interface surrenders control to the bus arbiter that is pulling CBRQ* low upon completion of the current bus cycle, regardless of the requester's priority.
	High	High	The bus arbiter that has control of the Multibus interface retains control until another bus arbiter pulls CBRQ* low. When CBRQ* goes low, the conditions are as described above.
3	Low (ground)	High	The bus arbiter that has control of the Multibus interface surrenders the use of the Multibus interface after each transfer cycle.

When configuring a system, the designer must decide whether to use CBRQ* and the proper modes of operation. By not carefully configuring a system using the CBRQ* signal, the system designer can inadvertently lock out one or more masters from the bus.

An example of this situation is a system that contains three masters. The highest-priority master supports CBRQ* but arbitrates for the bus in a normal manner. The middle-priority master is in common-bus request mode and retains the bus after its first access. The lowest-priority master does not support the CBRQ* signal and expects to arbitrate for the bus via the BPRN* signal. In this case, depending on the middle-master's bus utilization, the lower-priority master may never gain access to the bus. The middle-priority master will not release the bus unless the highest-priority master requests the bus. The simple solution to this problem is to give the master that does not support the CBRQ* signal the highest priority. Special care should be taken to ensure that each master can properly arbitrate for the bus in a CBRQ*-based system. If CBRQ* is desired for the system, the designer must ensure that all masters in the system that do not support CBRQ* are given higher priority than the master receiving CBRQ*.

To guarantee that a system will work with masters that contain various levels of CBRQ* support and in any priority configuration, each bus master should be so configured that it surrenders the bus after each transfer cycle. This mode allows masters that do not support CBRQ* to work with masters that do, but it does not provide any performance enhancement.

The decision to use CBRQ* is based on the application requirement. Normally, masters that perform sequential access to the system bus can obtain large performance increases by using CBRQ*. Typically, masters that are performing DMA on the system bus or masters that are executing code on the system bus benefit from the CBRQ* configuration.

9.1.2 Memory Configuration and Addressing

When configuring a system, the designer must be aware of the size and type of memory in the system. Specifically, the designer must pay close attention to the following areas:

- Address space

- Data width

- Access time

- Dual-port memory

- Read-only memory

- Special functions

These system memory requirements are discussed in the following sections.

ADDRESS SPACE

How a memory is mapped in a particular system is application-dependent, but there are common configuration requirements that are application-independent. The system designer must consider the size of memory on each memory board in the system and the proper starting address. Each memory board must be configured so that its starting address meets the application requirement. If continuous memory is required, the designer must ensure that the starting address of a memory card is selected to begin where the address space of the preceding card ended.

If your application requires overlapped memory, i.e., system bus memory arrays that share common address space, ensure that your memory cards can support overlapped memory via the Multibus inhibit signals. Otherwise, avoid overlapping the system memory. Also, in many applications the local memory of an SBC card may overlap a system memory card's address space. Although there is nothing electrically or architecturally wrong with this configuration, the system designer must be aware that the portion of system memory which is overlapped can never be reached by the SBC board.

DATA WIDTH

Eight-bit memory can pose a problem in a system with 16-bit masters. Specifically, a 16-bit master can communicate with 8-bit memories, but the master must be aware of this memory. Many 16-bit microprocessors require a 16-bit-data-width execution code space; therefore, the 16-bit master cannot execute code out of 8-bit system memory. The system designer must carefully review the application requirements and select the proper memory width.

ACCESS TIME

The Multibus specification ensures that masters and slaves of different speeds can transfer data correctly. When reviewing an application, the designer should consider the access time of the memory cards in the system. By proper choice of the memory access time, the system performance can be increased from 5 to 25 percent. On the other hand, just choosing faster memory may not increase performance at all. The designer should review the access time requirements of the masters in the system and then make the memory access time decision. Figure 9-3 is a graph showing various Intel SBC masters' wait states performance versus system memory access times. As can be seen from the graph, large changes in memory access time are required before a master's performance increases. This is primarily due to the acknowledge synchronization time

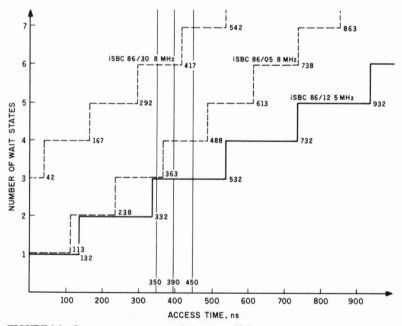

FIGURE 9-3 System memory access time versus SBC wait states.

required by the master. From the graph, Intel's iSBC 86/30 operating at 8 MHz can reduce the number of inserted wait states from seven to six by accessing system memory with an access time of 417 ns or less. However, the next performance increase does not occur until the memory access time decreases to 292 ns. Therefore, using memory boards with access times of 350 ns will not improve the system performance. Similar plots are shown for Intel's iSBC 86/ 05 and iSBC 86/12. The master's access time requirements must be reviewed for the best price-performance trade-off.

A similar plot should be developed to make an access time determination for the system. The specific SBC hardware reference manual should be checked for the first XACK* sampling point. To this the microprocessor cycle time for each wait state is added. For the iSBC 86/30 example, the XACK* is −208 ns. This means that, in order for a "one wait" cycle to occur, XACK* from the memory board must come a maximum of 208 ns prior to command. This, in Multibus-based systems, is illegal. The iSBC 86/30 microprocessor clock cycle time is 125 ns. The first legal XACK* sample point time is 42 ns, which occurs after three wait states. Every wait state boundary is a multiple of 125 ns. The optimum memory board access time requirement can now be determined by deciding which wait state boundary the access time should fall in. Ideally, the selected memory board's access time should be the farthest to the right of the boundary step before moving into the next wait state boundary. This yields the best price-performance trade-off.

DUAL-PORT MEMORY

Dual-port memory allows an SBC's on-board memory to be accessed from the system bus. This type of memory is beneficial in that data can be moved directly into an SBC's memory, but it can also pose a special problem to system designers in that it is "special" memory.

The first area a system designer must be aware of is "aliasing," which occurs when a location in dual-port memory has a different address from each port. On SBC boards this means that a memory location can have two unique addresses: one from the SBC's microprocessor and one from the Multibus system bus. The block diagram of Fig. 9-4 demonstrates the problem. In this diagram there are two SBC masters with dual-port memory. The first master has the on-board and system bus address based at 0000H. Therefore, each memory location has the same address from either port. Ideally, the second SBC would like to have the on-board and off-board addresses at the same location. Unfortuantely, the system bus side of the dual-port memory would overlap the address of the first SBC and cause system failures.

To overcome this problem, the system bus port is given a different base address into the memory. This offset prevents the overlap. For example, memory location 0000AH as addressed from the microprocessor has the address 1000AH when addressed from the system bus side. This problem occurs on most

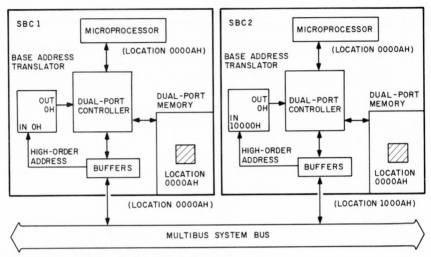

FIGURE 9-4 Multibus dual-port block diagram.

older SBCs that permanently fix the dual-port memory address from the micro-processor side at 0000H. Newer dual-port designs allow the configuration of the address from each port. This can prevent the aliasing problem, since the base addresses can be configured to be equivalent. However, many microprocessor families require RAM or ROM memory to be available for vector and register area. Failure to properly provide this area can lead to system problems. The designer should take both these situations into account when configuring the system and generating application software and firmware for it.

Another area to be aware of is a communication port located on a few SBCs' dual-port memory called the wake-up byte. This special memory location allows a Multibus master to interrupt another master by writing a value into it. It is primarily used for interprocessor communication. The user must be aware of each of these locations in the memory space or disable this feature on the SBCs that contain it. This precaution is especially necessary in systems that per-form power-up memory testing.

The final area for a system designer to be concerned with is in the use of the lock signal. There are two types of lock functions on the Multibus system bus. The first allows a bus master to keep the bus and prevent other masters from taking the bus away. This type of bus lock is extremely useful in real-time burst DMA transfers and semaphore exchange in a shared single-port system mem-ory. Dual-port memory poses a problem for semaphore exchanges in that the bus lock does not keep the on-board microprocessor from getting to its memory; the Multibus LOCK* signal is used for that purpose. The Multibus master sim-ply activates the LOCK* signal during a semaphore exchange and thereby pre-vents the on-board microprocessor from getting to its memory resource. Unfortunately, not all master boards or intelligent slaves support the LOCK signal. Also, lock is not supported on the early backplanes. The system designer must decide if the application requires a dual-port lock function and choose the master–intelligent slave combination accordingly. If the boards chosen do not support the dual-port lock function and a lock feature is required, then the lock function must be handled via software means or in global single-port RAM.

READ-ONLY MEMORY

Read-only system memory (ROM and PROM memory boards) does not pose any major system concerns unless the system performs a power-up memory test or the PROM board overlays system RAM memory. If a system performs power-up memory testing, then the system software must be aware of the location and size of the system PROM memory. When a PROM board overlays system RAM memory, the system designer must ensure that

1. The PROM board selected drives the inhibit signal.

2. The RAM board selected receives the inhibit signal.

3. The PROM board is configured to drive inhibit for the area affected by the overlay.

SPECIAL FUNCTIONS

Special functions include error-correction code (ECC) circuitry and parity-checking circuitry. ECC memory can be a problem if it is not properly designed into the system. Most of the available ECC memory boards do not self-initialize memory on power-up. This function is normally left up to the operating system. Some of the boards may not work unless they are initialized or the error-reporting portion of the ECC function is disabled.

Most parity and ECC memory boards have status registers which must be configured for unique I/O addresses on the system bus. The system designer must ensure that each memory register set has a unique address and that the operating system is aware of any special memory considerations. The system designer should also verify that the operating system can properly handle an ECC or parity error report.

9.1.3 Interrupt Configuration

The Multibus system bus supports interrupts of two types: non-bus-vectored and bus-vectored. In non-bus-vectored interrupts the bus vector is generated by the master device; in bus-vectored interrupts the vector is generated by the interrupting slave device.

Non-bus-vectored interrupts are the simplest to use and require no special consideration. The system designer must choose the interrupt sources, connect the interrupt sources to the programmable interrupt controller (PIC) properly, and initialize the PIC correctly. Non-bus-vectored interrupts are normally used when there are few bus interrupt sources or the system performance requirements allow the system interrupts to be "OR-tied." (Because of the open collector drivers, more than one interrupt source uses the same interrupt line.)

Bus-vectored interrupts have the same requirements as the non-bus-vectored ones and the additional requirement that all the slave PICs must be correctly initialized. The advantage of bus-vectored interrupts is that a total of 64 system interrupt sources can be allowed, each with its own unique vector address.

All Multibus masters accept non-bus-vectored interrupts, and many masters also accept bus-vectored interrupts. System designers should note that a master which has bus-vectored capability requires bus priority to service an interrupt (bus-vectored or non-bus-vectored, on-board-generated or system-generated). Some SBCs allow the bus-vectored capability to be disabled if it is not required for the application. Bus priority is not required for these boards to service on-board interrupts.

9.1.4 Time-Out

Time-out is a safety feature, located on most masters, that prevents system lockup when the bus acknowledge signal is not generated within a predetermined time limit. In normal system configurations the time-out option should be disabled. This ensures that bus operations (memory read, memory write, I/O read, I/O write, interrupts) that require longer times than are allowed by the time-out feature will not be corrupted. Also, the system will halt if nonexistent I/O or memory is accessed. This may prevent a "run-away" microprocessor.

On the other hand, time-out can be used to the advantage of a system. Many operating systems (e.g., Intel's iRMX[1] 86) calculate the size of available RAM memory by performing write, read, and verify operations until nonexistent memory is found. In this case time-out prevents the system from locking up and is required by the operating system. When the operating system is aware of the time-out, a controlled time-out operation is performed. Time-out can prevent special deadlock conditions such as the lock hang-up discussed in Sec. 5.3.1. The deadlock situation occurs when a dual-port RAM board, with one port on the Multibus system bus and the other port on the iLBX bus, is simultaneously locked from each port. This action can prevent both masters from getting to the resource. When boards are locked from their resource in this manner, the time-out prevents the system hang-up. For this type of time-out it is imperative that the master know a time-out has occurred.

The system designer must decide whether time-out is required for the system and ensure that the time-out option is properly configured for the application.

[1]iRMX is a trademark of Intel Corporation, Santa Clara, California.

It is recommended that the time-out option be disabled for each master in the system unless it is required by the operating system or application.

9.1.5 Bus Clocks

The two system bus clocks, BCLK* and CCLK*, are required to be enabled or disabled for proper system operation. BCLK* is used for bus arbitration and is required for the bus masters to arbitrate for the bus. CCLK* is a general-purpose system clock and may be required by some of the slave boards.

The system designer must configure one and only one board to drive BCLK*, and the BCLK* drivers of other boards must be disabled. If the application requires CCLK*, the system designer must also configure one and only board to drive CCLK* and the CCLK* drivers of all other boards must be disabled. It is recommended that the board which drives the clocks be placed in a slot that is farthest from the bus backplane termination circuitry. This location ensures that the clocks are driving into the termination, which helps reduce system noise. The boards that receive the clock signals should be as close to the termination circuitry as possible. Board positioning is covered in greater depth in Sec. 9.5.

9.1.6 Level of Compliance

Some Multibus-based boards comply to subsets of the full bus specification. Although these boards will work properly in many system applications, the system designer must be aware to what level each board in the system complies to the Multibus specification. Specifically, areas such as bus priority, memory address range, data width, interrupts, and lock must be reviewed to ensure proper system operation.

BUS PRIORITY

For bus priority, the bus master must be checked for full or partial bus master capabilities. Intel's iSBC 80/10B and National's BLC 80/10 are examples of boards with only partial bus master capability. Also, support of the CBRQ* signal must be checked if it is required for a specific application. Some older SBC boards either do not support CBRQ* at all or only partially support it. The board's hardware reference manual should be checked to verify the level of bus priority support.

MEMORY ADDRESS RANGE

The memory address range that can be decoded by the system memory must be verified to ensure proper addressing operation by the bus master. The basic rule is that the system memory should be able to decode the full address range of the system bus masters. An exception to the rule occurs when a system memory board decodes less than the available address range, but the application guarantees that the generated addresses can never go beyond the memory address decode range. Another area within memory address compatibility that the system designer should check is whether the memory is relocatable or is fixed in its decoded range. For example, a 64K-byte memory board may decode 20 bits (1Mbyte) of address space but is fixed on the lowest 64K-byte boundary, whereas a different 64K-byte memory board may be locatable on any 64K-byte boundary within the 1M-byte range.

Probably the largest variance in address range is in the generation and decoding of the four high-order address bits. Some boards, e.g., Intel's iSBC 286/10, generate a full 24-bit address. Other boards provide a paging method for the high-order address bits, and still other boards do not support these addresses at all. There is a similar variation of boards that receive the high-order address bits. The designer must be aware of the addressing variation and capabilities.

DATA PATH WIDTH

Data width compatibility must be checked to ensure that 16-bit boards can operate properly in the system. Specifically, 16-bit boards must know about 8-bit system memory. The system designer must ensure that the 16-bit bus master executes only out of 16-bit memory. The 16-bit bus master must perform byte operations when transferring data to 8-bit memory.

INTERRUPTS

The level of bus interrupt support for each bus master should be reviewed for consistent and reliable operation. A product may support no interrupts, non-bus-vectored interrupts, or bus-vectored interrupts. Also, the interrupt capability can support level interrupts and/or edge-level interrupts. It is necessary to so configure interrupt sources that the interrupt request method corresponds to the interrupt-sensing of all the bus masters.

LOCK

Lock is supported at many different levels by currently available SBCs. The level of support ranges from none to the capability to generate and receive lock. There are also boards which generate only or receive only. Table 9-2 is a partial list of boards and level of lock support. The system designer should review the application and decide what level of lock support is required.

9.1.7 Mechanical Considerations

In order to design a reliable system, the designer must be concerned with various mechanical aspects of the design, including such areas as thermal design, cabling, Multimodule mounting, and form factor. In the following sections those areas are discussed.

TABLE 9·2 iSBC CPU Boards LOCK* Signal Support

Neither generate nor receive LOCK*
   iSBC 80/10B[a]
   BLC 80/10[b]
   BLC 80/11A
   iSBC 80/24
   iSBC 80/30
   iSBC 86/12A†
   BLC 86/12B†
   iSBC 88/25

Generate LOCK* only
   iSBC 86/05
   BLC 86/05

Receive LOCK* only
   iSBC 589†

Generate and receive LOCK*
   iSBC 86/14†
   iSBC 86/30†
   iSBC 88/40†
   iSBC 88/45†
   DBC 86/50[c]
   iSBC 286/10†

Note: Boards marked with a dagger (†) contain dual-port memory.

[a]iSBC is a trademark of Intel Corporation, Santa Clara, California.

[b]BLC is a trademark of National Semiconductor Corporation, Santa Clara, California.

[c]DBC is a trademark of Microbar Corporation, Palo Alto, California.

THERMAL DESIGN

Probably one of the most overlooked areas is the proper thermal design of a board or a system. Improper thermal design decreases the MTBF of a board, which decreases the MTBF of a system. Board-level thermal design guidelines are covered in Chap. 10. In this section the guidelines for system-level thermal design are covered.

The area for system thermal design is the air flow through the system for board cooling. Most Intel board products require 200 linear feet per minute (LFM) of free moving air to operate properly in a 0 to 55°C (32 to 131°F) environment. The system designer should verify that the system package allows for this cooling over the entire board area. Some basic guidelines for the system packaging are as follows:

1. The boards with the highest power dissipation should be placed closest to the fan or the best air circulation.

2. Neither the I/O cabling nor other portions of the system enclosure should obstruct the air flow over the boards.

3. Board-to-board spacing should be as large as the system's mechanical design will allow.

4. In systems that do not provide adequate forced-air cooling, the boards should be oriented vertically so that the hot air between the boards is not trapped, and the system operating range should be reduced.

5. The power supply should have its own fan to ensure proper ventilation. The orientation of the supply should direct the supply-generated heat away from the boards.

CABLING

When a system design is planned, the I/O cable routing must be considered. Most I/O connectors on SBC boards are located on the top edge of the board. In addition, the I/O cable from SBX multimodules is oriented toward the top of the board. Some SBC boards with SBX multimodules can have as many as five or six cables coming from the top of the board. The system designer must ensure proper routing of cables and also not obstruct the air flow, as mentioned in the section on thermal design. The cables must be mechanically secured in the system chassis to prevent damage to them or the boards during shipping or use. One way to secure cables that do not have locking mechanisms is to lay foam rubber sheets between the top of the SBC boards and the chassis cover. This method has the advantage of securing the cable connectors to the top of the boards and providing a seal for the air flow through the system.

SHOCK AND VIBRATION

All of the Multibus SBC products meet strict shock and vibration standards (Chap. 2). However, once these boards are placed in a system environment, additional precautions are necessary.

It is highly recommended that all I/O connectors be mechanically secured. This will ensure that they will remain attached during shipping and, in some applications, use of the system. Some SBC cards and SBX multimodules have a locking-pin type of receptacle for mass-terminated cable that provides a mechanical lock for the connector. Most SBCs and SBXs use the standard edge connector. For this type of connector-receptacle pair a special connector-securing assembly should be designed for the system chassis.

In severe shock and vibration environments, SBC boards have a tendency to separate from the P1 Multibus connector. Card cages have mechanical board-locking devices that prevent the boards from separating from the P1 connector. It is highly recommended that these locking devices be used in your system. They must be used in any environment in which the boards and card cage in the system are mounted upside down.

BOARD-TO-BOARD SPACING

When a system uses SBX or SBC multimodules, the system designer must be aware of the increased board slot-spacing requirements.

In card cages with 0.7 in (17.7 mm) or less connector-to-connector spacing, host SBC boards with SBX multimodules require two slots. Host SBC boards with SBC multimodules (memory, mathematics, etc.) also require two slots unless the SBC board is placed in the end slot of any of the card cage modules. In that case the board requires only one slot. In some card cages certain slots are designed to accept host SBC boards with SBX multimodules without requiring extra slots. SBC boards with SBC multimodules can use any slot without requiring extra slots if the slot-to-slot spacing is greater than 0.8 in (20.3 mm).

In either card cage, the system designer must be prepared to use multiple slots if the boards used in the system design have requirements above what can be directly designed in one slot. The slot-board requirement must be reviewed early in the design phase to compute the exact size of the card cage assembly. Failure to do so could result in a card cage that is larger than is physically allowed by the system chassis.

9.2 BUILDING SYSTEMS WITH iSBX MULTIMODULES

The iSBX Multimodule approach allows a system designer to simply and quickly add extra I/O to the system design. In the following section we provide the information necessary to ensure proper iSBX operation in the system.

9.2.1 Addressing

The iSBX Multimodules connect to the I/O bus of a microprocessor and are addressed on the local (on-board) bus of the host SBC. Therefore, the addresses covered by the iSBX Multimodule, when connected, are not broadcast over the Multibus system bus. Most host SBC boards do not go to the system bus for the full range of the iSBX addresses even if only one iSBX Multimodule is connected. (Refer to Chap. 4 for the iSBX address ranges.) The system designer must be aware of the on-board–off-board address when an iSBX Multimodule is connected. Some SBC boards remain on-board for iSBX address only when an iSBX Multimodule is connected, but others remain on-board whether or not a module is present. This fact is extremely important when adapting a design from a system bus slave I/O expansion to an iSBX Multimodule.

The method by which an iSBX Multimodule is addressed varies with the data width of the baseboard. In a 16-bit baseboard, 8-bit iSBX module design, only the low-order data byte (D0 to D7) is used. This means that all data and status registers on the iSBX module are separated by 2-byte address locations. Therefore, each of these address locations is on an even I/O address boundary. For example, the Intel iSBX 351 serial communication module's data and status address could be assigned to I/O locations 0A0H and 0A1H, respectively, on an 8-bit baseboard. The same module on a 16-bit baseboard would have the same registers assigned to 0A0H and 0A2H, respectively. The hardware reference manual for each baseboard and iSBX Multimodule should be referred to prior to configuring the system.

9.2.2 Interrupts

The iSBX specification allows for two interrupt source connections to the baseboard. If additional interrupt connections to the baseboard are required, the two option lines can be used. The system designer must plan all interrupt sources and ensure that the iSBX module interrupts are properly connected on the SBC's interrupt controller.

9.3.3 DMA

The main concern to the system designer with regard to DMA is that the host SBC is responsible for transferring the data to or from the SBX module. The iSBX interface does not allow for an iSBX Multimodule to assume master capability to perform DMA directly between the module and on-board memory. If the host SBC does not have DMA capability, then the data must be transferred via interrupt signaling from the iSBX Multimodule to the host SBC. In that case, the designer must ensure that the software overhead to move the data can meet the transfer requirements of the iSBX Multimodule. For example, the iSBX 218A floppy disk Multimodule can not work reliably with double-density disk drives on the iSBC 80/10B. The software overhead requirement to move each byte of data exceeds the required data transfer rate. However, CPUs with faster operation can reliably transfer data.

Many iSBX Multimodules were not directly designed for DMA operation but may be used in a DMA mode on host SBCs with DMA controllers. In many cases the interrupt signal can be used as the DMA request signal and the host's chip select can provide the DMA acknowledge. The advantage of the DMA operation over the interrupt operation is that much less processor and local bus bandwidth is used to move the data. The designer must ensure that the interrupt and chip select signals can meet the DMA timing requirements and that the host and iSBX Multimodule can be configured to allow this operation. Also, as with the interrupts, any additional DMA signal requirements should be handled by the iSBX option lines.

9.2.4 Levels of Compliance

As with the baseboard SBCs, the iSBX Multimodules support various levels of compliance. The system designer must review each area to ensure proper operation in the system. The following are the compliance-level areas a system designer should be aware of:

1. Data path width

2. DMA support

3. MWAIT* support

Each of these areas is discussed in the following sections.

DATA PATH WIDTH

The system designer must ensure that the chosen iSBX modules support the data width requirements of the baseboard. The 16-bit baseboards which support the iSBX bus interface also support 8- or 16-bit iSBX Multimodules. For this environment, the designer must ensure only that all data transfers to an 8-bit iSBX module are on the low-order data byte (D0 to D7).

The 8-bit baseboards can operate only with 8-bit iSBX modules. Although a 16-bit iSBX module may mechanically attach to the 8-bit baseboard, the required data path for the module is not supported. Putting a 16-bit iSBX module on an 8-bit baseboard will result in random and incorrect results.

DMA SUPPORT

The DMA support compliance level affects both the iSBX module and the baseboard. Baseboards and iSBX modules may or may not support DMA. The system designer should review the level of DMA support required and ascertain the compatibility of the modules to the baseboard. Most iSBX modules that support DMA may also be programmed by conventional means, but that should be verified for each module. Also, a module designed for DMA operation will normally transfer data less efficiently when used with conventional data transfer means rather than DMA.

MWAIT* SUPPORT

As with the DMA support, support of the MWAIT* signal on the baseboards and the iSBX modules is optional. The system designer must review the module's capabilities and decide if MWAIT* support is required on the baseboard. If the baseboard's cycle time is faster than that of the iSBX module that is attached to the baseboard, MWAIT* support may be required to allow the baseboard to resynchronize to the module's cycle. Often the baseboard provides a jumper option to allow a fixed number of resynchronization cycles for the iSBX module. If so, MWAIT* support may not be required. However, if the resynchronization time is variable, then MWAIT* support is required.

9.2.5 Mechanical Considerations

The system designer should be aware of the baseboard-to-baseboard spacing, mounting considerations, and cable considerations when planning the system configuration.

SPACING CONSIDERATIONS

Baseboards with iSBX modules will take two slots when designed into backplanes with less than 1.0-in (2.54-cm) center-to-center spacing. Certain backplanes provide slots that give adequate spacing for baseboards with iSBX modules. The system designer must adequately plan for the slot requirements when iSBX modules are involved.

MOUNTING CONSIDERATIONS

The mounting hardware supplied with the iSBX module should always be used to secure the module to the baseboard properly. The iSBX connector alone does not provide adequate support for the module, and mechanical or electrical failure can occur in any normal shock or vibration environment.

The system designer must also review the number of modules the system requires and compare that number with the number of iSBX sockets available on the baseboards in the system. In reviewing the modules, the number of double-wide iSBX modules must also be considered. Most baseboards support single-wide and double-wide modules in some combination. If a baseboard has only one iSBX socket, normally it will support a single or double-wide Multimodule. (A baseboard's double-wide Multimodule support should be verified.) Intel's iSBC 80/10B is an example of a baseboard that supports one single- or double-wide Multimodule.

If a baseboard has two iSBX sockets, normally it will support two single-wide Multimodules or one single- and one double-wide Multimodule. Some host SBCs do not allow a single- and a double-wide Multimodule to coexist on the host board. For those SBCs, two single-wide Multimodules or one double-wide Multimodule can be accommodated. The baseboard should be reviewed for simultaneous single- and double-wide Multimodule support if that is a requirement for the application. Examples of baseboards that provide single- and double-wide Multimodule support are Intel's iSBC 80/24 and 86/30, National's BLC-80/11 and BLC-86/12B, and Heurikon's HK-68A.[2]

In some cases a baseboard may provide three iSBX sockets. For these baseboards, three single-wide Multimodules or one single- and one double-wide Multimodule can be simultaneously supported. In the latter case one socket cannot be used. An example of a baseboard with three iSBX sockets is Intel's iSBC 88/40.

CABLING

As iSBX Multimodules are added, more I/O cables must be properly planned for the system. In many applications the cable from an iSBX Multimodule will directly overlay the cable from the baseboard's I/O connector. The system designer must ensure proper routing and guarantee that the cables do not obstruct the air flow.

9.3 BUILDING SYSTEMS WITH THE MULTICHANNEL BUS

The Multichannel bus provides a high-speed I/O gateway to the Multibus system bus. To provide flexibility in many different system environments, the Multichannel bus makes many configuration options available to the user. The following areas should be considered by the system designer:

[2]HK is a trademark of Heurikon Corporation, Madison, Wisconsin.

- Device configuration

- Bus priority

- Time-out

- Cable and termination considerations

- Levels of compliance

- Mechanical considerations

9.3.1 Device Considerations

A slave on the Multichannel bus can be either a basic talker-listener or an intelligent controller. Both types of device have configuration requirements which must be considered by the system designer. Specific areas for the designer to be aware of are address, data width, parity, and autoconfiguration. In the following sections we will explore these areas.

ADDRESS CONSIDERATIONS

The Multichannel bus supports 16 devices each of which contains up to 16M bytes of unique memory space and up to 16M bytes of unique I/O space. Each device that is connected to the Multichannel bus must be configured with a unique device number (0 to 15) by the system designer. Care must be taken that every device number required by the application is covered and that no two devices have the same device number.

The Multichannel bus is a block transfer bus (i.e., one address for one to N bytes of data) with the transfer length dynamically set by the master. A slave is required to generate the on-board resource addresses for each data transfer. A lock-up condition can occur when the slave is reading from its memory and writing the data to the Multichannel bus and reads beyond the existing on-board memory boundary. Suppose, for example, that an application requires a transfer of 16K bytes of memory. The master, as per the bus specification, terminates the transfer after reading the last byte from the slave. The slave, which has been responding to the master, has exactly 16K bytes of memory (on board or on the Multibus system bus). After the master accepts the last byte, the slave's design may cause it to prefetch the nonexisting 16K + 1 byte, potentially locking the system. To prevent this type of system lock-up, the system designer must ensure that the available memory size is one byte or word larger then the application requires if the design uses boards that prefetch data.

DATA WIDTH

The bus supports 8- and 16-bit devices, and it is up to the master to ensure that the data transfer is properly aligned for the slaves. The system designer must ensure that all potential masters have knowledge of a bus that contains both 8- and 16-bit devices. The data width of each device is predefined at system configuration time, and its capabilities must be reviewed prior to configuring the system. The designer must also ensure that the 8-bit slaves have the address capability required for the system. Some 8-bit slaves may contain 256 bytes of local memory and I/O. This restriction is due to the 8-bit address width of a slave implementation.

PARITY

When a system is configured, there are two considerations for a designer with respect to parity. The first is whether a system requires parity, and the second is how the system should react when a parity error occurs.

The decision to use parity is usually application-dependent. Normally parity is used in noisy environments where the cable or boards may pick up electrical interference or electrostatic discharge (ESD). Parity should also be used when a data error could be extremely costly, as in a machine control environment. For most applications, bus parity is highly recommended. The main reason why a system designer may choose not to use parity is the overhead for parity checking and generation and the parity drivers and receivers required for each board. The system designer should be aware that parity checking over the bus only ensures that the bus drivers, receivers, and cable medium are working properly. Parity will not help if there are memory or I/O failures. If additional protection against failures is required, then block data check sums, error correction, or cyclic redundancy checking (CRC) should be used on the devices.

If parity is chosen for the system, then the system designer must ensure that all devices which drive the address-data (AD) lines generate parity and all devices that receive AD check parity to ensure system integrity. At a minimum, if parity is selected for the system, all devices which drive the bus must generate it. Otherwise, the system may generate parity errors even if the data is valid. If parity is not chosen for the system the designer must ensure that no devices check it on the bus; otherwise, parity errors may occur even if the data is valid.

The other area to consider is the action of the system when a parity error is detected. The action taken is also system application–dependent. In systems that buffer the data prior to moving the data to the final destination, the recommended action is to invalidate the data block and perform a retry on the block. In systems in which the data is used immediately after receiving each transfer, a system halt is required with some type of error status available to the system operator. For most applications that use parity, the buffered approach is recommended. Whatever action is chosen, the system designer must ensure that the system software can handle the action and that all devices comply with the requirements of the action.

AUTOCONFIGURATION

The Multichannel bus provides a means for a system to configure itself on power-up or when new devices are added after power-up. The system designer must decide if autoconfiguration is required for the system and how the auto-configuration "hooks" provided by the bus specification should be used.

The autoconfiguration allows a system to be dynamically configured. The system software does not need to be updated if devices change or memory size changes. The decision to use the autoconfiguration feature should be based on the application and the environment the system is in. If frequent updates are expected or the system supports many configurations, the autoconfiguration method should be employed. Another application in which autoconfiguration support may be beneficial is one in which the system cannot be brought down for repair of a device or when a device needs to be updated. Autoconfiguration allows devices to be interchanged while the system is running and keeps the system supervisor informed of the changes. On the other hand, if a system is statically configured and future updates to the configuration are not planned, the software overhead for autoconfiguration is not necessary.

The SRQ signal and register provide the hooks for autoconfiguration. It is up to the system designer to place the necessary information into a device's service request (SRQ) register for the Multichannel supervisor to interpret and store in a look-up table. The Multichannel specification designates one bit in the SRQ register for autoconfiguration so that a supervisor can determine whether a normal SRQ or an autoconfiguration SRQ has occurred. The remaining bits in the register can be defined by the user. The only requirement is that a consistent definition of the SRQ register bits be used to simplify the system software. The information contained in the SRQ register is application-dependent, but there is general information that should be provided. The device number and device type (talker, listener, talker-listener, or intelligent controller) should be included. Other information such as memory size, special functions, and/or level of intelligent controller may also be included as the application dictates.

An example of use of the autoconfiguration option is Intel's iSBC 589 board. It is a DMA board that has a Multichannel bus interface, which can be configured as a supervisor, intelligent controller, or basic device. As an intelligent controller or basic device it has a specific format for the SRQ register when used in autoconfiguration. Figure 9-5 shows the iSBC 589 SRQ register format when used for autoconfiguration. If additional information about a device is required, bits 4 to 6 point to other registers on the device which may be user-defined. As a supervisor, the iSBC 589 reads the SRQ register information and builds a look-up table in its memory. This table is then consulted whenever a bus transaction takes place. Figure 9-6 is the format used by an iSBC 589 supervisor when building a system configuration table. This is only an example; the format can be defined by the user.

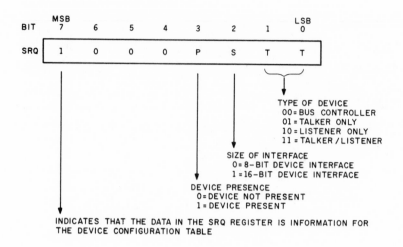

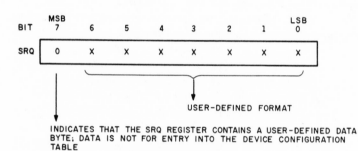

FIGURE 9-5 iSBC 589 SRQ register definition.

9.3.2 Cable and Termination Considerations

The system designer must consider the environment and devices when planning the system. The cable type and length, as well as the method of termination, are the keys to a reliable implementation.

CABLE

The designer has three types of cable to choose from: flat ribbon, twisted pair ribbon, and shielded ribbon. The use of these cables depends on the application. Flat ribbon cable can be used in a quiet environment and when all the devices connected to the cable are within the same system box. Normally, flat cable is used when there is close spacing between boards. Twisted pair cable provides greater noise immunity over distances, but it is generally more difficult to provide connector termination for it. One cable, Spectra-Strip's Twist and Flat,[3]

[3]Twist and Flat is a trademark of Spectra-Strip Corporation.

provides the advantages of twisted pair cable while providing evenly spaced flat sections (approximately every 2 ft or 0.6 m) for mass-terminated connectors. Shielded flat ribbon cable is highly recommended when the cable goes inter-system in noisy environments. This cable provides high noise immunity, but it is expensive and more difficult to mass-terminate.

After the cable type has been selected, the system designer must choose the cable length appropriate to the application; it should be the minimum required by the physical separation of the devices. Careful planning of the device locations may lower the cable length requirement and thereby reduce the overall system cost and the cable's susceptibility to system noise. The devices that attach to the cable should be connected directly to the cable; cable stubs should not be used for attaching them. Figure 9-7 shows the correct and incorrect methods of

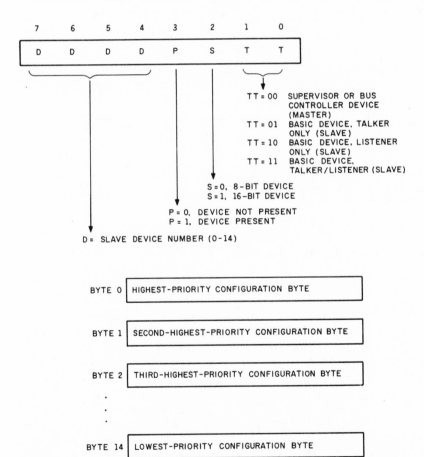

FIGURE 9-6 iSBC 589 Multichannel bus device configuration: byte format and table format.

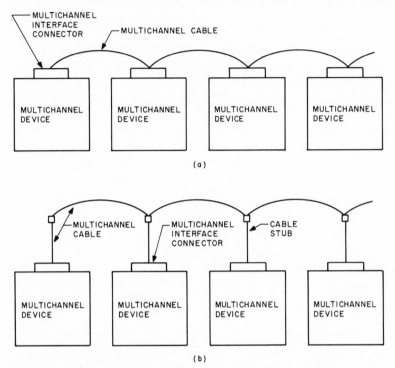

FIGURE 9-7 **Multichannel bus cable and device interconnect methods: (a) Correct method; (b) Incorrect method.**

connecting devices. The stubs cause signal reflections which reduce the reliability of the overall system.

SIGNAL TERMINATION

The Multichannel bus requires signal termination at both ends of the cable. The termination must be provided by the devices or termination modules. The system designer must ensure that the devices chosen provide the termination for the bus and that two of them are physically located at each end of the bus. Also, the designer must ensure that the termination is properly configured at each end of the cable and that no other devices are providing termination. Intel's iSBC 589 and iSBC 580 provide the capability to terminate the bus at either end of the cable. These products can have the termination removed if they are not at the end of the cable. Both products are shipped with the termination in place; therefore, the boards not required to provide termination must have the termination resistors removed.

In the event that the devices selected for an application do not have termination capability, pull-up or pull-down termination modules, or both, must be

designed and implemented on the bus. Chapter 3 explains the electrical requirements of these modules. Figure 9-8 is the schematic of a pull-down termination
module, and Fig. 9-9 shows the PCB layout of the module. The system designer
must choose the appropriate form factor to fit and mount the modules in the
system chassis. It should be noted that, by careful planning, one module design
can satisfy the termination requirements for both pull-up and pull-down
termination.

9.3.3 Levels of Compliance

The Multichannel bus supports various levels of compliance for devices that
attach to it. The system designer must be aware of the device's capability before
the system can be properly configured. The following areas permit variation:

- Data path width

- Address path width

- Parity support

- Interrupt register support

DATA PATH WIDTH

Data width compatibility must be verified when systems are designed with 8-
and 16-bit data width. The 16-bit devices must be checked to ensure that they
can transfer data with 8-bit devices. The 8-bit devices are required to receive
or transmit data only on the low byte of the A/D bus.

ADDRESS PATH WIDTH

The Multichannel specification supports both 8- and 16-bit addresses. The 8-bit-
address devices can support up to 256 bytes of memory and 256 bytes of register
or I/O. The 16-bit-address devices can support 16M bytes of memory and 16M
bytes of register or I/O. The system designer must verify the address range
capabilities of each device in the system; otherwise, an address generated may
go beyond the boundaries of the 8-bit device. In a system that consists of 8- and
16-bit-address devices, the 8-bit device must check parity for 16 bits of
addresses if parity is supported in the system.

PARITY

If the application requires parity, each device must be checked for parity support. The system designer must ensure that all talking devices generate parity
and all listening devices check parity. If parity is not selected, then all listening
devices must be configured to disable parity.

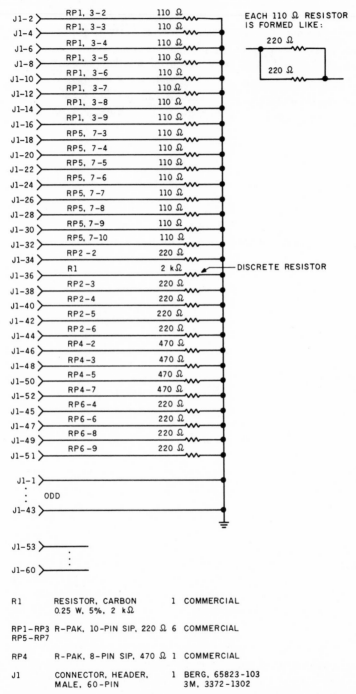

FIGURE 9-8 Schematic of pull-down termination module. (Note: Use SIP packages. Resistance values in ohms.)

330

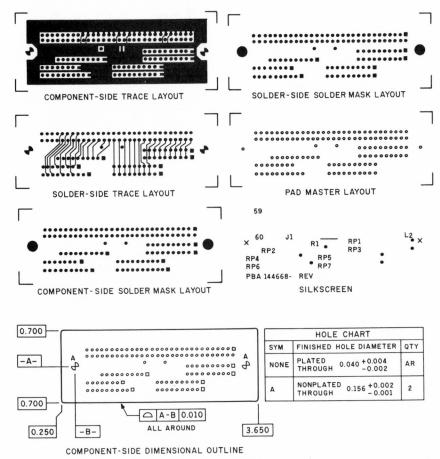

FIGURE 9-9 Pull-down termination module PCB layout.

INTERRUPT SUPPORT

The bus requires consistency in the support of supervisor request (SRQ) and supervisor take over (STO) signals and registers. If transfer error reporting or autoconfiguration is required for the application, then the devices must support these interrupts. The application should be reviewed to ensure the consistency of the devices and to verify that the devices are configured properly for the application.

9.4 BUILDING SYSTEMS WITH THE ILBX BUS

The iLBX bus provides a high-speed memory execution path for Multibus system–based iSBC boards. In order to provide flexibility in many different system environments, the iLBX bus makes many configuration options and requirements available to the user. The following areas should be considered by the system designer:

- Address space
- Secondary master
- Optimized operation
- Levels of compliance
- Mechanical considerations

9.4.1 Address Space

When configuring a Multibus system with the iLBX extension, the system designer must configure the iSBC board for the added memory on the iLBX bus. The design must be carefully partitioned to ensure that the executable code remains on the iLBX bus and does not spill over onto the Multibus system bus. Executing on the Multibus system bus causes a degradation of SBC execution speed and wastes system bus bandwidth for execution. Both actions cause an overall degradation of system performance. On the other hand, if the iSBC board is so configured that its memory address range is covered totally by the on-board memory and the iLBX bus, the processor can never go to global memory on the system bus. The application requirements and system configuration requirements must be closely reviewed prior to physical implementation of the system.

9.4.2 Secondary Master

A secondary master can greatly increase the performance and flexibility of a system. However, if the secondary master is not properly configured or has extremely high bandwidth requirements, the overall system performance may suffer because the primary master is prevented from executing. If the secondary master's bandwidth is high enough to cause performance degradation, then alternative architectural methods to handle the secondary master should be investigated.

The decision to use a secondary master rests totally with the application. In many applications high-speed mass storage devices can move the data to or from an iSBC board directly and not burden the Multibus system bus. In other applications the secondary master can extend the functionality of the iSBC board. Intel's iSBC 580 can provide a Multichannel bus interface capability to an iSBC board via the iLBX bus.

If secondary-master support is required for an application, the system designer must review the performance requirements of the secondary master and the length of time the bus is required by the secondary master. Because a secondary master can retain the bus for an indeterminate length of time, the secondary master can affect interrupt latency of the master board or the overall system performance. Also, the primary master must be verified for secondary-master support capability to ensure proper operation.

9.4.3 Acknowledge Timing

The iLBX bus allows a tight timing relationship between the master and the slave devices that greatly improves the memory access time, which directly affects the overall system performance. Optimized operation requires the system designer to study, understand, and configure the system with regard to CPU timing and memory access time. Also, increased overhead on the slave devices is necessary to provide the timing flexibility and the tight timing required.

In Sec. 5.3.1, three types of transfer acknowledge were developed. Type 1 acknowledgment allows a slave to acknowledge a transfer cycle any time after the slave receives the ASTB* signal; it provides the "optimized" operation. In type 2 acknowledgment the slave acknowledges the transfer cycle any time after receiving a DSTB* signal. Type 3 acknowledgment requires the slave to acknowledge the transfer cycle only when data is valid or accepted. Type 3 acknowledgments are considered nonoptimized operations. The main concern for a system designer is how to configure the acknowledge time for the slaves in the system. The problem becomes more complex if a secondary master also is part of the system. The bus allows optimized and nonoptimized slave devices to coexist on the same bus. However, if a secondary master is present, then both the primary and secondary master must be configured for optimized operation if any of the slaves are configured for optimized operation. If neither the primary nor the secondary master can support the optimized operation, the slaves must be configured for nonoptimized operation in order for the system to perform correctly.

For a system to be optimized, the slave must have the capability to vary its acknowledge timing with respect to the master. The variable acknowledge timing allows the slave to drive the acknowledge line active prior to generating or accepting valid data. This is known as advance acknowledge, or preacknowledge. The amount of preacknowledge can vary from 0 ns (acknowledge active when data is valid) to the maximum access time of the slave device. This variability allows a slave device to work in many different system configurations. For a particular configuration, once the preacknowledge time is set, it remains fixed. In general, the amount of preacknowledge time implemented must be less than or equal to the acknowledge acceptance overhead of the fastest master. Acknowledge acceptance overhead is defined as the difference in time between the master's acceptance of the acknowledge signal and sampling of data. The following general steps should be taken when a system is configured for optimized operation:

1. Check the slave's access time (t_{13}) and preacknowledge time increments (in the specific board hardware reference manual).

2. Compare the primary master's acknowledge overhead to the secondary master's and choose the lowest overhead time (see hardware reference manual).

3. Configure each slave to preacknowledge a time less than or equal to the lowest overhead time.

As an example, assume a system which consists of a primary master with an acknowledge overhead of 100 ns, a secondary master with an acknowledge overhead of 150 ns, slave A with 160 ns access time and preacknowledge increments of 40 ns, and slave B with 225-ns access time and preacknowledge increments of 25 ns. Comparing these times to the steps above, we find:

1. Slave A 150/40, slave B 225/25

2. System acknowledge overhead $=$ 100 ns

3. Slave A configured to preacknowledge 80 ns prior to data valid; slave B configured to preacknowledge 100 ns prior to data valid

The system acknowledge overhead of 100 ns was chosen because it was the lowest overhead time between the primary and secondary master. Slave A preacknowledge of 80 ns was chosen because it was the lowest preacknowledge time increment available without going over the 100-ns system acknowledge overhead. The next increment to the preacknowledge time was 120 ns, which exceeds the 100-ns limit. Slave B, with its 25 ns preacknowledge increments, can exactly meet the 100-ns system overhead time.

9.4.4 Levels of Compliance

The iLBX bus supports various levels of compliance of the devices that attach to it. The system designer must be aware of the device's capability before the system can be properly configured. The following areas permit variation:

- Data path width
- Secondary-master support
- Parity support

DATA PATH WIDTH

The bus supports 8- or 16-bit interfaces. The system designer must ensure that all device bus interfaces are the same width; otherwise, improper transfers will occur. Some devices can be configured for 8- or 16-bit operation. The designer must ensure that such devices are properly configured to match the other boards in the system.

SECONDARY-MASTER SUPPORT

The capability of a primary master to support a secondary master must be verified if secondary-master support is required for an application. Limited primary masters do not provide secondary-master support. The system requirements must be matched to primary-master capability before the primary master is selected.

PARITY SUPPORT

If the application requires parity, each device must be checked for parity support. The system designer must ensure that all devices that write data to the bus generate parity and that all devices that receive data check parity. If parity is not required for an application, then any devices that check parity must be configured to disable the parity option. Failure to disable the parity option can result in false transfer errors.

9.4.5 Mechanical Considerations

Since the iLBX bus uses the Multibus P2 connector, many of the mechanical attributes of the Multibus system bus are used. The following areas require special consideration by the system designer:

- Bus interconnect assembly
- Connector key slot
- Battery back-up–front-panel interface

BUS INTERCONNECT ASSEMBLY

The bus interconnect assembly can be either a mass-terminated cable assembly or the dual or tri-auxiliary connectors currently used in many of the Multibus board products. Connector assembly mounting and Multibus high-order address busing are the two main mechanical concerns of the cable assembly.

The cable assembly has the advantage of a flexible configuration ability and the support of up to five boards. Therefore, the system designer can design the cable assembly to meet the application requirements. The only requirement of the cable assembly is that its maximum length not exceed 4 in (10.16 cm) in overall length. The cable assembly can be constructed from standard off-the-shelf flat ribbon cable and mass-terminated connectors.

The cable assembly must be securely mounted to the backplane by using the P2 connector mounting holes provided on the backplane. This prevents undue stress to a cable assembly that supports multiple boards when one or more boards are removed. Cable failure will result when boards are constantly removed if the connector assembly is not properly secured.

If the high-order Multibus address lines (ADR14* to ADR17*, located on the P2 connector) are required for an application along with the iLBX bus(es), the cable assembly must also support those signals. The problem occurs when the Multibus signals must be bused to all boards in the system, while each iLBX bus assembly in the system extends across only two to five boards. For this situation a special cable assembly must be constructed that allows individual iLBX buses while connecting the high-order Multibus address lines to all boards. The system designer must recognize the application requirement and fabricate the proper cable assembly to match the application requirements. Many of the cable and connector vendors will fabricate special cables if the volume warrants outside vendor support.

KEYSLOT

Every iLBX-compatible board provides a special keyslot for a corresponding keyed connector. The use of a keyed connector is highly recommended to prevent mixing boards without iLBX support and battery backup P2 connector boards with iLBX connector boards. Placing a board in the wrong connector can destroy components on the board. The key and keyslot ensure that only iLBX-compatible boards are placed in iLBX connectors and that P2 battery backup–compatible boards are placed only in P2 battery backup connectors.

BATTERY BACKUP–FRONT-PANEL INTERFACE

Since the iLBX bus uses all of the P2 connector (except the four Multibus high-order address lines), battery backup support and front-panel interface (reset, halt-run, interrupt) are located on the top right of the boards on a connector labeled P3. A special cable assembly must be constructed if those features are required for the application. Also, special consideration must be given to systems that contain boards with these support signals on P2 and boards with the support signals on P3. The system designer must review the application requirements to ensure that the cable assembly matches the requirements.

9.5 REDUCING MULTIBUS SYSTEM NOISE

Since the Multibus was first introduced, many advances in VLSI have occurred. Faster microprocessors, faster memory, and faster buffers with 1- to 2-ns switching times and 48+ mA drive are now available. Heavily loaded systems that use these components may generate or induce enough system noise that the reliability of the transfer decreases. Although this chapter and book are based on the Multibus system bus, the information presented here pertains to any system bus.

In this section we will discuss three electrical phenomena that can introduce noise into the system:

- Signal-to-signal coupling

- Ground shifts

- Signal ringing

Although the causes of these noise problems differ, the effect on the data and the system is virtually the same. It is often difficult to distinguish between noises that cause problems in a system, since the effects are similar. The information given in the following sections will help in identifying the noise origin as well as suggest ways to reduce the noise in the system. In many applications the noise generated by the phenomena is substantially within the TTL threshold levels. For these applications following the suggestions made in this section will reduce the risk of noise-related problems. On the other hand, if the application does have noise-related problems, following these recommendations will help reduce the noise to an acceptable level.

9.5.1 Signal-to-Signal Coupling

When a signal on one trace affects the signal on an adjacent trace, the phenomenon is called signal-to-signal coupling. The signal that is induced on the adjacent trace is called coupled noise.

Problems in a system can occur when the coupled noise is severe enough to cause a TTL low logic state, which must be ≤ 0.8 V, to appear as a high logic state or when the coupled noise causes a TTL high logic state, which must be ≥ 2.0 V, to appear as a low logic state. Since there is sufficient noise margin in the high logic state, the coupled noise usually affects low logic levels. This occurs in TTL because a typical high logic level equals 3.5 V, leaving a 1.5-V noise margin. On the other hand, a typical low logic level equals 0.4 V, leaving only a 0.4-V noise margin. The main cause of coupled noise is inductive coupling, which can be expressed as

$$V_n = L\frac{di}{dt}$$

where L = total mutual inductance of parallel current paths

i = signal current in primary trace

$t =$ signal current transition time

$V_n =$ coupled voltage (noise) in adjacent trace

CHARACTERISTICS OF SIGNAL-TO-SIGNAL COUPLING

The mutual inductance L is a function of the length of the parallel paths and the cross-sectional area of those paths. The outcome of this statement is that backplanes are prime candidates for coupled noise. Boards also can have coupled noise, but normally the noise is insignificant because the trace lengths are generally short. However, if the trace lengths are 4 in (10.16 cm) or more and the primary signal has fast rise and fall times (<2 ns), then the board is a candidate for coupled noise.

To review the formula above, there are three ways to increase the magnitude of the coupled noise V_n: increase the inductance L, increase the current i, and decrease the time t. As the backplane length increases, the magnitude of the coupled noise may also increase because the mutual inductance L has increased. High-current drivers (such as the BCLK* and CCLK* drivers) may increase or cause coupled noise because they affect the current i. Fast-switching devices (such as TTL Schottky devices, AS[4] devices, FAST[5] devices) may increase or cause coupled noise because they reduce the current transition time t. Also, it should be noted that signal-to-signal coupling is additive. This means that 16 lines simultaneously transitioning in the same direction will cause more coupled noise then one signal transition. If two signal transitions simultaneously oppose each other, then their coupled noise components cancel each other.

REDUCING EFFECTS OF SIGNAL-TO-SIGNAL COUPLING

By following these guidelines, coupled noise can be reduced in most system configurations.

- Do not drive CCLK* on the bus unless it is required for the configuration. This eliminates any coupled noise generated by the CCLK* signal transitions.

- Keep backplane length as short as possible.

- Use backplanes that interleave ground traces between signal traces. The grounds absorb the radiated field from the signal traces.

- Keep BCLK* and CCLK* signals as short as possible and as close to the terminators as possible. This can be done by grouping the boards that use the clocks as close as possible to the termination.

- Drive BCLK* and CCLK* with masters that drive these signals 180° out of phase. This has a canceling effect on the coupled noise.

[4]AS is a trademark of Texas Instuments Corporation, Dallas, Texas.

[5]FAST is a trademark of Fairchild Corporation, Santa Clara, California.

TABLE 9-3 TTL Signal Driver Speeds

Fastest	Advanced Schottky
	Schottky
	Advanced low-power Schottky
	Low-power Schottky
	Standard
Slowest	Low-power

- Place boards with faster signal transition times closer to the terminators. This will reduce the length of the current-carrying path. Table 9-3 is a list of the drivers in order of their speed.

9.5.2 Ground Shifts

Ground shift is defined as the potential difference between the ground to which the receiver signal is referenced and the ground to which the driver signal is referenced. If the ground shift of a signal is large enough, it can cause signal failure. Figure 9-10 shows a model of ground-shift failure.

EFFECTS OF GROUND SHIFTS ON A SYSTEM

In Multibus systems there is a common ground path for all boards. Ground shifts have an adverse effect on a system by causing signals that are referenced to the ground to be incorrectly read by the receiving devices. For example, using Fig. 9-10, if the ground on board A is at a higher potential than the ground on board B, the potential difference is added to the signal S. If signal S is 0.8 V (TTL low logic signal) at driver A output as referenced to ground at board A and ground at board B is at $+1.2$ V as referenced to ground at board A, the signal at the receiver of board B will be 2.0 V (TTL high logic level) as referenced to ground at board B.

Normally, backplane ground shifts alone are insufficient to cause a signal error. However, backplane ground shifts coupled with board-level ground shifts and voltage drops through board and backplane connectors can cause problems. Ground-shift problems are difficult to trace because they occur around the signal transition time and are not traceable after a signal has reached steady state.

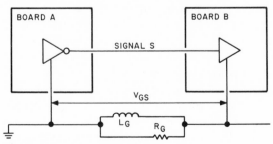

FIGURE 9-10 Ground-shift failure model.

EFFECTS OF GROUND SHIFTS ON MULTIBUS SIGNALS

Active-low signals that must be active during address and/or data transitions are primary candidates for ground-shift problems. Multibus signals such as LOCK*, BUSY*, and commands are most susceptible to ground-shift noise problems. A large amount of current is generated when 24 address and 16 data lines change state. Since 16-bit systems have eight address and eight data lines more than 8-bit systems have, ground-shift problems are more prevalent in 16-bit systems—there is additional current to transfer.

A BUSY* failure can occur when two or more masters require the use of the bus. If board A in Fig. 9-10 has the bus and is driving the BUSY* signal (signal S) and board B requires the bus and is receiving the BUSY* signal, a BUSY* failure can occur when board A drives address or data on the bus. In effect, there is a simultaneous ground shift between board A and board B bus arbiter chips. This is a combined ground shift of backplane, connector, and board grounds. When it occurs, board B's bus arbiter sees the bus in a nonbusy state and begins to drive the bus. This action results in corrupted data and system failure.

In a manner similar to the BUSY* signal, the LOCK* signal is susceptible to ground-shift problems. In this case board A in Fig. 9-10 is driving the LOCK* signal (signal S), to lock the dual-port memory of board B. If a combined ground shift occurs during board A's transfer cycle, the dual-port memory to board B may appear unlocked to board B. This allows board B to get to its memory during a message or semaphore exchange by board A and results in corrupted data and system failure.

Memory and I/O commands can cause system failures due to ground shifts. If board A in Fig. 9-10 is a master driving a command line (signal S) and board B is a slave receiving the command, a combined ground shift may appear as an early termination of the command to the slave. This false end of command can corrupt the data coming from or going to the slave. In either case the corrupted data can cause system failure.

REDUCING THE EFFECTS OF GROUND-SHIFT NOISE

Most ground-shift failures are due to the combined ground shift of the backplane, board, and connectors. The largest contribution factor in ground-shift failures is the backplane. Therefore, the first area to correct is the backplane.

There are two ways to reduce ground shift on the backplane. The first way is to reduce the distance between the boards that are communicating. This works because the magnitude of the ground shift is directly proportional to the distance a signal must travel. In other words, the backplane length should be kept as short as the application will allow and boards that communicate with each other should be placed in adjacent slots or as close together as possible. For example, if a system has multiple masters that may be susceptible to ground-shift problems, the masters should be placed in adjacent slots so that the BUSY* signal length is as short as possible. This reduces the chance of the BUSY* failure mentioned earlier.

The second way to reduce ground shift is to reduce the instantaneous current that the ground lines must handle. Although simple in theory, this may be difficult in practice. Most drivers are capable of sinking currents far above their specification. The instantaneous discharge of the bus capacitance can double the current through a given driver. On the other hand, choosing boards with the lower-current drivers may help.

Connector ground shifts due to voltage drops across the connector contacts can be greatly reduced by cleaning or replacing the connectors and boards. If an application requires the boards to be removed and reseated often, then a preventive maintenance schedule should be performed on the backplane. Consider 24 address lines each sinking 32 mA and a connector whose normal contact resistance of 10 mΩ is increased by wear and contamination to 600 mΩ. The voltage drop is calculated as follows:

$$\begin{aligned} V_{drop} &= I_{total}R \\ &= (24)(32 \times 10^{-3})(600 \times 10^{-3}) \\ &= 0.46 \text{ V} \end{aligned}$$

The effect of increased contact resistance is clearly demonstrated when 0.46 V is compared to a normal voltage drop of less than 0.01 V for a 10-mΩ contact. Normally the ground return path is divided among multiple contacts, but those contacts are also carrying the steady-state DC. This example demonstrates the importance of good connector contacts.

The last area to review for reduction of ground-shift problems is the board itself. Board ground shifts supply the minimum voltage differential of all three components. Normally, reducing the distance between boards and reducing the instantaneous current will rid most systems of a ground-shift problem. However, if a problem still exists, the boards in the system are suspect. The solution requires the isolation of the suspect board(s) and the replacement of the boards with boards that have an improved grounding network (if they exist). If the problem requires the replacement of boards, then the ground-shift component due to the backplane and the connector could not be sufficiently reduced.

9.5.3 Signal Ringing

Signal ringing is the damped oscillation of a signal when the signal performs a state transition. Typically, ringing problems occur when a signal changes state from high to low because of the TTL low-level threshold. Figure 9-11 is a graphic representation of signal ringing with respect to time. The magnitude of the ringing depends upon the signal transition speed and how a signal is terminated. Specifically, signal ringing increases as the signal transition time

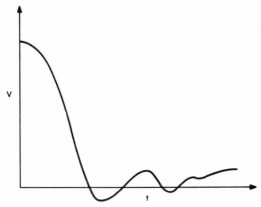

FIGURE 9-11   **Signal ringing with respect to time.**

decreases and the level of termination decreases. Normally, signals that require a clean edge transition, such as clocks and command-strobe signals, are affected by signal ringing.

ADVERSE EFFECTS OF SIGNAL RINGING

On the Multibus system bus ringing affects both BCLK* and CCLK*, since those signals normally drive edge-sensitive devices. Excessive ringing could inadvertantly clock those devices, which might result in system failure.

REDUCING THE EFFECTS OF SIGNAL RINGING

The way to reduce signal ringing on the system clocks is to ensure that the master that is driving the clocks is driving into the termination. Also ensure that all boards receiving the clocks are positioned on the backplane between the master and the termination. This practice ensures that the clocks are terminated and reduces the magnitude of the signal ringing in the signal lines.

9.5.4   Noise Reduction Summary

The three ways in which noise is generated in a system are signal-to-signal coupling, ground shifts, and signal ringing. Summarized below are the directions for keeping noise to a minimum. They should always be followed when building a system.

BACKPLANES

- Use backplanes that have interleaved grounds and/or ground planes.

- Use the shortest backplane length that an application will allow.

- Keep connector contacts clean and replace any worn connectors.

CLOCKS

- If CCLK* is not required for an application, do not drive it on the Multibus system bus.

- If your system requires CCLK*, drive it with a master that drives BCLK* and CCLK* 180° out of phase.

- Place the boards that receive the clocks between the master that drives the clocks and the bus termination.

- Place all boards as close to the termination as an application will allow.

BOARD PLACEMENT

- Place boards receiving a signal as close as possible to the board(s) generating the signal.

- Avoid empty slots between boards when possible.

- If empty slots are required, so configure the system that the empty slots are farthest from the termination and the boards are closest to the termination.

9.6 SYSTEM CONFIGURATION EXAMPLE

The fire and security system discussed in Chap. 8 will be used here as the system configuration example. The following are the board requirements for the system:

- Three masters (two 16-bit masters, one 8-bit master)

- Four iSBX modules (one double-wide, three single-wide)

- One memory module (128K bytes)

- 256K-byte system memory RAM board

- 64K-byte PROM board

- Custom Multibus-compatible I/O board

- Cables for I/O and sensors

In this system one 16-bit master, an SBC 86/X1, will be the system supervisor. The SBC 86/X1 has an 8-MHz 8086 microprocessor, 128K bytes of dual-port dynamic RAM, four 28-pin sockets to handle 64K bytes of PROM, one serial port, 24 lines of parallel I/O, two iSBX sockets, and eight interrupt inputs.

The other two masters, an SBC 86/X2 and an SBC 88/X3, perform specific system tasks. The SBC 86/X2 also uses an 8-MHz 8086 microprocessor, and it has many of the features of the SBC 86/X1. In place of the dual-port dynamic RAM is 8K bytes of single-port high-speed static RAM. The SBC 88/X3 is a special-function, intelligent analog I/O board that uses a 5-MHz 8088 microprocessor. The SBC 88/X3 contains sockets for PROM expansion and 16K bytes of dual-port RAM. A local interrupt controller handles the analog I/O interrupt sources. The 256K-byte system memory is for the supervisor and is contiguous with its local memory. The PROM card provides a look-up table for the system master and is located above the 256K-byte RAM board. Figure 9-12 is the block diagram for the system configuration. The memory map for the system is shown in Fig. 9-13. The number of masters is not expected to change, but the custom I/O boards can be increased for future expansion.

Step 1. Choose the bus priority technique. Since there are only three masters and the system is not expected to expand beyond that number, serial priority is chosen. Although all three masters fully support CBRQ, common-bus request is not required for the application.

Step 2. Compute the number of slots required. The locations of the iSBX modules and memory modules are first decided. The memory module is placed on the iSBC 86/X1. One double-wide and one single-wide iSBX Multimodule are placed on the iSBC 86/X2. The remaining two single-wide iSBX modules are placed on the iSBC 88/X3. A total of six slots

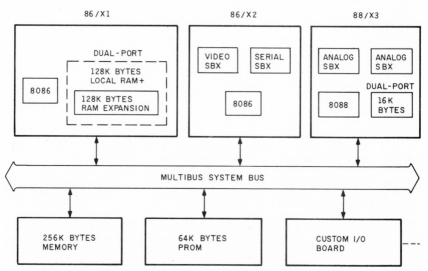

FIGURE 9-12 Block diagram for system configuration example.

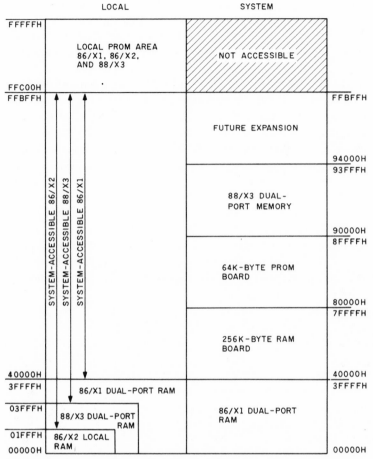

FIGURE 9-13 Memory map for system configuration example. (Note: Where local SBC memory overlaps system memory, that system memory is not accessible by the SBC board.)

are required for boards. In addition, two slots may be required for iSBX modules and one slot for the memory module.

Step 3. Choose the card placement. the Following variables are considered for board placement:

   a. *Termination.* The boards should start occupying slots beginning with the slot adjacent to the termination.

   b. *Interboard Communication.* The boards that require the greatest amount of communication should be placed in adjacent slots.

   c. *Clocks*. The board chosen to drive the system clocks should occupy
      the first empty slot farthest from the termination.

In this system design, the PROM board is used only for an occasional look-up value by the iSBC 86/X1; its system usage is relatively low compared to that of the other boards. Therefore, the PROM board is placed in the first slot adjacent to the termination. The iSBC 86/X2 communicates directly with and is the only board that uses the custom I/O board. Since there is a high utilization by the iSBC 86/X2, these boards should occupy adjacent slots. The iSBC 86/X1 executes code out of the 256K-byte memory board. This requires a high utilization by the iSBC 86/X1; therefore, the iSBC 86/X1 and the memory board should occupy adjacent slots. The iSBC 86/X2 and the iSBC 88/X3 exchange messages with the iSBC 86/X1 at a fairly regular frequency. The I/O card is placed in the slot adjacent to the PROM card. Next to the I/O card is the iSBC 86/X2. This satisfies the adjacency requirement.

There are three boards yet to place. The placement of the boards at this point is fairly arbitrary as long as the board that drives the bus clock(s) occupies the last slot and the memory board and the iSBC 86/X1 are adjacent. An additional consideration of memory module and iSBX module placement should influence the decision. The board with the memory module should be placed in the last slot if that is the card cage end slot. If the iSBC 86/X1 is placed there, only one slot is used, but if the iSBC 86/X1 is placed in any other slot, two slots are required. The iSBC 88/X3 will take two slots no matter where it is placed, because of the iSBX modules. Therefore, the iSBC 88/X3 takes the next slot available after the iSBC 86/X2. (One slot is skipped for the space taken by the iSBX modules on the iSBC 86/X2.) The memory card is placed next, after skipping a slot taken by the iSBX modules on the iSBC 88/X3. Finally, the iSBC 86/X1 is placed in the last slot. The iSBC 86/X1 is a good choice for the clock drivers because it drives BCLK* and CCLK* 180° out of phase. Figure 9-14 is a diagram of the board placement.

Step 4. Choose the card cage to fit the application. One iSBC 604A or equivalent termination backplane and one iSBC 614A or equivalent expansion backplane are chosen for the application. With the placement of the boards as stated above, only eight slots are required for this application. Furthermore, additional expansion backplanes, four slots at a time, can be added to support the additional custom I/O boards as they are required. This solution also keeps the number of empty slots to a minimum.

Step 5. Review special system considerations. For any application each board should be reviewed for special requirements. In this application

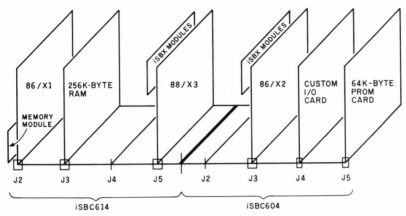

FIGURE 9-14   Diagram of final board placement.

CCLK* is required for the PROM board. The memory board can accept all 24 address lines, but the application requires only 20. The memory board must pull up the four high-order address lines. The iSBC 88/X3 has 8-bit dual-port memory. Any communication between the iSBC 86/X1 and the iSBC 88/X3 must be performed in 8-bit transfers.

Step 6. Configure the boards and backplane for the application.

   a. Connect the iSBC 86/X1 BCLK* and CCLK* drivers; disable all other masters' clock drivers.

   b. Configure the memory to the memory map diagram; verify that no gaps in the memory space are present; check that the iSBC 88/X3 dual-port memory has been accounted for on the system bus.

   c. Install PROMs where used.

   d. Configure all system interrupts.

   e. Configure parallel and serial ports with jumpers.

   f. To implement the serial-priority bus resolution, ground the iSBC 86/X1 BPRN* signal on the backplane. Connect the daisy chain for the iSBC 86/X2 and iSBC 88/X3 BPRO*/BPRN* signals.

   g. Securely fasten all iSBX and memory modules.

   h. Connect all I/O cables and route in a manner that does not obstruct air flow.

9.7 SYSTEM CONFIGURATION SUMMARY

The Multibus family is relatively simple to configure while providing the flexibility and performance to meet most application requirements. The guidelines discussed in this chapter will help in simplifying the system configuration and increasing the system reliability. The guidelines are not meant to cover every situation or configuration. The goal of this chapter is to educate the system designer on the key configuration areas of the Multibus family. Anyone building systems with standard SBC products should consult and review the hardware reference manuals of each board in the system.

10

Board Design Guidelines

This chapter provides information on designing boards which use the Multibus family of system structures. Included in the chapter are general guidelines for electrical, mechanical, and thermal design of Multibus family–compatible boards. Also included are design examples for interfacing to the various Multibus family structures and backplane layout considerations. This chapter is not intended to furnish an exhaustive list of board-level design rules. It is intended, however, to introduce the board-level designer to the concepts of interfacing to the Multibus family. The notation throughout this book is the same as that defined for the Multibus system bus covered in Sec. 2.1.

10.1 GENERAL DESIGN GUIDELINES

This section covers some general guidelines that are common to most board-level products. The concepts explained here pertain to the circuitry throughout the board as well as the bus interfaces. The board-level designer is faced with satisfying many areas in the design. The design must be both electrically and mechanically sound and provide adequate thermal dissipation while being manufacturable, testable, and serviceable. Each of these areas requires careful planning and design if all goals are to be achieved. The following sections expand upon each of the points.

10.1.1 Electrical Considerations

The proper electrical design of a board is more than one that is just "logically" correct or meets worst-case timing and loading. There are many considerations, such as PCB layout, grounding, driver-receiver selection, and voltage decoupling, that a designer should be aware of to ensure a sound, reliable design.

PCB LAYOUT CONSIDERATIONS

The basic rule is to keep stub and trace lengths to a minimum when laying out a PCB. Although this rule is extremely simple, many designs have proved to be unreliable because they did not follow it. As for the Multibus system bus, the rule means that the bus drivers and receivers should be located on the first row of ICs above the P2 connector. For the iLBX bus the bus drivers and receivers should be located on the first row of ICs above the the P2 connector. The Multichannel bus drivers and receivers should be located directly below or to the side of the Multichannel connector. The goal for all designs should be to keep the trace stub length less than 2 in (5 cm). If a signal, such as an address, is to be received in a number of locations throughout the board, it should be buffered by a single receiver close to the bus connector and the output of the buffer should be routed to the other locations. Figure 10-1 is diagram of the acceptable component-placement areas for the Multibus family boards.

Normally on intraboard signals, the trace lengths are short, but occasionally a signal must be routed throughout the board. The signals that are routed in this manner should be carefully reviewed for their effect on the board's operation. Normally signals with fast rise and fall times cause the problems. A typical fast edge problem is ringing on clock inputs; it can result in false clocking or excessive undershoot below 0.5 V which can extend a PROM's access time

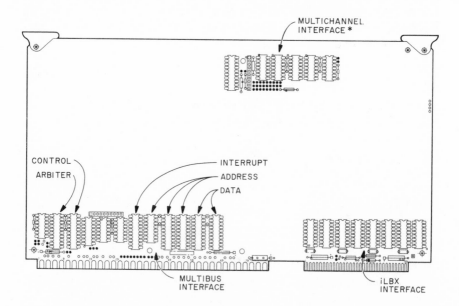

*MULTICHANNEL CONNECTOR
NOT SHOWN FOR CLARITY

FIGURE 10-1 Bus interface component placement.

beyond specification. Termination may be required at the receiver end to prevent signal ringing and reflections. Also, careful routing of the signal may be required to prevent coupling of noise into adjacent signals. Avoid routing a signal throughout the board unless absolutely necessary.

DRIVER-RECEIVER SELECTION

The general rule for selecting a bus driver is to pick a driver that comes closest to meeting the minimum bus drive requirements without going below them. Basically, LS-type drivers should be used for an interface design unless speed or drive requirements prevent their use. These rules help reduce signal-to-signal coupling and reduce the instantaneous current demands placed on a board and system when the drivers change state. Schottky drivers generate more signal-to-signal coupling than LS-type drivers because their instantaneous current changes with respect to time (di/dt) are greater.

Lower-power devices draw less alternating and direct current than standard Schottky devices. Besides providing a thermal advantage, the lower sink current minimizes the ground-current surges which can lead to inductive ringing on the board and backplane. Consider a Multibus board that simultaneously enables all 24 address lines and 16 data lines, with all outputs at a TTL low. The instantaneous current surge is significant. For example, a 74S240 driver can sink 60 mA, and a 74LS240 driver can sink 20 mA. The 74S240 interface would instantaneously sink 2.4 A for 40 lines versus 0.8 A for the 74LS240 interface. This current surge can create a large ground shift as discussed in Chap 9. Schottky drivers are more capable of generating the current surge and ground-shift problems.

GROUNDING

Proper board grounding and ground networking help limit the instantaneous current surges and help provide signal noise immunity. The main problem, as developed in Chap. 9, is ground shifts. The ground-shift noise can cause a generated TTL low-level signal to be sensed as a TTL high-level signal at the receiver because of a potential difference between the device's reference grounds. Improper grounds cause a high enough inductive impedance to cause the ground shift. Multilayer boards (four or more layers) with a solid ground plane usually provide a more than adequate grounding system. Boards with two layers or multilayer boards with traces on the ground plane may cause problems unless the grounding is adequately distributed.

In areas where there are bus interfaces, the multilayer board should keep the ground plane solid because of the high current demand of bus drivers. For example, on the Multibus interface the first row of ICs above the P2 connector should have a solid ground below it. The two-layer boards pose a greater problem. The ground trace that connects the Multibus interface ICs should be a minimum of 100 mils (0.025 mm) wide (assuming 2-oz (56.7-g) copper). This ground trace should be directly connected to all eight Multibus interface ground pins. Interface drivers that must remain active-low during multiple signal transitions (i.e., LOCK∗, BUSY∗) should be located as far to the left on the ground strap and as close to the Multibus ground pins as possible.

Two-layer designs must provide a good ground grid. The grounding grid system provides multiple return paths for the device current. This cuts down on the inductive impedance between devices. Ideally, the grid should be 1-in (2.54-cm) squares with a minimum of 12.5-mil-wide (0.32-mm-wide) trace. If this cannot be accommodated on the board design, then as much gridding as possible should be provided. A good grid system prevents ground differentials and on-board coupling.

DECOUPLING CAPACITORS

Decoupling capacitors provide a low-impedance path for transient currents to ground. A general rule is to provide a 0.1-μF capacitor for every two ICs. For high-current, fast-transition buffers a 0.1-μF capacitor should be used for each buffer. In order to prevent inductive impedance, the capacitor should be located as close to the IC power and ground pins as possible. Additional bulk capacitance on any power supply pins also is required, especially if the power supply cables extend more than 1 ft (30.48 cm) from the supply.

10.1.2 Thermal Considerations

Proper thermal design can improve the reliability of the board by increasing the MTBF of each component. The goal of good thermal design is to limit the absolute junction temperature of the component die substrate. It is the job of the IC package to remove as much heat as possible from the substrate. Packages with low thermal resistance, such as ceramic packages, remove heat more efficiently than plastic packages, which have a higher thermal resistance. The package's thermal resistance to the ambient air also is important. Low thermal resistance implies that a package can be more efficiently cooled by convection (forced-air cooling).

As stated earlier, reducing the junction temperature is the goal of good thermal design. Absolute junction temperatures are almost always specified for discrete semiconductors by component manufacturers; they are rarely specified for microelectronic devices. Normally only typical values of absolute junction temperatures are listed. The device will operate beyond the specified temperature, but the chemical reactions that are accelerated will reduce the MTBF of the device. A derated junction temperature value used by many designers is 125°C (257°F) for all package and device types.

The first step is to judge whether there are any hot components on the board. (A hot component is any component which, in operation, exceeds the manufacturer's power dissipation specification.) When there are any, the component's junction temperature can exceed the recommended value. Additional cooling techniques may be required for these components, or a package with a lower thermal resistance may be needed. The following are some of the key guidelines for proper board-level thermal design; for specific problems the books listed in the reference section should be consulted.

1. Avoid placing cerdip or ceramic ICs that dissipate more than 1 W below SBC Multimodule sites.

2. Avoid placing plastic ICs that dissipate more than 0.7 W below SBC Multimodule sites.

3. Avoid placing single-in-line package (SIP) components directly in front of a hot component. SIP components typically block the air flow.

4. Avoid placing hot components in the 1-in^2 (6.45-cm^2) area at each corner of the SBC. Because of typical card cage construction, these areas usually suffer from low-velocity air flow.

5. Avoid placing hot components near the P1 edge card connector. Because of typical card cage construction, these areas usually suffer from low-velocity air flow.

6. A socketed component in free convected air tends to increase in temperature, but in forced-air systems it tends to be cooler because more of it is exposed.

10.1.3 Mechanical Considerations

Careful mechanical design of a board is crucial to ensuring a reliable board and system. Specific areas of importance are component placement considerations for manufacturing, testing, and Multimodule placement. Other areas of importance are the component height restrictions for special areas of the board and designing a board to meet the shock-vibration specification. In the following section we will discuss these areas.

COMPONENT PLACEMENT CONSIDERATIONS

If iSBX and iSBC Multimodule boards are planned for a design, their placement must be considered in the early component placement phase of the baseboard design. With proper planning a board can simultaneously contain RAM, PROM, mathematics, and iSBX Multimodule boards. The key to the layout is to ensure that all the baseboard connection sockets are so placed that all the Multimodule form factors can fit simultaneously. Figure 10-2 is a layout outline of a baseboard and the location of the associated Multimodules.

Card cage guides place additional constraints on component placement. When card guides are used, no components must come within 0.25 in (6.35

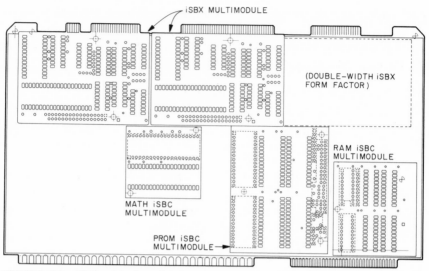

FIGURE 10-2 iSBC and Multimodule layout outline.

mm) of the card edges. This ensures that the components will not interfere with the card guides.

Manufacturing considerations also affect component placement on a board. Component placement and orientation can have a significant effect on automatic component insertion and board-level testing. A board layout review should be conducted early in the design phase by members of the manufacturing and test organizations.

COMPONENT HEIGHT

The Multibus specification states that the maximum component height must be no greater than 0.4 in (10.16 mm). However, there are additional restrictions if iSBC multimodules are used on SBC baseboards. Recall that there are two types of Multimodule boards: iSBX and iSBC Multimodules. Each Multimodule family has its own mechanical requirements. The iSBX bus mechanical specification allows for a maximum component height of 0.4 in (10.16 mm) under the iSBX Multimodules, whereas the maximum component height board underneath the iSBC multimodule is 0.2 in (5.08 mm). Figure 10-3 is a diagram of the component height specification when iSBC Multimodules are used. In addition, the overall height of the iSBC Multimodule on a iSBC baseboard must be no greater than 0.76 in (19.3 mm). This specification ensures both end and adjacent slot compatibility for backplanes with respecitvely less than and more than 0.8 in (20.3 mm) slot-to-slot spacing.

The use of iSBC Multimodules implies that no jumper option stake pins are to be designed in the area beneath the iSBC Multimodule. If this criterion cannot be met, then special stake pins that have a maximum height of 0.2 in (5.08 mm) must be used. The board designer must consider proper stake-pin placement early in the design phase.

SHOCK AND VIBRATION

Components with fragile leads, such as crystals, transistors, and light-emitting diodes (LEDs), should not be placed close to the top edge of the board. In handling the board during insertions and extractions, such components tend to break easily. In addition, crystals should be laid down if the board area permits. If it does not, the crystal should be supported in the upright position with a crystal holder or a wire-wrap post. The crystal should never stand vertically without some type of support. In general, for fragile components, the manufacturer's recommendations should be followed closely.

Selection of dual-in-line package (DIP) sockets is important in meeting a board's shock and vibration specification. Inexpensive, single side-wipe sockets have a tendency to allow the component to walk out in heavy shock and/or vibration environments. Their retention force declines rapidly after multiple insertions and extractions of components. This is especially true of heavy components such as 24-, 28-, and 40-pin ceramic DIP components. Sockets should be carefully selected for the environment in which they will be used.

Cables and cable connectors are another important aspect of proper shock and vibration design. The cabling that comes from the I/O edge of SBCs and iSBX Multimodule boards can easily vibrate off the edge connector on the board when the edge connectors are not mechanically tied down. Specialized strapping for the edge connectors is normally required. The pin connectors, such as the 3M 3372 connector header series, have built-in mechanical cable-locking devices. The connector mechanically attaches the cable to the board and is highly recommended for the board I/O connectors on all new designs. If the design cannot accommodate mechanically locking connectors, then it must ensure that the system chassis can keep connectors in place.

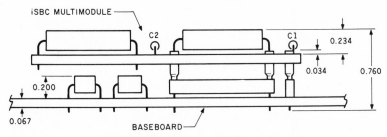

FIGURE 10-3   iSBC Multimodule component height requirements.

10.2 GENERAL BUS INTERFACE DESIGN GUIDELINES

The following sections provide general design guidelines for interfacing to the Multibus system, iSBX, iLBX, and Multichannel buses. Since these buses are established, time-proven structures, standard and accepted interface configurations have been developed. In addition, VSLI components have standardized much of the interface. The following guidelines, which are provided for direct interface application, may be modified for particular applications.

10.2.1 Multibus Master Interface

A basic Multibus master interface block diagram is shown in Fig. 10-4. It can be broken down into five elements:

- Control
- Bus exchange
- Address
- Data
- Interrupts

Figures 10-5 through 10-8 are the schematic representations of the interface block diagram for the 8086 family of components. In the following sections we will explain the implementation of these elements.

CONTROL

The control portion of the interface circuit is shown in Fig. 10-5. The bus control is provided by the 8288 bus controller chip, which runs synchronously with the 8086 microprocessor and monitors the 8086 status lines S0 to S2. The 8288 converts the 8086 bus structure to the Multibus system bus structure. When a Multibus bus cycle is requested via the status lines, the bus controller provides all the bus commands and the board's data buffer control lines: data buffer enable and data buffer direction (DT/R).

The 8288 provides standard Multibus system bus timing and drive capability for normal bus cycles. However, there are special timing considerations when a master keeps the bus for consecutive cycles (i.e., lock or common-bus request cycles). The 8288 does not enable commands on the bus until 105 ns after the master has been granted the bus. This ensures that the Multibus timing specifications t_{AS} and t_{DS} of 50 ns are met. When a master retains the bus for consecutive cycles, these timing parameters can no longer be guaranteed. Therefore, an additional logic must be added to ensure compatibility for these operations. The flip-flop in Fig. 10-5 disables the AEN* input (AEN* = high) at the beginning of every transfer operation. This guarantees that the proper

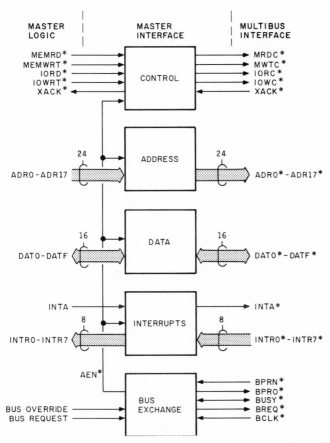

FIGURE 10-4 Multibus master interface block diagram (hexadecimal notation).

setup time is met for all bus operations. Specific details on the 8288 timing and interface requirements can be found on the manufacturer's data sheet.

BUS ARBITRATION

The bus arbitration section is shown in Fig. 10-5. The 8289 bus arbiter chip is used for the 8086 microprocessor family. As with the 8288, the 8289 converts the 8086 bus to the standard Multibus system bus interface. For other microprocessor families the 8218/19 bus arbiter chips can be utilized for Multibus system bus arbitration.

The 8289 runs synchronously with the 8086 microprocessor and monitors the 8086 status lines S0 to S2. When the microprocessor makes a system bus request, the signal line OBCY* (on-board cycle) goes inactive. This signal is generated by on-board–off-board address decoders which are not shown. The on-board– off-board decision is based on address information. The board is configured to

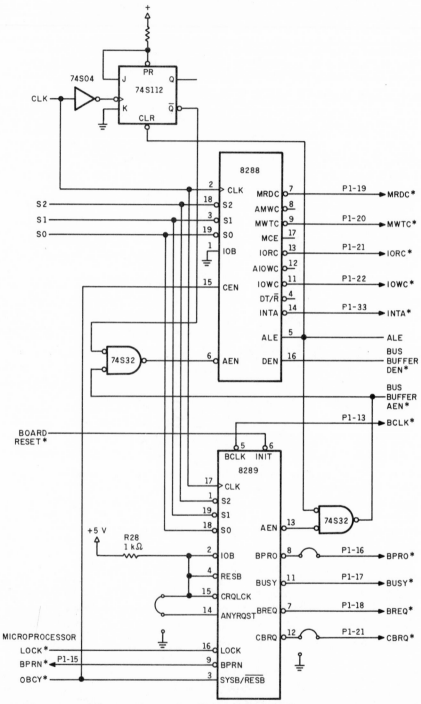

FIGURE 10-5 Multibus master control and bus exchange interface.

respond to a fixed set of on-board addresses. If an address is out of the range of the on-board address, the OBCY* signal goes inactive (OBCY* = high). Once this signal is received by the 8289, the 8289 begins to arbitrate for the bus by driving BREQ* active. Once the bus has been granted (BPRN* = low, BUSY* = high), the 8289 generates the control signal AEN. This signal, gated with address latch enable (ALE), enables the address buffers and the 8288 bus controller onto the bus. The gating of AEN* with ALE turns off the buffers during the ALE active time. Although this is not a requirement of the Multibus specification, turning off the buffers during ALE active prevents the buffers from turning on when the buffer inputs are at an indeterminate state. Otherwise, the buffers could generate multiple signal transitions on the bus, which could couple into adjacent signals on the bus. The undetermined input state while the buffers are enabled occurs when a microprocessor retains the bus for consecutive cycles (e.g., lock and CBRQ cycles).

The 8289 also provides bus lock capability and CBRQ* arbitration modes. The lock input, when active, allows a bus master to retain the bus once the bus has been granted. The CBRQ* input-output, along with the ANYRQST signal, allows a master to operate in common-bus request mode. The circuit shown in Fig. 10-5 also allows for the configuration of the different CBRQ* modes discussed in Chap. 9. Jumper stake pins are provided so that a user can configure the interface for the application. Specific details on the 8289 timing and interface requirements can be found in the manufacturer's data sheet.

ADDRESS INTERFACE

The address section of the interface is shown in Fig. 10-6. For this implementation, all 24 address lines are driven. The 8287 buffer is used in a unidirectional mode to drive the address lines. The address drivers are enabled by the AEN* signal generated by the 8289 bus arbiter chip. This ensures that the address drivers will not turn on until the master has control of the bus. The 8287 direction input, T/R, is set to a logic high by a pull-up resistor. This permanently sets the direction of the address drivers to the bus. For non-dual-port designs, 74LS240s also are a good choice for address drives.

In dual-port designs, the 8287 address buffers would be used in the bidirectional mode to allow Multibus system bus access to the dual-port RAM. Therefore, the direction input and enable input terms are modified to allow address signals to be driven on-board from the Multibus system bus. Dual-port designs are covered in more detail in Sec. 10.3.

DATA INTERFACE

The data interface implementation for the 8086 family is shown in Fig. 10-6. The basic 16-bit interface requires three 8287 buffers: lower data buffer, swap data buffer, and upper data buffer. The swap-byte buffer is required for com-

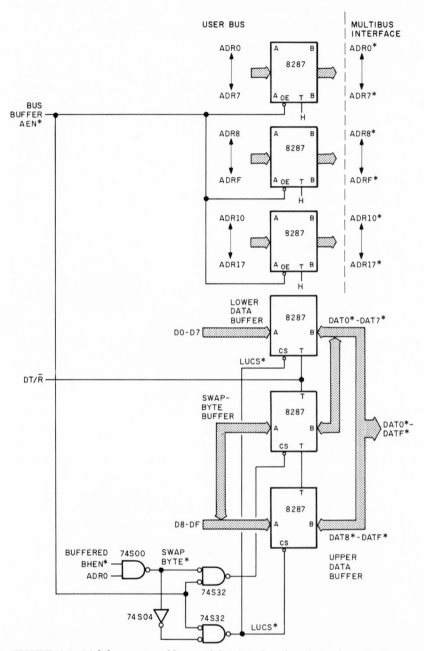

FIGURE 10-6 Multibus master address and data interface (hexadecimal notation).

patibility with 8-bit boards in 8- and 16-bit mixed systems. The swap byte places all byte operations on the low-order data bus (DAT0* to DAT7*).

The buffer chip select logic is responsible for turning the appropriate buffer(s) on or off depending on the operation. The basic algorithim is an even-byte operation performed on the lower data buffer, a odd-byte operation performed on the swap-byte buffer, and a word operation performed over the lower-byte buffer and the upper-byte buffer. The upper buffer chip select is simplified by allowing the upper buffer to turn on during a low-byte operation. This has no effect on the data, since the upper byte is ignored during byte operations. The chip select terms must also include the AEN* signal to ensure that the buffers turn on only when the master is granted the bus. The truth tables for the buffer chip selects are given in Fig. 10-7. The buffer direction input can be driven directly from the 8288 bus controller DT/R output or from other available board signals.

As with the address buffers, the data buffers require additional chip select and direction terms if a dual-port interface is used. For this case, the AEN* term is logically ORed with the dual-port slave request. The direction term is logically ORed with the slave direction term. Dual-port designs are covered in more detail in Sec. 10.3.

INTERRUPTS

There are two interrupt interface designs: non-bus-vectored (NBV) and bus-vectored (BV). The non-bus-vectored interface shown in Fig. 10-8 is straight-forward and does not require any special consideration other than buffering the bus interrupt signals as close to the Multibus edge connector as possible. The stake pins increase flexibility.

The bus-vectored interrupt interface is more complex and requires additional support logic. This type of interrupt interface allows slave programmable interrupt controllers (PIC) such as the 8259A to be present on the system bus. Anyone who is not familiar with bus-vectored interrupts should review the bus-

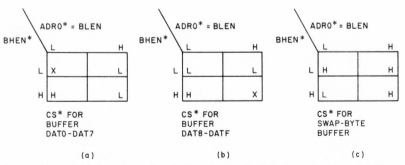

FIGURE 10-7   Multibus master data buffer select truth table (L ≤ 0.8 V; H ≥ 2.0 V).

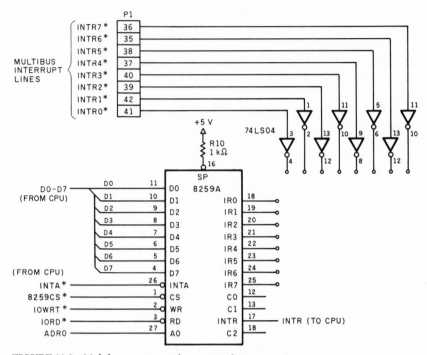

FIGURE 10-8 Multibus master non-bus-vectored interrupt circuit.

vectored interrupt section in Chap. 2. Figure 10-9 is a bus-vectored interrupt interface implementation for the 8086 microprocessor family, and Fig. 10-10 is the Multibus access timing. The circuit operation is explained in the following section.

When the 8259 receives an interrupt, it generates an INTR signal to the 8086 processor. The 8086 status lines (S0 to S2) inform the 8288 and 8289 that an interrupt cycle is occurring. Since, at this time, the 8086 does not know whether a BV or NBV interrupt has occurred, the first INTA cycle requests the system bus via the 8289. When the 8289 gains control of the bus, it locks the bus to guarantee back-to-back INTA* cycles and activates the bus AEN* signal, which generates the INTA* signal to the bus via the 8288. The INTA* signal causes the slave PICs on different Multibus slave boards to freeze the state of the priority resolution logic. Locally, on board, the first INTA* cycle requests the 8259 master PIC to place the highest-priority slave PIC identification on cascade lines CAS0 to CAS2. The three-state buffers for the cascade lines are enabled by the 8288 master cascade enable (MCE) output. The first INTA cycle also performs a "ready" signal to the microprocessor.

The second interrupt acknowledge bus cycle activates the MCE signal again

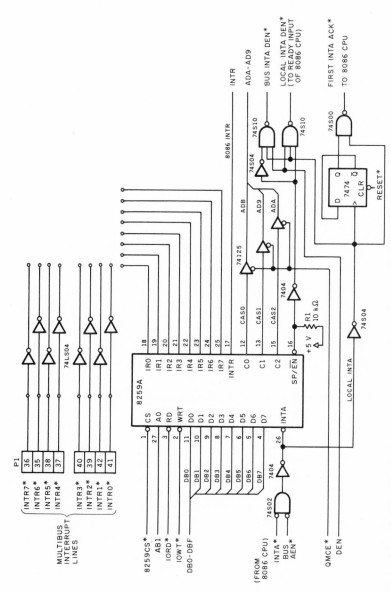

FIGURE 10-9 Multibus master bus-vectored interrupt circuit (hexadecimal notation).

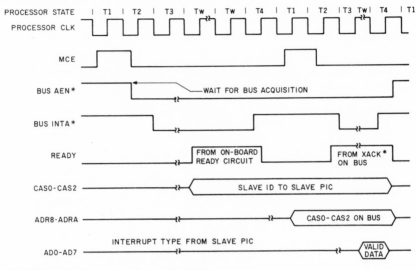

FIGURE 10-10 Bus-vectored interrupt timing sequence.

and generates a second INTA* to the Multibus system bus. The slave ID number on CAS0 to CAS2 from the master 8259 PIC is placed on the Multibus address lines ADR8* to ADRA*. The second INTA* signal causes the slave PIC to recognize its slave ID, place the interrupt vector on the Multibus data lines DAT0* to DAT7*, and generate the XACK* signal. If the interrupt is non-bus-vectored, the master PIC is responsible for generating its own interrupt vector. In this case the 8259 SP/EN signal will be active. This active output provides a local ready for the 8086. On the other hand, if the interrupt is bus-vectored, the interrupt vector comes from the addressed slave's PIC on the Multibus system bus along with its XACK* signal when the vector is valid. In this case the XACK* signal provides the 8086 ready. The circuitry also provides for a bus DEN* signal to enable the bus data buffers to accept the vector.

10.2.2   Multibus Slave Interface

A basic Multibus slave interface block diagram is shown in Fig. 10-11. The interface can be broken down into five elements:

- Address
- Address decode
- Control

- Data

- Interrupts

Figures 10-12 through 10-16 are the schematic representations of the interface block diagram.

ADDRESS INTERFACE

The job of the address interface is to buffer the Multibus address signals that are used on-board. The design is very straightforward and does not require any special consideration. For the implementation in Fig. 10-12, 74LS240 octal line drivers and receivers are used. The receivers are always enabled to monitor addresses on the bus. If an address is not used, it need not be buffered. Also, if

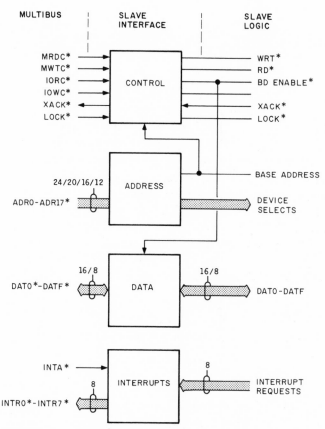

FIGURE 10-11   **Block diagram of multibus slave interface (hexadecimal notation).**

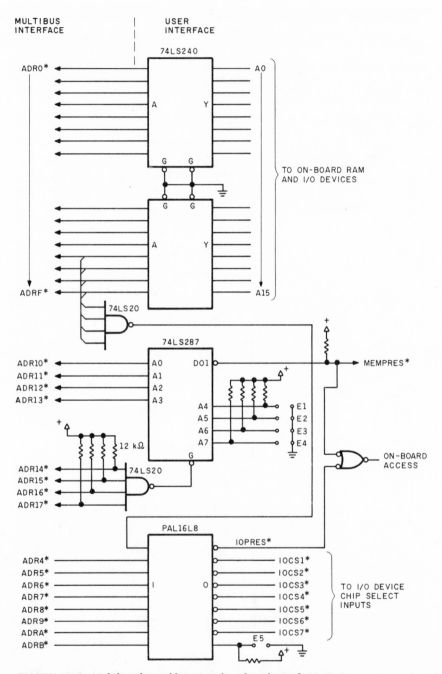

FIGURE 10-12 Multibus slave address interface (hexadecimal notation).

an address is terminated at an input close to the P1 connector, as in the case of an address line connected only to a decoder, it may not require a buffer. In the latter case, the decoder should be the only input on the board in order to meet the design guidelines of Sec. 10.1.

ADDRESS DECODE

The address decode circuits decide whether the requested resource is present on-board. The circuit shown in Fig. 10-12 takes advantage of programmable array logic (PAL) and bipolar PROMs for decode.

The decode PROM provides the memory decode for the slave board. Two functions are performed by the PROM. The first function is to generate the signal MPRES* when the requested memory is present on board via the address inputs. For this implementation, the memory array is a 64K-byte block that can be placed anywhere in the first 1M-byte address space. The four-input NAND gate decodes the high-order address ADR14* to ADR17* to the first megabyte page. If the address is greater than a megabyte, the NAND gate output will be high, which will disable the decode PROM. The pull-up resistors on the NAND gate inputs allow the slave board to work in 1M-byte-only systems, where the high-order address lines are not driven. The four jumpers on the decode PROM inputs (E1 to E4) provide the selection of one of sixteen 64K-byte spaces. The jumper selection addresses for this implementation are listed in Table 10-1.

TABLE 10-1 Multibus Slave Address Decoder Example

E1	E2	E3	E4	Starting address (hex)
O	O	O	O	00000
O	O	O	I	10000
O	O	I	O	20000
O	O	I	I	30000
O	I	O	O	40000
O	I	O	I	50000
O	I	I	O	60000
O	I	I	I	70000
I	O	O	O	80000
I	O	O	I	90000
I	O	I	O	A0000
I	O	I	I	B0000
I	I	O	O	C0000
I	I	O	I	D0000
I	I	I	O	E0000
I	I	I	I	F0000

Note: I = jumper in; O = jumper out.

The second function of the decode PROM is to provide address translation for the high-order Multibus address lines ADRD* to ADRF*. This function is required in most dual-port designs. As an example, the address translation allows the 64K-byte memory array, as seen by the Multibus system bus, to be placed on any 16K-byte boundary. This means the decoder must translate the high-order addresses to provide the proper mapping into the memory array.

The PAL provides all the decoding for the slave I/O resources. Its outputs generate all of the required chip selects when a valid address is detected. In addition, one of the jumper options allows all the on-board I/O to be offset by 80H. The PAL for this implementation has been socketed. This allows the intended users to design their own PAL code and place the I/O at virtually any address. The user can replace the PAL and reconfigure the I/O to meet the application needs. This implementation decodes all 64K-byte I/O spaces, with 4K bytes of address space directly input to the PAL. The I/O chip selects can decode down to a 16-byte address area.

CONTROL

The control section of the slave design provides the conversion and routing of Multibus commands (MRDC*, MWTC*, IORC*, IOWC*) to board-specific commands and generates the XACK* signal. Although the control implementation can be cleanly implemented in a PAL, a discrete implementation (which can be set into a PAL) is shown in Fig. 10-13.

The outputs of the OR gates provide address-qualified commands. These outputs are used by the respective I/O and memory devices. These signals also provide information for the start of the XACK* generator. The job of the XACK* generator is to send an XACK* signal back to the master when the slave has completed the requested operation. This is accomplished by counting CCLK cycles starting from the time when the bus command is received until the slave has completed the operation. The number of clock cycles required depends on the access time of the devices on the slave board. The generator consists of eight flip-flops wired together to form a shift register. In cases where the I/O and memory have different access times, a circuit at the output of the XACK* generator can differentiate between memory or I/O access and routes the appropriate XACK* signal. For this implementation CCLK* is used to drive the XACK* generator, and only memory requests are shown.

For memory modules, receiving the INH1* inhibit signal is required. In this implementation, the INH1* signal blocks the board enable signal, which in turn prevents any further board activity. Timing of this signal is critical to ensure that no buffer fights or false acknowledges occur. The timing parameter t_{ID}, which is the maximum inhibit delay from the inhibiting slave, must be valid less than 100 ns from valid address on the bus. If this parameter is not met, the inhibited slave may complete the cycle and place XACK* on the bus or the

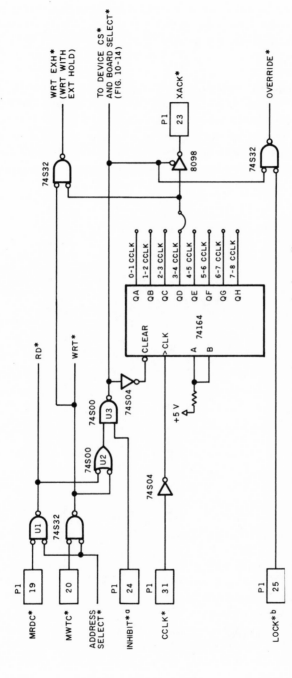

FIGURE 10-13 Multibus slave control interface. (Notes: ^{a} This term is used only on all RAM memory modules; ^{b} Used on dual-port slaves.)

369

inhibited slave may go into an unknown state. In a similar manner, the inhibited slave must ensure that it can reliably prevent the cycle when the inhibit signal is received at the maximum t_{ID} specification.

DATA INTERFACE

The slave data interface, which is similar to the master data interface, is shown in Fig. 10-14. Its implementation supports both 8- and 16-bit masters. The following is a discussion of the key interface features.

The 8- or 16-bit interface has a swap buffer similar to the master interface and follows the same rules as the master interface. An 8-bit-only interface would require one buffer for the DAT0* to DAT7* lines, with the board select term gated directly into the OE input. The key point for slave interfaces is that

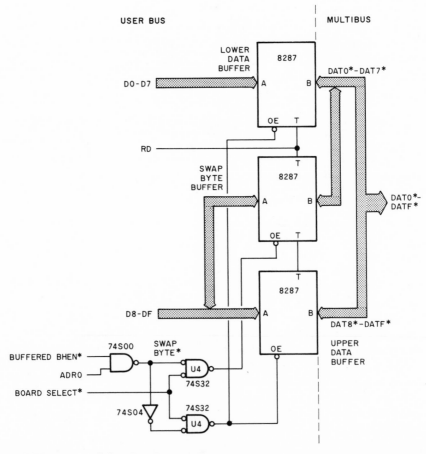

FIGURE 10-14 Multibus slave data interface.

the buffers must be turned on and off with command. Because of this require-ment, the designer must be aware of two key design parameters.

The first parameter is data hold time on a write cycle. If the buffers are gated with command (as in this example), the data is removed when command goes inactive. If the same write command is used on the slave's LSI devices, there can not be any guaranteed hold time for the data. If the devices require data hold time, then a special write signal must be generated for the devices. This write signal must end before the bus signal while providing the LSI devices with the proper data setup. The slave control logic shown in Fig. 10-13 generates a WRTEXH* signal. This signal is generated by gating the bus write command with an output of the XACK* generator. The output chosen guarantees that the data remains valid 20 ns after the internal write signal (WRTEXH*) goes away. The cost of this implementation is that XACK* may have to be delayed an additional 100 ns to meet the minimum command width.

The second parameter involves data turn-off on a read cycle. Once the bus read command, MRCD* or IORC*, is removed, the data buffers can remain active only 65 ns. For example, if the delay path of the critical ICs is added for the control interface shown in Fig. 10-13 and the buffer interface of Fig. 10-14, the control logic and the data buffer logic delay times are as follows:

$$74S32(U1) + 74S00(U2) + 74S00(U3) + 74S32(U4) + 8287_{\text{output disable}}$$
$$7 \text{ ns} \quad + 5 \text{ ns} \quad + 5 \text{ ns} \quad + 7 \text{ ns} \quad + 18 \text{ ns} = 42 \text{ ns}$$

This implementation left a 23-ns margin. However, if LS-type devices had been used instead of the 74S32 and one 74S00, the design would have been greater than the maximum allowable hold time specification.

INTERRUPT INTERFACE

Slaves can support NBV and BV interrupts. If the reader is unfamiliar with these types of interrupts, a review of Chap. 2 on Multibus interrupts is suggested.

The NBV interrupt case of the slave is straightforward, and its implemen-tation is shown in Fig. 10-15. The bus requires the NBV interrupt logic to latch and transmit the interrupt to the master and Fig. 10-15 covers these three requirements. The interrupt is latched by the 7474 D flip-flop. This signal is transmitted to the bus by the 7406 open collector driver. When the master reads the status of the interrupt at the correct address, the state of the interrupt flip-flop is latched into the status flip-flop (74S74). The command, along with the address-generated chip select (CS*), also enables the three-state buffer (8098). The output of the 8098 is connected to the user data bus for placement on the Multibus system bus. Once the master has read the status, it clears the interrupt by writing any value to the same I/O address.

A basic BV interrupt design is given in Fig. 10-16. This implementation works for both 8086 family and 8080/85 families. The responses of the two families to interrupts are different; therefore, the Multibus interface can support only one type of BV interrupt on a given system. For this example the 8086 family response is used.

When the 8259A receives a user interrupt on IR0 to IR7, it passes the interrupt on to the Multibus, buffered by a 7405 open collector driver. The bus master responds to the interrupt request by generating two INTA* commands (see Sec. 10.2.1). The first INTA* command freezes the internal state of all slave 8259As on the Multibus system bus. The second INTA* command requests a restart address from the interrupting bus slave. Address lines ADR8* to ADRA* are driven by the bus master, and the interrupt address code is generated by the master 8259A. When the slave 8259A receives the second INTA* command, it looks at the address lines ADR8* to ADRA*. If the address lines match the slave address, the slave will enable the data interface drivers by driving the EN* signal active. The slave 8259A then drives the data lines (DAT0* to DAT7*) with the vector address. Also, the slave is responsible for generating XACK* when the vector address is valid on the system bus. Once the master receives the XACK* signal, it goes to the vector address and begins servicing the interrupt.

The circuitry shown in Fig. 10-16 allows the interrupt interface to connect to the data interface. One 74S08 ORs the IORC* command with the INTA* command to ensure the buffers face in the right direction during read or inter-

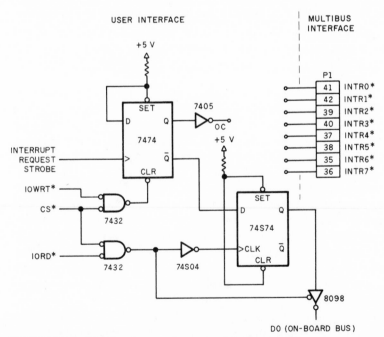

FIGURE 10-15 Multibus slave non-bus-vectored interrupt circuit.

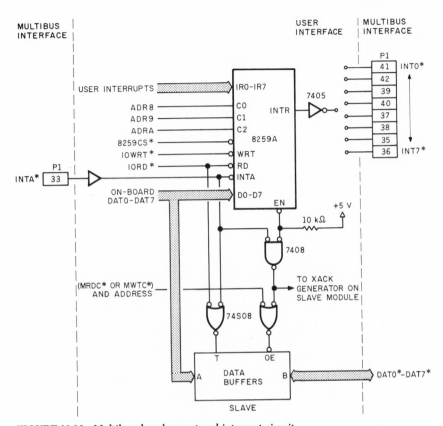

FIGURE 10-16   Multibus slave bus-vectored interrupt circuit.

rupt acknowledge operations. The second and third 74S08 ensure that the data buffers are enabled during a normal data cycle and an interrupt acknowledge cycle.

10.2.3   iSBX Multimodule Interface

The iSBX interface is basically an extension of the microprocessor bus, and therefore it is relatively simple to interface to. There are, however, certain design areas that require further explanation. Implementations in the area of MWAIT* handling and generation and chip select decoding are given in Figs. 10-17 and 10-18. These functions are described in the following sections.

MWAIT* GENERATION AND HANDLING

The MWAIT* signal is used by iSBX Multimodules to extend the I/O cycle. Normally an iSBX Multimodule generates an MWAIT* signal when it is not ready for the transaction with the host SBC. Intel's iSBX 331/332 mathematics

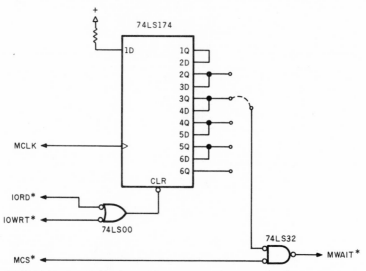

FIGURE 10-17 iSBX multimodule MWAIT* signal generation.

Multimodules generate MWAIT* for this purpose. The signal is derived directly from the peripheral chip on these Multimodules. Under normal conditions, the timing specifications of the iSBX bus are compatible with many peripheral chips currently on the market. However, because of some timing considerations, an MWAIT* may have to be generated to extend the cycle. The circuit shown in Fig. 10-17, when used on an iSBX Multimodule, will generate an MWAIT* to the baseboard on every selected cycle. In MWAIT* generation it is important that the MWAIT* signal be valid no later than 75 ns after the iSBX bus chip select is valid. Otherwise, the cycle may not be extended.

Baseboards have the responsibility for receiving the MWAIT* signal and integrating the signal into its READY circuitry. The circuit illustrated in Fig. 10-18 accomplishes this task. In this circuit the I/O ready is blocked whenever an MWAIT* signal is active. Once MWAIT* goes inactive, the READY is passed through to the microprocessor.

In many cases, the microprocessor can not meet the full AC timing specification of the iSBX bus. When it does not, the host SBC must artificaly extend the I/O cycle. As an example, an 8-MHz 8086 cannot meet some of the AC timing specifications without inserting two wait states. The ready circuit in Fig. 10-18 gates in selectable outputs of a T-state generator (similar to the one shown in Fig. 10-21) to ensure that the I/O ready signal to the microprocessor will be delayed.

iSBX MULTIMODULE CHIP SELECT GENERATION

The 16-bit SBCs that support 8- and 16-bit iSBX Multimodules need special decoding consideration. Table 10-2 gives the address and chip select require-

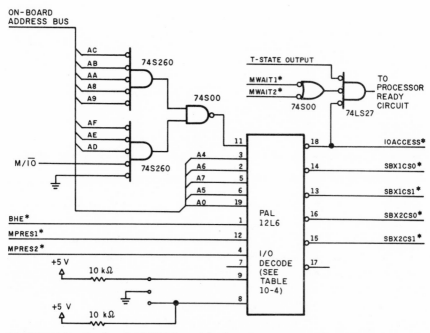

FIGURE 10-18   Baseboard iSBX Multimodule chip select generation (hexadecimal notation).

TABLE 10-2   iSBX Bus Chip Select Address Space (Hexadecimal Notation)

I/O port addresses	Device selected		Function performed
80,82,84,86, 88,8A,8C,8E	iSBX connector J4	Read/write	low-byte transfer (both 8- and 16-bit boards), or word transfer (16-bit boards only). Activates SBX1 CS0* for Multimodule boards.
81,83,85,87, 89,8B,8D,8F	iSBX connector J4	Read/write	high-byte transfer (16-bit boards only). Activates SBX1 CS1* for Multimodule boards.
90,92,94,96, 98,9A,9C,9E	iSBX connector J4	Read/write	byte transfer (8-bit boards only). Activates SBX1 CS1* for Multimodule boards.
A0,A2,A4,A6, A8,AA,AC,AE	iSBX connector J3	Read/write	low-byte transfer (both 8- and 16-bit boards), or word transfer (16-bit boards only). Activates SBX2 CS0* for Multimodule boards.
A1,A3,A5,A7, A9,AB,AD,AF	iSBX connector J3	Read/write	high-byte transfer (16-bit boards only). Activates SBX2 CS1* for Multimodule boards.
B0,B2,B4,B6, B8,BA,BC,BE	iSBX connector J3	Read/write	byte transfer (8-bit boards only). Activates SBX2 CS1* for Multimodule boards.

TABLE 10-3   iSBX Bus Width Select Implementation

PAL input		
Pin 9	Pin 8	Interface operation selected
Low	Low	16-bit operation for both connectors
High	Low	8-bit operation for connector J4, 16-bit operation for connector J3
Low	High	16-bit operation for connector J4, 8-bit operation for connector J3
High	High	8-bit operation for both connectors

ments of a 16-bit host SBC with two iSBX bus connectors (J3 and J4). Since the decoding is relatively complex and selectable (8- or 16-bit iSBX Multimodules), the method of generating the chip selects is performed via a PAL.

The PAL in Fig. 10-18 decodes the address lines to provide the I/O chip select terms required for the iSBX bus and other on-board I/O components. Two inputs of the PAL provide a user-selectable jumper option to indicate whether the devices installed on the iSBX interface are 8- or 16-bit devices. The functions of the two select signals are listed in Table 10-3. In Table 10-4 are listed the four iSBX bus chip select outputs and the conditions required to activate them.

10.2.4   iLBX Master Interface

A basic iLBX master interface implementation is given in Fig. 10-19. The interface can be broken down into five elements:

- Address space decode
- Address
- Data
- Control
- Secondary-master support

Most of the design implementations assume an 80286 microprocessor and 8086 family signal attributes. Design examples are also given for an 8086 microprocessor implementation and 8-bit microprocessor implementation. These implementations are explained in the following sections.

ADDRESS SPACE DECODE

The iLBX bus must be added to the board's on-board–off-board decoding scheme. The decoder in this implementation is designed to allow various memory sizes on the iLBX bus. The job of the decoder is to decide whether the requested resource is on-board, on the Multibus system bus, or on the iLBX bus.

The memory address space decode is performed by a PAL device (U7). The PAL in this implementation has four outputs: Multibus memory access (MBA-CESS*), on-board RAM access (OBRAM*), on-board ROM access (OBROM*), and iLBX memory access (LBXEN*). The PAL inputs include microprocessor addresses A14 to A23, M/IO, and three select inputs. The addresses allow decoding memory blocks down to 16K bytes. The M/IO signal limits the decoding to memory space only. The selectable inputs specify the upper boundary of memory on the iLBX bus. In this example there are eight selectable upper boundaries at 512K-byte increments. The base address for the iLBX bus is fixed at address 100000H. Table 10-5 shows the iLBX decoder for this example.

For example, assume that the SBC contains 256K bytes of RAM with a starting address at 00000H and 32K bytes of ROM with the starting address at 0FF8000H. Also there is 1M byte of RAM on the iLBX bus starting at 100000H. The memory map for this example is given in Fig. 10-20. The PAL was chosen for the added flexibility it gives to the design. It is socketed, so a different decoding scheme could be implemented by replacing the current PAL with a new

TABLE 10-4 ISBX Bus Chip Select Generation Example

Output signal name	Input signal combination	Output signal functions
SBX1 CS0*	A7 and $\overline{A6}$ and $\overline{A5}$ and $\overline{A4}$ and $\overline{A0}$ and $\overline{IO\ ADDR}$ and $\overline{MPRES1}$*	Provides the MCSO* chip select term for I/O addresses 80 through 8E (even addresses only) to an 8- or 16-bit iSBX bus device on J4.
SBX1 CS1*	A7 and $\overline{A6}$ and $\overline{A5}$ and $\overline{A4}$ and $\overline{BHE}$* and $\overline{IO\ ADDR}$ and $\overline{SBX1\ 8\text{-bit}}$ and $\overline{MPRES1}$*	Provides the MCS1* chip select term for I/O addresses 81 through 8F (odd addresses only) to a 16-bit iSBX bus device on J4.
	A7 and $\overline{A6}$ and $\overline{A5}$ and A4 and A0 and $\overline{I/O\ ADDR}$ and SBX1 8-bit and $\overline{MPRES1}$*	Provides the MCS1* chip select term for I/O addresses 90 through 9E (even addresses only) to an 8-bit iSBX bus device on J4.
SBX2 CS0*	A7 and $\overline{A6}$ and A5 and $\overline{A4}$ and $\overline{A0}$ and $\overline{IO\ ADDR}$ and $\overline{MPRES2}$*	Provides the MCSO* chip select term for I/O addresses A0 through AE (even addresses only) to an 8- or 16-bit iSBX bus device on J3.
SBX2 CS1*	A7 and $\overline{A6}$ and A5 and $\overline{A4}$ and $\overline{BHE}$* and $\overline{IO\ ADDR}$ and $\overline{SBX2\ 8\text{-bit}}$ and $\overline{MPRES2}$*	Provides the MCS1* chip select term for I/O addresses A1 through AF (odd addresses only) to a 16-bit iSBX bus device on J3.
	A7 and $\overline{A6}$ and A5 and $\overline{A4}$ and $\overline{A0}$ and $\overline{I/O\ ADDR}$ and SBX2 8-bit and $\overline{MPRES2}$*	Provides the MCS1* chip select term for I/O addresses B0 through BF (even addresses only) to an 8-bit iSBX bus device on J3.

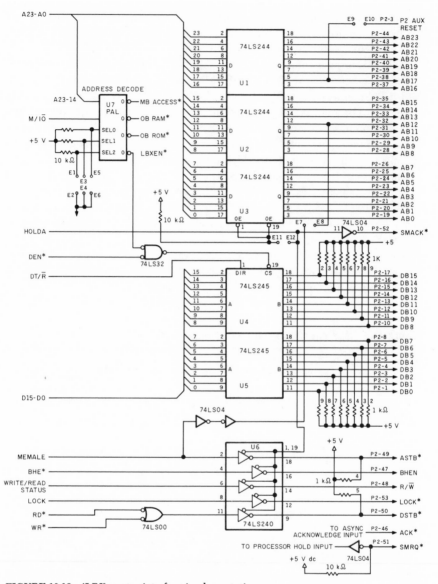

FIGURE 10-19   iLBX master interface implementation.

programmed PAL. Virtually any mapping is allowed for 16K-byte blocks of memory within 24M bytes of address space.

ADDRESS INTERFACE

The addresses are buffered by three 74LS244 octal buffers (U1 to U3). The input addresses to the buffers come directly from the microprocessor bus. The buffers are normally enabled to the bus unless the microprocessor HOLDA output goes active, which turns them off. The HOLDA signal is in conjunction with the secondary-master request (SMRQ∗) signal. This relationship is described later in this section.

DATA INTERFACE

The 16-bit data interface is composed of two 74LS245 octal transceivers. The transceiver chip select (CS) input is made up of the combination of the decode PAL's LBXEN∗ output and the microprocessor's control data enable (DEN)

TABLE 10-5   iLBX Bus Address Space Decoder Example

iLBX bus upper limit	Select jumpers		
	E1-E2	E3-E4	E5-E6
Reserved	In	In	In
Reserved	In	In	Out
17FFFFH	In	Out	In
1FFFFFH	In	Out	Out
27FFFFH	Out	In	In
2FFFFFH	Out	In	Out
37FFFFH	Out	Out	In
Disable iLBX access	Out	Out	Out

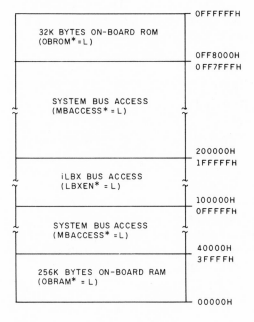

FIGURE 10-20   iLBX bus memory map.

output. The transceiver direction term comes directly from the control DT/R output.

CONTROL

All of the control outputs are driven by a 74LS240 octal buffer (U6). The 80286 SBC board's control signals are direct derivatives of the microprocessor's control outputs. Since the 80286 ALE output meets the iLBX ASTB* timing, it is used to drive the input of the ASTB* buffer. In a similar fashion, BHEN, R/W, and LOCK buffer inputs are driven directly from the 80286 bus. The data strobe (DSTB*) is an OR condition of the 80286 RD* and WR* commands. As with the address buffers, the command buffers typically are enabled unless the processor HOLDA signal becomes active.

SECONDARY-MASTER SUPPORT

The secondary-master support used in this implementation is straightforward and takes advantage of the 80286 internal control. The 80286 HOLD and HOLDA are used to provide secondary-master support. The secondary-master request (SMRQ*) is buffered and then directly connected to the 80286 HOLD input. The 80286 HOLDA output drives the input of the SMACK* buffer. The 10kΩ pull-up resistor on the SMRQ* input ensures that the SMRQ* signal will be inactive if the system does not contain a secondary master.

Although this secondary-master implementation is simple to perform in hardware, it can be costly in terms of overall system performance. When the microprocessor receives an active HOLD signal and the microprocessor generates a HOLDA, all microprocessor activity is stopped. This occurs even if the microprocessor is not using the iLBX bus. An improved implementation would allow the microprocessor to turn off its iLBX interface while maintaining the ability to execute on-board or on the Multibus system bus.

ADDRESS STROBE GENERATION

The address strobe signal can be derived directly from many microprocessors' ALE signal. Intel's 80286 microprocessor can directly drive the ASTB* signal with its buffered ALE. In 8086 and 8088 implementations, the ALE signal does not provide the proper address setup to generate ASTB* directly. Therefore, a circuit must be used to generate the proper ASTB* signal. The circuit given in Fig. 10-21 does the job with very little overhead. It takes advantage of a T-state generator, which is required on most board-level designs. The outputs of the T-state generator indicate the current 8086/8088 T state.

The basic T-state circuit operates as follows: The 74S175 is wired to form a four-bit shift register. When the 8086 ALE is generated, the shift register is cleared. On the first falling 8086 clock edge after ALE is removed, a 1 is clocked into the Q1 bit position. The first falling clock edge after ALE is removed is the

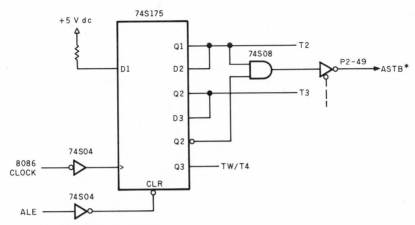

FIGURE 10-21 8088 and 8086 T-state generator.

T2 state of the 8086. Each successive falling clock edge shifts the 1 down a bit position. When the Q3 output goes high, the 8086 has entered the T4 or TW (wait state). All outputs will remain high until the next ALE is generated.

The ASTB* signal is generated by ANDing (74S04) the T2 state with the T3* state. This produces an ASTB* signal that starts at the beginning of T2, is one clock period in width, and provides the proper address set-up to meet the iLBX bus specification.

AN 8-BIT IMPLEMENTATION

An 8-bit microprocessor that requires only an 8-bit iLBX interface is virtually a subset of the 16-bit interface. Since the 8-bit interface does not use the higher-order data byte, the 74LS245 transceiver U4 and the byte high enable (BHEN) circuitry can be eliminated. The remainder of the interface design is equivalent to the 16-bit implementation.

If the requirement of an 8-bit board is to have the capability of interfacing with both 8- and 16-bit iLBX devices, a data interface circuit similar to the one shown in Fig. 10-22 should be used. To implement the circuit, both data transceivers are required. When the device is configured for 16-bit operations (E1 jumpered to E2), the low-order address line A0 is used to differentiate between the high and low bites. When A0 is low, the data is transmitted on the low-byte data transceiver U4 while the high-byte data transceiver U5 is turned off. Similarly, when A0 is high, the data is transmitted on the high-byte transceiver U5, while the low-byte transceiver U4 is turned off. The A0 address line is also used to generate the BHEN signal. To configure the 8-bit interface, the jumper is connected between E2 and E3. When the jumper is placed in the 8-bit mode, the high-byte transceiver U5 is permanently disabled and all data transfers occur over the low-byte transceiver U4.

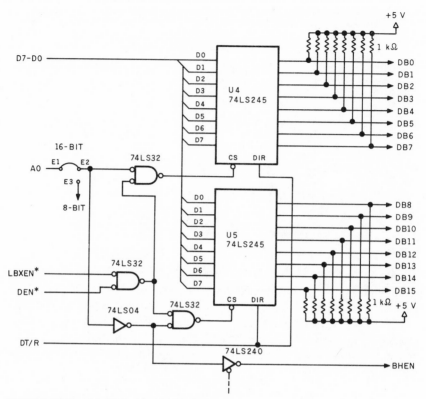

FIGURE 10-22 8-bit SBC with a 16-bit iLBX interface.

10.2.5 iLBX Slave Interface

Much of the slave interface circuitry is similar to the master interface circuitry. The key differences are in the address circuitry and the bus acknowledge (ACK∗) circuitry. The slave interface implementation is given in Fig. 10-23 and is explained in the following sections.

ADDRESS INTERFACE

Since the address does not remain valid throughout the entire transfer cycle, the slave must latch the bus address and control signals. The signals are latched by using 74S373 transparent latches. This implementation takes advantage of the address setup time (40 ns to ASTB∗ active) to give additional address decode time.

The circuit operates as follows: The D flip-flop is cleared on a board reset. The Q∗ output, which is connected to the 74S373 latch enable input, allows the address information to pass directly through to the address decoder. When the

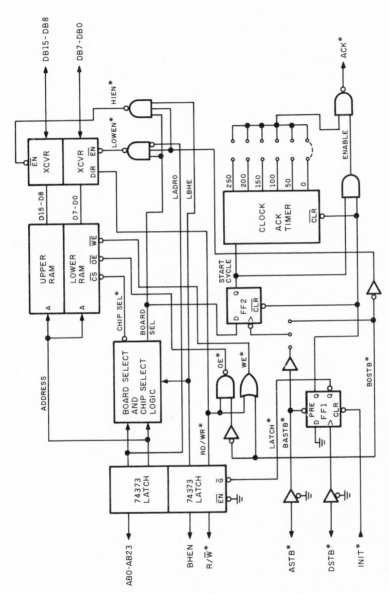

FIGURE 10-23 iLBX slave interface.

ASTB* signal goes active, the flip-flop is preset, which in turn latches the address. The information remains latched until the trailing edge of DSTB* (which signals the end of cycle) clocks the flip-flop and reenables the latches for the next cycle. If the address were for a resource on-board, the decoders would generate the proper chip selects (CHIP SEL*) and board select (BOARD SEL*). If the extra decode time of 40 ns is not required, then a clocked octal flip-flop, such as a 74(L)S374, could be used in place of the 74S373 transparent latch. In that case the ASTB* signal should be inverted and connected directly to the clock input of the flip-flop.

DATA INTERFACE

The data interface, which consists of two 74LS245 octal transceivers, allows the slave to transmit or receive a 16-bit word or either the high- or low-order data byte. The direction term for both buffers is derived from the latched iLBX bus R/W* signal. The enable circuit uses two three-input NAND gates to select the high or the low byte or both. The LOWEN* signal consists of the board select term, address signal AB0, and the DSTB* signal. The board select term ensures that the buffer turns on only when the board is selected. The AB0 term ensures that the buffer turns on only when the low byte is requested (AB0 low). This address will be low whenever a low byte or word value is requested. The DSTB* signal guarantees that the slave buffers turn on only when a valid data strobe is issued by the master. To ensure that a buffer fight cannot occur between the master and slave, the timing parameter t_{14} is critical. The slave has 45 ns from the trailing edge of DSTB* to turn off its data buffers. The TTL devices used in the buffer-enable circuitry must be carefully chosen in order to meet this parameter.

The high-byte enable circuit consists of the same terms as the low-byte enable circuit with the exception that the buffered BHEN signal replaces AB0. If a high byte or word is requested, the BHEN signal will be high, which will enable the buffer. If only the low byte is requested, the BHEN signal will be low, which will disable the high-byte buffer.

ACKNOWLEDGE INTERFACE

The circuit shown in Fig. 10-23 allows the slave to generate the type 1, type 2, or type 3 acknowledge. Basically, for type 1 acknowledges, the slave generates the ACK* signal based on address strobe. For type 2 and 3 acknowledges, the slave generates the ACK* signal based on data strobe. The interface timing of the master(s) determines if a type 1 acknowledge can be used or if a type 2 acknowledge must be used.

Connecting a jumper from E1 to E2 selects the address strobe as the clock to set the start cycle flip-flop FF2. The START CYCLE output activates the acknowledge timer, which can be implemented via digital delay lines or a shift register similar to the Multibus master T-state generator. Immediately following the START CYCLE output going active, the delay line outputs a sequence of six signals each delayed by 50 ns from the preceding signal. By connecting the output of the desired delay to the input of the ACK* driver, the proper delay time for the system configuration can be programmed for the ACK* signal.

The acknowledge hold time after the trailing edge of DSTB* t_{12}, is a critical parameter to be aware of. The iLBX bus specification allows a maximum of 45 ns to turn off the ACK* signal. As with the data buffers, care should be taken in choosing the TTL devices in the critical path. Failure to comply with this timing parameter could result in a false acknowledge on the next transfer cycle.

If a system is designed for type 1 acknowledges, it is possible for the primary master to run synchronously with its slave devices. This virtually means that the microprocessor on the master expects data relative to its clock. Although there is no requirement to run synchronously in a type 1 acknowledge system, the primary master's performance can be improved or the slave device's memory access time can be longer when they are synchronous. However, when designing slave boards capable of running synchronously with type 1 acknowledges, the designer must be aware of certain conditions that can cause the primary master to lose synchronization: dual-port memories and dynamic memories. Whenever the memory is being refreshed or the other port is accessed in dual-port slave designs, the primary master will lose synchronization with the transfer. To overcome this problem, the slave should dynamically change its acknowledge to type 3 whenever the memory will not be ready in the normal period. This type of implementation has little effect on system performance, since refresh and dual-port hits occur only a small percentage of the time. Also, it is far more efficient than slowing down all accesses to meet the worst-case requirements of the refresh and dual-port delays.

10.2.6 Multichannel Master Interface

A basic Multichannel master interface is shown in Fig. 10-24. This type of interface implementation can be used on Multichannel bus supervisors or intelligent controllers. The main difference between the supervisor and intelligent controller interface is that the supervisor drives the supervisor active (SA*) signal and the intelligent controller receives SA*. The interface can be broken into four elements:

- Address and data
- Parity
- Control
- Interrupts

Although not a requirement, the implementations discussed in the following sections assume an 8086-family processor design.

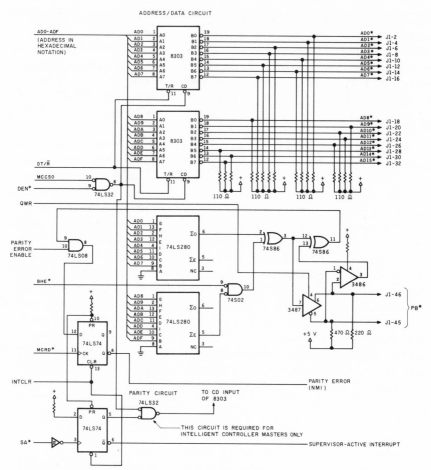

FIGURE 10-24 Multichannel master address-data interface.

ADDRESS-DATA INTERFACE

The address-data (A/D) interface shown in Fig. 10-24 uses the 8303 octal buffer transceiver to drive the bus. The buffer input signals come directly from the microprocessor A/D bus. The buffers are enabled by the chip select MCCS0* and the 8288 DEN. The chip select goes active whenever the microprocessor addresses its Multichannel interface. The DEN signal goes active whenever a data transfer takes place.

Intelligent controllers must also react to supervisor active (SA*). If an intelligent controller is active on the Multichannel bus, it must release the bus whenever the supervisor wants to regain control. When the supervisor asserts SA*, the intelligent controller must be off the bus in 75 ns maximum after receiving SA* active. The circuit shown in Fig. 10-24 implements this function. The SA* signal is the clock input to the D flip-flop. When SA* goes active, the flip-flop is clocked, which drives its Q* output low. The Q* output, which is a term in the buffer enable circuit, turns off the A/D buffers. This action also provides an interrupt to the microprocessor. When the microprocessor reads the status of the interrupt, the flip-flop clears, which allows the interface to be enabled for future transfer cycles.

PARITY INTERFACE

If parity is chosen for the system, all Multichannel devices that talk on the bus are required to generate parity and all devices that listen to the bus are required to check parity. The circuit shown in Fig. 10-24 both generates and checks parity. The basic circuit uses two 74LS280 parity generator-checker devices. When the master is talking, the microprocessor A/D bus, which is connected to the parity circuit inputs, sets the proper parity up on each byte. The outputs of the high- and low-byte parity circuit are "exclusive-ORed" to generate the proper parity signal. This signal is connected directly to the Multichannel bus parity differential driver. The driver is enabled whenever the device is talking on the bus. An intelligent controller also gates the enable with the SA* flip-flop as is done with the A/D buffers.

Parity checking uses the same circuits as parity generation, except that the data used to generate the parity check bit comes from the Multichannel bus via the A/D buffers. When the interface port is accessed by a microprocessor read, the A/D buffers are enabled and the data is directed toward the microprocessor local A/D bus. After the parity circuits generate it, the parity bit is compared with the bus parity bit (PB*) via the EXCLUSIVE-OR gate. When the microprocessor internally reads the data, the state of the parity check is latched. The output of this flip-flop generates a nonmaskable interrupt (NMI) if a parity error has occurred.

This parity implementation also allows parity generation and checking with 8-bit Multichannel devices. To accomplish this, the high-byte check bit is gated with the microprocessor's byte high enable (BHE*) signal. If a byte transfer occurs, the high-byte parity circuit is disabled. Therefore, it does not contribute to the parity bit on 8-bit reads or writes.

CONTROL INTERFACE

The control portion of the Multichannel interface consists of DRDY*, DACC*, R/W, and A/D. The control section of the Multichannel interface is given in Fig. 10-25. The implementation of each of these signals is explained in the following paragraphs.

The R/W and A/D signals are directly controlled by the microprocessor. The microprocessor sets the state of these lines by writing the appropriate data to the control latch under software control. This method, although relatively slow, gives the microprocessor full control over the state of the bus. The supervisor enables the bus control differential drivers by using the SA* signal as the

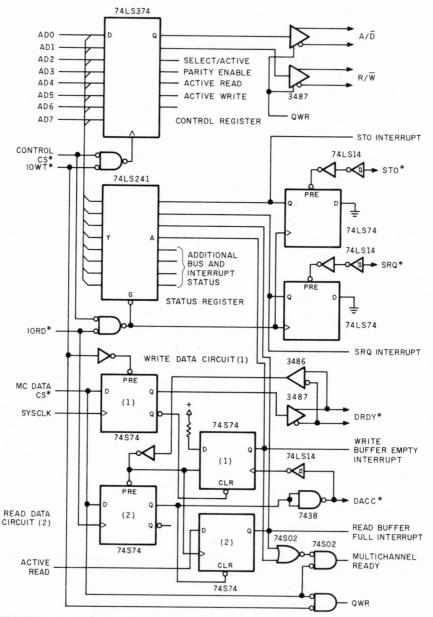

FIGURE 10-25 Multichannel master control interface.

enable. The intelligent controller enables its drivers when SA* goes inactive. The intelligent controller also gates the enable with the SELECT signal. This signal goes active only when the intelligent controller has been programmed to take the bus over when the supervisor goes inactive. This ensures that, in a configuration with more than one intelligent controller, only one will be enabled on the bus.

The DRDY* signal generation is performed via the DRDY flip-flop. When the microprocessor writes data to the Multichannel interface, the flip-flop preset input goes inactive and the D input goes low. On the next falling edge of the microprocessor clock (SYSCLK) after the write command goes active, the DRDY* signal is generated. This circuit provides the 60-ns data setup required before DRDY* becomes active. The DRDY* signal remains active until the DACC* signal is received from the listening device. The DACC* signal clocks the "ready" flip-flop, which generates a ready back to the microprocessor. The microprocessor completes the cycle by removing the write command, which in turn presets the DRDY flip-flop and forces DRDY* inactive.

The DACC* signal generator allows the microprocessor to read data from the Multichannel interface in two ways. In the first way the microprocessor reads the interface and waits for data to become valid. In this case the DACC flip-flop is held in a preset state by the DRDY* signal being inactive. The microprocessor reads the interface, which forces the D input to the DACC flip-flop to be low. However, the flip-flop does not clock, since it is the rising edge of command that clocks the flip-flop. Since data is not available, the ready flip-flop provides a not-ready signal to the microprocessor. When data is valid from the Multichannel bus, the bus DRDY* signal is generated. That removes the preset to the DACC flip-flop and clocks the ready flip-flop, which generates a ready signal to the microprocessor. The microprocessor responds by removing the read command, which clocks the DACC flip-flop and generates the bus DACC* signal. The ready signal is cleared once the DACC* signal is generated. The DACC flip-flop is preset when the DRDY* signal goes inactive.

The second way the DACC interface is used is by generating an interrupt to the microprocessor when data is available. In this case the ready flip-flop also generates an interrupt to the microprocessor when a bus DRDY* signal is received. The ready signal does not affect any microprocessor operation currently in progress, since the ready is gated with the Multichannel interface chip select term. When the microprocessor services the interrupt, it reads the Multichannel interface. Since the ready signal is valid, the cycle continues as previously described. The interrupt is also cleared when DACC* is generated.

INTERRUPT INTERFACE

The bus supervisor is the only device that receives and acts on the bus interrupts SRQ and STO. Only intelligent controllers and basic devices may generate those signals. Therefore, the interface requirements are different for those devices.

For supervisor devices, the circuit given in Fig. 10-25 is used. This circuit allows supervisors to accept, read status, and clear the bus interrupts. When a bus interrupt is received, the state of the interrupt is latched into the D flip-flop. The output of the flip-flop generates an interrupt to the microprocessor. When the microprocessor services the interrupt and reads the status, the read operation also clears the interrupt.

Intelligent controllers, as well as basic devices, must generate the bus interrupts. Besides the interrupt generation, the devices are responsible for providing the interrupt register data on an interrupt poll by the supervisor. The operation of these circuits is explained in the next section.

10.2.7 Multichannel Slave Interface

In the circuit implementations discussed in this section it is assumed that a microprocessor is not an integral element of the interface design. The following slave interface characteristics are considered:

- Device select-deselect

- Parity generation and checking

- Transfer handshake

This section provides basic circuit implementations to illustrate the considerations involved in the various signal line implementations. The circuits shown are not optimized or complete. In many cases the tasks performed by the circuits can be replaced by a microprocessor or microcontroller. In that case the circuit designer must decide where the price-performance trade-off is for the implementation.

DEVICE SELECT INTERFACE

The device select circuit shown in Fig. 10-26 allows a slave to scan the Multichannel bus for its device number and generate the proper on-board and bus control signals.

The device select circuit compares the device number field of the first word of the address transfer to the number selected on the four-bit switch SW1. If the numbers match, the flip-flop F2 clocks, thereby setting the internal control signal ACTIVE. That this signal is active implies that the device has been selected. The address mode synchronizer flip-flop F1 keeps track of the first and second address transfer. This flip-flop ensures that flip-flop F1 compares and clocks only on the first address transfer. Once the device is selected the switches are forced to compare to the deselect value 0FH, so that the circuit can be deselected by the master when the transfer is complete.

In this implementation the AACC signal is generated directly from the

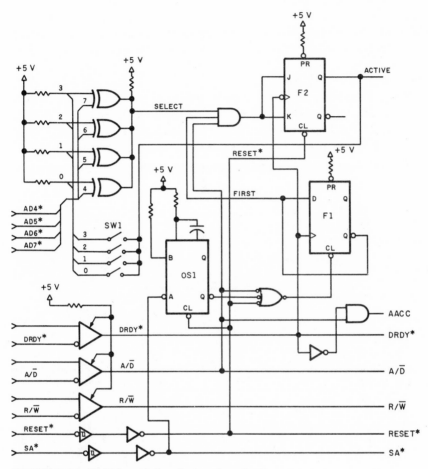

FIGURE 10-26 Multichannel slave device select circuit.

DRDY* signal. The signal is qualified by the bus A/D signal in that it can be active only during address transfers. If additional data hold time is needed after DRDY* is asserted, a delay must be incorporated before deasserting AACC.

PARITY INTERFACE

The basic parity circuit given in Fig. 10-27 is similar in operation to the master parity circuit. However, there is additional overhead to provide STO* signal generation and STO register support. If a microcontroller were used with this interface, the parity generation and check would be performed in hardware as shown but the register support would be handled by the microcontroller.

The parity bit circuit implementation for a slave device is similar to the master circuit. For the slave implementation the control signals such as R/W and

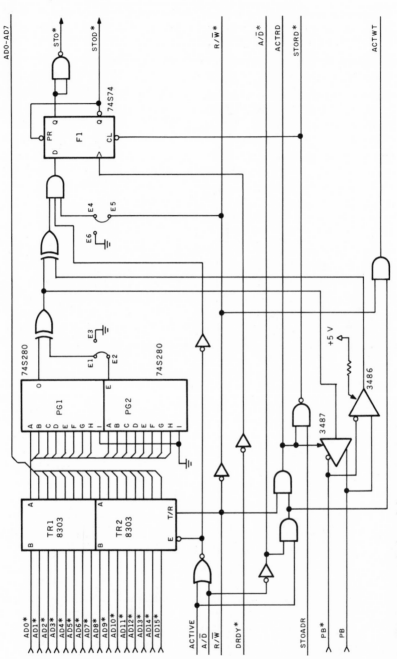

FIGURE 10-27 Multichannel slave parity circuit.

A/D come from the bus rather than being generated by a microprocessor. Slave and intelligent controller devices generate an STO interrupt when a parity error occurs. In this circuit implementation, when a parity error occurs, flip-flop F1 clocks and thereby generates an active STO* signal on the bus.

A basic slave STO register circuit is shown in Fig. 10-28. When a master addresses the slave's STO register and places the bus into the data mode, the signal STORD* becomes active. This signal enables the STO* buffer B1 and generates the DRDY* signal after the data setup time has been met. If a parity error has occurred, the input(s) to the buffer B1 will be high, which will cause the STO register data to be nonzero. If no parity error has occurred, the value in the STO register will be zero. After the register read cycle is completed, the parity error and STO register data are cleared. The nonzero STO register value is user-definable. For this example, the value chosen is 0FFH.

TRANSFER HANDSHAKE INTERFACE

The transfer handshake interface is composed of two circuits: the read hand-shake circuit and the write handshake circuit. The read handshake circuit, which is used by slave devices that talk on the bus, is shown in Fig. 10-29. The write handshake circuit, which is used by slave devices that listen on the bus (address or data), is shown in Fig. 10-30.

The read circuit is active whenever the device is a talker in a data transfer. In this case the slave device is responsible for asserting DRDY* when data is

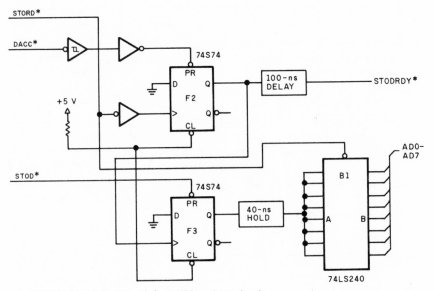

FIGURE 10-28 **Multichannel slave STO register circuit.**

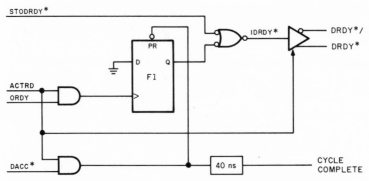

FIGURE 10-29 Multichannel slave read transfer handshake circuit.

valid and receiving DACC* to guarantee that data has been accepted. The ACTRD signal, which was developed earlier in the parity circuits, is a combination of the device select and data mode terms. This signal goes active whenever the slave device is selected as the bus talker and the bus is placed in data mode. Once the on-board data has met the required 40-ns setup, an ORDY (output ready) signal is generated. The signal clocks flip-flop F1 and thereby asserts DRDY* on the bus. The ORDY signal generation is a function of the devices that are on the slave. When the slave receives DACC*, the one-shot (OS1) is clocked, thereby generating a pulse that clears the DRDY* flip-flop F1. This pulse can also be used by the slave to advance the on-board circuitry for the next cycle. The cycle continues until the master places the bus in the address mode (A/D = high), which removes the ACTRD signal.

The write circuit is active whenever the device is the listener in a data transfer cycle. In that case the slave is responsible for receiving DRDY* and the bus data and generating DACC* when it has internally accepted the data. The ACTWT (active write) signal generated in the control circuit section is used to qualify the write cycle. When the slave receives a DRDY*, flip-flop F2 preset input is brought high, which allows the flip-flop to clock once the slave has internally accepted the data. The on-board slave circuit generates an IRDY (input ready) when it has accepted the data. This signal, qualified by ACTWT, generates a DACC* signal back to the master. Once the master removes the DRDY* signal, the flip-flop F2 is cleared, thereby removing DACC*. The signal WRTCMD (write command) can be used as a write signal by the slave's memory or I/O devices. The data hold time for these devices should be checked for actual signal use and implementation.

10.3 SPECIAL INTERFACE GUIDELINES

Special interfaces are specific interface designs that allow for a consistent and standard high-level hardware-software interface. The following design implementations are covered:

- Dual-port memory interface

- Interprocessor communication port

- 16M-byte addressing

- Standard I/O addresses

These design implementations are not part of the Multibus system bus structure specification, but they do implement a Multibus system architecture philosophy. Their goal is to provide a consistent interface and consistent functionality across the board product line.

10.3.1 Dual-Port Memory Interface

The dual-port RAM access control logic and buffers, shown in Fig. 10-31 and 10-32, allow the RAM on an SBC board to the shared by the local microprocessor and other Multibus masters. When accessing the RAM array, the local microprocessor request is given priority over the Multibus master's request. When a Multibus access is in progress, the dual-port control logic enters the slave mode and any subsequent local microprocessor requests are held off until the slave mode is completed.

The circuit is based on three flip-flop stages: synchronizer (U1), dual-port arbiter (U2), and command enable (U3). The synchronizer flip-flop synchronizes the asychronous Multibus RAM array request. The dual-port arbiter provides the second stage of synchronization and arbitrates between the local microprocessor request and the synchronized Multibus request. The command enable flip-flop enables the selected interface command to the RAM array.

When a Multibus request is made to the dual-port RAM, the OFF BD RAM REQ* signal goes active. This signal is the combination of the bus address chip select and the OR of the memory bus commands. It provides the input term to the synchronizer flip-flop U1. On the next rising edge of the dual-port clock (DP CLOCK) the signal is latched. The output of U1 is connected to the three-input NAND gate. This gate provides the block term for a local microprocessor

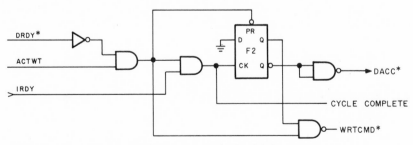

FIGURE 10-30   Multichannel slave write transfer handshake circuit.

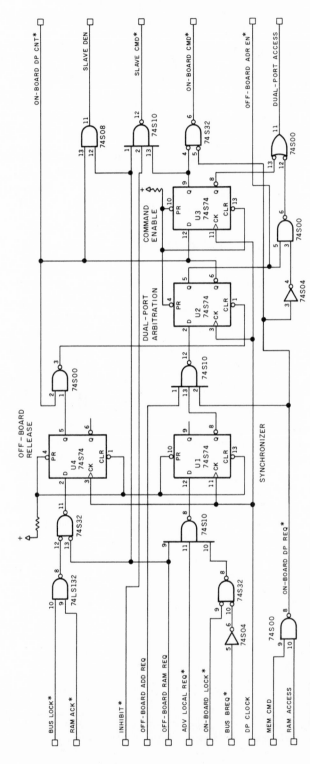

FIGURE 10-31 Dual-port control circuits.

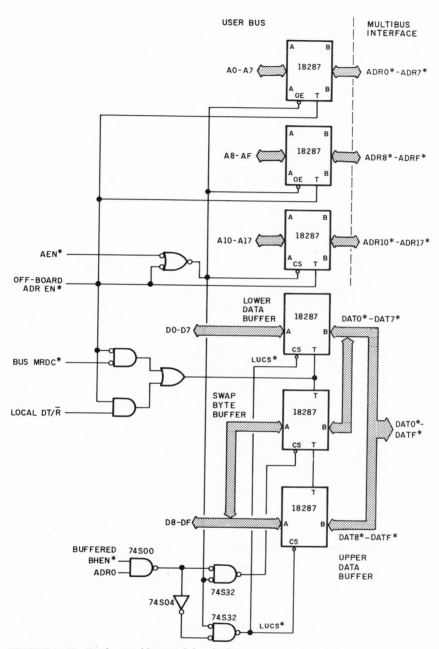

FIGURE 10-32 Dual-port address and data buffers.

access. If there is no pending local request, the synchronizer output goes to the dual-port arbiter flip-flop U2. This flip-flop provides the second stage of synchronization and enables the appropriate address buffers on the next rising clock edge.

Slave requests must be double-synchronized to help prevent arbitration failures. If the slave request does not meet the setup time of U1's D input, the Q output may go astable (i.e., walkout). The period of time during which the output remains astable varies with the flip-flop type. The clock period chosen for the arbitration circuit must be greater than the astable period to ensure the signal will be stable prior to clocking at the next stage. Care should be taken when choosing the arbitration flip-flops. Two criteria for choosing them are a low setup time requirement and an astable period less then the arbitration clock. The 74S74 D flip-flop has been characterized to work well in arbiter circuits because of slow set-up time requirements and a short astable period. Each vendor's flip-flop should be characterized carefully for use in arbiter circuits.

The Q output of U2 is connected to U3, which enables the appropriate commands to the RAM array on the subsequent clock edge. When the Multibus access is completed, the master removes the command, which causes the OFF BOARD RAM REQ* signal to go inactive. This allows the off-board release flip-flop (U4) to clock, thereby clearing the dual-port arbiter flip-flop which turns the dual-port RAM back to the local CPU.

This implementation also contains two lock circuits, one from the Multibus system bus side and one from the local CPU side. The bus lock signal, which is derived from the Multibus LOCK* signal, will prevent any local CPU access once the dual-port memory has been granted to the Multibus port. The BUS LOCK* signal prevents flip-flop U4 from clearing, thereby holding the dual-port arbiter flip-flop in the slave mode. The dual port will remain locked until the LOCK* signal is removed. The local CPU lock, ON BOARD LOCK*, prevents any Multibus system bus access to the dual-port RAM. When activated by the local CPU, this signal blocks any Multibus system bus request.

10.3.2 Interprocessor Communication Port

A common problem that systems with multiple microprocessors must overcome is the effective transmission of messages between SBC masters. Although multiple algorithims and methodologies can be developed to solve the problem, rarely is the same method used on each SBC board. The key area that is hindered by nonstandard communication methods is the system software. The software must be rewritten for each application; otherwise, it cannot take advantage of the hardware mechanisms provided.

The block diagram of Fig. 10-33 provides a signaling mechanism that is controlled by the system software. This implementation allows SBC boards to place messages in common (global) system memory (dual-port or shared Multibus sys-

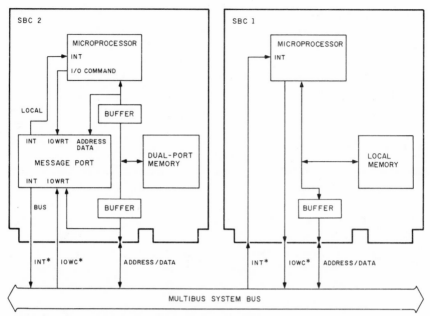

FIGURE 10-33 Interprocessor message byte block diagram.

tem memory) and signal the SBC that a message is valid. The procedure is as follows: SBC 1 places a message in the SBC 2 dual-port memory. After the message has been placed, SBC 1 writes a value into a designated I/O port on SBC 2. This action generates an interrupt to the microprocessor on SBC 2. When the interrupt is serviced, the local microprocessor reads the message and clears the interrupt by writing a value to the I/O port. If more then one master can use the communication port from the system bus side, then a semaphore (flag) must also be used so that the other masters do not contaminate the data. This test-and-set flag must also be placed in global memory. All masters must test, and set if open, this flag prior to using the communication port.

When SBC 2 wants to signal that it has completed the action requested by SBC 1, it places a return message into its dual-port memory. After the message has been placed, SBC 2 writes a value into its I/O port to interrupt SBC 1. When SBC 1 receives the interrupt, it services the interrupt by reading the return message and clearing the interrupt by writing a value to the I/O port of SBC 2.

Figure 10-34 is the decoding of the data written by the signaling SBCs to the communication I/O port. The values are symmetrical, so that the action performed by an SBC is the same for a given data value whether the I/O write is local or is from the Multibus system bus. The decoding scheme also allows a Multibus master to reset an SBC by writing a specific value into the I/O port.

This provides a remote reset for peripheral boards without resetting the entire system. Figure 10-35 shows a hardware implementation of the signaling mechanism. In this circuit two programmable array logic (PAL) ICs provide the entire signaling hardware. PAL U1 provides all the necessary handshake logic, and PAL U2 provides the Multibus I/O address decode.

When a Multibus write to the signal port I/O address occurs, U2 decodes the address. If the I/O port address is valid, the MBCS* signal goes active. This signal is connected to the U1 input. The data value comes from the Multibus data lines DAT0* and DAT1*. This selects the proper signal action. When the Multibus IOWC* command becomes valid, a signal operation takes place and a Multibus XACK* is generated. A similar operation takes place when the I/O write occurs from the on-board side. In this case the data comes from the local data bus (D0 to D1), the chip select (ON BD FLAG CS*) comes from the on-board address decoders, and the I/O write command comes from the local CPU. The Multibus system bus address decoder provides flexibility for the placement of the signal port I/O address. The I/O port can be placed in one of eight system bus I/O addresses. This is accomplished by placing the appropirate

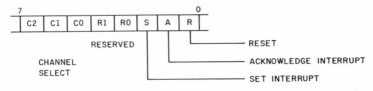

WAKE UP BITS			ACTION PERFORMED	
S	A	R	MULTIBUS WRITE	ON-BOARD WRITE
1	0	0	INTERRUPT ON-BOARD PROCESSOR	INTERRUPT TO MULTIBUS HOST
0	1	0	ACKNOWLEDGE INTERRUPT TO MULTIBUS HOST	ACKNOWLEDGE INTERRUPT TO ON-BOARD PROCESSOR
0	0	1	HARDWARE RESET THE BOARD	ILLEGAL

CHANNEL BITS			CHANNEL SELECTED
C2	C1	C0	
0	0	0	CHANNEL 0
0	0	1	CHANNEL 1
	•		•
	•		•
	•		•
1	1	1	CHANNEL 7

R1R0 = 00 (RESERVED FOR FUTURE USE)

FIGURE 10-34   Interprocessor flag byte message format. (Note: All other codes are reserved and will cause unpredictable results.)

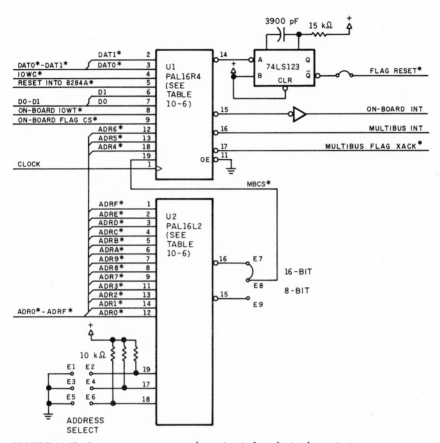

FIGURE 10-35 Interprocessor message byte circuit (hexadecimal notation).

jumpers between pins E1 and E2, E3 and E4, and E5 and E6. This decoding allows a maximum of eight unique signal ports with the same base address to coexist on the system bus. It should be noted that if additional I/O ports are required, other base addresses can be programmed into the PAL. To allow the decoder to work in 8- and 16-bit environments or 16-bit-only environments, a jumper select is provided. For the 8- and 16-bit mode, only the first eight addresses are decoded (ADR0* to ADR7*). Table 10-6 gives the logic equations for the decode and flag byte PAL. The decode implementation accepts 16-bit addresses 08A4H to 08A7H and 09A4H and 09A7H. For the 8- and 16-bit mode the addresses are 0A4H to 0A7H.

10.3.3 16M-byte Addressing

With the introduction of microprocessors that have a full 16M-byte address range, such as Intel's 80286, SBCs with microprocessors that can address only

TABLE 10-6 Flag Byte Generator and Address Decode Pal Example

---

FLAG BYTE PAL

BFLAGINT   := BFLAGINT * /D1
+ BFLAGINT * D0
+ BFLAGINT * IOWT
+ BFLAGINT * FLAGCS
+ RESET
+ DAT1 * DAT0 * /IOWC * ADR6 * /ADR5 * ADR4 * /MBFLAGSEL

FLAGINT   := /DAT1 * DAT0 * /IOWC * ADR6 * /ADR5 * ADR4 * /MBFLAGSEL * /RESET
+ FLAGINT * D1 * /RESET
+ FLAGINT * D0 * /RESET
+ FLAGINT * IOWT * /RESET
+ FLAGINT * FLAGCS * /RESET

FLAGRES   := DAT1 * /DAT0 * /IOWC * ADR6 * /ADR5 * ADR4 * /MBFLAGSEL

FLAGXACK := DAT1 * /DAT0 * /IOWC * ADR6 * /ADR5 * ADR4 * /MBFLAGSEL
* FLAGRES * /RESET

DECODE PAL

16BSEL   = FS2 * FS1 * FS0 * /AF * /AE * /AD * /AC
* AB * /AA * /A9 * /A8 * A7 * /A3 * A2 * A1
+ FS2 * FS1 * /FS0 * /AF * /AE * /AD * /AC
* AB * /AA * /A9 * /A8 * A7 * /A3 * A2 * /A1
* A0
+ FS2 * /FS1 * FS0 * /AF * /AE * /AD * /AC
* AB * /AA * /A9 * /A8 * A7 * /A3 * A2 * A1
* /A0
+ FS2 * /FS1 * /FS0 * /AF * /AE * /AD * /AC
* AB * /AA * /A9 * /A8 * A7 * /A3 * A2 * A1
* A0
+ /FS2 * FS1 * FS0 * /AF * /AE * /AD * /AC
* AB * /AA * /A9 * A8 * A7 * /A3 * A2 * /A1
* /A0
+ /FS2 * FS1 * /FS0 * /AF * /AE * /AD * /AC
* AB * /AA * /A9 * A8 * A7 * /A3 * A2 * /A1
* A0
+ /FS2 * /FS1 * FS0 * /AF * /AE * /AD * /AC
* AB * /AA * /A9 * A8 * A7 * /A3 * A2 * A1
* /A0
+ /FS2 * /FS1 * /FS0 * /AF * /AE * /AD * /AC
* AB * /AA * /A9 * A8 * A7 * /A3 * A2 * A1
* A0

8BSEL   = FS1 * FS0 * A7 * /A3 * A2 * /A1 * /A0
+ FS1 * /FS0 * A7 * /A3 * A2 * /A1 * A0
+ /FS1 * FS0 * A7 * /A3 * A2 * A1 * /A0
+ /FS1 * /FS0 * A7 * /A3 * A2 * A1 * A0

1M-byte or less cannot transfer data over the full 16M-byte address range. This becomes critical in systems that contain 16M-byte microprocessors and peripheral controllers that can provide addressing only in the first megabyte page. It would mean that a disk controller could read or write data only in the first megabyte of the 80286 address space.

To overcome this problem, a standard hardware mechanism has been designed to give 1M-byte microprocessors, such as Intel's 8086 and 80186, the ability to read or write data anywhere in the 16M-byte address space. The goal of this interface is to provide a consistent mechanism that the system software can take full advantage of.

The basic mechanism, given in Fig. 10-36, provides a 256K-byte window into the full 16M-byte address range for 1M-byte SBCs. The 1M-byte processor provides the window via its on-board address range 80000H to 0BFFFFH. The actual high-order address signals are generated by the data value written to the latch during an on-board I/O write. This value remains intact until overwritten by another value. When the decoder detects the 256K-byte memory space between 80000H and 0BFFFFH (A18 = low, A19 = high), it enables the latch

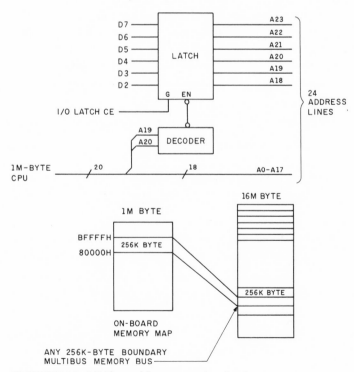

FIGURE 10-36 16M-byte address generation circuit.

onto the Multibus system bus. When the 1M-byte reads or writes data in the address range of 80000H to 0BFFFFH, the Multibus address generated will be offset by the value written to the latch. To place the 1M-byte SBC to the normal 1M-byte address range, the value 08H should be written to the latch. This places the actual microprocessor address on the Multibus system bus when the window is enabled.

The 16M-byte window should be used mainly for data movement and not for code execution. Care should be taken to ensure that all interrupt service routines are local to the SBC and that the service routines are aware of the window.

10.3.4 Standard I/O Addresses

Most operating systems expect certain I/O addresses to be fixed for proper operation. A typical SBC has on-board serial I/O, parallel I/O, timer-counter I/O, and an interrupt controller. The operating system expects to initialize and communicate with these devices at fixed locations. Although many operating systems can be reconfigured, the process is time-consuming and prone to error. Also, not standardizing the system I/O addresses prevents simple migration between board products. Another subtle problem occurs when I/O is allowed to be randomly placed. Each I/O address that is kept for on-board I/O prevents the microprocessor from going to the system bus for that I/O location. If the SBCs in a system use a large portion of the I/O space for on-board I/O, global system I/O may not have an address range that can be reached by all the SBCs. As an example, in a system with two SBCs, one with on-board I/O addresses in the range of 0 to 07FH and the other with on-board addresses in the range of 080H to 0FFH, the SBCs use the whole of the first 256-byte I/O address space. A global I/O controller that decodes only the first 256 bytes can not be placed where both SBCs can access its I/O ports.

To overcome these problems, a standardization of the on-board I/O addresses, with their associated functions, is required. The following rules should be followed:

1. CPU SBCs. Use I/O address space 0060H to 00FFH for on-board I/O resources. Table 10-7 is a list of specific I/O function-address requirements.

2. Peripheral SBCs. Design Multibus system I/O decoders for 16 bits (64K-byte address space) of address decode-selection. This ensures compatibility of the peripheral board with all CPU SBCs.

3. Peripheral SBCs (with on-board memory). Design memory address selection independently of I/O address selection. This allows the I/O to be mapped independently of the memory in the system address space.

TABLE 10-7 Standard Multibus System Bus I/O
Addresses

Port address	Function
0–5FH	Off-board I/O
60–7FH	Third SBX
80–9FH	Second SBX
A0–BFH	First SBX
C0–C3H	Master-slave pic or misc I/O
C4–C7H	Slave pic or misc I/O
C8–CEH	First parallel port
D0–D7H	PIT or second serial I/O
D8–DEH	Serial I/O (8251 uses D8, DA only)
E0–EFH	80130
F0–FFH	On-board or off-board I/O

10.4 MULTIBUS SYSTEM BUS BACKPLANE DESIGN

Proper backplane design is an important aspect of system reliability. Many system problems can be traced back to inadequately designed backplanes—a system is as reliable as its weakest point. If the boards in the system are designed to provide reliable operation but the backplane cannot transfer data between the boards reliably, system reliability is lowered to the level of the backplane. The following sections provide guidelines for designing reliable backplanes. Also included are three implementations for parallel-priority bus arbitration.

10.4.1 Backplane Layout Considerations

The simplest aspect of system design appears to be the backplane. At first glance no circuitry is involved and all traces run parallel to each other. The fact that the design appears to be simple is the reason for underestimating the importance of proper backplane design and layout. A number of layout techniques can enhance or reduce the reliability of the system.

The simplest backplane design is one that contains no solid ground plane or interleaved ground traces. This design is a two-layer layout with signals on both sides of the board. This simple backplane design will be used as a base for comparison of the techniques for improving the design. The simple design can cause two general problems. The first is that limited ground busing aggravates any inductive ground-shift problems. The second is that lack of a ground plane or interleaved ground traces can increase susceptibility to signal-to-signal coupling.

SOLID GROUND PLANE

A significant enhancement of backplane operation occurs when a layer which contains a solid ground plane is added. "Solid," in this sense, means that virtually no signal traces are placed on this layer other than ground. The solid ground plane helps reduce bus noise in three areas. First, it exhibits much lower inductance than the ground return traces of the simple backplane. This helps to limit the problems caused by current surge inductive ringing. Inductive ringing causes a ground shift between devices and is a function of the magnitude and frequency of the current spike. This problem is more prevalent in systems that contain boards with high-current bus drivers.

The solid backplane also helps to filter the high-frequency noise components of the signals on the backplane and reduce the signal edge transition rates. This is due to the distributed capacitance effect between the backplane and the signal traces.

The third, and most important, benefit is that the solid ground plane helps to reduce inductive coupling by providing the shortest signal ground return path for the high-current signals causing the coupling. The solid ground-plane implementation exhibits less than half the signal inductive coupling of the simple backplane discussed earlier.

INTERLEAVED GROUND TRACES

The interleaved ground trace implementation virtually means that every signal trace on the backplane has, on each side, an adjacent, parallel ground trace for the entire length of the backplane.

This implementation is electrically equivalent to that of the solid ground plane in that it exhibits less than half the signal inductive coupling over the basic backplane implementation. Also, as with the solid ground plane, it helps reduce the ground-shift noise due to the multiple ground return paths. To provide the most effective noise reduction, the ground traces must be tied to the system ground at both ends so they can conduct current. The advantage of the interleaved ground implementation is that the board layout can be in two layers.

There is a trade-off between solid ground-plane designs and interleaved ground designs. If a design must be in two layers, a solid ground plane exhibits the best electrical characteristics. However, if trace and layout options prevent a solid-ground-plane design, the interleaved traces offer greater layout flexibility because traces can be placed on the second layer. In the interleaved design, as much solid ground as possible should be placed on the second layer. The optimum design has a solid ground plane and interleaved traces.

MODULAR BACKPLANES

Modular backplanes offer the designer flexibility in adding boards to a system. An application can grow in size without requiring system backplane redesign. Also, the same backplane design can be used in different applications, regardless of the number of boards required for each application. Examples of card cages with modular backplanes are Intel's iSBC 604/614 and National's BLC 604/ 614.

Although modular backplanes offer system flexibility, they also pose a problem when an attempt is made to implement any of the noise reduction techniques mentioned. The first consideration is the existence of the current return path. If the interconnection between the modular backplanes does not provide for interconnection of the ground return lines, then any grounding effect is lost. If a design has interleaved ground traces, then the method used must be such that the grounds are kept continuous over the length of the backplane. Intel's iSBC 604/614 card cages have backplanes that allow the interleaved ground traces to cross the edge connector boundaries. This is made possible by providing a short flat ribbon interconnect cable and the connectors on each backplane, so that the ground traces on each module can be connected. The approach is illustrated in Fig. 10-37. Another approach is to provide a single connector-receptacle on each modular backplane that provides for the signals and interleaved ground traces. An example of this approach can be found in Intel's iSBC 608/618 card cages.

The second modular backplane consideration is total length. The Multibus specification allows for a maximum of 16 boards and a maximum trace length of 18 in (45.7 cm). The length of each module must be considered, so that the

GROUNDING CABLE

FIGURE 10-37   **iSBC 604/614 backplane example.**

maximum-length specification is not exceeded when modules are combined or added.

MONOLITHIC BACKPLANES

Backplanes are monolithic when they offer continuous traces and do not allow slot expansion. Although they do not provide the flexibility that modular backplanes offer, they can be designed to provide the best noise immunity of any approach considered thus far. For this implementation, all the requirements of each modular backplane (i.e., interleaved ground traces and ground plane) are met, and, in addition, the number of slots on the backplane meets the application slot requirement. In this case a true solid ground plane and continuous interleaved ground return traces are achievable.

One approach to this type of backplane is to put all signal traces on the inner layers with interleaved ground traces. Then two solid ground planes are placed on the outer layers to create a four-layer backplane. With this type of layout, each signal trace becomes a virtual shielded cable. This implementation has a lower characteristic impedance and more inherent capacitance ($\sim$35 pF/ft) than other implementations. Backplanes of this type display significantly less coupling than any others.

10.4.2 Parallel-Priority Arbitration Examples

Since parallel-priority techniques require a central arbitration circuit, the circuitry is ideally placed on the backplane design. The two main problems with this approach are that the circuitry takes up backplane area and that the backplane contains active components that may require service. One way around the problems is to dedicate a slot on the backplane for the parallel arbitration circuitry and design a specific arbitration board for the system.

The following three configurations can be implemented on the backplane or on a special module. The first configuration is the standard, fixed parallel arbitration method currently used on Intel's iSBC 608/618 card cages. The other two examples are implementations of a rotating-priority algorithim.

FIXED-PRIORITY IMPLEMENTATION

A fixed parallel-priority resolution example is given in Fig. 10-38. The circuit uses a 74148 encoder and a 74S138 decoder chip for each eight masters. The BREQ* for each master is connected to the 74148. When a BREQ* signal goes active, the 74148 output generates an encoded three-bit BREQ* number. The 74138 decodes the BREQ* number from the 74148 and drives the appropriate BPRN* line. The activation of the BPRN* line allows the selected master to access the Multibus interface. The priority is fixed by the 74148 encoder. This means that if two or more requests occur during the same arbitration cycle, the highest-priority request will be given the BPRN* signal. When a BREQ* signal

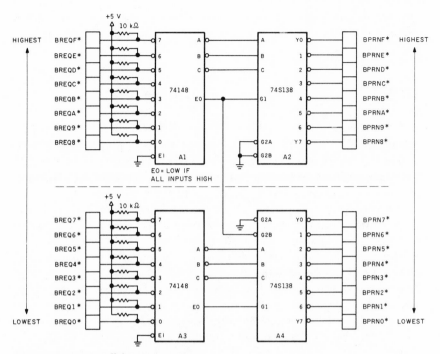

FIGURE 10-38 Parallel-priority circuit.

is attached to input 7 of the 74148, it has the highest priority. The priority decreases with each decreasing input number. Therefore, the lowest-priority input is 0. To connect a second set of eight masters, the circuit is duplicated. However, the second 74138 will not be enabled unless all of the high-order BREQ* signals (BREQ8* to BREQF*) are inactive. This is accomplished by connecting the higher-order 74148 encoder EO output to the enable input of the low-order 74S138 decoder.

The bus resolution timing is synchronous with bus clock and must start on a falling edge of bus clock and be completed by the next falling edge of bus clock. The following timing must be met for a proper bus exchange to occur.

$$\text{BCLK cycle} = t_{\text{BRQ}} + t_{\text{bd}} + t_{\text{prt}} + t_{\text{bd}} + t_{\text{su}} + \text{BLCK skew}$$

where t_{BRQ} = bus request output delay from BCLK
t_{bd} = bus signal delay
t_{prt} = maximum parallel resolution time
t_{su} = BPRN* setup time

$$100 \text{ ns} = 35 \text{ ns} + 2 \text{ ns} + t_{\text{prt}} + 2 \text{ ns} + 22 \text{ ns} + 2 \text{ ns}$$
$$t_{\text{prt}} = 37 \text{ ns (maximum)}$$

As can be seen from the above equations, there is only 37 ns in which to resolve the bus priority reliably. Reviewing the circuit of Fig. 10-38, the equations are

$$t_{prt} = t_{74148} + t_{74S138}$$

$$t_{prt} = 25 \text{ ns} + 12 \text{ ns} = 37 \text{ ns}$$

AUTOMATIC ROTATING-PRIORITY IMPLEMENTATION

In many applications all the masters may require equal priority to obtain the bus. In the preceding implementation the priority was fixed and could not be dynamically changed. Still, some method of arbitration is required when more than one master requests the bus during a BCLK cycle. The main problem facing a more complex implementation is the time available to resolve the priority. Reviewing the equations developed for the fixed priority implementation shows that a maximum of 37 ns is available to resolve the priority. This does not allow a designer too much flexibility in what is done with the time between receiving BREQ* and generating BPRN*.

The circuit shown in Fig. 10-39 allows for a simple priority rotation mechanism for up to eight masters. The rotating algorithim is as follows: A device, after being granted the bus, receives the lowest priority. Therefore, a device requesting the bus will have to wait, in the worst case, until each of the seven devices has been granted and has released the bus at most once. As an example, both BREQ3* and BREQ5* are active and BREQ5* has higher priority. The following is the setup prior to the rotation; in it 0 = highest priority and 7 = lowest priority:

	BREQ0*	BREQ1*	BREQ2*	BREQ3*	BREQ4*	BREQ5*	BREQ6*	BREQ7*
Request	1	1	1	0	1	0	1	1
Priority status	7	6	5	4	3	2	1	0

After the SBC that generated BREQ5* is granted the bus, the priority rotates. The following is the setup after the rotation:

	BREQ0*	BREQ1*	BREQ2*	BREQ3*	BREQ4*	BREQ5*	BREQ6*	BREQ7*
Request	1	1	1	0	1	1	1	1
Priority status	4	3	2	1	0	7	6	5

To implement this algorithim, a bipolar PROM is used to generate the priority and the rotation mechanism. To cover all of the conditions, a 2K-byte PROM

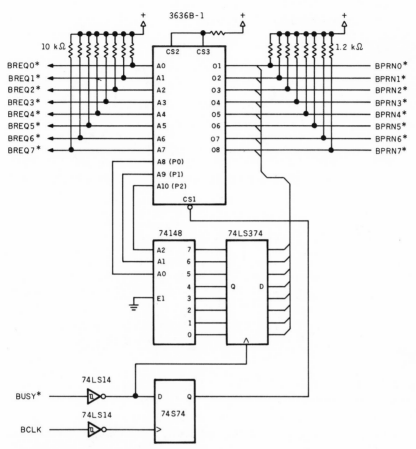

FIGURE 10-39 Automatic rotating-priority circuit.

is required. Also, the PROM must have an access time less than 38 ns. Because of the tight timing constraints, the PROM is directly driven by the Multibus BREQ* signals and the PROM directly drives the Multibus BPRN* signals. The PROM selected for this implementation is Intel's 3636B-1 or AMD's 27S191A and 27S291A bipolar PROMs. They are organized in 2K × 8 and have a maximum access time of 35 ns. The octal latch in the circuit is used to latch the last priority granted. The clock for the latch is generated directly from BUSY* going active, which means the requesting master was granted the bus and the priorities can change. The 74S74 D flip-flop ensures that the BUSY* signal attains a TTL high level to clock the latch. This is done by turning off the PROM decoder synchronously with BCLK. The 74148 priority encoder encodes the latched BPRN* signals into a three-bit binary number. The three-bit number provides the number of the BREQ* signal that will rotate to the lowest

TABLE 10-8   Rotating-Priority PROM Example

BPRN0* =	BREQ0*(P0 P1 P2 + BREQ7(P0* P1 P2 + BREQ6(P0 P1* P2 + BREQ5(P0* P1* P2 + BREQ4(P0 P1 P2* + BREQ3(P0* P1 P2* + BREQ2(P0 P1* P2* + BREQ1(P0* P1* P2*))))))))
BPRN1* =	BREQ1*(P0* P1* P2* + BREQ0(P0 P1 P2 + BREQ7(P0* P1 P2 + BREQ6(P0 P1* P2 + BREQ5(P0* P1* P2 + BREQ4(P0 P1 P2* + BREQ3(P0* P1 P2* + BREQ2(P0 P1* P2*))))))))
BPRN2* =	BREQ2*(P0 P1* P2* + BREQ1(P0* P1* P2* + BREQ0(P0 P1 P2 + BREQ7(P0* P1 P2 + BREQ6(P0 P1* P2 + BREQ5(P0* P1* P2 + BREQ4(P0 P1 P2* + BREQ3(P0* P1 P2*))))))))
BPRN3* =	BREQ3*(P0* P1 P2* + BREQ2(P0 P1* P2* + BREQ1(P0* P1* P2* + BREQ0(P0 P1 P2 + BREQ7(P0* P1 P2 + BREQ6(P0 P1* P2 + BREQ5(P0* P1* P2 + BREQ4(P0 P1 P2*))))))))
BPRN4* =	BREQ4*(P0 P1 P2* + BREQ3(P0* P1 P2* + BREQ2(P0 P1* P2* + BREQ1(P0* P1* P2* + BREQ0(P0 P1 P2 + BREQ7(P0* P1 P2 + BREQ6(P0 P1* P2 + BREQ5(P0* P1* P2))))))))
BPRN5* =	BREQ5*(P0* P1* P2 + BREQ4(P0 P1 P2* + BREQ3(P0* P1 P2* + BREQ2(P0 P1* P2* + BREQ1(P0* P1* P2* + BREQ0(P0 P1 P2 + BREQ7(P0* P1 P2 + BREQ6(P0 P1* P2))))))))
BPRN6* =	BREQ6*(P0 P1* P2 + BREQ5(P0* P1* P2 + BREQ4(P0 P1 P2* + BREQ3(P0* P1 P2* + BREQ2(P0 P1* P2* + BREQ1(P0* P1* P2* + BREQ0(P0 P1 P2 + BREQ7(P0* P1 P2))))))))
BPRN7* =	BREQ7*(P0* P1 P2 + BREQ6(P0 P1* P2 + BREQ5(P0* P1* P2 + BREQ4(P0 P1 P2* + BREQ3(P0* P1 P2* + BREQ2(P0 P1* P2* + BREQ1(P0* P1* P2* + BREQ0(P0 P1 P2))))))))

priority, which is the previously granted BREQ*. When BUSY* goes inactive, a new BPRN* signal is enabled on the bus if a BREQ* was pending. The trade-off of this circuit implementation is that a pending bus request may take an additional two BCLK cycles over the standard parallel-priority circuit before generating the BPRN* signal.

The core of this circuit is the code programmed into the bipolar PROM. The equations for each BPRN* output are given in Table 10-8; they can be modified to fit particular applications.

SPECIFIC ROTATING-PRIORITY IMPLEMENTATION

Specific rotating priority allows the user to control the rotation by programming the latch, via bus I/O writes, with the lowest-priority BREQ* number. Any BREQ* number can be written at any time. Priority selection is application-dependent. A priority, when set, remains intact until a new value is written into the latch.

The circuit shown in Fig. 10-40 is a specific rotating-priority implementation. In it the same PROM decoder, latch, and priority encoder that were used for the autorotating priority are used. However, in place of advancing the priority with BUSY*, an I/O write to the latch I/O address changes the priority. This is done by decoding an I/O address via a programmable logic array (PAL) decoder and gating the chip select output of the PAL with IOWC*. Since this is a bus command, an XACK∗ signal also must be generated. In addition, the PROM must be disabled synchronously with BCLK. This ensures that the new BPRN∗ signal will have the proper setup to BCLK as required by the Multibus specification. The synchronization is accomplished by the two 74S74 D flip-flops. In order for this circuit to operate properly, the priority circuit I/O port

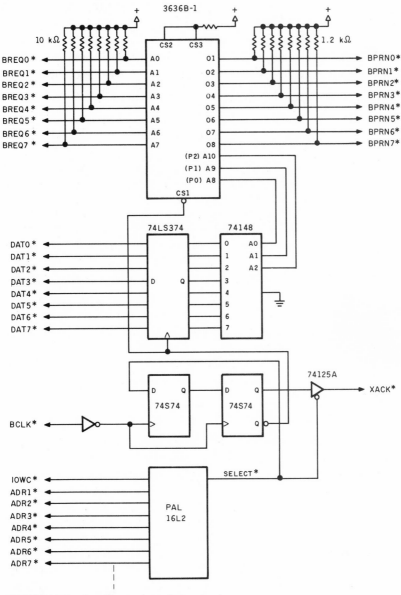

FIGURE 10-40   Specific rotating-priority circuit.

must be a global system resource. The bipolar PROM code from the priority algorithim can be altered to fit specific application requirements.

10.5 SUMMARY

The design guidelines discussed in this chapter are beneficial to the system designer of one custom board or 16 custom boards. The goal was to provide standard designs and implementations to simplify the board designer's job. The examples are based on many years of design experience and implementations. The guidelines, when implemented in the design, will ensure compatibility with other Multibus board products and system software. A major advantage of the guidelines is that, when they are followed, the reliability of each board, and therefore of the overall system, will be increased.

REFERENCES

Morris, Charles L., and John R. Miller: *Designing with TTL Integrated Circuits* (New York: McGraw-Hill Book Company, 1971) pp. 83–96.

Southard, Robert K.: "High-Speed Signal Pathways from Board to Board," (Harrisburg, Pa.: Amp Incorporated, 1981).

Steinburg, David S.: *Cooling Techniques for Electronic Equipment* (New York: John Wiley & Sons, Inc., 1973).

Reyner, E. M.: "Crosstalk Analysis of Digital Interconnection Systems," (Harrisburg, Pa.: Amp Incorporated).

Appendix:
List of Abbreviations

A list follows of the abbreviations used in this book, together with their definitions.

AC	alternating current
A/D	address-data
ALE	address latch enable
AU	application unit
B	binary
BD	basic device
BIU	bus interface unit
BV	bus-vectored
CHR	cache hit ratio
CON	controller
CPR	central parallel bus priority resolution circuitry
CPU	central processing unit
CRC	cyclic redundancy checking
CRT	cathode ray tube
D	decimal
DC	direct current
DEN	data enable
DIP	dual in-line package
DMA	direct memory access
DTL	diode-transistor logic
DT/R	data transmit-receive

ECC	error correction code
EEPROM	electrically erasable programmable read-only memory
EPROM	erasable programmable read-only memory
ESD	electrostatic discharge
EU	execution and control unit
GND	logic ground
GPIB	general-purpose interface bus
H	hexadecimal; high
IBM	International Business Machines Corporation
IC	integrated circuit
ICE	in-circuit emulator
ID	identification
IEEE	Institute of Electrical and Electronics Engineers
I/O	input–output
L	low
LDP	locally distributed processing
LED	light-emitting diode
LFM	linear feet per minute
LSI	large-scale integrated
MCE	master cascade enable
MIP	Multibus interprocessor protocol
MPSC	Multiprotocol serial processor
M/R	memory-register
MSI	medium-scale integration
MTBF	mean time between failure
NBV	non-bus-vectored
NMI	nonmaskable interrupt
OBCY	on-board cycle
OEM	original equipment manufacturer
OMO	OEM Microcomputer Systems Operation
PAL	programmable array logic
PCB	printed circuit board
PIC	programmable interrupt controller
PROM	programmable read-only memory

RAM	random access memory
ROM	read-only memory
RTL	resistor-transistor logic
R/W	read-write
SBC	single-board computer
SCU	surveillance controller unit
SDLC	synchronous data link control
SIP	single-in-line package
SNA	serial network architecture
SRQ	service request
SSI	small-scale integration
STO	supervisor takeover
SU	system unit
SUP	supervisor
TTL	transistor-transistor logic
USART	universal synchronous-asynchoronous receiver-transmitter
VCRU	video-camera reader unit
VLSI	very large scale integration

Index

About the Authors

James B. Johnson is the manager of Intel's OEM Microcomputer Systems Division board design group, and was responsible for the current published Multibus specifications which served as the basis of the IEEE-796 specifications. He and Mr. Kassel created the iSBX specifications, now in the process of getting IEEE approval. Author of several technical articles, he is the designer of the boards for seven single-board computers, the first three iSBX Multimodule boards, and various input-output boards. He obtained his M.S.E.E. from Stanford University in 1974.

Steve Kassel is project manager with Intel's OEM Microcomputer Systems Division board design group. Formerly involved with the design and development of a microprocessor-based laboratory controller, he has designed three single-board computers and one iSBX board. He was responsible for the definition of the Multichannel bus, the iLBX bus, and the iSBX bus along with Mr. Johnson. He obtained his M.S.E.E. from Washington State University in 1976.